AF684093

Law and Philosophy Library

Volume 122

Series editors
Francisco J. Laporta, Autonomous University of Madrid, Spain
Frederick Schauer, University of Virginia, USA
Torben Spaak, Stockholm University, Sweden

Editorial Board
Aulis Aarnio, Secretary General of the Tampere Club, Finland
Humberto Ávila, University of São Paulo, Brazil
Zenon Bankowski, University of Edinburgh, UK
Paolo Comanducci, University of Genoa, Italy
Hugh Corder, University of Cape Town, South Africa
David Dyzenhaus, University of Toronto, Canada
Ernesto Garzón Valdés, Johannes Gutenberg Universitat, Germany
Riccaro Guastini, University of Genoa, Italy
Ho Hock Lai, National University of Singapore, Singapore
John Kleinig, City University of New York, USA
Claudio Michelon, University of Edinburgh, UK
Patricia Mindus, Uppsala University, Sweden
Yasutomo Morigiwa, Meiji University, Japan
Giovanni Battista Ratti, University of Genova, Italy; University of Girona, Spain
Wojchiech Sadurski, University of Sydney, Australia
Horacio Spector, University of San Diego, USA; Universidad Torcuato Di Tella, Argentina
Robert S. Summers, Cornell University, USA
Michel Troper, Université de Paris Ouest - Nanterre, France
Carl Wellman, Washington University, USA

The Law and Philosophy Library, which has been in existence since 1985, aims to publish cutting edge works in the philosophy of law, and has a special history of publishing books that focus on legal reasoning and argumentation, including those that may involve somewhat formal methodologies. The series has published numerous important books on law and logic, law and artificial intelligence, law and language, and law and rhetoric. While continuing to stress these areas, the series has more recently expanded to include books on the intersection between law and the Continental philosophical tradition, consistent with the traditional openness of the series to books in the Continental jurisprudential tradition. The series is proud of the geographic diversity of its authors, and many have come from Latin America, Spain, Italy, the Netherlands, Germany, and Eastern Europe, as well, more obviously for an English-language series, from the United Kingdom, the United States, Australia, and Canada.

More information about this series at http://www.springer.com/series/6210

Pauline Westerman • Jaap Hage • Stephan Kirste •
Anne Ruth Mackor
Editors

Legal Validity and Soft Law

Springer

Editors
Pauline Westerman
Faculty of Law
University of Groningen
Groningen, The Netherlands

Jaap Hage
Faculty of Law
University of Maastricht
Maastricht, The Netherlands

Stephan Kirste
Faculty of Law
University of Salzburg
Salzburg, Austria

Anne Ruth Mackor
Faculty of Law
University of Groningen
Groningen, The Netherlands

ISSN 1572-4395 ISSN 2215-0315 (electronic)
Law and Philosophy Library
ISBN 978-3-319-77521-0 ISBN 978-3-319-77522-7 (eBook)
https://doi.org/10.1007/978-3-319-77522-7

Library of Congress Control Number: 2018945113

© Springer International Publishing AG, part of Springer Nature 2018
The chapter Unlocking Legal Validity: Some Remarks on the Artificial Ontology of Law is licensed under the terms of the Creative Commons Attribution 4.0 International License (http://creativecommons.org/licenses/by/4.0/). For further details see license information in the chapter.
This work is subject to copyright. All rights are reserved by the Publisher, whether the whole or part of the material is concerned, specifically the rights of translation, reprinting, reuse of illustrations, recitation, broadcasting, reproduction on microfilms or in any other physical way, and transmission or information storage and retrieval, electronic adaptation, computer software, or by similar or dissimilar methodology now known or hereafter developed.
The use of general descriptive names, registered names, trademarks, service marks, etc. in this publication does not imply, even in the absence of a specific statement, that such names are exempt from the relevant protective laws and regulations and therefore free for general use.
The publisher, the authors and the editors are safe to assume that the advice and information in this book are believed to be true and accurate at the date of publication. Neither the publisher nor the authors or the editors give a warranty, express or implied, with respect to the material contained herein or for any errors or omissions that may have been made. The publisher remains neutral with regard to jurisdictional claims in published maps and institutional affiliations.

This Springer imprint is published by the registered company Springer Nature Switzerland AG
The registered company address is: Gewerbestrasse 11, 6330 Cham, Switzerland

Preface

Philosophical analyses of concepts can be elucidating and clarifying but can also plunge us into despair by creating more problems. An investigation into the concept of validity seems to belong to the latter category. The notion of validity may make perfect sense if it is applied in everyday life by juridical decision-makers, who as a matter of routine decide on the validity of contracts, wills, or licenses. They seem to use the notion as unthinkingly as we use a knife and fork in eating our meals. As soon as one starts wondering what a fork or a knife *is*, how they evolved, whether or why they serve their purpose better than chopsticks (and what that purpose is), the more complicated they become and tend to absorb the mind to the point that one forgets eating.

So it seems to be with validity. Any investigation of the notion brings with it the comparison with adjacent notions. Is validity the same as the existence of rules? Can we say that invalid rules are not rules at all? Or should we say that invalid law exists but simply lacks a legal meaning? And what is the relationship between existence and binding force? Is it possible to conceive of valid—existing—rules that are nevertheless not binding? Or should we allow for the possibility that a rule is binding but is nevertheless invalid? And if we say the latter, what does this mean? Do we say that such a rule is simply denied membership of the extended family of law? Is it a bastard? Or should we say that validity tests are simply unnecessary and superfluous and that it is more important to assess the binding force of legal items? And if the latter is the case, what do we mean by binding force? Do we understand this as the degree to which a reason is a compelling one or as the chance that it will have legal effect, i.e. as efficacy? What is the relation between binding force, legal relevance, efficacy . . . and validity?

Indeed, one fool may ask more questions than seven wise men can answer. However, there is a good reason for the fool to ask these questions. New forms of (delegated or outsourced) rule-making involve numerous non-legal actors who lack the required formal and legal competences to create valid legal products. Nevertheless, they are daily engaged in producing agreements, covenants, treaties, standards, or codes. These products cannot unequivocally be called legally valid material but have yet some legal weight and relevance in legal discourse. Not only at the international level are such "soft law" arrangements created but also at the European and domestic levels. They may not have been created in accordance with legal rules and are therefore not part of the self-replicating legal system but nevertheless acquire a binding force that in some aspects resembles the force of law. That means that the daily routine of juridical decision-makers in attributing validity is much less self-evident and unproblematic than it appears to be at first sight. The fool's questions may haunt the minds of practitioners as well if they are confronted with the shades of softness that pertain to the typical products of "multilevel governance" and that resist treatment in terms of traditional dichotomous valid/ invalid assertions. If these products are members, they belong to different families at the same time; if "existence" can be attributed to them, they exist in the twilight zones of different discursive contexts in which they gain or lose weight.

Fortunately, more than just seven wise men tried to answer the fool's questions. They were addressed by a larger audience first in the Special Workshop during the IVR congress in Washington in the summer of 2015 and subsequently at a lively conference at the University of Groningen in December of the same year. Both events were meant as attempts to come to terms with the notion of validity and its adjacent equivalents in a world in which soft law arrangements are no longer exceptional. This book is the result of the discussions that took place among the contributors to this book. Since they come from all parts of Europe, their views are marked by a plurality of perspectives, as well as legal traditions.

After a historical overview and criticism of the concept of validity as such by von der Pfordten, several authors (Hage, Kirste, Carpentier, Sandro and Mackor) take a more analytical approach to the concept by distinguishing several aspects and meanings. The special relation between validity and efficacy is examined from different angles by Van Klink and Lembcke, Westerman, Goyal, Eliasz and Załuski, as well as Waltermann. The volume concludes by offering closer analyses of the phenomena of soft and international law (Bódig and Brus).

To pretend that there is a red thread running through all these contributions as though they would form together a coherent whole would unjustly and unnecessarily reduce the richness of the perspectives offered. Although the authors often refer to each other and to a web of shared notions, there is no common conceptual framework. We think that this is an advantage. It is for readers to marvel at the manifold new and refined distinctions that are made by the authors and to draw—provisionally—their own conclusions. Insofar as the new legal landscape of today is a *terra incognita*, these conclusions cannot be but temporary and provisional.

Groningen, The Netherlands — Pauline Westerman
Maastricht, The Netherlands — Jaap Hage
Salzburg, Austria — Stephan Kirste
Groningen, The Netherlands — Anne Ruth Mackor

Contents

Validity in Positive Law: A Mere Summary Concept

Dietmar von der Pfordten

Abstract One can distinguish at least four phases respectively consecutive properties of a legal norm: (1) A norm in positive law emerges and hence begins to exist as or by a thought and speech-act, as well as its intended language-manifestations in space and time. (2) A legal norm obligates, forbids, allows, authorizes, etc. those who are subject to the law. A legal norm also creates or affirms subjective rights or positions or changes a legal status. (3) A legal norm needs and gives justification because as free beings we primarily want to be guided only by our own will. (4) A legal norm obtains efficacy in a narrow sense as it is acknowledged and followed, at least partially. These four phases respectively properties of a positive, legal norm are very profound natural as well as social phenomena. In addition, the concepts corresponding to them, partly from antiquity, are in any case time-honored concepts of the everyday world, as well as for academics, and they have an unequivocal function and a fairly clear meaning. Why then do we need the much more obscure and problematic artificial concept of validity besides these four necessary and acknowledged phases resp. consecutive properties of a legal norm? The concept of validity seems to be, in its overwhelming importance, an invention of general philosophy, which some legal philosophers and legal theorists took up and overvalued in the second half of the nineteenth century and the first half of the twentieth century, with more harm than good to their own research and legal philosophy in general. Legal validity has become the most acclaimed concept of legal positivism in the twentieth and twenty-first century. In addition, even nonpositivists are infected by this virus. Today we still carry the burden of this overvaluing with far too much emphasis. There is only a limited, pragmatic area of application of the concept of validity in applied law: like other lately (and subsequently for pragmatic reasons) introduced summary concepts, e.g. "something," "entity," or "interest," which are much less directly related to reality, the concept of validity, firstly, summarizes the normative force or function of a legal norm, that is obligation, permission, authorization, status determination, etc., and, secondly,

D. von der Pfordten (✉)
Georg-August-University of Goettingen, Goettingen, Germany
e-mail: rechtsph@gwdg.de

© Springer International Publishing AG, part of Springer Nature 2018

P. Westerman et al. (eds.), *Legal Validity and Soft Law*, Law and Philosophy Library 122, https://doi.org/10.1007/978-3-319-77522-7_1

summarizes different types of legal norms by leaving open the author and addressee of the norm and thus includes also three- and multidimensional norms.

1 Introduction

What entities can bear the *property* of *validity*? Contracts, values, tickets, norms, etc. are considered to be *valid* or *nonvalid/invalid*. Since norms are often used in positive law,[1] *legal norms* can be considered to be bearers of the property of validity in positive law.[2] In order to understand the phenomenon of validity in positive law, a promising method is, therefore, to look more carefully at the *properties* of *legal norms*.

A *norm* in *positive law* passes through certain *phases/stages* and respectively has certain *consecutive properties*. One can distinguish at least four of these phases respectively consecutive properties: (1) A norm in positive law *emerges* and hence begins to *exist as* or *by*[3] a *thought* and *speech-act*, as well as its intended *language-manifestations* in space and time, e.g. an oral or written judgment, an oral or written contract, an oral or written order by a magistrate, or a decision and promulgation of a statute.[4] (2) A legal norm *obligates*, *forbids*, *allows*, *authorizes*, etc. those who are subject to the law. A legal norm also *creates* or *affirms subjective rights* or *positions* or *changes* a *legal status*. One could call all these *intended functions* or *effects* of a legal norm, which emerge in the realm of mental and communicative interaction,[5] the *mental* and *lingual results* or *normative forces* or *normative functions* of the

[1]Besides norms, we find other speech-acts in law, such as statements, definitions, descriptions etc. As different types of speech-acts are only arbitrary means to attain the aims of law, any type of speech-act can become part of the law. Hence, it is impossible to define law by reference to a specific type of speech-act, e.g. rules or norms or principles. Cf. von der Pfordten (2015), p. 172.

[2]One could also assume that a whole legal system might be qualified as valid or invalid. However, this qualification has the assumption and understanding of legal systems as necessary conditions, which is debatable. In addition, significant parts of law can be qualified as valid or invalid, e.g. the codification of an area of law, e.g. the Code Civil, Code Pénal, ABGB, StGB, BGB, etc. However, the necessary conditions for codifications are not clear. They might be, for our purposes, seen at least as a multitude of norms. Cf. for arguments attributing validity to norms: Grabowski (2013), pp. 242ff.

[3]There is a discussion as to whether speech-acts *are* themselves norms or only *create* norms. This discussion cannot be taken up here. However, the thesis that speech-acts only create norms seems to reduce the concept of a norm to the second element distinguished here, the result, function or force of the speech-act.

[4]These are the *locutionary acts* in the sense of the speech-act theory of Austin. See Austin (1962), pp. 94ff.

[5]And which therefore imply a sort of general duty of acceptance. Sartor (2000), pp. 585–625, has proposed characterizing this doxastic obligation as legal validity. The problem with this view is that legal validity is a property of legal norms and the description of validity a descriptive statement. The doxastic obligation is only the implication of a valid norm not identical with validity. See for a different approach: Sartor (2006).

existing legal norm.[6] Apart from these intended forces, functions or effects, legal norms might have several unforeseen and/or unintended consequences: e.g., a prohibition of vending certain goods can increase the black market for these goods as an unforeseen and unintended effect. (3) A legal norm *needs* and it *gives justification* because as free beings we primarily want to be guided only by our own will. The legal norm itself *needs* justification because it infringes upon our freedom and *gives* justification to the required act because if one obeys the norm, this obedience is justified at least partially by this legal norm. (4) A legal norm obtains *efficacy* in a narrow sense as it is acknowledged and followed, at least partially. Besides this efficacy in the narrow sense, it can also occur in a wider sense with at least three features: (a) the general authority of the lawgiver, (b) the threat of sanctions and the promise of rewards in order to secure acceptance and compliance, and (c) factual sanctions in the case of noncompliance or factual rewards in the case of compliance (about efficacy, cf. also Hage, Westerman, *supra*).

These four phases respectively properties of a positive, legal norm, that is, (1) *existence as a speech-act*; (2) *normative result, force*, or *function* (*obligation, prohibition, allowance, authorization, creation*, or *affirmation* of *rights* or *positions, change* of *legal status*, etc.)[7]; (3) the *needing* and *giving* of *justification*; and (4) *efficacy* (e.g., *acknowledgement of a norm, norm following, etc.)*, are very profound natural as well as social phenomena. In addition, the concepts corresponding to them, partly from antiquity, are in any case time-honored concepts of the everyday world, as well as for academics, and they have an unequivocal function and a fairly clear meaning. All of these phases, resp. properties of a legal norm, can be analyzed from different epistemological perspectives—(1) natural-scientific, (2) sociological, (3) historical, (4) juridical, (5) philosophical (ethics and theory of law)—and from some other scientific and academic perspectives, e.g. ethnological, psychological, theological, medical, etc. Several academic disciplines are institutionalizations of these different epistemological perspectives on law in general and legal norms: (1) the natural sciences, (2) sociology of law, (3) legal history, (4) legal dogmatics, (5) philosophy of law (ethics and theory of law), etc.

Why then do we need the much more obscure and problematic artificial concept of *validity* besides these four necessary and acknowledged phases resp. consecutive properties of a legal norm?[8] Why do we need a concept that obscures the clear differences between (1) existence; (2) normative force, result, or function; (3) needing and giving of justification; and (4) efficacy of a legal norm, as well as the different epistemological perspectives from natural sciences, sociology, history, law,

[6]These are both the *illocutionary* and *perlocutionary acts* in the sense of the speech-act theories of Austin and Searle. See Austin (1962), pp. 98ff. and 101ff.; Searle (1969), pp. 23ff. and 25ff.

[7]Some try to qualify all these functions or forces as *imperatives* resp. *obligations* (Befehle, Verbindlichkeiten), e.g. Meyer (2011), pp. 30ff. Already Larenz (1929), pp. 15, 25, has emphasized the obligatory, normative character of law. See for a general critique of these attempts: Hart (1994), pp. 20ff. This issue cannot be discussed here. If these attempts were successful, legal validity would indeed be identical with obligation.

[8]See for concepts in law in general: Hage and von der Pfordten (2009).

and philosophy (ethics and theory)? Why do we need a concept that is—as validity is—in its overwhelming, theoretical importance a *parvenu* of the *nineteenth* and *twentieth century*?[9]

In the course of engaging with this topic, my doubts about the concept of validity have grown. In view of the present hypertrophy of this concept in legal theory,[10] as a methodological guideline, one should at least try to see how far one could get without it.[11] A strong thesis fuels the debate: the concept of validity seems to be, in its overwhelming importance, an invention of general philosophy, which some legal philosophers and legal theorists took up and overvalued in the second half of the nineteenth century and the first half of the twentieth century, with more harm than good to their own research and legal philosophy in general. Legal validity has become the most acclaimed concept of legal positivism in the twentieth and twenty-first century.[12] In addition, even nonpositivists are infected by this virus.[13] Today we still carry the burden of this overvaluing with far too much emphasis.[14] There is only a limited, pragmatic area of application of the concept of validity in applied law: like other lately (and subsequently for pragmatic reasons) introduced summary concepts, e.g. "something," "entity," or "interest," which are much less directly related to reality, the concept of validity, firstly, *summarizes the normative force or function of a legal norm, that is obligation, permission, authorization, status-determination etc.*, and, secondly, *summarizes different types of legal norms by leaving open the author and addressee of the norm, and thus includes also three- and multidimensional norms.*[15] This useful and warranted area of application of the concept of validity as a pragmatic summary concept will be explained below in the first part on legal practice.[16] Then, in the second part, the historical development of the concept of validity in philosophy and legal theory will be critically retraced.

---

[9]Up until now there exists—as far as I know—no empirical historical study of the emergence of the concept of validity in positive law. Munzer (1972), p. 37, refers to the Oxford English Dictionary, which gives a first date of 1571 for the following sense of "valid": "Good or adequate in law; possessing legal authority or force; legally binding or efficacious." Munzer's study of 1972 is still the best treatment of the subject of validity, and one wonders why it has gained so little attention: one can imagine that his very careful, painstaking and convincing critique of validity in Ross, Kelsen and Hart was not very welcome to the leaders and followers of legal positivism as the hegemonic theory of our times. This is one striking example of how opinion is nudged in academia.

[10]See e.g. Habermas (1998). Despite its title, this book gives no definition or conceptual analysis of the concept of "Geltung" at all. Moreover, the juxtaposition of "Faktizität" and "Geltung" is wrong. The opposite of "Faktizität" is "Normativität" and of "Geltung" is "Nicht-Geltung."

[11]See for a careful critical analysis of several conceptions of validity: Grabowski (2013), pp. 247–357.

[12]It is no accident that Munzer (1972), discusses only three legal positivists: Alf Ross, Hans Kelsen and H. L. A. Hart.

[13]Radbruch (1999), § 10, pp. 78–85; Larenz (1929); Alexy (1992), pp. 139–153.

[14]See already my critique: von der Pfordten (2011a), p. 145.

[15]Moreover, "binding force" might be another expression of this summary-concept. Cf. Sartor (2006, 2007).

[16]See for a careful analysis of the discourse of validity: Grabowski (2013), pp. 455–535.

Afterward, an objection will be addressed: does the concept of validity denote the membership of a norm in a legal system? Five additional questions will be raised: What is the function of the summary concept of validity in metanorms? Is the concept of validity a continuum concept? What are the inner legal conditions for a legal norm to be valid law? What are the outer legal conditions for a legal norm to be valid law? What is the relationship of the summary concept of legal validity to the other phases resp. properties of norms mentioned in the introduction?

2 Legal Practice

For an analysis of the practical use of the concept of validity, take the example of the German Basic Law (*Grundgesetz*) (for a different account on this issue, cf. Mackor, *supra*). One finds the concept of validity in the German Basic Law in several instances but prominently at the beginning and at the end, in the Preamble, and in Article 146 of the *Grundgesetz*. The Preamble includes, as is well known, the following: "This Basic Law *is* thus *valid* [*gilt*] for the entire German People" (emphasis added). Moreover, in Article 146 of the Basic Law, it says: "This Basic Law, which *is valid [gilt]* since the achievement of the unity and freedom of Germany for the entire German people, loses its *validity* [*Geltung*] on the day on which a Constitution freely adopted by the German people takes effect."

Why does the *Grundgesetz* not just speak of the "obligation" but of the "validity" in these articles? One can assume that the concept of validity is essentially to be understood in the sense of the word "obligation" here but goes beyond this notion in at least two ways: it includes a summary not only of orders/commands and prohibitions, that is, obligations/duties, but also of permissions, authorizations, the recognition or promulgation of subjective rights, regulations of a status, etc., that is, different types of speech-acts that create different normative forces or functions, which singular legal norms can adopt. On the other hand, and unlike obligations, in the case of validity, it must not be clearly settled who the author and who the addressee of the legal norm are. As modern legal systems increasingly cover not only duties but also permissions, authorizations, rights, status provisions, etc., that is, very different forms of speech-acts and their results, and as there increasingly exists a multitude of obligated and authorized persons—e.g., in the case of fundamental rights, the State on the one hand and several citizens on the other—the summary concept of validity is—similar to the concept of norm as opposed to the concept of obligation—shorter and therefore more efficient for denoting this plurality of normative forces and addressed persons than the simple concept of obligation.

As a summary concept of the different functions, forces, or results of phase/property (2) of a concept, legal validity is used to deal with at least two phenomena, which may occur, in the realm of these different functions, forces, or results of a norm: (a) *collisions* of norms and (b) the *extent* resp. *limitation* of norms.

(a) Practically and more concretely, the concept of validity appears in the rare event of a *collision of two legal norms* (cf. Carpentier, *supra*). In this case, the more specific question of validity or invalidity is raised; firstly, if it is doubted whether an existing norm violates a higher, "superior" norm (e.g., the constitution) or, secondly, if the norm is not created in accordance with metanorms, which govern the production of norms.[17] Legal norms then declare other legal norms as invalid. In modern, highly differentiated and multilayered legal systems, this inner systemic function of guaranteeing consistency and coherence is needed more and therefore extended.

(b) A second field of practical application is the question of the *temporal*, *spatial*, and *personal extent resp. limitation of a legal norm*, e.g. whether such a law is already in force or is set out of force or whether it extends spatially to a case at hand, especially whether it is valid only nationally or also internationally, or what persons it is applicable to, e.g. only to persons over the age of 14. This is particularly important for the punishment of crimes. Sections 2–7 of the German Criminal Code read like this:

§ 2 Zeitliche Geltung: (1) Die Strafe und ihre Nebenfolgen bestimmen sich nach dem Gesetz, das zur Zeit der Tat gilt. (2) Wird die Strafdrohung während der Begehung der Tat geändert, so ist das Gesetz anzuwenden, das bei Beendigung der Tat gilt. (3) Wird das Gesetz, das bei Beendigung der Tat gilt, vor der Entscheidung geändert, so ist das mildeste Gesetz anzuwenden. (4) Ein Gesetz, das nur für eine bestimmte Zeit gelten soll, ist auf Taten, die während seiner Geltung begangen sind, auch dann anzuwenden, wenn es außer Kraft getreten ist. Dies gilt nicht, soweit ein Gesetz etwas anderes bestimmt. [...].

§ 3 Geltung für Inlandstaten: Das deutsche Strafrecht gilt für Taten, die im Inland begangen werden.

§ 4 Geltung für Taten auf deutschen Schiffen und Luftfahrzeugen

Das deutsche Strafrecht gilt, unabhängig vom Recht des Tatorts, für Taten, die auf einem Schiff oder in einem Luftfahrzeug begangen werden, das berechtigt ist, die Bundesflagge oder das Staatszugehörigkeitszeichen der Bundesrepublik Deutschland zu führen.

§ 5 Auslandstaten gegen inländische Rechtsgüter

Das deutsche Strafrecht gilt, unabhängig vom Recht des Tatorts, für folgende Taten, die im Ausland begangen werden: 1. Vorbereitung eines Angriffskrieges (§ 80); 2. Hochverrat (§§ 81 bis 83); [...].

§ 6 Auslandstaten gegen international geschützte Rechtsgüter

Das deutsche Strafrecht gilt weiter, unabhängig vom Recht des Tatorts, für folgende Taten, die im Ausland begangen werden: [...]

§ 7 Geltung für Auslandstaten in anderen Fällen

(1) Das deutsche Strafrecht gilt für Taten, die im Ausland gegen einen Deutschen begangen werden, wenn die Tat am Tatort mit Strafe bedroht ist oder der Tatort keiner Strafgewalt unterliegt.

(2) Für andere Taten, die im Ausland begangen werden, gilt das deutsche Strafrecht, wenn die Tat am Tatort mit Strafe bedroht ist oder der Tatort keiner Strafgewalt unterliegt und wenn der Täter

1. zur Zeit der Tat Deutscher war oder es nach der Tat geworden ist oder [...]

[17] Guastini (1994), p. 212.

§ 2 Jurisdiction ratione temporis; lex mitior: (1) The penalty and any ancillary measures shall be determined by the law which is in force at the time of the act. (2) If the penalty is amended during the commission of the act, the law in force at the time the act is completed shall be applied. (3) If the law in force at the time of the completion of the act is amended before judgment, the most lenient law shall be applied. (4) A law intended to be in force only for a determinate time shall be continued to be applied to acts committed while it was in force even after it ceases to be in force, unless otherwise provided by law. [. . .]

§ 3 Offences committed on the territory of the Federal Republic of Germany: German criminal law shall apply to acts committed on German territory.

§ 4 Offences committed on German ships and aircraft: German criminal law shall apply, regardless of the law applicable in the locality where the act was committed, to acts committed on a ship or an aircraft entitled to fly the federal flag or the national insignia of the Federal Republic of Germany.

§ 5 Offences committed abroad against domestic legal interests: German criminal law shall apply, regardless of the law applicable in the locality where the act was committed, to the following acts committed abroad: 1. preparation of a war of aggression (section 80); 2. high treason against the Federation (Sections 81 to 83); [. . .]

§ 6 Offences committed abroad against internationally protected legal interests: German criminal law shall further apply, regardless of the law of the locality where they are committed, to the following offences committed abroad: . . .

§ 7 Offences committed abroad – other cases: (1) German criminal law shall apply to offences committed abroad against a German, if the act is a criminal offence at the locality of its commission or if that locality is not subject to any criminal jurisdiction. (2) German criminal law shall apply to other offences committed abroad if the act is a criminal offence at the locality of its commission or if that locality is not subject to any criminal law jurisdiction, and if the offender:

1. was German at the time of the offence or became German after the commission; or [. . .].

For private law, these issues are addressed, e.g., by the metarules of private international law.

In all of these examples, one could replace "validity" (in German: "gilt") with "obligation" or "duty" if the underlying legal propositions in question are obligations/duties. The same holds for permissions, authorizations, rights, positions, status changes, etc. In addition, if it is unclear whether the norm in question is an obligation, a permission, an authorization, etc., one could replace "validity" which means "is valid" with a mere listing of these different functions. Therefore, in these cases, too, the concept of validity serves only as an efficient summary concept of different types of normative functions or results of positive law.

This higher level of pragmatic efficiency of word choice should not obscure the fact that the summary concept of validity essentially refers to the speech-act function of obligation and additionally to permission, authorization, subjective law, status determination, etc. However, this means that validity represents no new or different "physical state" or "normative state" of the law resp. the legal norm in addition to these forms of speech-act function. One must, in my view, use Ockham's razor and criticize all attempts at an ontological or metaphysical hypostatization of such a new, obscure "physical state" or "normative state" of validity (cf. Sandro, *supra*).

The concept of validity does not refer to the first phase of existence because the speech-act, which is or refers to (see above for this distinction) a legal norm, exists even if the norm only becomes valid in the future or becomes invalid, e.g. by lapse of time or collision with a higher norm.[18]

In order to clarify this fundamental critique of the theoretical hypertrophy of the concept of validity, the history of the concept will be sketched in the following.

3 History of the Concept of Validity in Philosophy and Legal Theory

The concept of validity is a philosophical and legal-theoretical child of the nineteenth century and specifically the value philosophy of neo-Kantianism. For 100 years, it has been the cornerstone of the theories of legal positivists such as Kelsen, Hart, Ross, and Raz (cf. Eliasz/Załuski, van Klink/Lembcke, *supra*). The concept has no Greek or Latin equivalent and no equivalent in Roman law. Moreover, in the natural law of the seventeenth and eighteenth centuries, e.g. in Grotius and Pufendorf, the concept had still not occurred, nor in Hobbes or Locke. Hobbes said, "auctoritas, non veritas facit legem." There is no mention of "validitas."[19] The same applies to the core of Kant's philosophy of law. Kant developed the criterion of law, to harmonize the "voluntary actions of any one Person with the voluntary actions of every other Person, according to a universal Law of Freedom" (*der Inbegriff der Bedingungen, unter denen die Willkür des einen mit der Willkür des anderen nach einem allgemeinen Gesetze der Freiheit zusammen vereinigt werden kann*[20]) as a material criterion, without mentioning the validity of law. Even in Hegel, in his *Elements of the Philosophy of Law* (*Grundlinien der Philosophie des Rechts*), validity plays no role. The same is the case in Fichte's *Foundations of the Natural Law According to the Doctrine of Science* (*Grundlagen des Naturrechts nach Prinzipien der Wissenschaftslehre*).

Only in the nineteenth century does validity first appear in the philosophy of neo-Kantianism but—surprisingly—not in the positivists, for example, John Austin in England. For the neo-Kantians, a conceptual reference point was Kant's qualification of judgments as "objectively valid." Kant writes in the *Critique of Pure Reason*: "Only in this way does there arise from this relation a *judgment*, that is, a relation which is *objectively valid*, and so can be adequately distinguished from a relation of the same representations that would have only subjective validity—as

[18]See for a similar critique of the identification of existence and validity of a norm: Munzer (1972), pp. 13ff. Munzer criticizes Alf Ross convincingly. However, the critique might be extended to all Scandinavian "realists." Scandinavian Realism considers law as fact and neglects the normative force or function. It cannot understand legal validity as a summary concept of normative function and so shifts it mistakenly to the existence of a norm.

[19]See Hobbes (1991), chap. 26.

[20]Kant (1968b), p. 230.

when they are connected according to laws of association."[21] The judgments, which are true, according to Kant, have *objective validity*. Alternatively, one could say, they are "universally valid" (*allgemeingültig*). This connection of the truth of judgments, sentences, or representations, with their qualification as valid or universal or universally valid (allgemeingültig) was expanded on by the influential nineteenth-century Goettingen neo-Kantian Hermann Lotze into a two-world theory of *being* (Sein) and *validity* (Geltung). Within a comprehensive reality, according to Lotze, there should be, besides the sphere of being, also a sphere of validity that is not part of being. Particularly in the third section of his book "*Logic*" (*Logik*), published in several editions, which deals with epistemology, under the heading "World of Ideas," he explains that the content resp. the truth of sentences or representations is not by itself real but "valid" (*geltend*).[22] The reality of validity should be a separate form of reality.[23] The validity cannot be inferred from other beings, according to Lotze.[24] It should be a fundamental concept in itself.[25] Plato, according to Lotze, had not claimed the existence of ideas but rather only their validity as a specific form of reality. Here, Lotze becomes the starting point for a new interpretation of Plato. Moreover, he follows Plato in another crucial point, too: logic and metaphysics should only be intermediate links, while the highest beginning of knowledge should be in *ethics*, namely in *values*, in the *good*. Therefore, Lotze maintained an *ethical* resp. *teleological idealism*. He was the author not only of the substantially expanded concept of validity but also of the substantially expanded concept of value. In addition, both concepts are combined: the ultimate truth of everything and all knowledge should be in values, which are valid.

Lotze's neo-Platonic but hardly neo-Kantian hypostatization of a separate sphere of truth, validity, and values was taken up several times: Lotze's student in Goettingen, Gottlob Frege, saw the meaning/reference (*Bedeutung*) of sentences in their truth-value.[26] Wilhelm Windelband, also a student of Lotze, took his teaching to southern Germany, especially to Heidelberg. Like Lotze, he distinguishes two spheres, which he describes in different terms, as validity (*Gelten*) and being (*Sein*), obligation (*Sollen*) and being (*Sein*), value (*Wert*) and reality (*Wirklichkeit*).[27] The concept of reality, which was all-encompassing for Lotze, is thus limited to the sphere of being (*Sein, Wirklichkeit*).

---

[21] Kant (2007), p. 159; Kant (1968a), p. 85.

[22] Lotze (1912), p. 511.

[23] Lotze (1912), p. 514.

[24] Lotze (1912), p. 512.

[25] Lotze (1912), p. 513: "One has to understand this concept as being a self-contained fundamental notion, of which everyone can know the meaning, but which we cannot construct from other components that do not already contain it (the concept) themselves." ("Man muss auch diesen Begriff als einen durchaus nur auf sich beruhenden Grundbegriff ansehen, von dem jeder Wissen kann, was er mit ihm meint, den wir aber nicht durch eine Konstruktion aus Bestandteilen erzeugen können, welche ihn selbst nicht bereits enthielten.")

[26] Frege (1986), pp. 48ff.

[27] Windelband (1920), pp. 213, 426.

In Heidelberg, Windelband's students, Heinrich Rickert and Emil Lask, also picked up this doctrine. Lask writes in 1911: "Lotze's carving out of the sphere of validity has shown the path to current philosophical research."[28] Moreover, already in his *Philosophy of Law* (*Rechtsphilosophie*) of 1905 he had written: "The formal positivity of law is nothing more than a kind of validity."[29] However, shortly afterward, Lask speaks revealingly of "obligation" instead of "validity" in one instance.[30]

In 1914, the Marburg neo-Kantian Arthur Liebert published a book called *The Problem of Validity* (*Das Problem der Geltung*) in a *Supplementary Series* of the *Kant Studies* (*Ergänzungshefte* der *Kant-Studien*), which appears to be the most comprehensive general monograph so far on the new concept of validity. It says at one point, and here we can already recognize the vagueness and dubiousness of the concept of validity: "You could with the same appropriateness replace the word validity with 'sense' ('Sinn'), 'value' ('Wert'), 'content' ('Gehalt'), 'meaning' ('Bedeutung'), 'justification' ('Rechtfertigung'), 'foundation' ('Begründung'), 'groundwork' ('Grundlegung')."[31]

The height of the theoretical hypostatization of the concept of validity was undoubtedly reached in Kelsen's so-called pure theory of law (*Reine Rechtslehre*). According to Kelsen, an act of law stating as mere subjective "willing" (*Wollen*) could and should be transformed by a higher positive norm of law into an "objective" "should" (*Sollen*), a "valid" norm, which binds the addressee.[32] The higher norms up to the basic norm (Grundnorm) are meant to create the "objective validity" of the subordinate norms.[33] The reason for the validity of a norm (Geltungsgrund) can only be, according to Kelsen, another norm.[34] Under validity, Kelsen wants to understand the "specific existence" (*spezifische Existenz*) of a norm, a "should" (*Sollen*) as opposed to a mere "being" (*Sein*).[35] In the posthumously published *General Theory of Norms* (*Allgemeine Theorie der Normen*), he speaks about validity as an "ideal existence" (*ideelle Existenz*).[36] The difference between being and ought is declared to be a not further explainable foundation for validity.[37] Validity does not mean efficacy, for Kelsen. Nevertheless, for Kelsen, efficacy must exist in order for the legal norm, as part of positive law, not to lose its validity.[38]

---

[28]Lask (1911), p. 12.

[29]Lask (1923), p. 283.

[30]Lask (1923), p. 283.

[31]Liebert (1914), p. 4.

[32]Kelsen (1960), p. 7.

[33]Kelsen (1960), p. 196.

[34]Kelsen (1960), p. 8.

[35]Kelsen (1960), p. 9.

[36]Kelsen (1979), p. 22.

[37]Kelsen (1960), p. 5.

[38]Kelsen (1960), p. 11.

How an additional "factual willing" can produce an "objective should" from a "subjective willing," is, however, totally unclear and doubtful. When two boys are arguing and one fetches his bigger brother, the supporting willing act of the bigger brother does not transform the subjective willing of the younger brother into a totally different sphere of objectivity. Here, Kelsen reinforces the metaphysical hypostasis of the second realm of obligation/should by the concept of validity. "Should", which is immunized as a nonexplicable basic concept, is expanded enormously and includes, according to Kelsen, allowance (*Dürfen*) and capacity (*Können*), too.[39]

Gustav Radbruch is known to have dedicated § 10 of his *Philosophy of Law* (*Rechtsphilosophie*) of 1932[40] to the validity of law, where the difference from Kelsen's hypostasis of validity is obvious. For the constitution of law in §§ 1–9 of the *Philosophy of Law*, validity does not matter at all. Validity is only introduced with the concretization of legal certainty in § 10. Radbruch initiated the treatment of validity with a reference to legal certainty as part of the idea of the law (Rechtsidee). He distinguishes three dimensions of validity: he noted, firstly, a legal validity doctrine of the will of the lawmaker; secondly, a socio-historical validity theory of power and recognition; and, ultimately, a philosophical natural-law theory or ethical theory of validity of right law (*richtiges Recht*) (the now claimed three dimensionality of validity). Radbruch provides different relationships between those aspects of the "legal should" (*rechtliches Sollen*), the sociological efficacy, and the philosophical rightness resp. natural-law rightness. Only the legal order is factually valid, which, as a whole, is able to gain factual efficacy.[41] As relativism does not allow for a final substantive decision on rightness, nobody can determine what is just. Thus, someone has to establish what should be legal.[42] While the individual must follow his conscience and can refuse to obey, the judge should—according to the earlier opinion of Radbruch—deliver, through his unconditional obedience to the law, at least legal certainty.[43]

As initially stated, I do not want to put these juridical, factual, and ethical dimensions of law into question. The same holds for the initially addressed four phases and properties of the legal norm, that is, the phases resp. properties of existence, normative function, justification, and efficacy. I only want to state that it makes more sense scientifically, in analyzing the reality, to dispense with the concept of validity, which is disciplinary and thus descriptively undifferentiated. It fosters a tendency to blur the distinctions between nature, sociology, history, law, and philosophy. It seems preferable to inquire, depending on the particular type of legal norm analyzed and carefully distinguishing the five perspectives of nature, sociology, history, law, and philosophy (ethics and theory), into the relationship

[39] Kelsen (1960), p. 5.

[40] This is an almost completely new version of his previous book "Grundzüge der Rechtsphilosophie" of 1914.

[41] Radbruch (1999), p. 79.

[42] Radbruch (1999), p. 82.

[43] Radbruch (1999), p. 82.

between existence, normative force or function, justification, and efficacy. Within the property of normative force or function, it is important to distinguish carefully between obligations, permissions, authorizations, subjective rights, status changes, etc. This will lead to different results, e.g. when a distinction is made between obligation, permission, and subjective rights. While, for example, a mere obligation might eventually, because of its loss of general compliance, lose its binding force, this does not seem to be the case for a permission or a subjective right. A permission holds, even if it is never used, just as a subjective right in no way loses its warranting and justification even if it is constantly flouted.

Stephen Munzer in his *Legal Validity* of 1972 has carefully distinguished legal validity from the existence and efficacy of a legal norm. With this distinction, he is, according to our analysis in Sect. 1, mostly on the right track. Legal validity is to be understood in his proposal as "legal strength or adequacy" or "sustainability in point of law."[44] He writes, "Here the fundamental idea is this: if something is strong or adequate in law, this means that it cannot be ignored or overthrown. If, for example, a person is judged to have made a valid will, the court of probate cannot simply ignore it and proceed as if he had died intestate. Rather, it must, within certain broad limits, see that the instructions of the testator are carried out."[45] This comes very close to the second phase of legal norms, mentioned above in the introduction, which we have called normative force, function, or result. However, Munzer has not realized that legal validity is only a summary concept, which summarizes several concrete normative forces or functions such as obligation, permission, authorization, status change, etc.

4 Validity as the Decision About the Membership of a Norm in a Legal System?

Now a possible objection should be addressed: H.L.A. Hart also took up the concept of validity and emphasized a dimension that was already implied in Kelsen's theory of the dependence of every valid norm in a legal system from the authorization by a higher valid norm up to the highest norm, the basic norm (Grundnorm). According to Hart, the "rule of recognition" is to decide on the validity of a norm and thus its status of belonging to the legal system.[46] The "rule of recognition" has to identify whether a norm belongs to the legal system. Does the validity concept not at least—as Kelsen and Hart believed—have its own importance as identification of belonging to a particular legal system (cf. Carpentier, Kirste, *supra*)?

A prerequisite of this assumption is of course that one regards the law, as Kelsen and Hart did, as a relatively closed system, which was denied by, among many

[44]Munzer (1972), pp. 3, 23, 37, 39f., 41.

[45]Munzer (1972), p. 39.

[46]Hart (1963), p. 103.

others, Eugen Ehrlich and the Free School of Law (*Freirechtsschule*).[47] To discuss this question, one would have to ask what is really meant when the law is seen as a system, which of course cannot be done here. However, if one at least concedes that the law as a particular legal system in specific contingent circumstances can take on such a system character, the question of belonging is raised. Stephen Munzer has criticized the belonging-conceptions of validity of Kelsen and Hart painstakingly and very convincingly.[48] This critique shall be reviewed here.

Only one decisive counterargument will be mentioned: there are cases in which a norm of the positive law is part of a legal system but loses its validity. Think of a statutory provision that is declared by the Constitutional Court to be in part unconstitutional and thus nonvalid. It is not claimed by this that the law in question does not belong to the legal system but only that it is in part no longer legally obligatory, permissive, etc. Therefore, there can be legal norms that are not valid but part of a legal system (cf. Carpentier for a similar example, *supra*).

If one accepts the characterization of the concept of legal validity as a summary concept for different normative forces or functions of legal norms, several questions remain. Five will be addressed in the following: What is the function of the summary concept of legal validity in metanorms (Sect. 5)? Is the concept of legal validity a continuum concept (Sect. 6)? What are the inner legal conditions for a legal norm to be valid law (Sect. 7)? What are the outer legal conditions for a legal norm to be valid law (Sect. 8)? What is the relationship of the summary concept of legal validity to the other phases resp. consecutive properties of legal norms mentioned in the introduction (Sect. 9)?

5 What Is the Function of the Summary Concept of Validity in Metanorms?

In law, especially in modern legal systems, one not only finds primary norms, which are addressed directly to addressees outside the law, but also metanorms, which refer to these primary norms. The concept of validity is used very frequently, perhaps one may assume nearly exclusively, in such metanorms. The German *Grundgesetz* and the German Criminal Code, cited above, show some examples. In order to understand the function of the concept of validity as a summary concept of the normative function of norms, it is important to understand this predominant use in metanorms.

An explanation might run as follows: a primary norm cannot leave open what normative force is intended by it. That is, it cannot leave open if it obliges, forbids, allows, authorizes, affirms, or gives a subjective right, changes a legal status, etc. Therefore, it would be inappropriate to use the summary concept of validity in these

[47] Ehrlich (1989).

[48] Munzer (1972), pp. 44–69.

primary norms. Nevertheless, the reverse holds for metanorms. Metanorms refer to primary norms, where the decision what normative force is intended is already made or must be made. Therefore, metanorms can refer to primary norms, without specifying their normative function. If the decision about the normative function of the primary norm *is not yet made*, the metanorm should not normally replace this decision of the normative function by the primary norm. In this case, the metanorm needs to leave open the specification of the normative function of the primary norm. So the unspecific summary concept of validity is needed.

Moreover, if metanorms refer to a *multitude of primary norms*, the specification of the normative functions of the primary norms is even impossible because the primary norms may have *different functions*. In this case, the metanorm needs to leave open the specification of the normative function of the primary norms. So the unspecific summary concept of validity is needed also in this case.

To sum up, one can identify two cases in which a metanorm needs to use the summary concept of validity: (1) where the decision about the normative function of the primary norm is not yet made and (2) where the metanorm refers to two or more primary norms, in which the normative function differs or might differ.

The last case—as shown by the examples above—occurs often in constitutional law with its more abstract norms and in the abstract part of criminal law, where the temporal, spatial, and personal applicability of a multitude of concrete crime-specifying norms has to be assessed. Therefore, it is no accident that the validity concept is used more frequently in constitutional law and in the abstract part of criminal law (cf. the examples in Sect. 3).

6 Is the Concept of Validity a Continuum Concept?

The qualification of a norm as valid or invalid by the summary concept of validity seems to be dichotomous/classificatory and not continuous/gradable (cf. Westerman, *supra*). However, secondary summary concepts like the concept of validity must follow the meaning of the primary concepts in this respect. If one takes obligation as one underlying primary concept, at first sight gradability is not applicable to this concept. However, if one considers the well-known distinction between rules and principles,[49] the picture changes. As far as principles are in question, the secondary qualification by the concept of validity might be continuous. Therefore, the gradability of the concept of validity depends on the gradability of the underlying primary concepts.

[49]Dworkin (1977), pp. 14–80.

7 What Are the Inner Legal Conditions for a Legal Norm to Be Valid Law?

In respect of different legal norms, different legal systems state different, arbitrary inner legal conditions for them to gain normative force or function, that is, to oblige, allow, forbid, authorize, change status, etc. and therefore be valid.

For example, in Germany, a federal statute (*Bundesgesetz*) becomes valid if several formal and material conditions are fulfilled, which are specified in Article 70 ff. of the *Grundgesetz*: e.g., as formal conditions, they have to be proposed either by the federal government (*Bundesregierung*), by the federal council (*Bundesrat*), or by some members of the parliament (*Bundestag*) (Article 76(1) *Grundgesetz* (GG)). It has to be accepted by the majority of the representatives of the *Bundestag* and under certain conditions by the *Bundesrat* (Article 77(1) GG). It has to be promulgated by the President in the Federal Law Gazette (Article 82(1) GG) etc. Afterward, it gains normative force on a specific date, determined in the statute.

A judgment of a court has very different inner legal conditions of normative force or function that are summarized as validity. For instance, for a judgment of a civil court in Germany to be valid, it has to be the final step of a civil trial; it further requires its oral promulgation in the courtroom and the written announcement to the parties (§§ 300, 310(1), 311, 313, 315 Zivilprozeßordnung (ZPO)).

8 What Are the Outer Legal Conditions for a Legal Norm to Be Valid Law?

There seems to be no outer legal factual condition for a legal norm to become valid law. Efficacy cannot be such a condition because after the specific legal speech-act is made and therefore existent, which satisfies the inner legal conditions (Sect. 7), it may take a considerable time until the norm becomes applicable to a first case and some further time until it is indeed applied to such a case. Nevertheless, the norm is already valid law—or so it is assumed.

There seems to be only one outer legal fact, which can turn a valid legal norm into an invalid one. This is the complete or nearly complete lack of efficacy over a prolonged period of time. However, it is open and uncertain what this lack of efficacy requires and how long exactly the prolonged period of time has to be (cf. Westerman, *supra*, for another perspective on this issue).

It is debated between positivists and nonpositivists whether a minimum of justice is a necessary condition for law to be valid. In the Radbruch formula, more precisely in the first part of the formula, such a condition of a minimum of justice is formulated.[50] Elsewhere I have endorsed a stricter criterion of what law is. Law must have the aim of mediation. Therefore, it is only law if all the persons affected by it are taken into consideration.[51] However, any positive legal system can incorporate the Radbruch formula as a positive legal metanorm as the German legal system did after 1945.

9 What Is the Relationship of the Summary Concept of Legal Validity to the Other Phases Respectively Consecutive Properties of Legal Norms?

If one distinguishes four phases resp. properties of a legal norm, that is, (1) existence; (2) normative result, force, or function (obligation, prohibition, allowance, authorization, creation, or affirmation of rights, change of legal status, etc.); (3) the needing and giving of justification; and (4) efficacy (e.g., acknowledgement of a norm and norm following), and identifies legal validity as a summary concept of the normative result, force, or function (phase or property (2)), the following question arises: what is then its relationship to the other three phases?

My thesis is this: each of the four phases of a norm of the positive law is a necessary but not a sufficient condition for the subsequent phase:

(1) To gain normative force and therefore oblige, forbid, allow, etc., summarized as being valid (phase 2), it is a necessary condition that the norm exists (phase 1). But existence is not a sufficient condition for normative force because in order to gain and retain normative force and therefore validity, several other inner and outer legal conditions have to be met, e.g. promulgation (Sect. 7) and no total lack of efficacy over a prolonged period of time (Sect. 8).
(2) To need and give justification (phase 3), it is a necessary condition for a legal norm that the norm exists (phase 1) and has normative force (phase 2). A norm that does not oblige, allow, forbid, authorize, etc. does not need and give justification. It is like a declarative speech-act and therefore like a statement of a fact, which does not impose upon the will of the addressee of the speech-act.

[50]Radbruch (1999), p. 216: "Der Konflikt zwischen der Gerechtigkeit und der Rechtssicherheit dürfte dahin zu lösen sein, daß das positive, durch Satzung und Macht gesicherte Recht auch dann den Vorrang hat, wenn es inhaltlich ungerecht und unzweckmäßig ist, es sei denn, daß der Widerspruch des positiven Gesetzes zur Gerechtigkeit ein so unerträgliches Maß erreicht, daß das Gesetz als 'unrichtiges Recht' der Gerechtigkeit zu weichen hat. Es ist unmöglich, eine schärfere Linie zu ziehen zwischen den Fällen des gesetzlichen Unrechts und den trotz unrichtigen Inhalts dennoch geltenden Gesetzen; eine andere Grenzziehung aber kann mit aller Schärfe vorgenommen werden: wo Gerechtigkeit nicht einmal erstrebt, wo die Gleichheit, die den Kern der Gerechtigkeit ausmacht, bei der Setzung positiven Rechts bewußt verleugnet wurde, da ist das Gesetz nicht etwa nur 'unrichtiges Recht', vielmehr entbehrt es überhaupt der Rechtsnatur."

[51]Cf. von der Pfordten (2011b, 2013), pp. 53ff., 66ff.

(3) To become efficacious, it is a necessary condition for a legal norm that the norm exists (phase 1), has normative force (phase 2), and needs and gives justification (phase 3). If a norm exists as a speech-act but is invalid because of defects in its making, one cannot qualify this norm as efficacious, even if the required act is performed.

To sum up, for positive law the concept of validity only has a minor function as a summary concept for the different forms of the phase/property (2) of norms, the normative result, force, or function (obligation, prohibition, allowance, authorization, creation, or affirmation of rights, change of legal status, etc.).

In respect of the function of the concept of validity in other areas and perspectives such as morals or social relations (cf. Kirste, *supra*) and ethics or sociology, it is crucial to differentiate these different areas. As validity is a very recent and subsidiary concept, one might suspect that in these other areas, too, the concept of validity has become hypertrophied and one should criticize this hypertrophy. For example, what does validity in morals add to obligation? What does validity in social relations add to factuality/efficacy? However, this would be another inquiry.

References

Alexy, Robert. 1992. *Begriff und Geltung des Rechts*. Freiburg/München: Karl Alber Verlag.

Austin, John Langshaw. 1962. *How to Do Things with Words*. Oxford: Clarendon Press.

Dworkin, Ronald. 1977. *Taking Rights Seriously*. Cambridge, MA: Harvard University Press.

Ehrlich, Eugen. 1989. *Grundlegung der Soziologie des Rechts*. 4th ed. Berlin: Duncker & Humblot.

Frege, Gottlob. 1986. Über Sinn und Bedeutung. In *Funktion, Begriff, Bedeutung. Fünf logische Studien*, ed. Günther Patzig, 6th ed., 40–65. Göttingen: Vandenhoeck & Ruprecht.

Grabowski, Andrzej. 2013. *Juristic Concept of the Validity of Statutory Law. A Critique of Contemporary Legal Nonpositivism*. Berlin: Springer.

Guastini, Riccardo. 1994. Invalidity. *Ratio Juris* 7: 212–226, Oxford: Wiley Blackwell.

Habermas, Jürgen. 1998. *Faktizität und Geltung*. Frankfurt a. M.: Suhrkamp.

Hage, Jaap C., and Dietmar von der Pfordten, eds. 2009. *Concepts in Law*. Heidelberg: Springer.

Hart, H.L.A. 1994. *The Concept of Law*. 2nd ed. Oxford: Clarendon Press.

———. 1963. *Law, Liberty, and Morality*. Stanford: Stanford University Press.

Hobbes, Thomas. 1991. *Leviathan*, ed. Richard Tuck. Cambridge: Cambridge University Press.

Kant, Immanuel. 1968a. *Kritik der reinen Vernunft*. Nachdruck Berlin: Akademie-Ausgabe. Vol. III/IV.

———. 1968b. *Die Metaphysik der Sitten*. Nachdruck Berlin: Akademie-Ausgabe. Vol. VI.

———. 2007. *Critic of Pure Reason, tr. Norman Kemp-Smith*. 2nd ed. Berlin: Springer.

Kelsen, Hans. 1960. *Reine Rechtslehre*. 2nd ed. Wien: Deuticke.

———. 1979. *Allgemeine Theorie der Normen*. Wien: Manz.

Larenz, Karl. 1929. *Das Problem der Rechtsgeltung*. Berlin: Junker & Dünnhaupt.

Lask, Emil. 1923 (1905). Rechtsphilosophie. In *Emil Lask: Gesammelte Schriften I*. Tübingen: Mohr.

———. 1923 (1911). Die Logik der Philosophie und der Kategorienlehre. In *Emil Lask: Gesammelte Schriften II*. Tübingen: Mohr.

Liebert, Arthur. 1914. *Das Problem der Geltung*. Berlin: Reuther & Reichard.

Lotze, Herrmann. 1912. *Logik*. Hamburg/Leipzig: Meiner.

Meyer, Stephan. 2011. *Juristische Geltung als Verbindlichkeit*. Tübingen: Mohr Siebeck.

Munzer, Stephan. 1972. *Legal Validity*. The Hague: Nijhoff.
Radbruch, Gustav. 1999. *Rechtsphilosophie. Studienausgabe*, hg. v. Ralf Dreier, and Stanley Paulson. Heidelberg: Müller.
Sartor, Giovanni. 2000. Legal Validity as Doxastic Obligation: From Definition to Normativity. *Law and Philosophy* 19: 585–625, Dordrecht: Springer.
———. 2006. *Validity as Bindingness. The Normativity of Legality*. Florence. EUI-Working Papers, Law No. 2006/18.
———. 2007. *Legal Validity: An Inferential Analysis*. Florence. EUI-Working Papers, Law No. 2007/24.
Searle, John. 1969. *Speech Acts. An Essay in the Philosophy of Language*. Cambridge: Cambridge University Press.
von der Pfordten, Dietmar. 2011a. *Rechtsethik*. 2nd ed. München: Beck.
———. 2011b. What is Law? Aims and Means. *ARSP* 97: 151–168, Stuttgart: Steiner Verlag.
———. 2013. *Rechtsphilosophie. Eine Einführung*. München: Beck.
———. 2015. On Obligations, Norms and Rules. In *Problems of Normativity, Rules and Rule-Following*, ed. M. Araszkiewicz et al., 165–176. Berlin: Springer.
Windelband, Wilhelm. 1920. *Einleitung in die Philosophie*. Tübingen: Mohr.

What Is Legal Validity? Lessons from Soft Law

Jaap Hage

Abstract The purpose of this article is to use the elusive phenomena of legal validity and soft law to illuminate each other. Three notions of legal validity are distinguished. Source validity and binding force (in a special technical sense) are internal legal notions that are used in legal argumentation. On the contrary, efficacy (also in a special technical sense) is an external notion, used in descriptive theories about law such as sociology of law or legal theory. Source validity is a characteristic of, among others, legal sources, and something was validly made in this sense if it was made by a competent agent in accordance with the relevant procedure. A rule has binding force if this rule exists and generates legal consequences when applied. A rule is efficacious if its consequences are accepted by the relevant legal subjects, including officials.

With these three notions of legal validity in place, the focus of the argument shifts to the nature of soft law and how it combines with the three notions of legal validity. For a proper analysis of soft law, three elements are required. First, it is necessary to replace the traditional rule-based view of legal reasoning by a view in which reasons, rather than rules, take the central place. For this purpose, a special logic for reasons, reason-based logic, is introduced into the argument. Second, it is necessary to replace the view of legal justification, according to which justification consists of an argument with the object of justification as its conclusion, with a view that emphasizes the dialogical nature of justification. For this purpose, a dialogical variant of reason-based logic is briefly explained. And third, the view of legal reasoning as a reconstruction of legal effects that exist independently has to be replaced by a constructivist view, according to which legal consequences are determined by means of legal argumentation.

On the basis of these three changes of perspective, the definition of soft law as law that can less easily be used in legal argumentation becomes understandable. Moreover, the tools that have become available by the introduction of the three notions of validity, dialogical reason-based logic, and constructivism make it possible to

J. Hage (✉)
University of Maastricht, Maastricht, The Netherlands
e-mail: jaap.hage@maastrichtuniversity.nl; http://www.jaaphage.nl

© Springer International Publishing AG, part of Springer Nature 2018
P. Westerman et al. (eds.), *Legal Validity and Soft Law*, Law and Philosophy Library 122, https://doi.org/10.1007/978-3-319-77522-7_2

identify different reasons why legal rules may be soft: limited applicability, dubious binding force, frequent exceptions, and weak reasons for the rule consequences.

1 Introduction

The nature of legal validity was and still is intensely debated. Highlights in the jurisprudential literature of the twentieth century are the works of Kelsen (1960), Ross (1946, 1959), Hart (2012), Dworkin (1978, 1986), Raz (1979), Alexy (1994, 2002), Munzer (1972), and Grabowski (2013),[1] and the contributions to the present collection testify to the continuation of this lively discussion. Looking at the ongoing discussion, one might wonder with Mackor and Westerman (present volume) whether philosophical hairsplitting has not sometimes taken the lead over practical relevance. Yet practical relevance there is, and this contribution will focus on one issue where the nature of legal validity plays a central role, that is, the validity of soft law.

Phenomena that are labeled as "soft law" are omnipresent. The expression "soft law" is often used to refer to rules based on quasi-legal instruments, which lack legally "binding force," whatever that may be, or whose binding force is somewhat weaker than the binding force of traditional law. Examples include the UN Declaration of Human Rights, recommendations in the law of the European Union, tax resolutions, published governmental policies, self-regulation in particular branches of society, codes of conduct for companies and governmental organizations, restatements of the common law, and case law in the civil law tradition. Despite this ubiquity of soft law—which, by the way, does not always go by that name—the precise nature of soft law is not yet clear, and it is possible that there is more than one kind of soft law (Westerman, present volume).

In the present contribution, the elusive phenomenon of soft law will be used to shed light on the at least equally elusive phenomenon of legal validity, and the other way round. As we will see, the binding force that soft law seemingly does not possess is often identified with legal validity. If that identification is made, an analysis of the binding force of soft law may shed light on the nature of legal validity, and the other way round. This mutual illumination, or at least an attempt to bring it about, constitutes the guiding principle of the present article.

To achieve this illumination, first a fundamental distinction between "internal" and "external" claims about the validity of rules will be made and elaborated (Sect. 2). Then an attempt will be made to give soft law a place in the preliminary account of legal validity that will by then be available. To that purpose, attention will be paid to a version of legal logic that takes reasons rather rules as its foundation (Sect. 3) and to a representation of legal reasoning as a real debate between parties (Sect. 4). The findings of Sects. 3 and 4 will be used to modify the existing account of validity

[1]The contributions of Von der Pfordten and Kirste to the present volume contain historical overviews with emphasis on the German-language literature.

and to give soft law a place in this account (Sect. 5). The contribution will be summarized and concluded in Sect. 6.

2 Internal and External Claims About Legal Validity

2.1 Binding Force

Because soft law is often considered to be law without or with weaker binding force, it is useful to first get some grip on the notion of binding force and its relation to legal validity. There are two fundamentally different views of law's binding force. One view sees the binding force of law as a causal influence. Law is binding because and to the extent that it influences human behavior. The other view emphasizes the immaterial nature of law's binding force: law is binding if it imposes obligations.

Law is almost literally binding if it is a causal influence in bringing about the behavior or the results that it prescribes. For example, if a person who has been sentenced to a term in jail is arrested by the police and handed over to the prison authorities, the law enforces the duty to go to prison in the strongest possible way. Almost the same holds when the law brings about the obligatory transfer of some real estate without the cooperation of the owner or when the law allows attachment in case a debtor does not perform. The binding force of law would in this case consist in being enforced.

A somewhat weaker way in which law can influence people is when law motivates people to behave in a particular way. If law directly motivates people, human behavior is the result of the internalization of legal obligations: the very awareness of an existing obligation normally suffices to motivate the agent to comply with the obligation. If law indirectly motivates people, the threat of sanctions, in a very broad sense, plays a role. Legal subjects are aware of existing obligations and of sanctions that may be applied if the obligations are violated. This combined awareness motivates them to comply with the law. The binding force of law would in this case consist in intentional—although not necessarily voluntary—compliance.

It is entirely possible to speak about the validity of law if one means to say that law is being enforced or intentionally complied with. However, this is not the meaning of binding force that Kelsen had in mind when he identified validity and binding force. According to Kelsen, validity in the sense of binding force is something that does not consist in facts alone (Kelsen 1960, p. 196). If we want to understand what is meant by the idea that the validity of a legal rule consists in its binding force, and we want to stay close to Kelsen's view on validity as binding force, we should look further than pure enforcement or compliance.

Law has obligatory binding force if it can create obligations. Since it is one of the purposes of law to guide human behavior by imposing obligations, it almost seems true by definition that law has this obligatory binding force. However, some legal rules impose obligations, while other legal rules have other functions. They confer competences or establish that some entities legally also count as entities of some other kind. For instance, a rule of constitutional law grants the formal legislator the competence to make statutes, and a definitional rule establishes that certain persons count as suspects in the sense of procedural criminal law. There should be one kind of binding force that applies to all legal rules in the same manner, and it should be the same for rules that impose obligations on the one hand and for competence-conferring and counts-as rules on the other hand. In the following discussion of this issue, I will use counts-as rules as representative of legal rules that do not impose obligations.

A rule of criminal procedure might be that a person about whom a serious suspicion exists, on the grounds of facts and circumstances, that he has committed a crime counts as a criminal suspect.[2] This rule establishes that a person who satisfies its conditions is a suspect in the sense of the law. It does not impose any obligation, in particular not the obligation (or even the permission) to consider or treat a person as a suspect. Somebody who does not recognize a person as a criminal suspect, even though the latter is a suspect according to the law, makes a legal error. But this error is an error of misclassification, not the violation of an obligation.

In general, it holds that counts-as rules do not impose legal obligations and therefore cannot have binding force in the sense of imposing obligations. Therefore, if binding force is to be the same thing for all legal rules, it cannot consist in the fact that they impose legal obligations. Not all individual legal rules have the obligatory force that is the topic of this subsection. This means that if we are looking for a kind of binding force that all legal rules have in common, it must be something other than obligatory force.

When we look for a notion of binding force that is equally applicable to obligation-imposing, competence-conferring, and counts-as rules, a suitable candidate presents itself. A rule has binding force if and only if it attaches legal consequences to operative facts. For instance, a rule of contract law attaches the existence of obligations to the operative fact that a contract has been concluded; a rule of constitutional law attaches the legal consequence that some governmental body has the competence to make statutes to the operative fact that this body is the formal legislator; and a rule of procedural criminal law attaches the legal consequence that a person is a suspect to the operative fact that there are serious suspicions about this person based on facts and circumstances.

2.2 *Introducing Validity Claims*

The claim that a particular rule is valid can be made both in legal discourse and in discourse about law. For example, a lawyer who wants a particular rule to be applied

[2]The content of this example rule was inspired by Article 27 of the Dutch Code for Criminal Procedure.

may argue that this rule is valid because it can be distilled from the case law of the court. A sociologist of law may argue that a particular rule has lost its validity because after many years of use, it has become obsolete and the rule is not complied with and no longer enforced by the courts. The former use of the notion of validity is part of legal reasoning. Rules play an important role in establishing the legal consequences of a case and therefore also in legal disputes. A claim that a rule is valid can be made in such a dispute, and then its import is that the rule can or should be used in assigning the rule's consequences to a case. Such a claim, made with the purpose of justifying the use of the rule, is an internal validity claim.

A sociologist who studies the phenomenon of law will obviously find that rules play an important role in law. Part of his research may concern the issue which rules exist and what the defining characteristics of rule existence are. This sociologist may report on his findings by making claims about the validity of rules, and he may provide criteria for validity as part of a methodological underpinning of his research.[3] Such claims about the validity of rules and about the nature of legal validity are typical examples of external claims about validity.

The purpose of internal and external validity claims is very different, and it should not be surprising that the truth conditions of internal and external validity claims differ. Since internal validity claims are part of legal discourse, the truth conditions of these claims are governed by law. In the next section, we will pay more attention to these conditions, but legal sources often play an important role in this connection. Moreover, because the law of different countries may differ, the truth conditions of internal validity claims may also differ slightly between countries.[4] The truth conditions of external validity claims may depend on the purpose of these claims. Is the theory in which these claims play a role predictive or explanatory,[5] and in the latter case what kind of explanation is aimed for? At first sight, one should not expect differences between different countries, however.

[3]To avoid ugly "he/she"-constructions, I will adhere to the convention that the gender of the author is used when the gender of the person referred to in the text is immaterial: in the present case this means that "he" is so used. I can only encourage female authors to use "she" in this connection.

[4]If the differences between the truth conditions for internal validity claims were to be large, the question should be raised whether they are really truth conditions for the same claims. Suppose that German and English law have very different conditions for the validity of legal rules, can we then still say that the German "*Geltung*" as applied to legal rules means the same as the English "valid"?

[5]As Westerman and Mackor (this volume) both point out, claims about validity in the sense of efficacy, the kind of validity-claims one can expect in external discourse about law can sometimes be used to justify claims about the binding force of some rule. The latter kind of claim is most typically made in internal legal discourse. See also Sect. 5.4 of the present contribution.

2.3 *Internal Validity Claims: Binding Force and Source Validity*

Claims that a particular rule is valid, or that it is not valid, often play a role in disputes about the legal consequences of a case. In a somewhat simplified representation, a solution for a case is argued by adducing a rule that leads to this conclusion and by pointing out that the case at hand satisfies the conditions of this rule (cf. MacCormick 1978, pp. 19–52).

An attack on such a rule-applying argument may consist in contesting the validity of the rule that is used. In that case, an additional argument is required to argue that the rule is valid. The validity at issue then means that the rule may be used in arguments that support claims about the legally correct outcome of a case.[6] We will denote this kind of validity as binding force. A claim about binding force is an internal validity claim, typically made to support a rule-applying argument.

How can a claim about validity in the sense of binding force be supported? As we shall see in Sect. 5, the answer to this question is controversial, but there is agreement that legal sources play an important role in establishing the binding force of a legal rule. A rule may be said to bind if it stems from such a validity source. What these validity sources are depends on the legal system at issue, but sources that are usually recognized are legislation, international treaties (conventions), custom (mainly in international law but also in private law), and also, in the common law tradition, judicial decisions (case law).

Three of the main validity sources concern rules that have been explicitly created: legislation, treaties, and court decisions. Not everybody has the power to make legal rules, and those who do have this power are typically subject to procedures for doing so. As a consequence, disputes may arise on whether some person or body had the power to create a rule or whether the correct procedure was followed. Confusingly, such disputes are often also conducted by means of validity claims. However, this time the validity concerns not the rules that were created but the instances of the legal source by means of which they were created.[7] Was this particular bill validly passed in the legislative chamber? Was the court competent to decide this case? Was the treaty already ratified by sufficiently many parties? These are the kinds of questions that may arise in disputes about the source of an alleged legal rule, and these disputes are about the validity of the source.[8] Therefore, we will from now on call this kind of validity "source validity."

---

[6]This point was already made by Sartor (2005, pp. 335/6).

[7]Mackor (present volume) disagrees here, but the difference seems superficial. According to Mackor, a rule is (source) invalid if the rule stems from a defective source.

[8]To avoid misunderstandings: they are disputes about the validity of the instance of the source. So the validity of a particular bill may be questioned in this connection, but not the role of legislation in creating law. The latter discussion is also possible, but that would again be a discussion about the binding force of a rule, namely the social convention (the "rule of recognition") that identifies the

Source validity plays an important role in legal arguments because one of the main reasons why a rule is binding is that it stems from a source that is valid: binding rules often stem from source-valid legislation. The validity of legislation is not the same as the validity of the rules created by that legislation. In the case of legislation and rules, this is easy to see because of the different words used ("legislation" as opposed to "rules"). It is far less clear when the so-called process-product ambiguity applies, as is the case with contracts. A contract as a meeting of wills—if that is how one sees the creation of a contract—is not the same as a contract in the sense of a set of obligations. The set of obligations can be terminated and then its validity (binding force) ends, while the meeting of the wills is an event that cannot be turned back.[9]

2.4 *External Validity Claims: Validity as Efficacy*

External validity claims can be defined as validity claims that are not used to support legal conclusions in general and that are in particular not used in rule-applying arguments. Such claims are typically made by social scientists who are interested in the existence of rules, and they are discussed for methodological purposes not only by social scientists but also by legal theorists, such as the Scandinavian realists, for example, Olivecrona and Alf Ross, as well as by Austin. Although the precise criteria for when a legal rule is valid in this sense are disputed, there seems to be no reason to assume that more than one external notion of validity is in use.

The hot issue with regard to this kind of validity is whether it can be defined in "naturalistic" terms.[10] The Scandinavian realists made it a part of their research program to give such a naturalistic definition (e.g., Ross 1946), while Kelsen made it a starting point of his *Reine Rechtslehre* that such a naturalistic definition is not possible (Kelsen 1960, p. 1).

The internal validity claim when applied to legal rules boils down to the fact that the rule generates legal consequences. But how can it be established that a rule actually does so? In other words, is there a way to check whether a valid rule really does what it should do given its binding force? Some authors might claim that it is a priori given that legal rules lead to legal consequences and that no independent evidence is possible, let alone required. However, theorists with a more sociological mind-set would look for evidence in social reality and more in particular in the recognition of these consequences by relevant persons. Such a search only makes

validity-sources of a particular legal system. This distinction is emphasized in Carpentier's contribution to the present volume.

[9]However, it is in principle possible to "avoid" juridical acts, including legislation and contracts. Such avoidance means that the legal consequences are no longer attached to the event in question and these consequences lose their validity in the sense of binding force.

[10]The term "naturalistic" is put between quotes, because it is not very clear what it means. The idea is often associated with empirical verifiability, or with physical properties. Cf. the distinction between methodological and substantive naturalism in Leiter (2014).

sense if the facts embodied in the legal consequences are facts in social reality that can exist through being collectively recognized as existing. What would such recognition amount to? Important aspects of collective recognition are that sufficiently many and/or sufficiently important members of a social group believe the fact to be present, believe that sufficiently many and/or sufficiently important other members also believe the fact to be present, and believe that these mutual beliefs constitute the believed fact. Perhaps some examples can illustrate what this involves for different kinds of social facts.

Suppose that about 20 persons together make a trip on foot to the top of a mountain. They each believe that they are *as a group* walking to the mountain top, they each believe that each of the others also believes that they are walking as a group to the top, and they all believe—minimally in the sense of not denying it when asked—that their mutual beliefs about acting together establish that they are walking as a group to the mountain top rather than as a set of individuals.[11] In this case, the people in the group make a trip on foot to the mountain top as a group.

The above example deals with collective recognition of acting together, but collective recognition does not always deal with collective action. Suppose that one member of the group, say Henriette, utters strong opinions about which path to take to the top of the mountain and that most of the group members tend to act on these opinions. After having several times chosen a particular path for the reasons that Henriette proposed for taking it, most group members recognize the leading role of Henriette. They believe that Henriette has become the leader of the group, that most other group members hold the same belief, and that Henriette is the leader of the group because she is recognized as such by most group members. In this example, the social fact concerns the possession by Henriette of the status of leader of the group.

In the two examples above, recognition took the form of believing. However, sometimes mere believing does not suffice. If the leadership of Henriette in the group of mountain climbers has been sufficiently established, the group members may collectively recognize an order from Henriette as a reason for acting. Suppose that Henriette ordered Susan to walk at the back of the group to see to it that nobody stays behind. Then Susan is considered to be obligated to walk at the back on the basis of collective recognition. This involves that she is liable to be criticized by group members, including herself, if she does not walk at the back. This also involves that group members who recognize that they have an obligation will typically, but not without exceptions, be motivated to do what they believe they are obligated to do. Existence of an obligation as a social fact requires this "critical reflective attitude" (Hart 2012, p. 57), which goes further than mere belief that the obligation exists, although it includes that belief.

[11]It is presupposed here that if the members of a group collectively believe that they are walking, they are actually walking. Collective delusions are somewhat problematic for social facts. This is not the place, however, to elaborate a theory of social actions that deals with this complication.

Susan is obligated to walk at the back in the sense of collective recognition, but Henriette's competence to create such a duty for Susan is also based on this collective recognition. The group members collectively recognize an order from Henriette as creating a duty for the person who was ordered. They do this by collectively recognizing the duties that ensue from the orders. In combination, this amounts to the recognition of a power to create duties by giving orders. This power actually exists through being recognized. This is an example of a fact—the existence of a power—that exists in the sense of collective recognition, where the recognition consists not in a belief but in a complex set of dispositions to act.

The last two examples illustrate how the consequences of counts-as rules and mandatory rules can exist in social reality in the form of recognition. Rules may be said to be valid in the sense of being efficacious if this kind of recognition of their legal consequences takes place. Following Hart (2012, p. 60/1), it is important to point out that in this connection, there may be a division of recognition-labor. The recognition of legal consequences may be delegated by the legal subjects to officials, who must in turn be recognized as officials by the "people."[12]

We see that it is possible to verify whether people recognize the consequences of rules and therefore also whether they consider a rule to bind. It must be emphasized, however, that what is verifiable is whether people consider a rule to have binding force, not whether a rule actually has this binding force. The claim that a rule is binding is a claim from the internal point of view, a claim that can be justified, but not one that can be verified independently.

The recognition of the legal consequences of a rule is not an all-or-nothing matter. A single person may recognize the consequences of a rule once, quite often, or always, and from a group of persons, one, some, or practically all may recognize the consequences.[13] It is clear that recognition comes in degrees, and since validity in the sense of efficacy is defined in terms of recognition, it comes in degrees too. This was recognized by Ross, who identified the validity of a rule with the probability that the rule would play a role in court decisions, and acknowledged that this probability may have different values (Ross 1959, p. 45; see also the contribution of Eliasz and Zaluski to the present volume). In the eyes of Ross, this was a feature that distinguished his theory of validity from other theories (e.g., the Kelsenian) according to which the notion of validity must be absolute, an all-or-nothing matter. We can now see that this difference can be explained by the fact that Kelsen wrote about validity as binding force, while Ross was discussing validity as efficacy. Kelsen and Ross did not necessarily have different views of legal validity; they were writing about different kinds of validity.

[12]In her contribution to this volume, Waltermann explores this role of the people and how this role sits together with different views on the nature of law.

[13]This observation plays an important role in the contributions to this volume of Van Klink and Lembcke and Westerman.

3 Reason-Based Logic

3.1 Introduction

We have an overview of what is involved in validity, with the distinction between on the one hand source validity and validity as binding force, which play a role in rule-applying arguments, and on the other hand validity as efficacy, which primarily plays a role in external discourses about law such as sociology of law and legal theory. It is now time to pay more attention to the phenomenon of soft law, to see whether it can still improve our insight into the nature of legal validity.

According to a popular view,[14] soft law consists of rules, in a broad sense, that were created by means of legal instruments that are not valid. This means that these instruments were made either by a body that did not have the power to do so or by means of a procedure that is not suitable for creating binding legal instruments. In the eyes of a hard legal positivist who identifies validity of rules with being validly made, this means that soft law is not valid or—which boils down to the same thing—has no binding force.[15] Moreover, if soft law lacks binding force, meaning that it has no legal consequences, soft law is not law either. This still leaves the possibility open that some instruments, which are seemingly legal, influence the behavior of people, including legal officials such as courts. They might therefore have some validity in the sense of efficacy, but efficacy cannot play a role in legal arguments and is from an internal perspective of limited interest.

However, it is not necessary to adopt a hard legal positivist view and to demand source validity as a condition for binding force. In Sect. 5, we will pay some attention to the possibilities of assuming binding force for rules that were not validly created. However, before doing so, we need an account of how soft law can seemingly exist without having binding force or with only a limited amount of it. That account will be presented briefly in the present and the following sections. It consists of two steps. The first step deals with the logic of legal reasoning and presents a logic based on reasons as a subtler alternative to a logic based on rules. This is necessary to account for the "weaker binding force" of soft law. The second step replaces the view of legal reasoning as an argument leading from a case description and legal rules to a legal consequence by the view that legal argumentation consists in a debate between two or more parties, a debate in which the outcome of a case is fixed. This is necessary to translate the logical possibilities of reason-based logic into a characteristic of rules belonging to soft law.

---

[14]This view is represented by the rough delineation of soft law in the contribution of Mackor to this volume.

[15]This is emphasized in the contribution to this volume of Van Klink and Lembcke.

3.2 Reasons Instead of Rules

Traditionally, legal reasoning on the basis of rules is represented as a kind of syllogism. We have a rule with the following structure:

IF Conditions, THEN Legal Consequences.

This rule functions as the major premise of the syllogism. The minor premise consists of a description of the facts of a case that satisfy the conditions of the rule:

Conditions.

Together they allow the derivation by means of a modus ponens-style argument of the legal consequences:

Conclusion.

This argument is deductively valid, which means that if both premises are true, the conclusion must logically also be true. There is no room for exceptions to the rule as it is formulated in the major premise, and neither is there an opportunity for balancing this argument against other arguments. Replacing this rule-based model of legal reasoning by a model where reasons take a central place makes it easy to account for the balancing of arguments (or reasons), and it also facilitates an account of exceptions to rules.[16]

3.3 Reasons

A reason is a fact (expressed by a true statement) that pleads for or against a particular conclusion. Some examples:

a. The fact this this body is the formal legislator is a reason why (pleading for the conclusion that) this body is competent to legislate.
b. The fact that Jane is a thief is a reason to punish her.
c. The fact that Jane is a minor is a reason not to punish her.
d. The fact that Gerald promised to return Jane's money to her is a reason why Gerald is obligated to return Jane's money.

A reason is characterized by two properties. The first is that something can only be a reason if it is really the case. Hypothetical facts can only be hypothetical reasons, not real ones. So if the present author had been the head of state of Belgium, that would be a reason to treat him in a ceremonial way. However, since he is not the head of state, this merely hypothetical fact is not an actual reason.

[16]The logic proposed here is in the eyes of the author the most elegant way to deal with balancing, but during the last few decades many different logics for "defeasible" legal reasoning have been developed. See: Verheij (1996), Hage (1997), Prakken (1997), and Sartor (2005).

The second characteristic is that reasons are relevant for some conclusion, either in a positive way (a pro reason) or in a negative way (a con reason). Moreover, this relevance is not confined to individual facts. If the fact that Jane is a thief is a reason to punish her, the fact that John is a thief is (normally) also a reason to punish him. Reasons can be universalized: if some fact of a particular kind is a reason for a particular kind of conclusion, then in principle all facts of that kind are reasons for conclusions of that kind.

3.4 Nexus

If a reason is universalized, the result is a general connection between kinds of facts. An example of such a connection would be that being a thief is a reason for being punished or—somewhat ambiguous—that thieves should be punished. The ambiguity of the latter formulation rests in the fact that it may be the expression of a connection between kinds of facts that *establishes* that persons who are thieves are persons who should be punished but that it may also be a descriptive sentence that claims that persons who happen to be thieves also happen to be persons who should be punished (for whatever reason). The connection between types of facts is a kind of rule that exists (has binding force) or not but that cannot be true or false. The descriptive sentence is true or false.[17]

The connection between kinds of facts that establishes that facts of one kind tend to be reasons for or against facts of the second kind may be (legal) rules and also (legal) principles. We need a term that covers both possibilities and therefore adopt the technical term "nexus" for this purpose. So a nexus is a connection between two kinds of facts that established that facts of the former type are reasons for or against facts of the latter type. Nexus are not true or false but are valid or invalid in the sense of binding force.[18]

It is possible to give reasons for or against the binding force of nexus. A typical example would be a discussion in legal interpretation where different interpretations of a legislative text are defended. Each interpretation leads to a different rule, and a reason that pleads for a particular interpretation is also a reason for the binding force of the rule that corresponds to that interpretation of the text and against the binding force of rules based on different interpretations (Hage 1997, p. 197). A different example would be an argument about the binding force of a rule of soft law such as the Charter of the United Nations. The authority of the General Assembly pleads as a reason for the binding force—and therefore the validity—of the rules based on the

[17]Cf. the discussion of rules and their factual counterparts in Hage (2015).

[18]Legal rules are one kind of nexus, but there are many other examples. For example the facts that somebody is a male and that he is unmarried are together a reason for the conclusion that this person is a bachelor. This reason is based on the definition (a nexus) that unmarried males are (count as) bachelors. The fact that the train departed too late is a reason why the train will probably not arrive on time. The underlying nexus is that trains which depart too late will probably arrive too late.

Charter, while the lack of competence of the General Assembly pleads against the validity of these rules.

3.5 *Balancing*

If there are several reasons pleading for or against a conclusion, these reasons need to be balanced, unless all the reasons point in the same direction. The outcome of this balancing operation is a decision on which set of reasons, the pro reasons or the con reasons, outweighs the other set.

It is possible to give reasons for (or against) the conclusion that one set outweighs the other set. Take the following example. The issue at stake is whether a motorized wheelchair counts as a vehicle under the prohibition on using vehicles near the soccer stadium. That a motorized wheelchair satisfies the definition of vehicles in a bylaw is a reason to count it as a vehicle. That a prohibition of motorized wheelchairs near the stadium would make it practically impossible for some handicapped persons to attend soccer matches would be a reason against counting them as vehicles. The newly adopted policy to give handicapped persons as much as possible equal opportunities to participate in social life is a reason why the con reason outweighs the pro reason. Therefore, on the balance of reasons, the conclusion should be that a motorized wheelchair does not count as a vehicle for the purpose of the prohibition.

As this example illustrates, the presence of a reason for or against a conclusion in itself cannot determine whether the conclusion should be adopted. Only on the balance of all pro and con reasons can the decision be taken whether the conclusion should be adopted. That is why these ordinary reasons are sometimes called "contributory reasons": they only contribute to the overall picture of reasons, which together determine the status of the conclusion.

3.6 *Exclusionary Reasons and Rules*

Facts that satisfy the conditions of a nexus are normally reasons for the conclusion of the nexus. Take for instance the nexus that contracts must be complied with. This nexus normally makes the fact that X has contracted to do Y into a reason why X has an obligation to do Y. The existence of the nexus establishes that there is a general connection between the conditions and the conclusion of the nexus. However, there may be exceptional circumstances that establish that this general connection is blocked. For example, if X was forced into the contract, the fact that he contracted to do Y is no longer a reason why he should do Y. Raz dubbed such exceptional circumstances "exclusionary reasons," and exclusionary reasons are best interpreted as reasons that block the operation of nexus.[19] If an exclusionary reason is present, a fact that would normally be a reason for a conclusion exceptionally does not count as such a reason.

Legal rules are often the result of a legislative decision-making process, in which a number of reasons based on policies, goals, values, interests, principles, etc. are weighed to achieve a balanced result. In many of the cases to which these legal rules may be applied, the underlying goals, principles, etc. would also be relevant. However, if the rule is applicable, there is no longer any need for the policies etc. underlying the rule because if the reasons based on those were also taken into account, they would be counted twice: once as reasons based on the underlying policies etc. and once as reasons based on the rule. Therefore, if a rule is applicable to a case, it excludes all nexus that are already incorporated in the rule. The application of a rule to a case establishes not only that the rule generates a reason to resolve the case in a particular way (the way of the rule) but also that potential other reasons, based on the policies etc. underlying the rule, no longer count as reasons in this case.[20] As a consequence, the reason generated by a rule typically does not have to be balanced against other reasons because the potential other reasons were accounted for in the rule formulation and are excluded by the application of the rule. Normally, when a rule is applicable to a case, there is only one reason indicating what the legal consequences of the case are: the reason generated by the applicable rule. Therefore, rules take a special place among nexus.

3.7 Exceptions to Rules

A rule is applicable to a case if the case satisfies the conditions of the rule. Normally, this means that the rule should be applied and that it generates a reason to attach particular legal consequences to a case. However, sometimes an applicable rule should not be applied, and we then say that there is an exception to the rule. Two major reasons to make an exception to a rule are, first, that application of the rule would violate the purpose of the rule and, second, that there is also another applicable rule with an incompatible conclusion, which prevails in the case at hand over the first rule.

Take for example the rule that farmers are obligated to combat thistles that grow on their land and that thistles can only be combated by using certain kinds of herbicides. The rule normally gives farmers a reason to use these herbicides to combat the thistles. Assume that there is also another rule that prohibits the use in open air of a chemical substance that is the main ingredient of the herbicide in

[19]This interpretation underlies the use of the term "undercutters" or "undercutting defeaters" for what Raz dubbed exclusionary reasons in the theory of defeasible reasoning. See Pollock and Cruz (1999), p. 196.

[20]Raz (1975), pp. 73–76.

question. Given this second rule, farmers are not allowed to use the herbicide. Let us also assume that, for reasons that are not relevant here, the second rule prevails over the first. This would create an exception to the first rule, and farmers would no longer have a reason to use the herbicide to combat thistles.

If there is an exception to a rule in a particular case, the rule should not be applied to that case and then it does not generate a reason.

3.8 Conclusion

Suppose that we have an argument in which a rule is applied to argue for particular legal consequences. To give a very simple example:

Thieves are punishable.
John is a thief.
Therefore, John is punishable.

Under a legal logic based on rules, the conclusion can be avoided in two ways. First, it is possible to deny that John is a thief, and second, it is possible to attack the rule that thieves are punishable. Under reason-based logic, both possibilities still exist, but there are two more possibilities. The one is to argue that an exception should be made to the rule, for example because the rule conflicts with some other applicable rule. The second possibility is to argue that the reason generated by the rule must be balanced against one or more other reasons and that these latter reasons outweigh the former reason. For instance, the reason that John is a thief must be balanced against the reason (against punishability) that punishment would in this case lead to heavy riots, and this latter reason is stronger than the former.

4 Legal Reasoning as Dialog

We have seen that the replacement of a logic based on rules by a logic based on reasons provides legal reasoners with two more opportunities to challenge conclusions based on rule-applying arguments. However, traditional logic consists of chains of propositions, and opportunities to challenge only make sense in a pragmatic setting in which arguments are moves in real dialogs. In this section, we will study a second deviation from the traditional logic for legal reasoning. After the replacement of rule-based logic by reason-based logic, we will replace monological logic, in which arguments are treated as timeless chains of propositions, with dialogical logic, which treats argumentation in the setting of real dialogs between parties who must reach an agreement on the outcome of a legal case. In this connection, we will first consider an argument as to why it is important to treat legal reasoning in the context of real-life dialogs, to continue with the development of a dialogical version of reason-based logic. After this has been done, we are finally in a position to analyze the phenomenon of soft law in Sect. 5.

4.1 Legal Constructivism

According to Kelsen, legal systems are characterized by the *Grundnorm* on the one hand and facts about rule creation on the other hand. Given the *Grundnorm* and the facts, the content of a legal system is fixed, to be discovered by the investigation of rule-creating facts or, in other words, by reading the official legal sources.

This view on the existence of legal rules is supplemented by a similar view on legal positions and legal status, such as a person being the owner of a good or being a criminal suspect. These facts, which are the result of rule application, are treated as if they existed in some independently existing "world of law." Legal decision-makers such as courts are sometimes presented as bodies that "find" and "apply" the law, with a silent presupposition that there is law to be found and applied. According to this view of law, legal reasoning is not necessary to bring about the legal consequences of concrete cases, but it is only necessary to obtain knowledge about the consequences that already exist independently. Legal reasoning is there to *reconstruct* the legal consequences, not to construct them.[21]

And yet when we look at legal practice, we can see that this picture of law is at least incomplete. If law is a system, as Kelsen would have it, it is at best an open system. The insight that law is not merely a rule-based part of social reality has given rise to a different view of law. This other view is that legal rules etc. are tools that are used in legal argumentation to *construct* the legal consequences of cases. These consequences are not already there, merely to be reconstructed through reasoning. They only exist as the *result* of legal arguments; legal argumentation is on this view constructive. Let us therefore call this view *legal constructivism*. According to legal constructivism, the quality of legal arguments determines the truth of legal propositions and not the other way round. Among others, through the influence of Dworkin,[22] who proposed a theory of law according to which legal judgments are the result of constructive interpretation, constructivist views of law have become quite popular, although not necessarily under that name.

On the constructivist approach that is proposed here, law is not a closed system. What may count as law depends on the quality of arguments that are *actually* adduced for a legal position. As a consequence, soft law can, at least in theory, play a role in legal arguments, and this may in turn be interpreted as the attribution of at least some kind of legal status to soft law. This is still very abstract, but in the following section we will go into some detail to make this argument about the legal status of soft law more explicit.

[21] Hage (2012).

[22] Dworkin (1986), chapters 2 and 7.

4.2 Reasons in a Dialogical Setting

To become more concrete about the role of soft law in a constructivist approach to law, it is necessary to provide some background knowledge on how argumentation in a legal setting works, and in particular on its dialogical setting. The following account tries to be not too far removed from actual legal practice. However, it is an account that is remotely based on formal logic and is therefore more structured than actual legal practices.[23] This should not vitiate its usefulness for understanding the constructive nature of legal reasoning, however.

Legal reasoning is not the mere production of arguments but an attempt to convince an audience to adopt a particular thesis. Examples of such theses are that a claimant is entitled to an unemployment benefit, that a state is obligated under international law to intervene in a civil war in a neighboring country, or that a suspect is liable to be punished for stealing an object in a computer game. The audience that needs to be convinced may be an opponent in a legal dispute, a forum of legal scholars, the producer of the argument who tries to convince himself, or a court.[24]

An important purpose of argumentation is to commit the audience to a thesis. For example, the court should become committed to the view that the suspect is to be convicted of stealing a virtual amulet. If a party in a dialog has become committed to a thesis, then the thesis may be said to have been justified to that party.

An audience can be convinced to accept a thesis by adducing reasons for the thesis. The audience may, if it wants, adduce reasons against the thesis, and whether the thesis should ultimately be accepted depends on the balance of the adduced reasons. If an audience is to be convinced that a particular fact is a reason to adopt a thesis, it must first be convinced that it is a fact and not a falsehood, and second it must be convinced that this alleged fact is relevant, a reason, to adopt the conclusion. For instance, if a court is to be convinced that John is guilty of theft because he forced Pancho to give away an amulet in a computer game (a virtual amulet), the court must be convinced first that John forced Pancho to give away a virtual amulet (truth) and second that forcing somebody to give away a virtual amulet makes one guilty of theft (relevance). As the latter formulation already indicates, relevance is not confined to a single case: all facts consisting in forcing somebody to give away a virtual amulet should in principle be relevant to the conclusion that somebody is guilty of theft. Acceptance of relevance boils down to accepting the binding force of the nexus (often the rule) that makes a fact of a particular kind relevant for a particular kind of conclusion.

---

[23]More details on dialogical reason-based logic can be found in Lodder (1999).

[24]The description of an argumentative process as a dialog between the proponent of a thesis and his audience suggests that there are always two parties involved in a legal dialog. That does not have to be the case. It is possible to devise a model of "dialogical" argumentation in which an arbiter plays a role who mediates between the other parties.

4.3 Commitment

A characteristic of dialogs that is important for our purposes is that the commitment of a party in the dialog to a particular thesis can—and often will—be the result of acceptance of the thesis by that party and in that sense voluntary. For example, the court accepts the thesis that John forced Pancho to give the virtual amulet to him (in the game, that is), and having accepted this thesis it also accepts that John should be sentenced to some punishment. Since acceptance is a voluntary act, it may be done for any reason, including a confession by the suspect, or even without a reason.[25] This establishes that legal argumentation is "open" in the sense that new and possibly unexpected facts may play a role.

However, commitment is not always a matter of voluntary acceptance. Somebody may become committed to a thesis even if he is reluctant to accept it. Take for example the thesis that the municipality Zutphen must grant an unemployment benefit to Denise. This thesis is justified for the audience consisting of Zutphen if either Zutphen directly accepts that it must grant the benefit or Zutphen is committed to other theses from which the duty to grant the benefit follows. This would, for instance, be the case if Zutphen is committed to

- the rule (nexus) that it should grant the benefit to a citizen if this citizen believed she would receive the benefit and this belief was justified on the basis of the behavior of the municipality,[26] and also
- the theses that Denise believed that she would receive an unemployment benefit and that this belief was justified because Zutphen published its policy for granting unemployment benefits and Denise met the conditions for a benefit as stated in the published policy.

Admittedly this is a simple example, but it illustrates two points. One is that commitment can be forced because of logical considerations. Given the two theses to which Zutphen is already committed, it is merely "logical" that it must provide the benefit, and this establishes that Zutphen is committed to the thesis that it should provide the benefit, even though it did not voluntarily accept this thesis. The important point here is that although commitment may be based on acceptance and is voluntary, it may also be forced. Forced commitment is often a matter of logic: a party in a dialog is committed to a thesis because the thesis follows logically from other theses to which that party was already committed.

The second point is that dialogical argumentation works backward: it starts from a thesis and works backward to the premises needed to justify acceptance of this

[25]A court will not normally accept theses without reasons, but in the end it must accept *some* theses without additional reasons, for instance the thesis that the suspect is telling the truth when he confesses his crime.

[26]Normally there would be additional conditions, for instance that the citizen undertook obligations because of her justified belief, but to keep the example manageable I will make some concessions on legal precision.

thesis. If the opponent in the dialog is already committed to the required premises, then he is also committed to the thesis and the thesis has been justified for the opponent. If the opponent is not yet committed to one or more of the required premises, the same procedure can be used to justify those premises. Theoretically, the justification process may go infinitely deep, with justifications for premises that function as justifications for premises that . . . and so on.

4.4 The Role of Law

A possible misunderstanding about the dialogical approach to legal reasoning is that there would be no special role for the law because the participants in a dialog can freely determine what they want to accept. There would only be one exception to this freedom, which exists when they are committed to a thesis because it "follows" from what they were already committed to. But even then, they ultimately determine for themselves what they will be committed to because in the end, every chain of commitments must end with premises to which a dialog party is committed because he accepted them.

This picture according to which dialog parties are ultimately free to accept what they want may be suitable for dialogs on unregulated topics, but it is not appropriate for legal dialogs. In legal dialogs, parties are committed to the law. By means of forced commitments, it is possible to mimic not only the demands of logic but also this commitment to the law. By assuming that all parties in a dialog are from the beginning of the dialog committed to the positive law, whether or not they accepted it spontaneously, it is possible to give law its rightful place in legal dialogs.

Commitment to the positive law would not make that legal reasoning on the dialogical approach work with a closed system of law because parties can always accept other premises next to the fixed legal ones, thereby allowing more rules than only those of the given positive law. In this way, the dialogical approach, even if it assigns a special place to positive law, allows more "legal" arguments than Kelsen would allow.[27]

However, there is more. Until now it was assumed that a dialog starts from some (zero or more) commitments at the beginning and gradually adds more commitments until eventually the thesis defended by the proponent is added.[28] Although it is possible to work with such dialogs, in which the commitments of the parties can only expand, this is not very attractive. In realistic dialogs, it should be possible to end commitments that were undertaken during the dialog or that were assumed from the

[27]There is no room to elaborate the following point, but it nevertheless deserves mentioning. Even where the body of valid laws is assumed to be fixed, the number of exceptions, and exceptions to exceptions, to these rules may still be open. This means that, even if the set of binding rules is closed, legal reasoning may still be open.

[28]A dialog also stops when both parties are committed to the negation of the main thesis, or if the parties stop adducing arguments.

very beginning of the dialog. However, ending a commitment should not be possible without good reasons. Therefore, a party who wants to end a commitment must commit his audience to recognize that the thesis to which he was originally committed is wrong. For example, if Zutphen originally accepted that Denise satisfied all the conditions for an unemployment benefit but wants to renege on this, it must commit Denise to the thesis that she does not satisfy all the conditions. So where originally Denise would have had the burden of proving that she satisfied the conditions, the burden of proof shifts at the moment Zutphen accepts this. From that moment on, Zutphen has the burden of proving that Denise does not satisfy all the conditions.

This may be interesting as a general aspect of dialogical justification, but it becomes particularly important in connection with the commitment to positive law. It means that a party who is committed to positive law at the beginning of the dialog has at least theoretically the possibility of convincing his opponent that a particular rule is not binding after all. One way to do so is, for instance, to argue that the present rule is based on a wrong interpretation of the legislation and that some other interpretation is to be preferred. Most often, this will not be an easy task, particularly if the opponent in the dialog has an interest in maintaining the existing commitments, and thus the commitment to the positive law will most likely remain as it was. However, theoretically, every commitment, including the commitment to the positive law, can be undone.

5 The Nature of Soft Law

Soft law is like efficacy because it comes in degrees: a rule of soft law may have less binding force than a rule of hard law. It is therefore tempting to identify soft law with law that has less efficacy than hard law. Yet this temptation is misguided because efficacy is an external notion of validity, while the claim that a particular rule is a binding legal rule, even if it is not very hard, is still an internal legal claim.

Can soft law then be interpreted in terms of source validity or binding force? To some extent it can be since typical soft law has not been made in a legally valid manner. However, this is only a negative characterization, which gives us no clue what soft law may be.

Binding force is an all-or-nothing matter: a rule is either legally binding or is not; there is no in-between. And yet for the characterization of soft law, we need a notion that allows for degrees. There must be the possibility for a legal rule to be more or less soft. This eliminates the possibility of a satisfactory characterization of soft law in terms of binding force.[29]

[29]Westerman, in this volume, seems to overlook the possibility that soft law comes in degrees, and is nevertheless fully binding. In that case, the required graduation of soft law can only be bought at the cost of allowing degrees of binding force. In the present author's opinion, not all reasons as to

Neither one of the three notions of validity we distinguished above can be used to define soft law, and yet all three of them are useful to better understand the nature of soft law. Running ahead of the argument in the following subsections, I want to put forward the hypothesis that soft law is law that can less easily be used in legal arguments than hard law. Or more precisely, a legal rule is softer the less easy it is to use in legal arguments, with as lower boundary the place where a rule stops to be binding law.

The idea of a rule being more or less easy to use in legal arguments is quite vague as it presently stands, but in the following subsections it will be substantiated by using the tools that were introduced in the sections above about reason-based logic and the dialogical approach to legal reasoning. A theory about the usability of rules in legal arguments can easily grow into a general treatise on legal argumentation, but this is not the place to present such a treatise. Therefore, the following account will necessarily remain superficial, focusing on the logical aspects of rules and not on the substantial reasons for or against applying a rule.[30]

5.1 Two Sides of Soft Law

The idea of soft law is typically associated with rules that somehow play a role in legal argumentation but that were not validly made, either because they were made by a body that lacked the relevant competence or because a body with the relevant competence did not follow the appropriate procedure. If a rule was not validly made, this is a contributory reason why this rule cannot easily be used in a legal argument, but it is not possible to argue backward: if a rule cannot easily be used, this may have many different reasons, and it is not justified to assume that there must be something wrong with the way the rule was created. So although the notion of soft law is connected to the notion of source validity, this connection is one-way only.

Soft law in the narrow sense has two sides. One side is that it was not validly created; the other side is that it cannot easily be used in legal arguments. It is also possible to work with a broader notion of soft law. This broader notion only focuses on the usability of soft law in legal argumentation and ignores the aspect of source validity. Soft law in the narrow sense can then be defined as rules that cannot easily be used in legal arguments—and which are therefore soft law in the broad sense—for the reason that they were not validly made.

why a legal rule is soft lend themselves to support the claim that the rule is less binding. However, in the end the matter is mostly semantic: it is possible—although not elegant—to use a notion of graded binding force to play the logical role of the graded notion of softness in this contribution.

[30]The contributions of Bódig, Brus, Mackor, Van Klink and Lembcke, Yugank and Westerman pay more attention to these substantive reasons. Most of what these authors write is highly compatible with the more abstract and logical account of the present contribution.

5.2 Applicability

Even if a rule is binding, this is no guarantee that it will play an important role in legal arguments. To play a role, a rule must not only exist, but there must also be reasons for applying it. By far, the most important reason for applying a rule is that it is applicable, meaning that a case satisfies the conditions of the rule. If hardly any cases satisfy these conditions, the rule may exist, but then it has little practical relevance.

This possibility of limited relevance seems to be quite uninteresting, but its relevance in the present connection lies in the fact that the applicability of one rule may be determined by other rules, which may be more or less easy to use in legal arguments. For example, a rule may create a strict liability for damage caused by persons for whom the liable person has a "special responsibility." The existence of such a "special responsibility" depends on the application of other rules defining it. If these other rules are unwritten or are for some other reason quite soft, the softness of these other rules translates into the applicability of the rule assigning strict liability and indirectly also into the softness of that rule.

5.3 Binding Force

A rule can only play a role in a rule-applying argument if it is binding. The easier it is to substantiate that a rule is binding, the harder is that rule. And the other way round, the harder it is to show a rule to be binding, the softer is that rule.

In a legal dialog, there are three possibilities with regard to showing a rule to be binding:

1. The dialog parties may be initially committed to the binding force of the rule.
2. The dialog parties may be initially committed to rules that make it easier to create "semi-forced commitment" to the rule.
3. Commitment to the rule depends completely on voluntary acceptance.

A rule to which parties are initially committed will normally be quite hard. However, this possibility will seldom occur. Parties are more typically committed to legal sources and their content than to the rules that are based on these sources. For example, dialog parties are committed to legislation as a source of law and to the presence of a particular rule formulation in the legislation. The translation from the rule formulation to the actual rule, which typically goes under the name "interpretation," is then still a matter that needs to be settled in a dialog.

The second possibility will be the most frequent one. In legal dialogs, the parties are typically committed to what the sources of law are. The typical reason that pleads for the binding force of a rule is then that the rule stems from a recognized source, which in turn typically boils down to the reason that the rule was validly made. For example, the rule that recommendations of the Commission provide binding rules for interpretation of EU regulations may be included in the initial commitment sets of legal dialog parties. Suppose that two dialog parties voluntarily accept the thesis that a particular recommendation by the Commission entails that some regulation has to be interpreted in a certain way. Given this voluntary acceptance, the parties are forcedly committed to this interpretation of the regulation. Because this forced commitment depends on an earlier voluntary acceptance of the interpretation of the recommendation, we speak of semi-forced acceptance.

In general, the parties in legal dialogs are from the beginning committed to a set of rules that specify what kinds of reasons can be adduced for and against the legal validity of a rule. These rules are the rules and principles used for identifying legal rules by the officials of a legal system and other influential participants such as legal scientists. The dialog parties are similarly committed to rules that specify when a rule is not legally binding. Let us call the rules belonging to either one of these two sets the 'validity rules' of a particular legal community. Together these sets of validity rules, to which the dialog parties are from the outset committed, partially determine which facts can be adduced to argue that a particular rule is or is not legally binding in order to obtain semi-forced acceptance.

Moreover, the dialog parties are also initially committed to rules that specify the relative weights of the reasons based upon the two validity sets and to the facts that are generally known to obtain, including the texts of the recognized sources of law. In other words, the initial commitments of the dialog parties determine which facts are decisive for the binding force of legal rules and also to some extent to which of these the parties are committed. It depends on the facts and on the dialog moves made by the parties which legal rules will be assumed to be binding in the dialog.

If the binding force of a rule depends on semi-forced commitment, the degree of softness of the rule depends on how easy it is to substantiate this semi-forced commitment. If a rule was validly made, the rule will typically be hard. If a rule was not validly made, it depends. For rules that were created, the fact that the creation was not valid will typically be a reason why the rule does not bind. However, many legal rules, or—perhaps better—nexus, were never created at all. Think in this connection of rules that indicate when particular terms are applicable (rules of meaning) or rules that give content to evaluative standards such as the standard of good faith. For these rules, the fact that they were not validly created is unproblematic because they were not created at all. Therefore, some of these rules will be quite hard, even though they were not created.

The third possibility is that parties in a dialog voluntarily agree on the binding force of a rule. Suppose that in a legal dialog one party claims the validity of the rule that forcing somebody to give away an amulet in a computer game counts as theft for the purpose of criminal law and that the opponent voluntarily accepts this claim. Then this counts-as rule can be considered as binding for the purpose of this dialog. In a dialog between two parties with opposite interests, this possibility will not be very relevant. However, if the legal debate is construed as a trialogue, in which both opposing parties are in a dialog with a neutral judge, this possibility becomes much more realistic.

The likelihood that parties in a legal dialog will voluntarily accept the binding force of some rule is nothing other than the efficacy of that rule. The likelihood that a party will accept a rule cannot be adduced as a reason why that party should accept the binding force of that rule, and therefore efficacy does not have an important role in legal dialogs.[31] However, efficacy is very important for the hardness or softness of a rule since a rule with high efficacy is typically a relatively hard rule.

5.4 Substantive and Formal Reasons for Binding Force

There are both substantive and formal reasons why a particular rule should (not) count as valid law.[32] The substantive (material) reasons are the most difficult to list because they depend on substantive theories about the desirable content of law.

The fact that a particular rule is broadly accepted as legally valid is a formal reason why this rule is legally valid. There are three variants of this first formal reason. A rule may be recognized as a legally valid rule because it stems from an official source of law. (Source-)valid legislation is typically considered to be such a source of law. The fact that a particular rule is based on the correct interpretation of such a legislative text tends to be a very strong reason why this rule counts as valid law. Legal certainty plays an important role in this connection[33] but also the idea of political obligation. Something similar holds for rules created by international organizations, such as the EU. The second variant is that a rule has a long history of being used, which may be seen as a reason to continue to use it. In this case, we speak of customary law. This reason is closely related to legal certainty. The third variant is that a rule is broadly accepted because it is seen as reasonable. This reason borders on substantive reasons for counting a rule as valid law. Moreover, if rules have a long tradition of use, this is a sign that this rule is considered to be reasonable. Variants two and three therefore overlap.

A second formal reason why a rule should be counted as binding is that legal subjects reasonably expect that this rule should hold. It is both necessary and desirable that legal subjects may know what the law is that applies to them, and therefore the fact that they expected a rule to apply is a reason to consider the rule as valid law. Publicly announced codes of corporate conduct belong to this category, as do published administrative policies and recommendations by the European Commission.

[31] However, parties may be committed to the rule of recognition that a reason why a rule is binding is that this rule is broadly accepted as such. This broad acceptance is efficacy and efficacy may therefore play some role in legal dialogs as a reason for binding force. Then we are talking about semi-forced commitment.

[32] This is elaborated as the difference between formal and material validity in the contribution of Sandro to the present volume.

[33] See the contributions of Sandro and Mackor to the present volume.

This second reason is closely related to the formal conditions for the existence of law that were listed by Fuller.[34] These conditions are that the law

1. consists of rules;
2. is accessible to the public;
3. does not work retrospectively;
4. is understandable;
5. is consistent;
6. does not require the impossible;
7. does not change too frequently;
8. is applied in adjudication.

If one or more of these conditions are not fully met, this is a reason why the law in question should not be considered as binding. Because the failure to meet the requirements comes in degrees, the corresponding reasons against the legal validity of the laws have a varying strength.

A third formal reason why a rule should be counted as binding is that the rule is a member of the legal system. This idea can of course be traced back to the work of Kelsen and Hart and is elaborated in the contribution of Carpentier to this volume.

5.5 *Exceptions and Strength of Reasons*

The more exceptions there are to a rule, the softer the rule is. There are two factors that determine how many exceptions a rule is amenable to. The first factor is how many different kinds of facts count as exceptions to the rule. For instance, if a rule potentially conflicts with many other rules, there will be many opportunities for making an exception to the former rule. The same holds if a rule is overinclusive in the sense that it is applicable to many cases that fall outside the purpose of the rule. The second factor is how often potential reasons for making an exception actually occur. For instance, if a rule potentially conflicts with some other rule, which would prevail over it, there may be many opportunities for making an exception. However, if the latter rule is seldom applicable, the opportunities for exceptions will seldom be realized, and the former rule may be very hard.

If a rule is applied to a case, this will "only" generate a reason for the conclusion of the rule. This reason may still have to be balanced against other reasons, and if this balancing leads to the conclusion that the other reasons outweigh the reason based on the rule, the conclusion of the rule is not attached to the case. The more often this happens, the softer the rule is.

Also in this connection, two factors play a role. The first, least important, factor is how strong the reason based on the rule is in comparison to the reasons against the rule conclusion. The weaker is the reason, the softer is the rule. However, it seldom

[34]Fuller (1963), Chapter 2. See also the contribution of Van Klink and Lembcke to this volume.

happens that a reason that results from rule application needs to be balanced against other reasons because the application of the rule excludes the existence of most other reasons. The greater the number of considerations that were taken into account in creating the rule, the greater the number of potential reasons that will be excluded if the rule is applied, and the harder the rule is.

For this latter reason, created rules will typically be harder than nexus that were not created or based on decision making at all. Created rules, in particular if they were validly created, typically exclude most if not all of the opposing reasons; reasons based on nexus that were not created, or that were not created validly, typically do not exclude many opposing reasons, and it depends on their strength whether they will outweigh these opposing reasons. Therefore, validly created rules are typically harder than nexus that were not created at all.

6 Conclusion

The purpose of this contribution was to shed light on the phenomenon of legal validity by means of soft law, and the other way round. A summary of the main findings may be helpful to see the connections between validity and soft law.

Soft law plays a role in legal argumentation, and understanding soft law therefore means understanding this role. There are two notions of legal validity that also play a role in legal argumentation. Source validity concerns legal sources, and the claim that something is source valid involves that this something was made by an agent that has the relevant competence and is in accordance with the relevant procedure. Validity in the sense of binding force concerns nexus, including legal rules, and boils down to the specific mode of existence of these nexus, which is that they attach consequences to fact situations or that they can be used in arguments supporting those consequences. It turned out that soft law is binding but not necessarily validly created law.

The hardness or softness of legal nexus depends on the usability of this nexus in legal argumentation. They are a matter of degree, and only if law becomes too soft does it lose its binding force, meaning that it loses its relevance in legal argumentation. Binding force is not a matter of degree, and therefore soft law cannot be characterized as law with limited binding force. It is possible that a legal rule, or—more generally—a legal nexus, is binding, though it may nevertheless be quite hard to use in legal argumentation. In such a case, a legally valid nexus is quite soft.

There is also a kind of validity, efficacy, that comes in degrees. However, the claim that a rule or some other nexus is valid in the sense of being efficacious is an external legal claim, used in sociology of law or in legal theory but not often in legal argumentation. Therefore, it is not possible to identify soft law with a low degree of efficacy. However, it was argued that low efficacy may be a way in which a rule is hard to use in legal argumentation and therefore soft.

In general, four kinds of formal grounds were found that can be used to argue why a particular nexus cannot be used in legal argumentation. The nexus may be seldom applicable, it may be invalid, it may be subject to many exceptions, and the reasons it generates may be relatively weak. These four grounds could be identified easily after the move was made from a rule-based logic for legal argumentation to a reason-based logic and from a monological view of legal reasoning to a dialogical, or—more generally—a procedural, view of it.

It turns out that the softness of some kinds of law does not impact the validity of that law in either one of the three senses of validity. However, all three kinds of validity turned out to be relevant for how hard or soft a legal nexus is, with a central role for validity as binding force.

Acknowledgements The author thanks Stephan Kirste, Anne Ruth Mackor, Pauline Westerman and Mark Rogers for useful comments on earlier versions.

References

Alexy, Robert. 1994. *Theorie der juristischen Argumentation*. 7e Auflage. Frankfurt a/M: Suhrkamp.

———. 2002. *The Argument from Injustice. A Reply to Legal Positivism*. Oxford: Oxford University Press.

Dworkin, Ronald. 1978. *Taking Rights Seriously*. 2nd ed. London: Duckworth.

———. 1986. *Law's Empire*. London: Fontana.

Fuller, Lon L. 1963. *The Morality of Law*. rev. ed. New Haven: Yale University Press.

Grabowski, Andrzej. 2013. *Juristic Concept of the Validity of Statutory Law. A Critique of Contemporary Legal Nonpositivism*. Berlin: Springer.

Hage, Jaap. 2015. The (Onto)logical Structure of Law: A Conceptual Toolkit for Legislators. In *Logic in the Theory and Practice of Legislation*, ed. M. Araszkiewicz and K. Pleszka. Cham: Springer.

Hage, Jaap C. 1997. *Reasoning with Rules*. Dordrecht: Kluwer.

———. 2012. Legal Reasoning and the Construction of Law. *i-Lex* 7 (16): 81–105. http://www.i-lex.it/us/previous-issues/volume-7/issue-16/103-legal-reasoning-and-the-construction-of-law.html.

Hart, H.L.A. 2012. *The Concept of Law*. 3rd ed. Oxford: Oxford University Press.

Kelsen, Hans. 1960. *Reine Rechtslehre*. 2nd ed. Wien: Franz Deuticke.

Leiter, Brian. 2014. Naturalism in Legal Philosophy. In *The Stanford Encyclopedia of Philosophy* (Fall 2014 Edition), ed. Edward N. Zalta. http://plato.stanford.edu/archives/fall2014/entries/lawphil-naturalism/ (last consulted on 28-01-2016).

Lodder, Arno. 1999. *Dialaw. On Legal Justification and Dialogical Models of Argumentation*. Dordrecht: Kluwer.

MacCormick, Neil. 1978. *Legal Reasoning and Legal Theory*. Oxford: University Press.

Munzer, Stephen. 1972. *Legal Validity*. Den Haag: Martinus Nijhoff.

Pollock, John L., and Joseph Cruz. 1999. *Contemporary Theories of Knowledge*. 2nd ed. Lanham: Rowman and Littlefield.

Prakken, Henry. 1997. Logical Tools for Modelling Legal Argument. In *A Study of Defeasible Reasoning in Law*. Dordrecht: Kluwer.

Raz, Joseph. 1975. *Practical Reason and Norms*. London: Hutchinson.

———. 1979. *The Authority of Law*. Oxford: Clarendon Press.

Ross, Alf. 1946. *Towards a Realistic Jurisprudence*. Copenhagen: Einar Munksgaard.

———. 1959. *On Law and Justice*. Berkeley: University of California Press.

Sartor, Giovanni. 2005. *Legal Reasoning. A Cognitive Approach to the Law*. Dordrecht: Springer.

Verheij, Bart. 1996. Rules, Reasons, Arguments. Formal Studies of Argumentation and Defeat. Dissertation University of Maastricht.

Concept and Validity of Law

Stephan Kirste

Abstract This paper argues that there is a difference between the concept of law and the validity of law. Whereas the concept of law provides the criteria of what law is, its validity signifies that law belongs to a certain system of meaning (e.g., a social, moral, or legal order). Accordingly, a norm that can properly be called law may or may not have legal, social, or moral validity (first thesis: separation of concept and validity of law). The first function of validity is to distinguish a particular system of meaning from others (second thesis: separation of different forms of validity). The validity of legal norms may depend on other systems of meaning such as morals (justice, equality, etc.) or social behavior (effectiveness, enforcement, acceptance, etc.) or not (third thesis: moral or social validity is not a necessary condition for the validity of law). Only norms that are law and are legally valid are also legally binding (fourth thesis: validity of law is a necessary condition for its bindingness).

1 Introduction

There is an ongoing debate in legal theory about the meaning of the concept and the validity of law.[1] These differences not only concern the criteria of law and the conditions of its validity; they also concern the question whether the concept of law and the validity of law have a necessary connection or even converge. If they do, then either only valid law would be law or we could omit the concept of validity altogether. The answer to this question presupposes a determination of what we mean by "validity of law" and what function validity has. In the theoretical debate, these questions are often presupposed. Instead, conceptions of validity often begin with the distinction of different kinds of validity and determine their relation.

[1] Grabowski (2013) provides an excellent overview and discussion from an analytical point of view.

S. Kirste (✉)
University of Salzburg, Salzburg, Austria
e-mail: Stephan.Kirste@sbg.ac.at

© Springer International Publishing AG, part of Springer Nature 2018
P. Westerman et al. (eds.), *Legal Validity and Soft Law*, Law and Philosophy Library 122, https://doi.org/10.1007/978-3-319-77522-7_3

Authors who assume that only valid norms are law, i.e., that validity is a necessary element of the concept of law, argue that only valid norms would indeed exist.[2] Only existing norms could fulfill the function of law, namely to motivate their subjects.[3] These authors understand validity in the sense of social efficacy.[4] Joseph Raz assumes that norms are true only if they really exist, like a nonexisting stone would not be a stone at all. The concept of validity would express exactly this existence.[5] However, the assertion that a nonexisting stone was a stone is wrong only in the sense that it expresses the assumption of the existence of the stone. The concept of a stone can be determined independently of any existing stone and even of the possibility that the imagined stone could exist at all, just as we can construct geometric forms that we have never seen before and that may perhaps never be seen. The same applies to norms: why shouldn't we be able to determine what a norm is, even if norms or a particular norm do not exist or at least do not exist in the usual forms of validity? It is not only possible to ask—as some legal positivists in the tradition of Hart do—if social facts have legal validity, but also if a presumed norm has legal, social and moral validity.

I will not follow this path. Instead, I will defend the thesis that the concept of law only determines what law is. Its sole function is to define the criteria for the understanding of a norm as law. The concept neither creates norms, nor would it lose significance if there were no positive norms. In contrast, the validity of law integrates a legal norm into a system of meaning. The concepts of law and of the validity of law have to be determined independently and have distinct meanings. However, both are necessary for the binding force of law. A norm is only legally binding if, *first*, it is law and, *second*, it is legally valid. The legal, social, and moral validity of law then observes legal norms from different angles[6] and answers the question whether the respective legal norm can be integrated into social practices or morals. Accordingly, I will discuss the concept of law (Sect. 2); the concept of validity of law and, specifically, the meaning of validity, the distinction between the forms of validity, and their significance for validity of law (Sect. 3); and, finally in my conclusion (Sect. 4), the binding force of law.

[2]Cf. Raz (1977), p. 339: "A rule which is not legally valid is not a legal rule at all. A valid law is a law, an invalid law is not."

[3]Jellinek (1959), p. 333: "All Law has as a necessary feature, that of validity. A legal sentence is only part of a legal order if it is valid; law that is no longer valid or not yet valid is not law in the proper sense of the word. A norm is valid if it is capable of working to motivate, to determine the will. This ability stems from the conviction that cannot further be deduced that we are obliged to follow it" (my translation, SK).

[4]Again Jellinek (1959), p. 334.

[5]Raz (1977), p. 341.

[6]Verdroß (1950), p. 98: "The question of validity (efficacy) of a legal order leads us into sociology, the question of the positive legal validity of a single norm is a problem for legal theory, the question of obligation finally is a problem of the philosophy of values" ("Wertphilosophie"), (my translation, SK).

2 The Concept of Law: Law as a Reflective Normative System

The function of the concept of law is to define what law is and how it can be distinguished from other social systems. If something meets its criteria, it is law; if not, it is something other than law. Understood in this way, the concept of law does not tell us that such laws belong to a particular legal order. It has nothing to do with "source" in this sense. This is just like an apple is an apple if it meets the criteria of an apple (genetic code, shape, taste, etc.), no matter if it has grown on this or that tree. Even if we disregard those theories doubtful about the possibility of defining something as heterogeneous as the various kinds of law,[7] sufficient substantial problems remain. They concern the general elements (*genus proximum*) of law just as much as the particular delimiting criteria. I cannot elaborate this here to the necessary extent but can only sketch a few aspects.[8]

2.1 *The Definition of Law*

Already the general characteristic of the concept of law (*genus proximum*) is dependent on the epistemic interest. A sociological theory of law will define law as a form of social action, practice, or communication. Many legal theories take the concept of the norm as the basis of definition. This point of departure for the understanding of law is justified by the difference of normative from other forms of social control. Law does not force behavior. It is intended to direct action through obligations, be they prohibitions, duties, or permissions. This includes the decisions to enact and adjudicate law. As a secondary function, it also stabilizes expectations.[9]

From this follows that non-normative sentences may be parts of laws and give cognitive orientation to action but cannot be considered law. Accordingly, because they are not normative sentences, some forms of soft law cannot be considered law. The disparate notion of "soft law" encompasses regulative means of governance such as open or teleological "final programs," recommendations, or opinions (as in Article 288 (4) TFEU) and private norm setting or informal acts of public institutions.[10]

---

[7]Henkel (1977), pp. 13 and 15; Hart (1983), pp. 21 f.

[8]For more detail Kirste (2010), pp. 62 ff.; Hoerster (2006), pp. 79 ff.; Alexy (1992), pp. 27 ff.; for different concepts of law Griller and Rill (2011), pp. 1–81.

[9]Luhmann (1993), p. 144. "We can define law … as a structure of a social system that rests on congruent generalization of normative expectations of behavior", Luhmann (1987), p. 105 (my translation, SK).

[10]Different opinion: Peters (2011), p. 21 ff., who takes soft law to be normative sentences and law (p. 23). She has to admit though that the binding force of European law does not stem from the respective regulations, but from Article 42 TEU, the general duty to cooperate (p. 24): "The legal duty of cooperation is the source of a legal obligation of the member states to take European Union soft law into account in some way or the other - without being directly bound by it."

Accordingly, since some forms of so-called soft law do not intend to have binding force, they cannot be law but only part of laws or referred to by legal institutions. This is the case with technical standards. These standards work as orientations for the market, but they become part of obligations only if referred to by hard law or courts, e.g. as benchmarks for negligence. NGOs or agencies may monitor these or ethical standards and publish their observations as reports, but no immediate legal consequences follow from this monitoring. Other principles may be so vague that they do not yet contain substantial obligations but only include the duty to be optimized or taken into consideration in balancing processes by legally competent institutions ("aim-oriented programs," legal goals and values, policies). The consequences that this kind of soft law may have are factual ones, not normative: an institution may not pay subsidies if potential beneficiaries do not adhere to their recommendations. This may raise the question of whether these recommendations are legitimate, but they do not themselves obligate the potential beneficiary. They function as incentives, orientation, and information and may have legal value in supporting laws[11]; they may coordinate but do not impose duties. As Bodig shows in this volume, CESCR Reports may establish a standard of rationality that can impose a burden of argumentation on parties, who do not meet them. There may even be social pressure to obey them, but this pressure is political,[12] not pressure in procedures regulated by norms.[13] Nonbinding soft law may be transformed into binding law by competent authorities, as the European Charter for Fundamental Rights was by the European Court of Justice, before formally being integrated into the corpus of the European Treaties (Article 6 (1) TEU). Because of their openness they may even substitute law in areas that are so dynamic or diverse that hard law would not be effective. They may prepare the formal transformation of their regulations into hard law as legal experiments,[14] but until then and apart from this, they are not norms and therefore not law. Sometimes normative regulations that stem from nonpublic authorities are also called "soft law." This is the case with the "self-regulation" of private companies, NGOs, and associations. They may be considered law (if they meet the further criteria to be discussed below) because they are norms ("best practice," "codes of ethics," "codes of conduct"[15]) and intend to obligate persons. The instance that they are self-imposed obligations does not hinder the fact that they are obligations and therefore norms. Remarkably, the sanction for violating them can be exclusion from the organization.[16] Thus, the institutional membership of persons in these organizations is a condition for bindingness, whereas hard law can achieve general applicability on a more abstract basis because the validity of laws follows the attribution to a legal order—but here, I am getting ahead of later

[11]"Promoting function," Peters (2011), p. 35.

[12]Goodin (2005), p. 240.

[13]For this element of legal norms, see below.

[14]"Evolution" or "growth" of soft law, Goodin (2005), pp. 239 f.

[15]For examples cf. Peters (2011), pp. 27 f.

[16]Luhmann (1987), p. 257.

argument. Their relation to other forms of law (namely public law, national laws) is a problem of legal pluralism.[17] The problem is not that they are law but whether they are valid. Thus, some forms of "soft law" lack normativity and therefore cannot be called law; others are norms, which raises the question of how they relate to other forms of law.

To determine that law is a norm is not specific enough, however. Morals and religion, too, influence actions through norms. Apart from possible overlappings, normativity is a common feature of law and morals.

This raises the question whether legal norms can be distinguished from moral norms and, if so, what criteria should be invoked. At this point, positivist and nonpositivist legal theories part company. Epistemologically skeptical and noncognitivist theories consider law but not morals as appropriate objects of knowledge.[18] Others, especially the theories of legal principles of Ronald Dworkin and Robert Alexy doubt that law and morals can be sharply distinguished. To justify this assumption, they point to principles we find in both fields[19] such as human dignity, liberty, and equality. Again, I will not unfold the debate here. We can well admit the similarities of legal and moral principles. However, we can distinguish them by their form. Principles of morality are—following different approaches—either expressions of knowledge of values, rational discourses, or different interests and convictions. They enter into modern differentiated constitutional systems with catalogs of basic rights only on the basis of the decisions of the constituent power, the legislator, or judges, and the latter two only if they are permitted to adopt them. From the moment of their inclusion, their extent and meaning depend on systematic coherence with other constitutional principles and not (only) the following of moral insights.

It seems then that we can distinguish law from other norms in that only the former norms are based on decisions. In this sense, law has been defined by imperative[20] or decisionist[21] theories. Theories that base law on forms of acknowledgement in so far follow a similar idea.[22]

---

[17] Cf. Seinecke (2015), pp. 3, 25, 34, 62, 298; Teubner (1996), p. 282 too considers this kind of soft law (e.g. the lex mercatoria) and considers its softness as an advantage. For reasons to be discussed later, I will follow him here.

[18] Hoerster (1993), p. 418. Kelsen (1960), p. 71.

[19] Dworkin (1986), p. 413.

[20] John Austin: "A law is a command which obliges a person or persons. But, as contradistinguished or opposed to an occasional or particular command, a law is a command which obliges a person or persons, and obliges generally to acts or forbearances of a class [. . .] a law is a command which obliges a person or persons to a course of conduct," Austin (1832), p. 18.

[21] Schmitt (1989), p. 22: "Every law as a normative regulation, including the constitutional law, in its ultimate foundation needs a previous political decision that has been reached by a politically existing power or authority" (my translation, SK). Or Coleman (1982), p. 148 assumes "that the authority of law is a matter of its acceptance by officials."

[22] "Law in a juridical sense in general is everything that human beings who live in some kind of community together, mutually acknowledge as a norm or rule for this coexistence," Bierling (1894), p. 19 (my translation, SK).

Still other theories are doubtful about the realism of these approaches and—instead of relying on the origin of these norms—emphasize their efficiency. Law could be distinguished from morals by its enforcement.[23] Both genetic and efficiency-oriented theories are mistaken in a twofold way: first, they ignore the well-established distinction—since Hume and Moore[24]—between normative and empirical utterances, and second, they ignore that modern law regulates both the origin and enforcement of legal norms.

Hans Kelsen's Pure Theory of Law emphasizes the first aspect. Based on the dualism of facts and norms, he understands law as a normative connection of the creation of norms (*Erzeugungszusammenhang*), in which norms can only be produced based on norms. To avoid an infinite recursion and also as a tool to understand the meaning of a willfully enacted norm as a norm, Kelsen presupposes a fictional or hypothetic basic norm. The basic norm is the transcendental condition for the possibility of recognizing an act of the legislator or any other person who attempts to produce law as normative.[25] The problem of the basic norm is, however, that although it can justify the pure normativity of law out of this norm itself, law is not pure normativity but a special form of normativity. This specific feature is the target of the delimitation of law and morals. For this delimitation, it is insufficient to understand, in a noncognitive way, moral norms as pure subjective facts that still have to be interpreted. Because of this, the critique of moral arguments does not positively define what law is. I do not think that Kelsen would claim that law is the only form of normativity.

This critique of Kelsen's does not mean abandoning his normative approach but means modifying it. This is further justified by a second objection against genetic and efficiency-oriented theories of the abovementioned kind: law is not a merely arbitrary decision. On all levels of the legal order, procedural rules organize the enactment of norms. Even the framing of a constitution is not in itself a revolutionary act—the revolutionary act can only negatively destroy the old order. Rather, the framing—like other lawmaking—seeks justification from higher norms such as (natural or higher ranking) human and civil rights (e.g., Declaration de Droit de l'Hommes et du Citoyen) or traditional rights (e.g., Declaration of Independence) or emerges from procedural norms or is both substantially and procedurally legitimated. From this constitutional foundation through the enactment of formal laws, statutory instruments, the procedural preconditions of judicial decisions down to the signing of contracts—and including international law—the production of norms follows procedural and material regulations in the form of norms. Naturally, in the

[23]Cf. von Jhering (1893), p. 177; Weber (1980), p. 17.

[24]Moore (1903), p. 10.

[25]*Kelsen* (1960), S. 47. Instead of a formal, Kant presupposes a material basic norm: "An External Legislation, containing pure Natural Laws, is therefore conceivable; but in that case a previous Natural Law must be presupposed to establish the authority of the Lawgiver by the Right to subject others to Obligation through his own act of Will," Kant, Law, p. 33.

framing of a constitution, they need not belong to the same legal order, the origin of which they regulate.

The same applies to efficiency. The enforcement of norms in a legal order is regulated by norms, too. It is a necessary element of modern states under the rule of law or legal states (*Rechtsstaaten*) that they are not only *founded* on the law but that the use of force to realize them is *limited* by norms. Enforcement laws (laws of punishment, police laws, etc.) regulate exactly this and sanction, if necessary, the violation of these norms. Not that law is enacted and enforced is relevant then but that this enactment and enforcement are regulated by norms. Accordingly, it is not force that renders a norm law but, the other way around, the norm that legitimizes force as a legal means to enforce law. In short, in the realm of law, force does not determine what law is; rather, law determines what kind of force is legitimate and legal. In the form of law, norms break both the facticity of the origin of legal norms and the facticity of their enforcement.

No other social order achieves this reflective normative mechanism. Therefore, we can define a norm as law if its enactment and enforcement are regulated by norms. Law is a system of normed norms or a reflective normative system. The norm is not only the general term of the concept of law, but the reflectivity of the norm is also the limiting term in the definition.

This concept of law determines the criteria for a norm to be law. The sentence "X is law" is a judgment based on the concept of law and further criteria that a particular norm fulfills the criteria of the concept of law. According to our definition, this sentence is true if X is generated in a normatively ordered procedure and can be enforced in a respective procedure. Although, generally, the further qualifying criteria will stem from a particular legal system, it is not necessary that X belongs to this particular system. X still meets the criteria of the concept of law if it had once been enacted and could have been enforced according to this system but not anymore, not yet, or if other legal norms of this system compete with X.

2.2 Possible Objections to This Definition

Four remarks are necessary here in order to meet possible objections: *firstly*, this definition does not mention the state. As modern public authorities under the rule of law, states are founded on and limited by law. In this perspective, the state presupposes law and is not part of the explanation or justification of law. From the proposed concept of law as a reflective order of norms, the assumption of legal pluralism follows: whenever a certain norm is enacted in a normed procedure and can possibly be enforced in a regulated procedure, it is law—be it a norm in a "primitive society," which is investigated by legal anthropologists, or soft law of international private law regimes. One may object that, under this definition, even normative structures of criminal organizations like the Mafia or similar organizations in the favelas of Brazil would be law, and indeed this consequence is necessary if the commands and their enforcement follow certain self-imposed procedural rules. As we will see, however, their claim to be valid will usually be rejected by public legal orders.

Secondly, it is not necessary that the procedural and competence norms that regulate the enactment of a legal norm are themselves legal norms. To avoid the naturalist fallacy, it is sufficient that they are norms at all. It is decisive to explain the legal norm as derived from a norm—be this norm formal in the sense of the regulation of the procedure or material in the sense of a moral or customary justification. The content of the founding norm may be the result of moral knowledge, moral discourse (I am not deciding the question of the origin of moral knowledge here), or a decision. Hans Kelsen was thus mistaken in the conception of "origin" in a "basic norm": to avoid the naturalist fallacy, it is sufficient to trace norms back to a norm; one does not also have to share his noncognitivism.[26] In order to understand the decision of the constituent power, the legislator, a judge, or the contracting parties as law, these decisions only have to meet the criteria of the concept of law. In a Kantian (or Hegelian) sense, "origin" means originating from a concept, not historical origin. Therefore, we do not have to create long chains of norms to explain the meaning of "lower" or conditioned norms as law. The concept of law, as developed here, considers reflective norms as law. Thus, whenever we have such a norm at any position in a hierarchy of norms, they are law. This can apply to the highest norm in the hierarchy as well. We do not presuppose another "basic norm" as the explanatory ground for law but only presuppose the concept of law. This concept, of course, is a concept and not itself a norm. The question of hierarchy, as I will show below, is a question of validity.

Thirdly, natural law is considered not to be law but moral provisions directed at legal action.[27] Norms of natural law can be justified like other moral norms can. They are aiming at directing legal behavior, where there are no legal norms for the respective action or as external measures of legal norms. This formal assumption about the status of natural law does not say anything about the possibility of recognizing these norms.[28] It also leaves open the question whether natural law has a higher or lower rank and if the norms of positive law that contravene natural law would be void. Given the formalized procedure of the enactment of positive laws, it could well be that natural law has inferior legitimation.

Finally, custom does not become law as factual practice that is accompanied by the conviction of the binding force of this practice because this could be the case with other non-legal practices as well. Rather, the recognition in a normatively ordered procedure—usually litigation—leads to the recognition of a custom as positive law.

These examples may already illustrate the potential of the concept of law presented here. By the criterion of the reflectivity of norms, we can distinguish law from orders of mere power—if they exist at all—tradition and morals that do not consist of such reflective norms. The distinction between law and morals is merely

---

[26]Kelsen (1960), pp. 65 f., 68 f., 198 f.

[27]Dreier (1996), p. 580.

[28]For this discussion in Germany in the twentieth century, cf. Kirste (2015a), pp. 91 ff.

formal: differing from law—although containing norms—morals do not consist of reflective norms, the enactment and enforcement of which are regulated by norms. This distinction does not refer to the *content* of morals and law: it is well possible—though not necessary—that they have similar content, as is the case with legal principles such as fundamental rights to freedom, equality, and human dignity.

However, the concept of law also has limits: neither can it solve the question of rival norms in legal pluralism, nor can it decide the question whether these legal orders contain binding norms. In other words, the concept of law neither decides the competition between public and private, national and inter- or supranational legislation, nor can it rule out the norms of a robber band, if they are established following a normed procedure. For both purposes, we need the concept of validity.

At this point, we can also refute the assumption that only valid law is law. A norm, rather, is law if it meets the criteria of the concept of law. This also applies to a norm before it has entered into force or after it has concluded its legal force, if its enactment or enforcement is regulated by another norm. Moreover, norms that regulate different consequences for one and the same fact are also law. Otherwise, we could not understand how they should be contradictory. However, the solution of such a concurrence of norms is dependent not only on the concept of law itself but also on other norms. Even extreme injustice would have to be called law, as long as it fulfills the abovementioned criteria of the concept of law. In the case of merely arbitrary acts, this will often not be the case. A conflict of a legal and a moral norm is impossible on a conceptual level because this conflict concerns two different kinds of norms.

3 The Concept of the Validity of Law

3.1 Validity

The philosophical concept of validity does not have a long tradition. Up until the second half of the nineteenth century, the concept was known and used but mostly not elaborated in a systematic way. Only a few examples can be mentioned here: whereas Gottfried Wilhelm Leibniz holds that law draws its validity from the accordance of the people,[29] John Locke thought that positive laws contradicting natural laws would not be valid.[30] Positivists also sometimes used the term. John

[29]Liebnitz (2003), pp. 70 f.: "Unde pater, Iegem ex conventione populi valere;" in German: "Hieraus erhellt, daß das Gesetz seine Geltung aus der Übereinkunft des Volkes bezieht."

[30]Locke (1824), p. 418: "Thus the law of nature stands as an eternal rule to all men, legislators as well as others. The rules that they make for other men's actions, must, as well as their own and other men's actions, be conformable to the laws of nature, i.e. to the will of God, of which that is a declaration; and the 'fundamental' law of nature being the preservation of mankind, no human sanction can be good or valid against it." Locke uses the term very rarely, though.

Austin gave it some interest when he discussed invalid unconstitutional laws,[31] and William Blackstone speaks of the religious validity of positive laws[32] but confounds the term with legal bindingness.[33] Bentham casually mentions moral validity and considers utility the reason for validity,[34] before he states: "No contract is void in itself; none is valid in itself. It is the law, which in either case grants or refuses validity."[35]

Kant did use the term "validity," though he elaborated no theory about it. Following him, Johann Gottlieb Fichte spoke of the validity of the rational law (*Vernunftrecht*).[36] Only the neo-Kantian debate gave it more precise contours.[37] In German, the meaning of validity is more telling perhaps than in English. If we claim or assert something (*geltend machen*), we want the claim to be objectively

---

[31]"...any law of the ordinary legislature, which conflicted with a constitutional law directly proceeding from the extraordinary, would be treated by the courts of justice as a legally invalid act" (Austin 1832, p. 244 cf. also p. 265, note). So Austin obviously knows the term, also when he speaks of "solemnities or formalities which are essential to the validity of certain contracts" (1832, p. XXXIX) but finds no systematic use for it, even where one would expect it.

[32]Austin (1832), pp. 278 f.: Blackstone "tells us 'that the laws of God ... are superior in obligation to any other laws: that no human laws are of any validity, if contrary to them: that all human laws which are valid, derive all their force, and all their authority, mediately or immediately, from those divine originals... to say that a human law which conflicts with the law of God, is therefore not *binding*, or not *valid*, is to talk stark nonsense... Numberless human laws adverse to general utility, have been and are enforced in every age and nation: and yet such human laws conflict with the law of God as known through the very exponent adopted by Blackstone himself..."—making it clear that "validity" was a useful concept for both Blackstone and himself.

[33]Austin (1832), p. 269: "If a law which it sets to its subjects conflict with a law of the kind, the former is legally valid, or legally binding."

[34]Bentham (1840), p. 104: "If a king had taken an oath to render his subjects unhappy, would such an engagement be valid?... It cannot be denied then, that the validity of the contract is at bottom, only a question of utility, a little wrapped up, a little disguised, and in consequence, more susceptible of false interpretations." For the causes of invalidation of exchanges: p. 172.

[35]Bentham (1840), p. 207. He adds though: "But for granting or refusing it reasons are necessary."

[36]Fichte (1845), p. 89: "So viel läßt sich einsehen, dass eine Gemeinschaft freier Wesen, als solcher, nicht bestehen könne, wenn nicht jeder diesem Gesetze unterworfen ist; und dass sonach, wer diese Gemeinschaft wolle, notwendig das Gesetz auch wollen müsse; dass es *a*lso hypothetische Gültigkeit habe. *Wenn* eine Gemeinschaft freier Wesen, als solcher, möglich sein soll, so muss das Rechtsgesetz gelten." Cf. also p. 91 where validity ("Gültigkeit") of law for one is made dependent on the acceptance of the other.

[37]Kant rarely applies the term "Geltung" ("validity") or "gelten" (to be valid) and does not elaborate a systematic use of the term. However, he does not omit the term, even in his legal philosophy, cf. in the introduction of the *Metaphysics of Morals* he writes "Nur sofern sie [die Sittengesetze, SK] als a priori gegründet und notwendig eingesehen werden können, gelten sie als Gesetze"/Moral Laws "in contradistinction to Natural Laws, are only valid as Laws, in so far as they can be rationally established a priori and comprehended as necessary." In this context Kant applies the term "validity" to signify different preconditions for natural and moral laws as means of explanation or comprehension. In more legal context he states, "Also gilt der Satz: 'Kauf bricht nicht Miete,' "The proposition, then, that 'Purchase breaks Hire' holds in principle," Philosophy of Law, pp. 15 and 132.

recognized.[38] In the retaliation (*Wiedervergeltung*), the objective law is established against the individual claim to validity in its violation. Also, "Geld" (money) is connected to "gelten" because in mass usage, it is accepted as a (legal) means for the exchange of goods.[39] This indicates that validation means the process of testing and recognizing a subjective assertion in a somehow objective context, even if the assertion does not have this status by nature. This is why neo-Kantian philosophers such as Hermann Lotze (1817–1881) or Heinrich Rickert (1863–1936) speak of an antagonism of "being" and "being valid." Assertions in the form of an argument, a conclusion, or a norm are valid if the subjective meaning the speaker connects with it can be objectively reconstructed. A great variety of possible meaning systems comes into play as objective references for such a reconstruction: social practices, recognized ethics, or legal systems. In this respect, validity would mean that a single social behavior could be attributed to a system of social practices, ethical or legal orders. This attribution can be normative, through material deduction of "lower" or "dependent" norms from "higher" norms, or formal, by the adherence of procedural and competence rules. Public law positivism considered this attribution to be based on decision, in a way that the norm could be justified by a state imperative[40] or a state decision[41] that would attribute it to the legal order of the respective state. Apart from these examples and insofar following the neo-Kantian tradition, to be valid shall be understood here as the attribution of an assertion to a system of meaning. Validity would then be the status of the affiliation of an assertion to the respective system of meaning.[42]

The attribution decides about competing claims of validity (*Geltungsansprüche*): e.g., between different kinds of knowledge, claiming to be true. They are valid if they can be justified in a system of scientific assumptions as true. A claimed right would then be valid if it can be justified within a certain legal order. Based on this justification, claims to validity that belong to a system can be distinguished from others that do not.

[38]Cf. Hegel Grundlinien: § 217 Z, p. 619: "Mein Wille ist ein vernünftiger, er *gilt*, und dies *Gelten* soll von dem anderen anerkannt sein. Hier muß nun meine Subjektivität und die des anderen hinwegfallen, und der Wille muß eine Sicherheit, Festigkeit und Objektivität erlangen, welche er nur durch die Form erhalten kann" [my emphasis, SK].

[39]Weber (1974), Col. 224–226: The ancient greek "νόμισμα" for money relates it to νόμῳ (custom) and νόμος (law) as Aristotle said in his *Nicomachean Ethics* V, 5, 11: "money has become by convention a sort of representative of demand; and this is why it has the name 'money' (nomisma) because it exists not by nature but by law (nomos) and it is in our power to change it and make it useless." Just like conventional laws, money does not exist naturally, but is valid based on our changeable recognition.

[40]Lasson (1882), p. 424.

[41]Schmitt (1993), p. 25.

[42]For concepts of validity as attribution or "membership", cf. Grabowski (2013), pp. 271 ff., which he rejects, pp. 279, 311.

Other than explained here, validity is often equated with existence.[43] Against this assumption, to avoid ontologizing norms, Heinrich Rickert rightfully proved that facts "exist," whereas norms or values are "valid."[44] Ignoring the difference between existence and validity tends to disguise the relational nature of validity. Something that exists seems to plainly exist; validity, however, is the status of being attributed relative to a certain system of meaning. In other words, legal norms do not exist; they make sense. This sense is relative to a certain system of meaning.

Statements about validity are then relative and immanent. This means that validity does not exist in general or in the absolute or in the singular. It is always related to a particular system of meaning; it is systematic validity. The respective system itself establishes the criteria of validity that justify a certain assertion to belong to a particular system. The range of validity follows the kind of respective system and may be universal with respect to moral systems, whereas ethical or legal systems establish a context-relative validity.[45] Accordingly, it is possible that a certain assertion does not only belong to a particular system of meaning—moral and ethical—or only to one—e.g., the ethical convictions of a certain community may not be valid in another. The objectivity of the validity then only refers to this particular system.

The attribution to a legal system is not a factual decision. The decision (e.g., of a legislator, a court, or contracting parties) can be attributed to a particular legal system if it shares the normative sense of the respective system. It does so if it follows the procedures, competences or rights, and material preconditions that the respective system sets for making this decision. This applies to the decision about the legal revision of them as well. A constitutional court can render a norm invalid only if it is competent to do so (this may be a problem in a federal state), if it follows the procedural rules for this decision and the decision is constitutional altogether. Only legal norms can claim to be attributed to a legal system, and only legally acting and competent gatekeepers can decide on this attribution; otherwise, they would leave the meaning system of a particular legal order.

Again, the *concept* as such does qualify a norm to belong to a particular legal system. It only states the abstract attributedness of norms to legal systems. The concept of validity points to the relatedness of legal norms to legal systems. Yet the concept cannot determine the criteria according to which a particular norm belongs to a particular legal system. This is to be decided by particular legal systems themselves. Whereas the concept of law qualifies a norm as legal, the concept of validity qualifies them as being related to some legal system. The sentence "legal norm X is legally valid" is a judgment based on the concept of validity and certain further premises from a particular legal system, attributing X to it.

---

[43]Kelsen (1960), p. 9; Weinberger (1988), p. 116.

[44]Rickert (1921), p. 122: "Something that merely exists, is not valid... Who says that 'facts' that are not values, are valid, talks imprecisely, or nonsense" (my translation, SK).

[45]Forst (1996), p. 53.

3.2 *Validity of Law*

If validity is relative to a certain system of meaning, law can be attributed to different systems of meaning; it can therefore have different forms of validity. Validity of law then means the attribution of law to a particular system of meaning.[46] By "validity of law" I mean the abstract attribution to a system of meaning, whatever that system is. In a substantial sense, this is the case, first, if a legal norm belongs to a certain system but not to another one. Here we can distinguish between competing claims of validity and delineate legal and illegal norms.[47] If we do distinguish between the concept of law and the validity of law, we can recognize the difference between law and nonlaw on the one hand and legal and illegal laws on the other.[48] Nonlaw encompasses all norms that do not meet the concept of law. Illegal are all laws meeting the criteria of law without having validity. Already Hegel made it clear that a person violating the law does not altogether deny the meaning of law, e.g. does not deny that there is property at all but only makes a claim that does not meet the requirements of objective law.[49] The ruling of a court thereby confirms the tested validity of law by rejecting the unjustified legal claim.[50] On the other hand, the claimant does not merely fight for a certain object but claims his right that has been contested by the illegitimate claim of the defendant.[51] Illegal norms are norms, only they cannot be attributed to a particular legal order.

Second, we can attribute a norm to a system of meaning in a temporal sense. This is the case when a norm does not yet belong or no longer belongs to a particular legal order, i.e. if it has not yet entered into force or has been invalidated.[52]

Some authors consider the attribution of a norm to a certain system of meaning irrelevant. Dworkin, for example, holds that principles that collide with other principles do not mutually exclude each other but can be optimized. Therefore, the

---

[46]Lippold (1988), p. 465: "Validity is defined as: Attribution of a certain norm to a certain order of norms" (my translation, SK).

[47]In the perspective of his social concept of validity of law, Jellinek correctly writes, "das Unrecht bricht dasjenige, was unverbrüchlich gelten soll; es zeigt, daß das, was sein soll, nicht sein muß; es beweist, daß die Autorität nicht mächtig genug ist, ihren Geboten unter allen Umständen Geltung zu verschaffen," Jellinek (1908), p. 62.

[48]For this discussion cf. Grabowski (2013), pp. 71 ff. Against him (2013, p. 79), I would take the concept of law as the criterion between law and non-law and would consider illegal laws ("Unrecht") still law, although somewhat deficient law even up to the "unbearable thesis" in Gustav Radbruch's Formula. Norms that meet the criteria set by the concept of law are law. If they are immoral they lack moral validity and, if the respective constitution permits moral norms, may even lack legal validity, cf. Kirste (2011), pp. 78 ff. and below here.

[49]Hegel, Grundlinien, § 81, p. 272 u. § 82 Z, p. 279.

[50]Until this authoritative decision about competing validity claims, validity may only be supposed ("vermutet"), but not be proved, Paulson (1979), pp. 12 ff.

[51]Rudolf von Jhering hits the point, writing that it would not be the plaintiff's goal to merely recover his object, but to make valid his right, von Jhering (1872), p. 19.

[52]Cf. Heckmann (1997).

concept of validity would not be appropriate for them.[53] However, even principles belong to a particular legal order and not to another one. Their range and the parameter of the optimizing program will be determined by this legal order and not by another one. Thereby, the principles of the European Declaration of Human Rights can be unfolded differently to those, say, of the Charter of the Organization of American States or of national constitutions. Other than perhaps in case-law systems, canonization of norms in codified systems can establish a defined lists of principles, even if there may be an undetermined list of concretizations possible.[54]

3.3 *Forms of the Validity of Law*

Reasons for the Distinctions of the Forms of Validity

Up to now, I have discussed a little vaguely validity as the attribution of a norm to a system of meaning. This has to be specified now with respect to different systems of meaning. Whereas we understand law as everything that meets the criteria of the concept of law, the concept of validity enables us to attribute laws to particular systems of meaning. Based on this, we can now distinguish different forms of the validity of law. Usually we distinguish between the legal/juridical, social, and moral validity of law. These three forms need not be conclusive, though. We could perhaps also speak of the political or cultural validity of law if we looked for the meaning of law for the respective systems of meaning.[55]

We can speak of legal validity if a legal norm has been enacted following the relevant formal and material norms. A norm has social validity if it is part of a certain social practice and in this sense efficient. Moral validity of law requires the justification of a norm within a realm of morals, or as Robert Alexy puts it, "right and valid are exactly those norms that in an ideal discourse could be judged as right by everybody."[56]

Epistemological interest theories emphasize rather one or the other form of the validity of law. Many theories assume though that law is only valid if the criteria of

---

[53]Dworkin (1967/68), p. 42.

[54]Dworkin (1967/68), p. 45 holds a different position: "If ... we tried actually to list all the principles in force we would fail. They are controversial, their weight is all important, they are numberless, and they shift and change so fast that the start of our list would be obsolete before we reached the middle. Even if we succeeded, we would not have a key to law because there would be nothing left for our key to unlock. I conclude that if we treat principles as law we must reject the positivists' first tenet, that the law of a community is distinguished from other social standards by some test in the form of a master rule... We might want to say that a legal obligation exists whenever the case supporting such an obligation, in terms of binding legal principles of different sorts, is stronger than the case against it."

[55]Larenz (1967, p. 19).

[56]Alexy (2009), p. 156 [my translation, SK].

more than one form of validity are fulfilled.[57] Positivist theories, for example, assume that law is only valid if it is legally valid and at the same time efficient to a certain extent.[58] Nonpositivist theories on the validity of law, on the other hand, presume legal validity and at least a minimum of moral justification, and in this sense validity is important.[59] Dialectical neo-Hegelian theories suppose both that the existence of law includes its ought and that the ought of law includes its being.[60] Thereby, the neo-Kantian dualism of ought and being would be overcome.

Finally, there are theories that postulate different criteria for the validity of a legal norm and that of a legal order. Hans Kelsen, too, distinguishes between the legal validity of a legal norm qua the cohesion of origin (*Erzeugungszusammenhang*) of the legal order and the validity of the legal order that presupposes its effectiveness.[61] However, in a neo-Kantian perspective, for Kelsen the effectiveness of a norm is the empirical occasional cause (*Veranlassungsgrund*) to examine the fact of the enactment of a norm. Without an efficient norm, there is no epistemological problem because there is no object of knowledge.[62] Common to these theories is the assumption that law is not valid if it lacks legal validity. Legal validity can thereby be understood as the core of the validity of law. Surprising is the conception of the validity of law as a combination of different forms of validity because the elements of the forms of validity and their mutual relation are all but unproblematic.

Up until here, I only assume then that the term "validity of law" is the encompassing concept of the three forms of validity—legal, moral, and empirical—and that without legal validity, the other forms do not really make sense in legal theory. I will therefore investigate the forms closer.

Legal Validity of Law

What sounds like a pleonasm—"legal validity of law"—is the expression of the fact that law is not only an object of validity (validity of law) but can also provide criteria for validity (legal validity). Laws are legally valid if they can be attributed to a particular legal order in a material or temporal sense. This attribution is a matter not of mere decision but of normative regulation.[63]

Legal validity seems to be easiest to determine. A norm is valid because of its coherence of origin or source. In the formalist reading of Hans Kelsen, this means that lower ranking or conditioned legal norms are valid if they fulfill the criteria legally established for their enactment. This also applies to the origin norm

[57]Hoerster (2006), p. 63.

[58]Kelsen (1960), pp. 219 f.

[59]Alexy (1992), p. 148 f.

[60]Larenz (1967), p. 22.

[61]Kelsen (1960), p. 219.

[62]Kelsen (1960), p. 215 f.

[63]For an early positivistic view cf. Lasson (1882), p. 423.

(*Erzeugungsnorm*). Kelsen attempts to avoid the pending infinite recursion by the assumption of a basic norm. This norm is not itself created but assumed as a transcendental condition for legal knowledge.[64] The respective basic norm is supposed to guarantee the unity of the normative order.[65] Here, again, the problem occurs that the basic norm can found normativity logically and not legally and also the validity only hypothetically but not in reality. The question remains open, how a hypothetically valid norm can found a norm of completely different validity, namely the legal validity of law.

One could assume that the validity of law can only be founded on a decision as the origin of a legal order. This argument does not justify the basic norm, however. It can also be neglected. If one defends an immanent concept of validity, as I do, according to which the validity of law is the affiliation of a legal norm to a system of meaning and the legal validity of law is the affiliation of law to a particular legal order, each legal order sets the criteria for this legal validity. The legal order closes itself if it forbids the amendment of particular norms. An amendment can only be attributed to such a constitution and is valid if the constitution contains a rule of change for this amendment. If this does not—for example in the case of formal or material "eternal clauses"—norms changing or amending the constitution could not be attributed to the respective constitution. This applies to the "eternal clause" as well. For its change, there exists no rule of change. According to its meaning, it excludes its own change. Otherwise, the "eternal clause" could not forbid the change of the explicitly named constitutional norms. At least implicitly, therefore, it regulates its own unchangeability. Neither can this rule of unchangeability be attributed to a "higher" legal norm, nor could a "higher" norm of this legal order that is excluded by this stop rule of change be attributed to the particular legal order. This is the reason why we do not need a basic norm, because the impending infinite recursion of validity can be stopped by the highest rule of unchangeability itself. This norm is valid in a legal sense because it excludes any change of itself and certain other norms. Its change could not be attributed to itself and would therefore have no validity in this particular legal order. It is a different thing to assume that this rule of change could be morally or socially valid. We can also consider such a highest rule of immutability to be law if its enactment followed certain norms for the enactment of the constitution, on which the constitutional convention previously agreed, even if these norms for the procedure on framing the constitution later do not become part of it because, according to the concept of law, necessary to the qualification of a norm as law is only that its enactment be subject to a norm, not that this norm is part of the legal order or law at all.

If a norm or even a legal system cannot be attributed to another legal system, it is not legally valid in the sense that this other legal system establishes. If we assume, as

[64]Kelsen (1960), p. 203: "Because the basis for the validity of a norm can only be another norm, this precondition can again only be a norm: not one, enacted by a legal authority, but a presupposed norm…".

[65]Kelsen (1960), p. 197.

I did above, that the norms of a criminal organization such as the Mafia or in the favelas in Brazil are law, they still lack the validity of state law for this reason because they are counter to public criminal laws. Accordingly, following the command of a Mafia boss cannot operate as a justification for committing a murder, whereas the command of a competent officer who adheres to the public laws can.

A particular legal system as a whole is not legally valid with respect to this same legal system because, evidently, as a whole it cannot be attributed to this very system. Yet it can be attributed to another particular legal system and be legally valid with respect to it. This might be the case with respect to a state legal order within a federal legal system or following monistic conceptions of a national legal system with respect to supranational or international legal systems. The federal constitution could provide criteria for the legal validity of the constitutions of the member states of this federal state. Such a legal system may also have moral or factual validity if it meets the respective requirement (see below). The fact that it cannot be legally valid does not infringe the legal validity of its norms since they can be attributed to the respective legal system and hence meet the criteria for their validity. Furthermore, as I argued before, its highest rules of change can be legally valid, even if the system as a whole is not.

Legal validity can be further distinguished into spatial, temporal, and material or substantive validity. Based on its reflective structure, law decides when its norms enter into force and often also when they cease to exist. During the time of their legal validity, these norms are detemporalized because while other social times pass on, law has an extended present in Bergson's sense.[66] Spatial validity concerns questions such as the validity of national law on airplanes and ships outside of the territory of the respective state or matters of so-called international private law, let us say with respect to marriages of couples with different citizenships. Material or substantive validity deals with statutes conflicting with constitutional principles, for example. In all of these cases, a norm is legally valid if it has better reasons to prevail in a temporal, extensive, or substantive conflict and therefore belongs to the respective legal order.

Only legally valid norms can produce legal consequences such as legal obligations (duties, prohibitions, or permissions) because only then can these obligations be attributed to a particular legal order. And only valid obligations in the former sense can be legally binding. The question remains, however, if this is only a necessary or already a sufficient condition.

An invalid norm does not belong to a legal system and hence may not be applied. It is possible, though, that a norm, which belongs, let us say, to a national legal system and is valid, may not be applied due to partly higher supranational law as in the European Union. In such federal systems, the infringement of national law may be less severe if the national law is valid, but only with respect to cases contradicting supranational is it not applicable.

[66]Kirste (2015b), pp. 63 ff.; Kirste (2002), pp. 36 ff.

In this sense, law is almost like Midas, as Kelsen stipulated: whatever it attributes a legal meaning to becomes legally valid.[67] Moral norms, social standards, even mathematical assumptions become legally valid if and insofar as law gives them legal significance. This does not mean that they thereby lose their validity in other social or natural systems because validity is only relative.[68] Since law is a particularly efficient social means, the question, however, is how to avoid that the Midas "Law" foolishly makes all it touches legal, even that which—like Midas' daughter or his food—is better remaining outside the realm of law. The increasing juridification (*Verrechtlichung*) of many social fields such as families shows that this is not a peripheral problem. There may be areas where soft law could work beneficially, if not touched by hard law. However, it is also clear that law can safeguard zones free from law (*Rechtsfreie Räume*) only by means of law itself, namely by permissions, autonomies, etc.

The Social Validity of Law

Law is valid in a social sense if either its subjects recognize it or the legal authorities enforce it against its attempted violation.[69] According to MacCormick's and Weinberger's institutionalist legal theory, law is valid only if it is efficient as a framework of action.[70] Georg Jellinek, too, assumed that the act of recognition would have the force of an origin of validity.[71] Similarly, Pauline Westerman in this volume considers belief in authority or its perception the relevant criterion for validity. Others put less emphasis on emotional or motivational recognition, but on application or—already an idealization—applicability,[72] or consider validity to be a prediction of future legal practices, namely by the courts, as Alf Ross does.[73]

[67] Kelsen, Allgemeine Staatslehre, p. 44.

[68] This is often misunderstood, cf. e.g. Green, Leslie, "Legal Positivism", *The Stanford Encyclopedia of Philosophy* (Fall 2009 Edition), http://plato.stanford.edu/archives/fall2009/entries/legal-positivism/, under 3.

[69] Geiger (1963), p. 205.

[70] Weinberger (1988), p. 119.

[71] In his well-known "normative force of the factual", Jellinek (1959), p. 339 f.: "Because the factual everywhere has the tendency to transform itself into the valid, in the whole range of the legal system it generates the precondition that a given social state rightfully exists, thus everybody, who wants to precipitate a change of this state, has to prove his better right" (my translation, SK). Validity is based on our feeling of being bound by a norm, 1959, p. 223.

[72] O.W. Holmes, A. Ross would be among them, cf. Grabowski (2013), pp. 312 ff., 321 ff.

[73] Ross (1958), p. 45: "a rule can be valid to a greater or lesser degree varying with the degree of probability with which it can be predicted that the rule will be applied. This degree of probability depends on the material of experience on which the prediction is built," cf. the article by Eliasz/ Zaluski in this volume.

The justification of the social (and moral) validity of law is debated. It is still not easy to reach a consensus on the meaning of recognition.[74] Further questions of social recognition are still open. Should factual recognition or the mere use of force be relevant for social validity?[75] If recognition is decisive, who is the subject of this recognition: the people[76] or rather the legal authorities?[77] If it were recognition by the people, would the irrelevance of recognition be the decisive criterion for a conventional rule in opposition of a legal norm?[78] It is certainly a positive feature of social validity that it is gradable because law can be more or less recognized and more or less enforced. Yet the reverse of this coin is the question how much recognition is needed for social validity? Are lesser valid norms also less obligating? Shall we really assume that if a norm is not applied by 51% of the courts, I (and also the courts) have no duty to obey it? Different from legal and moral validity of law, social validity is relative to social circumstances. Legal validity and moral validity are disjunctive and lead to clear results: a legal norm is either legally and/or morally valid or not; it is not more or less morally or legally valid, as it is socially. If, however, average recognition is sufficient, how can we justify the validity of a legal norm toward the rest of its subjects?

Furthermore, a norm may still be legally valid if it is actively or passively rejected by its subjects, even if no one thinks about it. It is also legally valid if the legislator has enacted it but no one even considers applying it. Gerhart Husserl hits the point writing, "A legal right is valid, even if all its subjects dreamlessly sleep" [my translation, S.K.].[79] Even if there is no actual, present reaction to this norm, it is still legally valid. In such cases, we can rely not on factual efficiency but only on the nonempirical term of "chance of efficiency," as Hans Kelsen and Robert Alexy do.

We face similar difficulties if we rely not on recognition but on the enforcement of a norm as the relevant criterion for its social validity because not any use of force by anybody can make a norm efficient but only that by legally empowered authorities, they have to respect their jurisdiction and the procedural rules for the use of force.

---

[74]Bierling (1877), p. 8.

[75]Bierling (1877), p. 7: "Law exists only as long as it is valid, i.e. as long as it is being recognized (respected, felt or looked at as binding or decisive" (my translation, SK).

[76]Bierling (1894), p. 47.

[77]Ross (1958), p. 35: "Only the legal phenomena in the narrower sense, however the application of the law by the courts are decisive in determining the validity of the legal norms. In contrast to generally accepted ideas it must be emphasized that the law provides the norms for the behavior of the courts, and not of private individuals. The effectiveness which conditions the validity of the norms can therefore be sought solely in the judicial application of the law, and not in the law in action among private individuals."

[78]Stammler (1896), p. 129.

[79]Husserl (1925), p. 6.—Gerhart Husserl (1893–1973) was son of Phenomenologist philosopher Edmund Husserl and a legal philosopher and civil law professor at different German universities and, during World War II, in Washington.

Differences occur within theories of recognition: in cases of a general—but not individual—recognition of legal norms by citizens, legal authorities can correct deviating presumptions of validity and enforce the law. A merely general recognition of a norm by the legal authorities, though, may be corrected by higher instances. This is not possible in cases in which the highest authority does not recognize the respective norm. This shows that for social recognition, the recognition of legal authorities is relevant. If these authorities do not recognize the respective norm, people can only protest and make use of the ambivalent means of resistance. This right is also a proof for the attempt to legalize even the preconditions and limits of the enforcement of social validity of norms against legal authorities denying legal recognition. In differentiated legal systems, similar assumptions can be made for all forms of recognition. In the democratic state under the rule of law, constitutional provisions on the right to vote or statutory provisions on litigation regulate the preconditions for the recognition of law. Accordingly, the observation of the social validity of law makes sense especially in the context of the analysis of the means of social engineering; the criteria of social validity are contested, however, and therefore often law itself regulates them and the procedure in cases of violations of recognition. This refusal is at the same time a deviating supposition of the validity of another norm that can be identified and refuted by the legal order.

Leonard Nelson rightly emphasized that just as a legal norm does not become a naturally existing fact through its fulfillment, the respective norm does not lose its validity because it is not part of the social practices.[80] Rather is an authoritative annulment necessary as the same is required for its enactment. Gustav Radbruch, too, distinguishes precisely between the facticity of the enforcement of law and its normative meaning. For him, enforcement is important for the value of legal security. This importance does not rest in mere facticity. Facticity is instrumental for the value of legal security, but only efficient law can provide legal security as one of the three elements of the idea of law.[81] Even Niklas Luhmann's "Theory of Social Systems," which analyses law as a form of social communication in the first place, considers validity not as equivalent with this practice but as a symbol that is being passed on.[82] The facticity underlying the social validity of law is a normatively broken facticity, even for theories accepting it as relevant for the validity of law. Accordingly, we can distinguish sentences uttering that law "should" be observed from others that law "is" actually observed.[83]

[80]Nelson (1917), p. 9.

[81]Radbruch (1993), p. 314.

[82]Luhmann (1993), p. 107: "Following Talcott Parsons we can label validity as a circulating symbol that is being passed on with every use – just as solvency in the economy or the collective binding in politics" and on p. 98, "We chose the concept of 'symbol', because the point is to respect and reproduce the unity of the system in the variety of its operations. In the legal system this is achieved by the symbol of the validity of law" (my translation, SK).

[83]Kelsen (1965), p. 467: "Daß das Recht 'gilt', bedeutet, daß es befolgt bzw. angewendet werden *soll*; daß es wirksam ist, bedeutet, daß es befolgt bzw. angewendet *wird*". "That the law is 'valid'

The Moral Validity of Law

Law is morally valid if its norms can be justified morally. In these cases, law appears almost as a reification or legalization of morals.[84]

The moral validity of law is no less debated than its social validity. This primarily concerns the criteria of validity. The possibility to recognize or justify the relevant moral norms, to which legal norms can then be attributed, is a matter of discussion. Optimists oppose noncognitivists in the estimation of moral knowledge. Procedural theories try to mediate but are dependent upon moral prerequisites in the foundation of just procedures. Even if we suppose the chance of a justification of moral norms, their content is subject to debate: e.g., what does justice mean? And even if all these questions could be answered, the question remains whether a legal norm is only valid if it meets a maximum amount of justice or if a minimal amount of justice suffices. I can neither elaborate on this here, nor is it my intention to criticize the search for morality that—to say the least—has a value of its own because it has produced so many legally important moral values and norms.

Given all these controversies with respect to morality, it seems reasonable that modern legal orders regulate materially moral questions in human and basic rights and enhance legal values themselves. To refrain from doing so or even to violate historically established values means a de-differentiation of law by shifting these questions back to other systems such as morals or other social practices that are less qualified to decide these questions and therefore may provide only arbitrary and imbalanced results.

Taken together, it is remarkable that around the core of legal validity, other forms of the validity of law are more and more legalized because their criteria of validity are unclear and debated. By its reflective structure, especially through legitimate and efficient procedures for its decisions, law provides the form for deciding the questions of its own validity. To keep the other forms of validity as a perspective of research for the sociology or ethics of law does still make sense, especially for a critique of law. To concede the social or moral validity of law, legal influence on its legal validity would be problematic, though.

The Mutual Relation of the Forms of Validity

This leads to determining the relation of the forms of validity of law. Often customary law is considered as an example for the origin of legal validity out of social practice. However, we have to take into account that according to the above-sketched concept of law, customs become law only if their origination is subject to regulation. This is often not the case with the standards and norms practiced in

means that it *ought* to be observed or applied; that it is efficacious means that it *is* observed or applied" (my translation, SK).

[84]Lask (1905), p. 5.

society. A norm that has grown out of social practices becomes law only if it is recognized by the competent legal authorities or is protected on the basis of group or individual human rights. The social practice then prompts the origin of law by judicial or international legal recognition. This assumption seems to be directed against Eugen Ehrlich's legal pluralism. However, legal pluralism can be justified based on the concept of law presented here. A norm is law if its enactment and enforcement is subject to norms. This can apply to competing norms within a legal order—if they have private or public origin. Validity deals with the question of how to decide this competition. If there are normed procedures, e.g. if there are arbitration courts agreed upon, the respective norms are law.

Some authors assume that the forfeiture of the social validity of law would also lead to a loss of legal validity.[85] Some positivist[86] and a few nonpositivist[87] theories of validity presume that cessation of a minimum of social efficiency or chance of efficiency of legal orders or single legal norms would lead to the end of legal validity, too. Since H.L.A. Hart, the conviction has been spreading that we would have to distinguish between single norms and a whole legal order. Whereas the efficiency of single norms is irrelevant, it is decisive for the validity of the whole legal order. In such cases, the rule of recognition of law in an internal perspective determines the criteria for the validity of legal norms.[88] This rule is itself independent from efficiency. As with the basic norm, the question of validity is not supposed to be applied to the rule of recognition. It is supposed to be a rule of mere means of

[85]For an analytical—critical—discussion of these concepts, cf. Grabowski (2013), pp. 344 ff.

[86]An early example of a positivistic theory of validity can be found in Thomas Hobbes. He assumes that there would be no valid contracts without a positive constitution, "And therefore where there is no Own, that is, no Propriety, there is no Injustice; and where there is no coercive Power erected, that is, where there is no Common-wealth, there is no Propriety, all men having Right to all things: therefore where there is no Common-wealth, there nothing is Unjust. So that the nature of Justice consisteth in keeping of valid Covenants, but the Validity of Covenants begins not but with the Constitution of a Civil Power sufficient to compel men to keep them: and then it is also that Propriety begins," Hobbes, Leviathan XV, S. 202 f.

[87]Ralf Dreier (1994, p. 123 f.): "Law consists of those norms which belong to the constitution of a system of norms organized in a state or on the international level, if this system is on the whole socially effective and, in a minimal sense, ethically justifiable, and of those norms which are laid down according to this constitution, if these, taken by themselves, are socially effective or have at least the chance to become socially effective and which are, in a minimal sense, ethically justifiable." Speaking of the concept of law here, his definition is relevant for validity as well, because he advocates unity of concept and validity of law.

[88]"Validity is a function in part of the internal point of view: a law is valid if it passes all the tests provided by the rule of recognition. The criteria for efficacy are different, however: a law is efficacious if it is obeyed more often than not. That a law is valid is no guarantee that it is efficacious, and that it is *not* efficacious is no proof that it is invalid"... "It would however be wrong to say that statements of validity 'mean' that the system is generally efficacious. For though it is normally pointless or idle to talk of the validity of a rule of a system which has never established itself or has been discarded, none the less it is not meaningless nor is it always pointless...," Hart (1991), p. 103 f.

knowledge.[89] Dworkin attempts to justify this with the assumption that the rule of recognition would not be the utmost rule, if there were criteria for its validity. However, the rule of recognition could establish criteria of validity that only the rule itself could fulfill. Following Hart, Joseph Raz holds that the legal system answers the question what law is, whereas a legal norm would be valid.[90] However, a legal order, if it is not merely a system of knowledge about law—a system of declarative sentences—but a system of norms, would have to be valid itself, to found the validity of legal norms.

Both in the case of a single norm and on the level of the legal order as a whole, it is not comprehensible if the obligated addressee of a norm by his refusal to fulfill his obligations can decide about the validity of the obligating norm. He is bound to recognize the legal norm, if it is legally valid, and not whether the norm is valid, if he adheres to it. Certainly, aspects of legitimation require that a person, who is the subject of an obligation, takes part in the foundation. Admittedly, a norm that is not being followed loses its social significance. From a legal point of view, it is still valid and as such can give the justification for a certain action and be binding. This is also the foundation of a right to resistance: if the institutions do not recognize and effectively defend the constitution, although they should, every citizen is justified in disobeying the acts of these institutions. Should he be successful and reestablish the general recognition for the old constitution, his acts would be justified by this. Once established, he cannot unilaterally renounce it. It is therefore convincing that in cases of social change, only the person legally permitted may decide about the forfeiture of validity.

Finally, the relation between moral and legal validity of law is problematic. What are the criteria for the moral validity of legal norms? Should only grossly unjust legal norms lose their legal validity or would each violation of justice or even merely of good practice suffice? With his unbearability formula, Radbruch tries to give an answer that certainly meets the feelings for justice of many. However, the criteria of an "unbearable measure" still need sufficient concretization. Maybe the hint of the development of human rights may prove to be helpful in establishing permanently accepted measures in future.

---

[89] "No such question can arise as to the validity of the very rule of recognition which provides the criteria; it can neither be valid nor invalid but is simply accepted as appropriate for use in this way," Hart (1991), S. 109.

[90] Raz (1977), p. 341: "These remarks may lead one to conclude that explaining what is legal validity is no more nor less than explaining what is law. This, however, is a mistake. The nature of law is explained primarily by explaining what are legal systems. Validity, on the other hand, pertains to the rules of the system."

4 Conclusion: The Bindingness of Law

The concept of law and the concept of validity have to be theoretically distinguished. Whereas the concept of law provides the criteria to decide the question if a norm is *law or nonlaw*, meaning something different than law, legal validity concerns the attribution of thus classified norms to a certain system of meaning. The criteria of a concept of legal validity permit it to decide the question if a legal norm is *legal or illegal*. Criticized by some authors, the disjunctive, nongradable, and clear valid/nonvalid criterion of legal validity is a major advantage to decide these claims. Validity of law decides controversial claims of validity. According to the systems of meaning the legal norms can be attributed to, different forms of validity can be distinguished. I have discussed legal, social, and moral validity of law here. I did not want to criticize these perspectives, but we can summarize that the internal problems of justification of these forms of validity and their mutual relation lead to an increasing juridification of them. Accordingly, legal validity of law is at the core of the validity and provides a solution to the tendency to subject the other criteria of validity to a norm.

Only a legal norm, the validity of which was founded, imposes an obligation on the addressee. Whereas some authors presume that a norm is valid if one ought to obey it,[91] we consider obligatory force not as a defining element of validity but a consequence thereof. The reason is that all obligations need a justification because they infringe freedom. This justification stems from properly enacted norms that can be attributed to a certain system (social practices, morality, law). Furthermore, validity does not mean the same as bindingness. Whereas validity of law concerns the relation between a legal norm and a legal system, obligation concerns the relation between this valid norm and a person. A norm as a sentence containing an obligation is legally binding only if it is law (i.e., can be subsumed under the concept of law) and is legally valid (i.e., can be attributed to a particular legal order). Thus, there may be a social (for example, arising from customs or conventions), a moral, and a legal bindingness. Norms that are legally valid can be binding, even if they lack social and moral validity. The sentence "the legally valid law X is binding" is then the judgment that the respective norm is law, belongs to a particular legal system, and the preconditions for the legal consequences the norm contains are given and therefore the respective subject should obey it.

Without the concept of law, we cannot justify that a norm creates legal obligation; without the concept of the validity of law, we cannot justify that the respective obligation is the obligation of this particular legal order. Only the concept of legal validity provides the possibility of deciding collisions of concurring legal obligations. The concept of law and the concept of the validity of law are necessary conditions for the justification of a legal duty. Legal obligation is not equivalent

[91] Kelsen (1960), p. 196; Kelsen (1949), p. 39: "Validity of law means that the legal norms are binding, that men ought to behave as the legal norms prescribe, that men ought to obey and apply the legal norms"; Grabowski (2013), p. 413 f.

with the foundation of a legal duty because there may be valid legal norms such as individual rights that contain an obligation but entitle the benefitted addressee, i.e. they establish a permission. Factually enforced norms that lack legal validity do not create this obligation, just as morally right norms do not. The modern differentiated law transforms both kinds of norm by its reflective form and bestows them in a well-ordered and just procedure, legal form, legal validity, and legal obligation.

References

Alexy, Robert. 1992. *Begriff und Geltung des Rechts*. Freiburg: Alber Verlag.

———. 2009. Hauptelemente einer Theorie der Doppelnatur des Rechts. *ARSP* 95: 151–166.

Aristotle. 1984. The Nicomachean Ethics. In *The Complete Works of Aristotle*, ed. J. Barnes, Revised Oxford Translation, vol. 2, Trans. W.D. Ross, 1729–1867. Oxford: Oxford University Press.

Austin, John. 1832. The Province of Jurisprudence Determined. In *The same: An Outline of A Course of Lectures on General Jurisprudence, or the Philosophy of Positive Law*, 1 ff. London: John Murray.

Bentham, Jeremy. 1840. *Theory of Legislation. Vol. 1: Principles of Legislation. Principles of the Civil Code*. Boston: Weeks, Jordan and Company.

Bierling, Ernst Rudolf. 1877. *Zur Kritik der juristischen Grundbegriffe. 1. Teil*. Gotha: Pertes.

———. 1894. *Juristische Prinzipienlehre. Bd. 1. Freiburg und Leipzig*. Freiburg: Mohr.

Coleman, Jules L. 1982. Negative and Positive Positivism. *Journal of Legal Studies* 11: 139–164.

Dreier, Ralf. 1994. Some Remarks on the Concept of Law. In *Prescriptive Formality and Normative Rationality in Modern Legal Systems*, ed. W. Krawietz, 109–124. Berlin: Duncker & Humblot.

———. 1996. Was ist Gerechtigkeit? *Juristische Schulung*, 580–584.

Dworkin, Ronald. 1967/68. The Model of Rules. *Chicago Law Review* 35: 14–46.

———. 1986. *Law's Empire*. Cambridge, MA: The Belknap Press of Harvard University Press.

Fichte, Johann Gottlieb. 1845. Grundlage des Naturrechts nach Prinzipien der Wissenschaftslehre. In *Johann Gottlieb Fichte's sämtliche Werke*, ed. J.H. Ficht, vol. 3, 1 ff. Berlin: de Gruyter.

Forst, Rainer. 1996. Kontexte der Gerechtigkeit. In *Politische Philosophie jenseits von Liberalismus und Kommunitarismus*, ed. Rainer Forst. Frankfurt/Main: Suhrkamp.

Geiger, Theodor. 1963. *Vorstudien zu einer Soziologie des Rechts*. Neuwied: Luchterhand.

Goodin, Robert E. 2005. Toward an International Rule of Law: Distinguishing International Law-Breakers from Would-Be Law-Makers. *The Journal of Ethics* 9: 225–246.

Grabowski, Andrzej. 2013. *Juristic Concept of the Validity of Statutory Law. A Critique of Contemporary Legal Nonpositivism*. Heidelberg, New York, Dordrecht, London: Springer.

Griller, Stefan, and Heinz Peter Rill. 2011. *Rechtstheorie. Rechtsbegriff – Dynamik – Auslegung*. Wien, New York: Springer Vienna.

Hart, H.L.A. 1983. Definition and Theory of Jurisprudence. In *Essays in Jurisprudence and Philosophy*, 21–48. Oxford: Oxford University Press.

———. 1991. *The Concept of Law*. Oxford: Clarendon Press.

Heckmann, Dirk. 1997. *Geltungskraft und Geltungsverlust von Rechtsnormen*. Tübingen: Mohr.

Hegel, G.W.F. 1985. *(Grundlinien): Grundlinien der Philosophie des Rechts. Naturrecht und Staatswissenschaft im Umrisse*. Frankfurt/Main: Ullstein Verlag.

Henkel, Heinrich. 1977. *Einführung in die Rechtsphilosophie*. München: C. H. Beck.

Hobbes, Thomas. 1968. *Leviathan*. Harmondsworth: Penguin.

Hoerster, Norbert. 1993. Richtigstellung über den Rechtspositivismus. *ARSP* 79: 416–420.

———. 2006. *Was ist Recht*. München: Beck Verlag.

Husserl, Gerhard. 1925. *Rechtskraft und Rechtsgeltung*. Berlin: Springer.

Jellinek, Georg. 1959. *Allgemeine Staatslehre*. 3 Aufl. Darmstadt: Wissenschaftliche Buchgesellschaft.

Jellinek, Georg. 1908. *Die sozialethische Bedeutung von Recht, Unrecht und Strafe*. 2nd ed. Berlin: Verlag O. Häring.

Kant, Immanuel. 1887. *The Philosophy of Law. An Exposition of the Fundamental Principles of Jurisprudence. The Science of Right*. Trans. W. Hastie. Edinburgh: Clark.

Kelsen, Hans. 1949. *General Theory of Law and State*. Cambridge/Mass.: Harvard University Press.

Kelsen, Hans. 1960. *Reine Rechtslehre*. 2. Aufl. Wien: Deuticke.

———. 1965. Was ist juristischer Positivismus? *Juristenzeitung*: 465–469.

Kirste, Stephan. 2002. Einleitung. In *Die Sophistik - Entstehung, Gestalt und Folgeprobleme des Gegensatzes von Naturrecht und positivem Recht*, ed. S. Kirste, K. Waecher, and M. Walther, 7 ff. Stuttgart: Steiner.

———. 2010. *Einführung in die Rechtsphilosophie*. Darmstadt: Wissenschaftliche Buchgesellschaft, Reihe: Einführung Philosophie.

———. 2011. Rechtsidee und Elemente der Gerechtigkeit bei Gustav Radbruch. In *Rechts- und Staatsphilosophie des Relativismus. Pluralismus, Demokratie und Rechtsgeltung bei Gustav Radbruch*, ed. W. Pauly, vol. 38, 57–83. Baden-Baden: Nomos, Reihe: Staatsverständnisse.

———. 2015a. Natural Law in Germany in the 20th Century. In *Legal Philosophy in the 20th Century in Civil Law Countries: The Civil Law World, (Vol. XII, tome II of Enrico Pattaro (ed.) A Treatise of Legal Philosophy and General Jurisprudence*, ed. Francesco Viola, 91–109. Heidelberg etc.: Springer.

———. 2015b. Longue Durée de la Loi. In *De La Pérennité et de la Temporalité du Droit*, ed. George Kadige, 67–83. Beirut: Èditions de l'USJ.

Larenz, Karl. 1967. *Das Problem der Rechtsgeltung*. 2. Aufl. Darmstadt: Wissenschaftliche Buchgesellschaft.

Lask, Emil. 1905. 'Rechtsphilosophie'. In *Die Philosophie im Beginn des 20. Jahrhunderts. Festschrift für Kuno Fischer*. 2. Band., 1–50. Heidelberg: Carl Winter.

Lasson, Adolf. 1882. *System der Philosophie*. Berlin und Leipzig: de Gruyter.

Liebnitz, G.W. 2003. In *Frühe Schriften zum Naturrecht*, ed. H. Busche. Hamburg: Meiner.

Lippold, Rainer. 1988. Geltung, Wirksamkeit und Verbindlichkeit von Rechtsnormen. *Rechtstheorie* 19: 463–489.

Locke, John. 1824. Two Treatises of Government. In *Works of John Locke*, vol 4, 12th ed., 209 ff. London: Rivington.

Luhmann, Niklas. 1987. *Rechtssoziologie*. 3. Aufl. Opladen: Westdeutscher Verlag.

———. 1993. *Das Recht der Gesellschaft*. Frankfurt/Main: Suhrkamp.

Moore, G.E. 1903. *Principia Ethica*. Cambridge: Cambridge University Press.

Nelson, Leonard. 1917. *Rechtswissenschaft ohne Recht*. Leipzig: Veit und Comp. - Vereinigung wissenschaftlicher Verleger.

Paulson, Stanley L. 1979. Neue Grundlagen für einen Begriff der Rechtsgeltung. *ARSP* 65: 1–19.

Peters, Anne. 2011. Soft law as a new mode of governance. In *The Dynamics of Change in EU Goverance*, ed. U. Diedrichs et al., 21–51. Cheltenham: Edward Elgar.

Radbruch, Gustav. 1993. Rechtsphilosophie. In *Gustav Radbruch Gesamtausgabe*, ed. A. Kaufmann, Bd. 2. Heidelberg: C. F. Müller.

Raz, Joseph. 1977. Legal Validity. *ARSP* 63: 339–353.

Rickert, Heinrich. 1921. *System der Philosophie: Allgemeine Grundlagen der Philosophie*. Tübingen: J. C. B. Mohr.

Ross, Alf. 1958. *On Law and Justice*. London: Stevens.

Schmitt, Carl. 1989. *Verfassungslehre*. 7.Auflage. Berlin: Duncker & Humblot.

———. 1993. *Über die drei Arten rechtswissenschaftlichen Denkens*. 2. Aufl. Berlin: Duncker & Humblot.

Seinecke, Ralf. 2015. *Das Recht des Rechtspluralismus*. Tübingen: Mohr Siebeck.

Stammler, Rudolf. 1896. *Wirtschaft und Recht*. Leipzig: Veit und Comp.
Teubner, Gunther. 1996. Globale Bukowina. Zur Emergenz eines transnationalen Rechtspluralismus. *Rechtshistorisches Journal* 15: 255–290.
Verdroß, Alfred. 1950. Zur Klärung des Rechtsbegriffs. *Juristische Blätter*: 88–90.
von Jhering, Rudolf. 1872. *Der Kampf um's Recht*. Neudr. herausgegeben und mit einer Einleitung versehen von H. Klenner. Freiburg/Berlin: Rudolf Haufe Verlag.
———. 1893. *Der Zweck im Recht*. Erster Band, 3. Aufl. Leipzig: Breitkopf und Härtel.
Weber, Max. 1980. *Wirtschaft und Gesellschaft. Grundriss der verstehenden Soziologie*. 5. Rev. Aufl. besorgt v. J. Winckelmann. Tübingen: Mohr Siebeck.
Weber, W. 1974. Geld. In *Historisches Wörterbuch der Philosophie*. ed. J. Richter, Bd. 3, Col. 224–226. Basel: Schwabe Verlag.
Weinberger, Ota. 1988. *Norm und Institution. Eine Einführung in die Theorie des Rechts*. Wien: Manz Verlag.

Sources and Validity

Mathieu Carpentier

Abstract This article proposes a "Simple Model" of the role that sources (mainly social sources) play in modern legal systems. Sources are described as legality-endowing facts. They give norms their legal quality. A norm is a *legal* norm (and not a moral or social one) if and only if it is traceable to a source. To understand how this works, I introduce the notion of source statements, which allows the Simple Model to eschew the usual questions about law's ontology: source statements are statements of fact that give an absolute reason to hold some legal statements (such as "if condition C obtains, then one ought to φ"). In such an outlook, sources, being facts, are not persons or authorities; they are (in most, but not all cases) facts about what authorities do.

This Simple Model allows us to disambiguate the notion of legal validity and to solve some classical jurisprudential puzzles. There are, basically, two concepts of validity: validity as membership—does a norm N belong to a given legal system?—and validity as conformity—does a norm N or, for that matter, does whatever X conform to higher-ranking norms of the legal system? If we follow the Simple Model, whether a norm belongs to a given legal system is *prima facie* independent from its lawfulness, that is, its conformity to, or consistency with, higher-ranking norms of the system. This is so because sources, being legality-endowing facts, are criteria of validity in the membership sense. The rule of recognition picks out the facts that are sources of law. It is not a set of constitutional requirements; there is an essential distinction to be made between the rule of recognition and the Constitution. The former is a set of membership criteria; the latter is a set of normative requirements that laws ought to be consistent with. We can therefore understand why "unlawful laws," such as unconstitutional statutes, may thus be valid norms and belong to the legal system until they are repealed.

The article concludes with some considerations on the relationship between validity (membership), bindingness, and publicity and why contracts and wills are never sources of law *stricto sensu*.

M. Carpentier (✉)
Toulouse-Capitole University, School of Law, Toulouse, France
e-mail: mathieu.carpentier@ut-capitole.fr

© Springer International Publishing AG, part of Springer Nature 2018
P. Westerman et al. (eds.), *Legal Validity and Soft Law*, Law and Philosophy Library 122, https://doi.org/10.1007/978-3-319-77522-7_4

1 Introduction

The notion of sources of law is pervasive both in contemporary legal philosophy and in legal discourse.

On the one hand, contemporary legal philosophers use a highly abstract notion of sources designed to serve their defense of their brand of legal positivism—legal positivism being discussed as a thoroughly philosophical thesis or set of theses. On the other hand, lawyers, jurists, and the like frequently talk of legal sources. First-year law students are taught about the main sources of law. Legal dogmatics have been feuding for years, at least in continental countries, over the respective merits and legal value of case law, custom, statutes, treaties, etc. On both sides, the concept of source is underconceptualized. The philosophers' source thesis is but a conceptual tool to show the social nature of legal facts. Lawyers presuppose that law "stems" from sources, without inquiring what such a "stemming" means.

In this paper, I am going to try and show that the notion of a legal source is a self-standing notion, one that should be inquired into regardless of any particular jurisprudential agenda. I will argue that contemporary philosophers are right to claim that sources of law—or rather a norm's traceability to such sources—are an essential component of legal validity. However, validity itself is a multifaceted, not to say straightforwardly ambiguous, notion, and we should not take it as if all its meanings depended on sources of law.

In the first part, I will propose what I call the Simple Model of sources of law, according to which sources are legality-conferring facts and not norm-creating authorities. As I will try to show later on, sources are not persons but facts, possibly facts about what some persons did or said.

In the second part, I will try to disambiguate the notion of legal validity. Under the Simple Model, the notion of a source is essential to only one of the notions of legal validity, i.e. the notion of validity as membership. It has no direct bearing on the other notions of legal validity. Furthermore, I will argue that sources may operate as a function of legal validity—itself understood as the membership of norms within the legal system—only under the assumption that they respect a condition of publicity. Although there are sources of private law, there is no private source of law.

2 Sources of Law: The Simple Model

2.1 Sources as (Generic) Facts

Everybody seems to agree that sources of law are facts. As the great Romanian jurist Mircea Djuvara wrote in 1939 in a very influential article (influential in France at least), "Every source of law is a fact. It is a fact from which norms that are to be applied to social activities stem" (Djuvara 1939, p. 219). Or as a more familiar legal philosopher would put it, "the sources of law are those facts by virtue of which it is valid and which identify its content" (Raz 2009, p. 47). In my previous work, I have claimed that validity and content are two different questions altogether. I will not rehearse my arguments here, but suffice it to say for present purposes that, to my mind, sources bear only on the validity of norms, not their content.

So sources are facts. Some of those facts are constituted by actions or complex sets of actions, for instance the complex action of passing and enacting a statute. But nothing prevents brute, natural facts to be used as sources of law. Facts about human nature have been described, by classical natural law theory, as being sources of law, and, as a matter of strict definition, there is not much of a difference between those facts and the complex social facts that constitute much of the sources of positive law.[1] I am aware, of course, that the facts referred to by natural lawyers are not really brute facts. But we could imagine a legal system where brute facts, under the relevant interpretation, could be used as a source of law. For instance, from the fact that it rains, we could infer that it is the law that such and such actions ought to be performed,[2] e.g. because rain is a sign of Gods' will. Of course such a legal system would exist in a world that is quite remote from ours. Ours is a world where legal sources are complex social facts whose content depends heavily on a set of interrelated constitutive rules. Sources are institutional facts—which should not come across as very surprising.

Although I think the sources-as-facts picture is basically correct, it does not come without a few caveats. It bears noticing that a fact, however complex, is not by itself a source of law. A single, specific act of legislation is not a source of law. It is an instantiation of a source of law, namely legislation. Sources of law are generic facts (or sets of facts): they are types, not tokens. So when we say, for instance, that a norm is traced back to a source, we must be aware that the norm in question is only being traced back to an instantiation of a source. This means that law, or at least positive law, is by its nature a cumulative enterprise. There are as many laws as there are facts that posit them.

I have referred to legislation as a topical example of a source of law. What I call "sources of law" need not be limited to so-called formal sources of law (statute, precedent, and so forth). It is hardly deniable that precedent is a source of law in France, but it is, however, not a "formal" one. And we could imagine sources that do not fall under the usual categories. However, it should be stressed that "sources of law" are only meant to designate facts from which laws derive their legality, their being laws in the first place. I will not use this phrase to refer to facts from which laws derive their content.[3] So-called interpretive sources, e.g. *travaux preparatoires*,

[1]On the role of sources in natural law theory, see O'Donnell and Day (2017).

[2]Note that in our rain example, the fact that it is raining is not the antecedent of a conditional norm, such as: *if it rains, one ought to do such and such*. Rather, the fact that it rains "gives birth" to a self-standing legal norm. More on this later.

[3]This is why sources of law are not identical, and not to be confused, with legal *texts*, that is, the products of law-making activities. For such an understanding, see Shecaira (2015, pp. 16–18), Pino (2014, pp. 199–200). The text is the vehicle of the law's communicative *meaning*; but the text itself does not give the norm it expresses or purports to express its *legality*. What does that is the fact that

are not sources of law in the sense I am using here. Some jurisprudents, such as Raz (2009, p. 47), have claimed that interpretive sources were sources for the purpose of their own theory. But even if we concede to Raz that validity and content are in some ways linked to each other, it does not help to mesh two very different concepts of sources into a single one.[4] The "sources" to which a judge resorts to ascertain the content of a statute are not conceptually different from the "sources" a student uses to write a paper. Legal sources do not primarily serve an epistemic function, even if they may occasionally serve such a function. They are not epistemic sources—by which I mean "stuff (or—if you're a journalist or a CIA agent—people) you take information from"; they are normative sources, the sources of legal norms. It is true that from the consideration of a source in the preferred stricter, normative meaning, one can derive information about the laws that exist by virtue of that source. But it is also obvious that in ordinary legal talk, sources are not meant to serve merely this information-giving role. Sources are what give laws their existence *qua* laws, not just what gives information about their existence, let alone their content.

The Simple Model of sources is thus the following. (a) Sources are generic social facts defined by a set of interrelated institutional rules. (b) By virtue of those facts, legal norms "exist" in some meaningful sense. (c) Sources are facts, not persons.

2.2 *Source Statements*

Claim (b) is familiar yet puzzling. What does it mean to claim that laws "exist" *by virtue of* their sources? One way to answer this question is to resort to an oblique explanation. Sources are truth conditions of source statements. Source statements may be defined as statements whose basic structure is the following:

(1) *Because* of facts $F_i \ldots F_j$, *it is the law* that P.

P may in turn be developed into the familiar conditional legal norm:

(2) *Because* of facts $F_i \ldots F_j$, *it is the law* that if condition C obtains, then one ought to φ.

Drawing on Kelsen's conception of *Sollen* (Kelsen 1967, pp. 117–119), I hasten to add that "ought" is meant to cover all deontic modalities understood here *lato sensu* (i.e., not only obligations, prohibitions, and permissions but also power-conferring norms, rights, and so forth). Also, it should be remembered that in (2), $F_i \ldots F_j$ are instantiations of a generic fact, whereas condition C is left unspecified. In

the text itself is the outcome of a law-creating fact. Of course, a single text can express multiple, even contradictory, norms, depending on the way you interpret it. But here I will assume that there are, at least in some cases, uncontroversial, easy interpretations.

[4]On this matter, I have nothing to add to the points made by Shecaira (2013, p. 10).

most cases, C will be a generic fact or a definite set of facts, but it could be a specific, individual fact as well.

Statement (2) should not be taken as implying a specific theory of the individuation of laws. I do not mean to claim—as Kelsen did—that all legal norms, and indeed all norms, are conditional norms (Kelsen 1967, pp. 100–101). Such a move was crucial for Kelsen since in his theory, all legal norms must be individuated around the delict-sanction relationship, which is conditional by nature. But here it does not matter whether legal norms are categorical or conditional.

However, taking conditional norms as an example may prove more problematic than it seems as it may lead toward a quite regrettable confusion. The reader certainly has noticed that I have left the type of relation expressed by "because" totally unspecified. I have replaced "by virtue of" with "because," which (arguably) does not help a lot. Before explaining why I did so, I must warn that this relation, whatever it may be, is not identical, or analogous, with the material implication used to link the antecedent with the consequent of the conditional norm. This should prevent us from incorporating the mention of the source into the antecedent of the norm.

Such a disastrous move is made by Kelsen in the *Pure Theory of Law*, and it is yet another consequence of his unfortunate theory of the individuation of laws. Kelsen is confronted with the existence of norms that do not provide any sanction but that only confer powers,[5] such as constitutional norms, and he does not seem to know what to make of them. So in order to save the simplicity of the theory, he resorts to the following reconstruction:

> The legal proposition that describes this situation says: "if the individuals authorized to legislate have **issued a general norm** according to which a thief is to be punished in a certain way; and if the court (...) has ascertained that an individual has committed theft; then a certain organ ought to execute the legally determined punishment" (Kelsen 1967, p. 47).[6]

This is very wrong.[7] Such a norm-individuation principle leads to obviously self-referential statements. Its basic structure is as follows: "If the legislature **has issued the norm** that thieves must be punished **and** if someone is a thief, then they must be punished." In such a statement, the norm referred to in the antecedent is nothing but the norm expressed by the whole statement itself. Of course there are self-referential laws. But it is just wrong to assume that all laws are self-referential. Moreover, it

[5]Actually sources are *not* power-conferring norms (they are not norms at all), and neither is the rule of recognition. I will say more about this later. But this point does not matter here since what Kelsen incorporates in the antecedent of the rule is not the power-conferring rule itself, but the acts that the addressee of that rule is supposed to perform—which is the very notion of a source such as has been defined in this paper. Kelsen does not say: "if the constitution empowers the legislature to perform such and such acts, then..." but: "if the constitutionally empowered legislature has performed such-and-such acts, then...".

[6]I have modified the translation. I gloss over details of the quotation that are either unimportant for the present purposes or very problematic (including those that incorporate not only constitutional norms but what Hart would call rules of adjudication into the norm-antecedent).

[7]For another (and very apt) line of criticism, see Duarte d'Almeida (2013, pp. 268–275).

leads to a very frequent error according to which the realization of the antecedent brings into existence not only the obligation (or prohibition, etc.) expressed by the consequent but also the norm itself. If nobody steals, then obviously nobody ought to be punished. But this does not imply that there is no law that provides that thieves must be punished. If we go with Kelsen's model, then the fact that the legislature has enacted a piece of legislation, joined with the fact that John is a thief, implies that John ought to be punished. But this piece of legislation is the very fact that created the **norm** that "**if** a piece of legislation is passed to the effect that there is a norm that if one is a thief then one should be punished, **and** if one is a thief **then** one should be punished." So we get to a point of maddening recursivity. "**If** a piece of legislation is passed to the effect that there is a norm that {if a piece of legislation is passed to the effect that there is a norm (. . .) that if one is a thief then one should be punished and one is a thief, then one should be punished}, **and** if one is a thief **then** one should be punished"—and so on *ad infinitum*.[8] We can of course accept this recursivity and live with it, but we can also agree that it leads to very unfortunate consequences.[9] Luckily, we can avoid them by extracting the source reference from the norm formulation and by distinguishing source statements from legal statements.

2.3 Source Statements and Legal Statements

Under the Simple Model, source statements are distinct from legal statements such as below:

(3) If condition C obtains, then one legally ought to φ.[10]

Source statements comprise legal statements: they state under what conditions legal statements are justified in a particular legal system. Source statements stand with legal statements in a relationship that is expressed by the word "because" in proposition (2). There are many ways to define this relationship; most of them are not oblique in the way proposed here. Most theories explain the way facts create law. My theory is much more modest, as we shall see.

[8]Things would be different if the "and" in bold had been a "then": "If the legislature has enacted the norm that thieves must be punished **then** if someone is a thief, then they must be punished". But this move is forbidden to Kelsen, because the whole proposition "if someone is a thief, then they must be punished" does not express a sanction, only its own consequent does. So under Kelsen's model the source-instantiating facts are as much a condition of the realization of the deontic consequent of the norm as the usual factual antecedent of the norm.

[9]For instance, the complete formulation of a norm is necessarily an infinite sentence comprised of embedded conditionals. Bentham would not be pleased.

[10]Notice that such legal statements may be internal statements, detached statements or moderate external ("hermeneutic") statements. It makes no difference for present purposes. For my own take on legal statements, see Carpentier (2014, pp. 54–85).

The classical positivist way to view it is to qualify legality through a set of attitudes of members of the legal community, or some of them, for instance officials of the legal system. Let me call this the Attitude Model. It covers both Austin's habit of obedience, which is a nonnormative attitude, and Hart's internal point of view, which is, as Hart showed at length, a normative attitude. A Hartian, philosophical account[11] of (2) could be that because of facts $F_i \ldots F_j$, or, rather, because those facts are source instantiations, it is accepted among officials that if C, then one ought to φ (Hart 1994, pp. 100–117). We can also think of (early) Raz's Belief Model (Raz 1999, p. 170), according to which because of facts $F_i \ldots F_j$, it is believed that if C, then one ought to φ. To take just one last example, Shapiro's Perspectival Model entails that because of facts $F_i \ldots F_j$, *from the legal point of view*, if C, then one *morally* ought to φ (Shapiro 2011, pp. 184–188).

Another possibility is what could be called the Hermeneutic Model, famously endorsed by Kelsen (1967, pp. 3–4). According to Kelsen, norms expressed or referred to by (3) are *meanings*. They are the meanings of the facts that "posit" them. Norms are objective meanings of acts of will. Their objective meaning depends on the existence of another, higher norm, which serves as a scheme of interpretation of the acts in question. The act of will by which the legislature states that thieves ought to be punished means (objectively) that thieves *ought* to be punished. The ultimate scheme of interpretation is the basic norm.

Yet another possibility is explored by some antipositivist theories that assume that because of facts $F_i \ldots F_j$, if condition C obtains, then one (*morally*) ought to φ, skipping altogether the "it is the law that" part of proposition (2). With a lot of caveats, I take Greenberg's Moral Impact Theory (Greenberg 2014) to be an instance of such a claim.

I do not need a particular theory of the normativity of law for my purposes in this paper since I do not purport to show how social facts "give rise" to a certain type of normative requirements. My approach to sources being oblique, I only need to show in what way first-order source statements uttered by members of the legal community (officials and laymen alike) aim to justify legal statements. This is why I will make a rather modest claim regarding the relation between source statements and legal statements. Source statements are justifications for legal statements insofar as they give what Raz calls *absolute reasons* to hold legal statements.[12] If John asks

[11]All these variations on the Attitude Model are *not* source-statements, but philosophical explanations of how source-instantiating facts cause a set of attitudes among the members of the legal community.

[12]It was Joseph Raz, to whom I am deeply indebted here, who coined the phrase "absolute reason" in *Practical Reason and Norms*. However, the definition of source-statements as reasons should not be confused with the claim that sources are reasons. Such a claim was made by Raz in a famous article (Raz 2009, pp. 65–66). Sources are not reasons, unless we confuse sources with facts that give rise to particular legal duties. Such facts are specified in the antecedent of the norm or of the legal statement. Such a confusion is exactly what Raz does when he puts on the same level a Parliamentary enactment, contracting with someone, marrying someone, etc., all of them being reasons for action.

why all Xs ought to φ, James replies: "Because it's the law." If John still asks why, James will reply: "Because the legislature said so." In that respect, James' statement gives John an absolute reason to hold the legal statement that all Xs ought to φ. In Raz's terms, it means that such a reason, though cancelable, cannot be overridden (Raz 1999, pp. 27–28): there is no other statement that would justify replacing our original legal statement with a contrary or contradictory legal statement. I will argue later that even a statement describing a higher-ranking source-instantiating fact would not be able to override—and could not be overridden by—our reason to hold the initial legal statement. In this case, we have a classical conflict of norms situation, whose resolution depends on default rules, metarules, and the like but not on the weighing and balancing of reasons.

Absolute reasons cannot be overridden, but they obviously can be canceled when the facts that constitute such reasons do no longer obtain or never obtained in the first place. For instance, the statement "actually the statute was repealed yesterday" or "actually the statute does not require *φ-ing*" cancels the reason given by James' statement.

Our oblique way of characterizing sources aims to show how facts "posit" norms by showing how certain statements are justified.[13] Therefore, saying that a norm is a legal norm amounts, in our view, to saying that in the relevant legal system, a source statement can be made that links the (true) reference to source-instantiating facts with the legal statement referring to the norm or to one of its logical consequences. If such a source statement can be made, then one has an absolute reason to hold the corresponding legal statement. Most obviously, the oblique way does not explain why one has such an absolute reason. But none of the nonoblique theories I have summarily sketched above provide such an explanation. And maybe such an explanation is impossible after all: I will make an attempt at giving one in the last two sections of this paper.

The oblique way allows us to stay clear of any ontological presupposition about the way facts "posit" norms—assuming such a thing is indeed possible. We do not need to endorse any of the theoretical models I have sketched out above or any theory of law's normativity. All that is needed for a norm to be traced back to a source is a source statement, together with the (true) statement of the existence of facts $F_i \ldots F_j$ mentioned in the source statement.

2.4 Sources, Persons, and Authorities

According to the Simple Model, sources are facts; they are not persons. Legislation is a source of law; the legislature is not. Obviously, persons (including institutions in

[13] Paolo Sandro tells me that in his opinion my oblique way is some sort of magic trick. He may be right, but at least I am in a good company of magicians. See e.g. the way Raz defines rules: "Rules are things the content of which is described by some normative statements" (Raz 2009, p. 148).

the usual sense) are not irrelevant to the existence of sources. In most cases, some of the facts that constitute a source are actions, which obviously—and trivially—have to be performed by someone.

It is naturally tempting to analyze sources as persons. After all, laws are in most cases created by persons: they are authoritative directives issued by certain persons, which can be called *legal authorities*. Legal authorities are a subset of public authorities. Public authorities are persons (*lato sensu*: individuals, institutions, public bodies) who claim to have practical authority over a certain group of people. What makes them *public* authorities is that they are somehow entrusted with the task of exercising authority over a certain group of people. This is due to a set, or sets, of legitimizing conditions (such as democracy, popular sovereignty, representation, fairness, rule of law, *Etat de droit*, and so on). The important point is that public authorities differ from private authorities in that they are, or at least claim to be, serving public interests—or the interests of the public if you like. A judge differs from a private arbitrator precisely in this way.

Legal authorities are public authorities that are entrusted with the task of issuing legal directives, that is, directives that express norms that belong to the legal system and are *prima facie* binding on legal officials. Not all public authorities are legal authorities—think for instance of merely consultative institutions, such as the French *Conseil économique, social et environmental*. But all legal authorities are public authorities.

The decisive, but wrong, move is to equate sources with legal authorities. The most famous author to err on this side is (again) Joseph Raz.[14] In "Authority, Law, and Morality," Raz writes: "the fact that law claims authority supports the (...) source thesis" (Raz 1985, pp. 315–316). The reasons for this support are due to Raz's service conception of authority about which I have nothing to say here. But Raz goes on: "Hence, the identification of a rule as a rule of law consists in attributing it to the relevant person or institution as representing their decisions and expressing their judgment (...) Such attributions can only be based on factual considerations" (and not on moral considerations[15]).

This is where it goes awry. Identifying a norm as a legal norm is of course dependent on factual considerations, but it is a long stretch to argue that such considerations are only concerned with the determination of what some persons said. Do not misunderstand me. I agree that legal authorities play a decisive part in the law-creating process. Denying this would imply a peculiar view, to say the least, of our modern legal systems. Obviously, there is no legislation without a legislature. Still, confusing the two amounts to a subtle, albeit important, category mistake.

[14] I realize I have been attacking Raz's theory quite a lot in this paper. This nitpicking is rather unfortunate since I do agree with many aspects of Raz's theory.

[15] Of course, Raz's aim, as I mentioned in the Introduction, is to prove a jurisprudential point about law and morality. I happen to agree with that point, but the ways he uses to get to it seem quite wrong to me. As I said, I am not trying to further any jurisprudential agenda here, although my positivistic tendencies should be obvious by now.

There is an important difference between the source of a law and its so-called creator. Strictly speaking, nobody "creates" law. What the legislature creates is a text, which aims to express some kind of normative requirement. The legislature is by no means the only one doing that. Many public and private authorities do quite as much. The question whether the legislature has issued such and such directive is distinct from the question of the *legality* of the norm it was aiming to express. What gives the directive its legality is a set of facts, including the fact that the legislature has created a text saying so and so. But not everything the legislature says (*qua* legislature) is always law: such is the case, for instance, of parliamentary resolutions under Article 34-1 of the French Constitution. Moreover, the fact that the legislature said so and so, that is, passed a statute, is seldom sufficient for there to be a law. Very often one needs a royal assent, a formal enactment, a signing into law by the head of state, etc. That does not make the Queen[16] or the President a legislator. They do not take part in passing the statute—the statute's text, that is—except perhaps when they can veto it. They are not, in that very respect, *legal* authorities.

A source of law is not what gives a given text its existence or what gives a given norm its content but what gives the norm the text aims to express its own existence *qua* law. Among the facts that perform that job, the facts about the legislature's actions play a decisive role. However, the legislature is *not* a source of law: only those facts are. Sources and authorities are two distinct conceptual categories, even if, in most cases, sources are generic facts (at least partially) constituted by some authority's actions. Sometimes, as the example of custom shows, sources of law are constituted by facts, which are not about any authority whatsoever.

If a source is what gives a norm its existence *qua* law, it must be what gives it its *legal validity*. This, however, is only partly true.

3 Sources, Membership, Conformity

3.1 Two Notions of Validity

Consider the following cases:

(a) I take the metro, and I reuse an already used ticket. The ticket inspector tells me that my ticket is *invalid*.
(b) I sign a contract stipulating that I agree to be eaten by my cocontractor. A judge tells me my contract is *invalid*.
(c) A court reviews a piece of legislation and declares it unconstitutional: the statute is thereby *invalid*.

[16]I am aware that the UK's legislator is, from a strict constitutional point of view, the Queen-in-Parliament. But conventions of the constitution forbid the Queen to withhold her Royal Assent. So maybe, from a strict legal point of view, she *is* a co-author of Parliamentary Acts, but this is a clear legal fiction.

(d) I am tried in France for murder, and I invoke an exculpatory circumstance provided for in Section 213.4 of the Syldavian Penal Code: the judge tells me that the norm I refer to is not a *valid* norm of French law.

Contrary to what would seem to be the case, I will argue here that cases (a), (b), and (c) roughly use the same concept of validity. I will argue that case (d) is somehow unique and corresponds to a separate notion of validity. And I will argue that sources *are* criteria of validity only on this second notion of validity.

It is commonplace that "validity" is ambiguous. My own distinction is the following. We use generally the word "valid" or "invalid" as a pretentious way to say "good" or "no good" or, if you will, "lawful" or "unlawful." When we say that a ticket, a contract, or a statute is *invalid*, we mean that they are "no good" in the eyes of the law. Notice that "valid" here is predicated of both material things and norms. For something to be "good" in the eyes of the law, i.e. for something to be lawful, it has to conform to some legal norms: the purchase of metro tickets ought to be made in conformity with the metro company bylaws; a contract ought to be made in conformity with legal requirements; statutes must conform with constitutional requirements; and so forth. Let me call this *validity as conformity*.

On the other hand, when we say that norm X is a valid norm of French law, we do not mean that it conforms to higher-ranking norms. What we do mean is that X belongs to the French legal system, that it possesses some quality that Section 213.4 of Syldavian Penal Code does not possess. Let me call this *validity as membership*.

There is therefore a crucial distinction to be made between the assertion "N is an invalid norm under French law" and the assertion "N is not a valid norm of the French legal system." Of course this distinction is a matter of stipulation. Be that as it may, I must make it clear that I am not dealing here with the subtle nuances of the *word* "validity" and of the way lawyers and jurisprudents use it. I am dealing with two different *concepts* of validity, and I think that these concepts, though overlapping, are not reducible to each other.

This distinction may look like the familiar distinction between material *v.* formal validity (Guastini 1992, p. 22; Pino 2014, pp. 207–208). But this is somewhat misleading. The formal/material distinction applies only to laws, and it assumes that both kinds of validity are two sides of the same coin, i.e. the validity of laws. But remember that validity as conformity applies to everything, laws as well as anything that can be regulated by law. When I say that "your ticket is invalid" or that it is "no good" from a legal point of view because you did not purchase it according to the rules, the concept of invalidity as nonconformity is the same as I would use about a statute. Moreover, the formal/material distinction is somewhat obscured by the fact that lawyers, especially contract lawyers, use it sometimes to refer to formal validity as the satisfaction of formal or procedural requirements. In that sense, both formal validity and material validity are instances of what I call validity as nonconformity.

What, then, is the difference between *membership* and *conformity to a higher-ranking norm*?[17] Inquiring whether N is a valid norm of French law amounts typically to asking two distinct questions:

(1) Does N *belong* to French law?
(2) Does N conform to—or does it conflict with—higher-ranking norms of French law? (Those higher-ranking norms[18] are typically the Constitution when N is a statute and statutory law when N is an administrative regulation or bylaw).

What is at stake in question (1) is primarily a demarcation problem.[19] If N is a norm of French law, then *ipso facto* it does not belong to the American legal system. If N is, e.g., a moral norm that does not meet certain criteria set by the French rule of recognition, then it is not a valid legal norm of the French system, and if it does not meet any criteria set by any rule of recognition of any legal system, then it is not a legal norm altogether. In that respect, membership is defined as the specific mode of existence of legal norms.[20] A legal norm exists *qua* legal norm if and only if it belongs to a legal system.[21] In that sense, validity is defined in terms of existence, *à la* Kelsen—but contrary to Kelsen's views, existence is not to be equated with bindingness (more on which later) but with membership.

What is at stake in question (2) is different. To ask whether a norm is consistent with a higher-ranking norm is independent of its membership within the legal system. Obviously, it generally only makes sense to ask this question when the norm does actually belong to the legal system, but it need not be so. One could ask this question about a fictitious or hypothetical norm or about a norm that belongs to another legal system. For instance, it can be asked whether French laws banning so-called Islamic headscarves from schools or criminalizing Holocaust denial would

[17]For related, but not exactly similar, distinctions see Ross (1998, pp. 158–159), Rodriguez and Vicente (2009, pp. 188–189), Lamond (2013, pp. 113–114). S. Munzer distinguishes validity (understood as conformity) and existence but nevertheless claims that both concepts are extensionally equivalent (Munzer 1970, p. 43).

[18]A norm is usually defined as being of higher rank than another norm if it regulates the way that other norm is to be "created" and/or that other norm's content. Since, as I have noted before, the notion of "law creation" is a bit confused, such a definition needs to be modified: a norm is of higher rank than another if it defines (and restricts) the scope of the powers of legal authorities; more specifically such norms regulate the way those authorities ought to issue legal directives and they also regulate those directives' content. On such an understanding, only what Hart called *rules of change* are liable to be called "higher-ranking norms".

[19]I would readily agree with Brian Leiter that the so-called "demarcation problem" as applied to *jurisprudence and legal philosophy* leaves a lot to be desired and should be abandoned altogether (Leiter 2011). But it is nevertheless an important feature of the activity of *lawyers*. The demarcation aspect of legal validity is a matter of *quid juris*, not *quid jus*. Part of lawyers' routine is to find out what the legal rules are, that is, the rules that belong to their legal system, that are relevant to a particular case or legal question. They will therefore "demarcate" without even realizing it.

[20]For brevity's sake, I brush over very important and intricate issues, on which see Kirste (2018) in this volume. It bears noticing that I am only concerned with what Kirste calls "legal" validity, and not with other spheres of validity (moral or social).

[21]For related arguments on the same point, see Lamond (2014, p. 39).

be consistent with the First Amendment of the US Constitution (obviously they would not). It is true that we would not normally say that those French laws are "invalid" under the First Amendment, the reason being that they are not valid laws of the American[22] legal system in the first place. But if anything, it shows that it makes sense to talk about a norm being invalid or unlawful, i.e. inconsistent with a higher-ranking norm, mainly, if not only, when that norm is *actually* a valid norm within a particular legal system, i.e. belongs to this legal system. *To put it in a nutshell, in order to be invalid, a norm must be a valid norm of the system in the first place!*[23]

There is a logical difference between a norm's belonging to a legal system and a norm's conformity with higher-ranking norms of the same legal system. Obviously, nonconformity is often a ground for suppressing the norm from the legal system; in the case of constitutional courts, it is a necessary condition. The difference between the French Constitutional Council abrogating a statute and the French Parliament doing the same is that the former may only do so if the statute is unconstitutional—or at least if it declares it to be unconstitutional—whereas the latter may do so for whatever reasons it wishes, among which is, most obviously, political expediency. In any case, the fact that the Constitutional Council abrogates[24] a law *because* it is unconstitutional does not mean that that law does not belong to the legal system *because* it is unconstitutional. What makes it no longer belong to the legal system is not its unconstitutionality but the *decision made* by the Constitutional Council to abrogate it. We must then distinguish between what *makes* a norm belong or cease to belong to a legal system and what are the *grounds* for its suppression from it.

3.2 Sources as Criteria of Membership

If the Simple Model is right, then sources are criteria of membership: sources give laws their existence *qua* laws, and such existence is nothing but the laws' membership within the legal system. The rule of recognition specifies which facts are sources of law. This is basic Hartian orthodoxy, and I see absolutely no reason to depart from it. When a norm can be traced back to a source, then it belongs to the legal system: it is a legal norm. If it cannot be traced back to such a source, it is not a legal norm. This, if anything, is a consequence of the Simple Model. According to it, sources are facts by virtue of which norms are legal norms (in the legal system considered). Then

[22]For brevity's sake, when I mention the "American legal system", I mean both the US federal legal system and the legal systems of the States.

[23]Of course, this is not always the case. Take for instance *a priori* constitutional review. A constitutional court adjudicates on a statute's constitutionality after its adoption by the Houses, but before it is signed into law by the President. In this case, the statute is not yet valid (not yet a member of the legal system), and if it is deemed unconstitutional by the Court, it will actually never be valid, but we nevertheless talk of its invalidity (its unconstitutionality).

[24]I take the example of the French Constitutional Council, because it is empowered by article 62 of the French Constitution to abrogate unconstitutional statutes.

the rule of recognition must be understood as the rule specifying which facts are legality endowing. It picks out which facts are sources. Since, according to the Simple Model, sources are facts and not persons, the rule of recognition is conceptually distinct from Hartian *rules of change*, which are power-conferring rules directed at lawmaking authorities.[25]

Therefore, the rule of recognition is not a set of constitutional requirements directed at legal authorities in their law-giving capacities. Sources have *prima facie* no bearing on validity understood as conformity to higher-ranking norms. Of course those norms must themselves be source based. However, the consideration of sources plays no part in determination of whether a law—or anything else—conforms to (higher ranking) norms. Sources have already done their job in allowing us to ascertain that the norm had legal status in the first place. This is the consequence of the fact that source statements are absolute reasons for holding legal statements. Such reasons cannot be overridden. From the fact that two norms are in conflict, one cannot infer that one of their corresponding source statements overrides the other and that one of the conflicting norms does not belong to the legal system.

It may be objected that whether a norm belongs to a legal system depends precisely on its *conformity* to the criteria of validity set out by the rule of recognition. I will answer by pointing out that, contrary to the notion of "conformity with higher-ranking norms," the notion of "conformity with criteria of membership" is not a *normative* but a *conceptual* kind of conformity. When we say that a law is unconstitutional, that is, invalid, we mean that, according to constitutional law, it *ought to be*, or *should have been*, made in conformity with constitutional norms. This is a normative requirement from the legal point of view. But when we say that a norm that does not meet a particular legal system's criteria of validity is not "in conformity" with those criteria, we mean a strictly conceptual claim: this thing is not what they call "law" in this legal system. Membership is a matter of conceptual conformity. Whether a given cat conforms to the criteria of catness is a purely conceptual matter: if it does not display certain cat properties, it is not a cat. It would make no sense to claim that it *ought* to be the case that it displays such properties. The same goes for laws and criteria of membership.[26] Whether a norm can be traced back to a

[25]Some claim that the rule of recognition is a power-conferring rule or a rule of change: see e.g., Mullock (1974), Waluchow (1985, p. 43), Waldron (2009). Pino (2011, p. 282) says that the rule of recognition is both a power-conferring and a duty-imposing rule. For a powerful refutation, see Raz (2009, p. 93). More recently, Matczak (2017) uses speech-act theory to show the nonredundancy of the rule of recognition, which is not a rule of change in disguise. One of the most illuminating points he makes is about the very different chronological nature of these two kinds of rules (Matczak 2017, p. 11): the rule of recognition always has an *ex post facto* function, it is a reconstructive generalization of acts of recognition that are already there, so to speak, since it presupposes an existing practice of recognition.

[26]I certainly do not mean to deny that our use of concepts is normative. But when we talk about the normativity of concepts, such normativity is directed at the speaker: in that perspective, to say that concept C means Y amounts to saying that only in conditions where Y-properties are displayed is it permissible for the speaker to say that an X is an instance of C. But the normativity of (*prima facie* nonnormative) concepts does not entail that the *predicandum* (X) *ought* to display Y-properties,

law-creating fact (a source) is a conceptual condition of its membership within the legal system. Whether a norm is consistent with higher-ranking norms, including norms specifying the formal and procedural requirements that legal authorities must satisfy, is a normative matter.

This is why there is an important distinction to be made between criteria of membership of laws set out in a rule of recognition and formal and procedural requirements set out by constitutional norms. Satisfying the former is a matter of conceptual conformity, whereas satisfying the latter is a matter of normative requirements. Modifying those procedural requirements does not amount to changing the rule of recognition. The rule of recognition states that legislation is a source of law, and the Constitution determines what procedural and substantive rules the legislature ought to follow. These are two very different things. Of course they interact to some extent. At some point, a norm violating core procedural constitutional requirements may lead legal scholars and officials alike to wonder whether it is a law at all. For instance, in French constitutional law, a bill must have been passed in identical terms by both Houses of the legislature (the National Assembly and the Senate[27]) and signed into law by the President of the Republic.[28] If the President "enacts" a bill that has been passed only at first reading by the National Assembly, not only does he violate a core constitutional requirement, but legal scholars and officials are bound to wonder whether such a "statute" is a law in the first place. This is because, as Hart observed in the *Concept of Law*, the rule of recognition itself is open textured. Sometimes we sincerely do not know whether some set of facts qualifies as "legislation" for the purposes of the rule of recognition. But those are simply exceptional cases. In most cases, even when Parliament violates the Constitution, it is obvious that what it produces is still law in some meaningful sense. Only in cases of gross violations of constitutional requirements will the question arise as to whether there is a law in the first place.

As far as membership is concerned, the crucial point in our example is not that the President or the National Assembly may have acted *ultra vires* or unlawfully: the point is that the basic legality-endowing facts are liable to be missing. There is not much of a difference between the President "enacting" a "statute" that would not have been passed in either House—and me, a private citizen, doing the same.

e.g. that a cat *ought* to display cat-properties. So when we say that X does not belong to the French legal system because it does not display certain properties which are part of the intension of the concept "membership in the French legal system", we do not express a normative requirement directed at the norm in question. By contrast, when we say that a norm is invalid, in the sense that it is unlawful, we *prima facie* express a normative requirement, through what one would call an "internal statement". (Many thanks to Anne Ruth Mackor and Paolo Sandro for raising strong objections regarding this point).

[27]French Constitution, Article 24 and Article 45 §1.

[28]French Constitution, Article 10. For simplicity's sake, I shall ignore here the various procedures by which disagreements between Houses are resolved as well as exceptional procedures by which the passing of a bill is forced upon either one of the Houses or both, such as the so-called "accelerated procedure" (see French Constitution, art. 45§2), the special provisions of Article 49§3, and so on.

Whatever "norm" is expressed by this directive is not a legal norm. The fact that the President is a public, legal even, authority is irrelevant as far as membership is concerned: lawmaking authorities cannot violate the rule of recognition. Such a "violation" would simply not make any sense. The fact that they can, and quite often do, violate the Constitution and the procedural and substantive norms contained therein is another matter entirely. Of course, the rule of recognition *is* normative.[29] But its normativity is directed at *law-applying* organs, which are under the *prima facie* obligation to apply the laws identified by it. The rule of recognition does not create any obligation for *law-creating* organs, and it does not confer on them any power. As I noted earlier, this is the job of Hartian rules of change. By contrast, conformity with a higher-ranking norm is typically an obligation for law-creating organs, one that will later be enforced by the courts.

We can therefore understand, and solve easily, the puzzle of illegal laws, such as unconstitutional statutes.[30] We can understand how it can be the case that some laws, though unconstitutional *ab initio*, are still laws until they are struck down, maybe dozens of years after they were first enacted. Whether a statute is unconstitutional has *prima facie* no impact on its membership within the system. Such a claim does not amount to saying that the constitutionality of a norm depends on what judges say it is. No such move is needed here. We may agree that a statute's constitutionality is a matter of objective judgment and also agree that only a source-instantiating fact (such as an act of repeal) is able to make it disappear from the legal system.

There is therefore more than a grain of truth in the Kelsenian adage according to which "the legal norms that belong to a legal order cannot be null, but only annullable" (Kelsen 1967, pp. 276–278).[31] In non-Kelsenian terms, if a norm can be traced back to a source, its own nonconformity to a higher-ranking norm, *even to*

[29]This is a somewhat contested topic in jurisprudence. Most writers agree that the rule of recognition is normative, insofar as it is a duty-imposing rule (we have already seen that it cannot be a power-conferring rule). See, a.m.o., Raz (1980, p. 197), Raz (2009, p. 93), Shapiro (2009, p. 240), Perry (2006, p. 1183), MacCormick (2008, p. 109), Coleman (2001, p. 86), Ruiz Manero (1990, p. 133). But some writers argue that the rule of recognition is not a normative rule, but a merely conceptual rule; see for instance Bulygin (1991, pp. 311–318). My own account is syncretic, more on which below.

[30]On this puzzle, see Sandro (2018) in this volume. For a modern illustration provided by an internal debate within inclusive positivists, see Himma (2005, 2009), Kramer (2003, pp. 115–140) and Waluchow (2009).

[31]I hasten to add that, although this slogan is true, it is inconsistent with many aspects of Kelsen's own theory of validity, which rests on a confusion between membership (or rather, existence, understood in a normative sense) and conformity. If a norm's validity (qua existence) depends on its conformity to procedural requirements set by higher ranking norms, as Kelsen famously argued, then one does not see why a norm which does not respect these requirements would not be null *ab initio*: annullability (*via* judicial review for instance) would then be a useless conceptual tool. Kelsen's solution to this dilemma is his well-known theory of "alternative dispositions": the Constitution empowers the legislature to make law according to procedural and substantive constitutional requirements and it also empowers it to make law in any other way that is inconsistent with the Constitution. On this strange theory, see Moreso (1993, pp. 83–92), Tur (2013) and Hochmann (2017).

the formal/procedural requirements set out by it, it does not entail that the norm does not belong to the legal system. If it is to cease to be a member of the legal system, the norm has to be suppressed by a normative act, such as an abrogation or repeal or annulment, performed by an authority empowered to do so,[32] such as a constitutional court. There is only one significant difference between the Constitutional Council abrogating a statute and the legislature repealing it: the Constitutional Council must *justify* its decision, which may only be grounded in the unconstitutionality of the statute. By contrast, when Parliament repeals a statute, it may do it for any reason it wishes, within certain limits of course,[33] and generally both the previous and the new laws are consistent with the Constitution.

3.3 Sources, Validity, and Publicity

I have talked about the validity of statutes. What about contracts? Are contracts more like legislation or more like metro tickets? Are contracts sources of law in the sense we have just expounded?

For present purposes, contracts may be defined as the set of facts by virtue of which contractual norms (so-called *negotia*) exist. This sounds very much like sources as defined by the Simple Model. I will argue that this resemblance is misleading. Even though contracts are norm-creating facts and even though those facts are regulated by law, contracts are not sources of law. This means that contracts are never picked out by the rule of recognition as criteria of membership. This seems to be a preposterous claim. I will defend it nevertheless. Incidentally, my point is not about contracts specifically. Through the example of contracts, I will try to show that there are no *private sources* of law.

As I have hinted, the rule of recognition is normative, insofar as it imposes duties on officials. This is commonplace, although contested. Sources are tools used by officials to determine which rules they are legally bound to apply. There is a *prima facie* relationship between membership and bindingness. Of course, Eugenio Bulygin has rightly insisted on the necessity of drawing a clear conceptual distinction between them (Bulygin 2015, p. 171). As a pure conceptual matter, validity is not a sufficient condition of bindingness, as the notion of *vacatio legis* shows. A statute enacted on January 1 might become binding ("enter into force," as is sometimes said) on July 1. It is nevertheless valid no later than from January

[32]Here I put aside the case of customary norms, which, in order to be suppressed, have to stop being practiced over a reasonably long time. I shall come back later to the problem of custom.

[33]As a matter of fact, some reasons are not constitutionally permissible. See e.g. the doctrine of *animus* in American Constitutional Law and the (rarely used) doctrine of "*détournement de pouvoir*" in French Constitutional Law. There are also specific constraints on abrogation or repeal by the legislature, such as the so-called "effet cliquet" (*ratchet-effect*) concerning specific legal rights. See also, in French Law, the doctrine of "negative incompetence" (by delegating too much to executive action, the legislature fails to do its job to the full extent required by the Constitution).

1 since it can be repealed on January 2. Membership is not a necessary condition of bindingness either,[34] as the classical example of choice-of-law rules shows (Raz 1980, pp. 196–197; Raz 2009, p. 149).

Following Stephen Munzer (1970, p. 58; 1973, pp. 1149–1150) and modifying his views a little,[35] I nevertheless argue that there is a *prima facie* link between membership and bindingness (or applicability). The rule of recognition is therefore a default norm of applicability (Carpentier 2014, pp. 154–155). Valid norms are *by default* binding, unless some further norms see to the contrary.

So bindingness is an important, albeit defeasible, feature of the job that sources perform. Now, it is a well-known fact that in most legal systems, contracts, wills, etc. *are not binding on the courts*. Of course, courts are under a duty to apply them—or sometimes to declare them null and void—but this duty is not a result of the contract itself but arises from statutory rules or other norms of the legal system. The mere fact that Jones and I sign a contract creates no particular duty for the courts to fulfill. It obviously creates a duty for Jones and me. But that does not suffice to make it a binding *legal* norm.

It is quite telling that most continental legal systems have a unified theory of "obligation" that encompasses both contract law and tort law. If contracts were a source of law, so would any tortious fact—any "delict" in the private law sense of the word. A contract is no more a source of law (or, rather, a source-instantiating fact) than my letting a flowerpot fall on your head is a source of law. The source statement for norms of tort law (e.g., Article 1240 (former 1382) of French Civil Code) is the following:

(4) Because of facts $F_i\ldots F_j$ (e.g., the fact that the legislature enacted the relevant civil code article), it is the law that if someone tortiously causes damage to another, he is under a duty to repair.

Analogously, the source statement for contractual obligations is as follows:

(5) Because of facts $F_i\ldots F_j$, it is the law that if someone contracts with another, both are under a duty to execute.[36]

Therefore, the facts that make up a contract are not included among law-creating facts, but they are embedded within the norm antecedent. Even in legal systems where there is no unified account of legal obligation as a private law concept, I think

[34] *Contra* see Schauer (1991, p. 119): "Validity… is a necessary condition of applicability".

[35] I think Munzer commits a mistake when he claims that normative conflicts defeat this *prima facie* link. This seems just wrong to me. Two conflicting norms are equally binding, equally applicable. The point is that they *cannot* (materially) be applied at the same time, but that does not mean that it is not the case that they both *ought* to be applied. Metarules (*Lex Posterior*, *Lex Superior* and *Lex Specialis*) serve as norms of applicability allowing law-applying organs to prioritize one of the conflicting norms over the other. But they presuppose the existence of a genuine conflict to be resolved in the first place.

[36] I realize this is very simplistic, as any contract lawyer would rightly argue. But contract law is only an illustration of a larger point here.

that (5) is a pretty accurate representation of why contracts are binding on its parties but never on third persons or judges. The norms (statutory or otherwise) that regulate contracts are, on the other hand, binding on judges, just as they are on everybody. To put it in a nutshell, *there are sources of private law; there are no private sources of law.*

Note that I do not mean to claim that facts constituted by actions performed by private persons can never be sources of law. Quite the contrary, customary laws derive their validity from such facts or, rather, from the repetition over time of such facts. So, of course, private persons can "create" law—so to speak: if one subscribes to the Simple Model, it will be agreed that persons do not "create" law. But it bears emphasizing that custom, however brought about by private persons, is not a *private source* of law.

So my point is that for there to be a legal source, or for there to be a norm that is *prima facie* binding on officials, there needs to be an element of publicity involved. The notion of publicity is obviously ambiguous, and I will not study all its relevant aspects here. Suffice it to say that the element of publicity I refer to here is not the notion of a law being made public. Such is the Fullerian notion of publicity, as opposed to the notion of secret laws, and true—or false—as it may be, it has no bearing on the present subject matter. Contracts can be made public: sometimes being made public through some registration scheme is a condition for a contract to be valid—to be "good" in the eyes of the law.

Remember my definition of public authorities. A public authority is a person (*morale* or *physique*) who is entrusted with the task of exercising some kind of authority (not necessarily legal authority) over a certain group of people because of certain background conditions of legitimacy. First, publicity depends on the size and nature of the group over which authority is exercised. It must be something like a political community or a subset of such a community. Then publicity depends on background conditions of legitimacy. I have no substantive account of those conditions to offer, and I do not need such an account. I would not be so arrogant as to presume to know what makes authority legitimate. This is a topic for substantive political philosophy.

From a purely metatheoretical point of view, I would argue that a common ground for conflicting theories of political legitimacy would be an account of the ability to further public interests. The content of the concept of public interest will depend on the theory or theories of legitimacy that are deemed correct by the political community, or at least by most of its officials, and it will be developed by concepts and doctrines that are highly context-dependent (see, e.g., the French notion of *service public*, which has no equivalent in the US or the UK or even in most non-French-speaking continental legal systems). This is why my notion of a public interest is purely formal and metatheoretical. An authority is a public authority if there is at least one acceptable theory according to which granting this person authority over the group satisfies the realization of what that theory defines as a public interest. Otherwise, the authority is private—and may well also be legitimate in its own way.

The example of customary law shows that law may emerge in a context where there are no legal authorities. Ours is a world where such a hypothesis is seldom verified, except in the realm of international law.[37] In most municipal legal systems, custom is today a residual source of law, but it is as much a legal source as the so-called formal sources. A customary norm is brought about by the repetition of private persons' actions. None of those persons are entrusted with a public interest. But the whole customary scheme, i.e. the whole scheme of having repeated actions give rise to a binding norm, clearly corresponds to a certain horizontal conception of the public interest, which may justify that the customary norm be binding for the whole legal community.

Therefore, I would argue that legal sources in general, whether or not legal authorities play a role in the way they operate, are meant to correspond to a certain conception of the public interest. Of course they may fail to do so. My point is only that for a source to be accepted as a legality-endowing fact by a political community, or the public officials thereof, it must at least be designed to have a defeasible built-in legitimacy. Even a dictator must claim to further the public interest and be accepted as doing quite as much, even if in the end he will only have served her own private interest.

When sources involve authorities (which is not always the case), that is, when the law-endowing facts are about some authorities' actions, they necessarily involve public authorities. Cocontractors are not such public authorities, and contracts themselves are not public sources. Cocontractors are private authorities: they posit private norms, which happen to be regulated by law (statutory or otherwise). Cocontractors are never entrusted with the task of exercising any authority whatsoever beyond the parties to the contract. Obviously, the very existence of contracts is very valuable and furthers undoubtedly some public interests. But from that trivial consideration, it does not follow that cocontractors are entrusted with some kind of public authority over the community or a subset of it, and it does not follow that it would be valuable that they be granted such authority.

This is why contracts, wills, etc. are never binding on officials and, therefore, can never be picked out as sources of law by the rule of recognition.

[37]I am putting aside the problem of customary international law, but I would argue that it vindicates my theory rather than pose problems for it. Of course customary international law is about the actions of public authorities (that is, states and state organs, international organizations etc.), but it does not involve authoritative directives, which is the case in treaties or unilateral decisions. However, it is plain that customary international law exists because of the convergent practice of state authorities *qua* authorities: the analogy between custom in domestic law and customary international law is likely to prove quite deceptive. But this matter is quite intricate and complex and I could not hope to do it justice here.

4 To Sum Up and Proceed Elsewhere

I have tried to show that sources are legality-endowing facts: they give laws their existence *qua* laws, their legality—their "legalness" so to speak. They are not persons or authorities. They are not the persons who create texts or who issue directives. They are facts that, when referred to by a source statement, give rise to legal norms, in the sense that they give purported norms their legal character. Legality, or existence *qua* law, has to be understood in terms of membership. As such it corresponds to a very specific use of the term "validity." Under the concept of validity as membership, sources are criteria of membership—whether you understand sources in a positivist fashion, i.e. as social facts, or in another way is irrelevant. However, there is another concept of validity, which has to be understood in terms of conformity with higher-ranking norms. Those two concepts are independent. A norm's invalidity (in terms of conformity) has no impact on its membership; only sources and source-instantiating facts, among them acts of repeal or abrogation, can suppress a norm's membership within the legal system.

The distinction between the two concepts of validity allows us to see why contracts, wills, and other "acts in the law" are never sources of law, even though the norms (the *negotia*) they give rise to may be valid or invalid, lawful or unlawful. Cocontractors and testators are private authorities, and they do not create binding norms beyond the private relationships instituted by their contracts and wills. The obligation of a judge to uphold a valid contract is the same as her obligation to sentence a criminal: both derive from legal norms grounded in source-instantiating facts. This is so because of the element of publicity involved in the very definition of a source of law.

Obviously the notion of publicity here expounded is tentative and undertheorized. It is also excessively formal and metatheoretical. But it shows, if anything, that the question "why" may prove to be less interesting than it would seem at first sight. Why do some facts give rise to obligations and rights or, at least, to what seem to be obligations and rights? The answer has varied to a great extent throughout the centuries. What has not changed, in my opinion, is the very thin fact that law claims to take charge of public interests and is generally accepted as doing just that, but the very content of the notion of public interest and the very justifications for law and legality have evolved and diversified greatly over time.

If anything, this conclusion shows that although law and legal validity ultimately depend on background conceptions of legitimacy, we do not need an all-encompassing theory of law's legitimacy to understand how validity works. The way law operates (the "how") is perhaps more interesting than the justifications given for it, and maybe we do not need those justifications to give a philosophical account of law and legality.

References

Bulygin, E. 1991. Regla de Reconocimento: ¿Norma de obligación o criterio conceptual? *Doxa* 9: 311–318.

———. 2015. Time and Validity. In *Essays in Legal Philosophy*, ed. E. Bulygin, 171–187. Oxford: Oxford University Press.

Carpentier, M. 2014. *Norme et exception. Essai sur la défaisabilité en droit*. Paris: LGDJ.

Coleman, J. 2001. *The Practice of Principle*. Oxford: Oxford University Press.

Djuvara, M. 1939. Quelques considérations sur la nature des sources et sur la formation du droit positif. In *Etudes de droit civil à la mémoire de Henri Capitant*, 219–234. Paris: Dalloz.

Duarte d'Almeida, L. 2013. In Canonical Form: Kelsen's Doctrine of the "Complete" Legal Norm. In *Kelsen Revisited*, ed. L. Duarte d'Almeida, J. Gardner, and L. Green, 259–282. Oxford: Hart Publishing.

Greenberg, M. 2014. The Moral Impact Theory of Law. *Yale Law Journal* 123 (5): 1288–1342.

Guastini, R. 1992. Rules, Validity and Statutory Construction. In *Italian Studies in Law*, ed. A. Pizzorusso, 11–27. Dordrecht: M. Nijhoff.

Hart, H.L.A. 1994. *The Concept of Law*. 2nd ed. Oxford: Clarendon Press.

Himma, K.E. 2005. Final Authority to Bind with Moral Mistakes: On the Explanatory Potential of Inclusive Legal Positivism. *Law and Philosophy* 24 (1): 1–45.

———. 2009. Understanding the Relationship between the U.S. Constitution and the Conventional Rule of Recognition. In *The Rule of Recognition and the U.S. Constitution*, ed. M. Adler and K.E. Himma, 95–121. New York: Oxford University Press.

Hochmann, T. 2017. Les théories de la "prise en compte des défauts" et de l'"habilitation alternative". In *Un classique méconnu: Hans Kelsen*, ed. T. Hochmann, X. Magnon, and R. Ponsard. Paris: Mare & Martin.

Kelsen, H. 1967. *Pure Theory of Law*. 2nd ed. Berkeley: University of California Press.

Kirste, S. 2018. Concept and Validity of Law. In *Legal Validity and Soft Law*, ed. P. Westerman, J. Hage, S. Kirste, 47–73. Heidelberg: Springer.

Kramer, M. 2003. *Where Law and Morality Meet*. Oxford: Oxford University Press.

Lamond, G. 2013. The Rule of Recognition and the Foundations of a Legal System. In *Reading HLA Hart's The Concept of Law*, ed. L. Duarte d'Almeida, A. Dolcetti, and J. Edwards. Oxford: Hart Publishing.

———. 2014. Legal Sources, the Rule of Recognition and Customary Law. *American Journal of Jurisprudence* **59** (1): 25–48.

Leiter, B. 2011. The Demarcation Problem in Jurisprudence. *Oxford Journal of Legal Studies* 31 (4): 663–677.

MacCormick, N. 2008. *HLA Hart*. 2nd ed. Stanford: Stanford University Press.

Matczak, M. 2017. 'On the Alleged Redundancy of the Rule of Recognition'. (unpublished manuscript).

Moreso, J.J. 1993. Sobre normas inconstitucionales. *Revista Española de Derecho Constitucional* 38: 81–115.

Mullock, P. 1974. Power-Conferring Rules & The Rule of Recognition. *University of Pittsburgh Law Review* 36 (1): 23–33.

Munzer, S. 1970. *Legal Validity*. The Hague: Martinus Nijhoff.

———. 1973. Validity and Legal Conflicts. *Yale Law Journal* 82 (6): 1140–1174.

O'Donnell, M.E., and C. Day. 2017. Sources and the Legality and Validity of International Law: Natural Law as Source of Extra-Positive Norms. In *The Oxford Handbook of the Sources of International Law*, ed. J. d'Aspremont and S. Besson. Oxford: Oxford University Press.

Perry, S. 2006. Hart on Social Rules and the Foundations of Law: Liberating the Internal Point of View. *Fordham Law Review* 75 (3): 1171–1209.

Pino, G. 2011. Farewell to the Rule of Recognition. *Problema* 5: 265–299.

———. 2014. Positivism, Legal Validity and the Separation of Law and Morals. *Ratio Juris* **27** (2): 190–217.

Raz, J. 1980. *The Concept of a Legal System*. 2nd ed. Oxford: Clarendon Press.
———. 1985. Authority, Law and Morality. *The Monist* 68 (3): 295–324.
———. 1999. *Practical Reason and Norms*. 2nd ed. Oxford: Oxford University Press.
———. 2009. *The Authority of Law*. 2nd ed. Oxford: Oxford University Press.
Rodriguez, J.L., and D. Vicente. 2009. Aplicabilidad y validez de las normas del derecho internacional. *Doxa* 32: 177–204.
Ross, A. 1998. Validity and the Conflict Between Legal Positivism and Natural Law. In *Normativity and Norms*, ed. S. Paulson and B. Litschewski-Paulson. Oxford: Clarendon Press.
Ruiz Manero, J. 1990. *Juridiccion y norma*. Madrid: Marcial Pons.
Sandro, P. 2018. Unlocking Legal Validity: Some Remarks on the Artificial Ontology of Law. In *Legal Validity and Soft Law*, ed. P. Westerman, J. Hage, S. Kirste, 99–123. Heidelberg: Springer.
Schauer, F. 1991. *Playing by the Rules*. Oxford: Clarendon Press.
Shapiro, S. 2009. What Is the Rule of Recognition (and Does it Exist)? In *The Rule of Recognition and the U.S. Constitution*, ed. M. Adler and K.E. Himma, 235–268. New York: Oxford University Press.
———. 2011. *Legality*. Cambridge, MA: Harvard University Press.
Shecaira, F.P. 2013. *Legal Scholarship as a Source of Law*. Dordrecht: Springer.
———. 2015. Sources of Law are Not Legal Norms. *Ratio Juris* 28 (1): 15–30.
Tur, R.M. 2013. The Alternative Character of the Legal Norm. Kelsen as Defeasibilist? In *Kelsen Revisited*, ed. L. Duarte d'Almeida, J. Gardner, and L. Green, 259–282. Oxford: Hart Publishing.
Waldron, J. 2009. Who Needs Rules of Recognition? In *The Rule of Recognition and the U.S. Constitution*, ed. M. Adler and K.E. Himma, 123–144. New York: Oxford University Press.
Waluchow, W. 1985. Hart, Legal Rules and Palm Tree Justice. *Law and Philosophy* 4 (1): 41–70.
———. 2009. Four Concepts of Validity. In *The Rule of Recognition and the U.S. Constitution*, ed. M. Adler and K.E. Himma, 327–349. New York: Oxford University Press.

Unlocking Legal Validity: Some Remarks on the Artificial Ontology of Law

Paolo Sandro

Abstract Following Kelsen's influential theory of law, the concept of validity has been used in the literature to refer to different properties of law (such as existence, membership, bindingness, and more), and so it is inherently ambiguous. More importantly, Kelsen's equivalence between the existence and the validity of law prevents us from accounting *satisfactorily* for relevant aspects of our current legal practices, such as the phenomenon of "unlawful law." This chapter addresses this ambiguity to argue that the most important function of the concept of validity is constituting the complex ontological paradigm of modern law as an institutional-normative practice. In this sense, validity is an artificial ontological status that supervenes on that of the existence of legal norms, thus allowing law to regulate its own creation and creating the logical space for the occurrence of "unlawful law." This function, I argue in the last part, is crucial to understanding the relationship between the ontological and epistemic dimensions of the objectivity of law. Given the necessary practice-independence of legal norms it is the epistemic accessibility of their creation that enables the law to fulfill its general action-guiding (and thus coordinating) function.

1 Introduction

Can anything interesting at all still be said on the topic of legal validity ("validity" hereinafter)? Many scholars would reply negatively, given that this concept has been at the forefront of the jurisprudential debate for the last few decades, in particular as one of the elected "battlegrounds" between legal positivists and nonpositivists. The real scope of this debate has been far from clear, however, for what positivists and antipositivists have been debating are the "grounds of validity," rather than the concept of validity *per se* (Sartor 2000). Does this suggest then that any form of

P. Sandro (✉)
Business School, University of Salford, Salford, UK
e-mail: p.sandro@salford.ac.uk

© The Author(s) 2018

P. Westerman et al. (eds.), *Legal Validity and Soft Law*, Law and Philosophy Library 122, https://doi.org/10.1007/978-3-319-77522-7_5

consensus on the concept has been reached? Hardly so, as shown by the different contributions in this volume.

As we shall see, due mostly to what is a major misconception in Kelsen's influential theory, "validity" has been used to refer to different properties of law. The result is that the use of the concept in legal discourse is inherently ambiguous, and so it is still unclear what is at stake when we discuss it. My aim in this chapter is to dispel this ambiguity in order to reveal what I see as the most important function played by the concept of validity, namely constituting the complex ontological paradigm of modern law as an institutional-normative practice. Far from being "a mere summary-concept" (von der Pfordten, in this volume), validity is an artificial ontological status that supervenes on that of existence of legal norms, thus allowing law to regulate its own creation. This function, I argue in the last part, is crucial to our understanding of the relationship between the ontological and epistemic dimensions of the objectivity of law. Given the necessary practice-independence of legal norms, it is the epistemic accessibility of their creation that enables the law to fulfill its general action-guiding (and thus coordinating) function.

The chapter proceeds as follows: in Sect. 2, I analyze the source of ambiguity in Kelsen's equivalence of existence, validity, and bindingness of law and show its counterintuitive consequences vis-à-vis our current legal practices. In Sect. 3, I offer some remarks on normative ontology and in particular on the difference between the *epistemic* and *metaphysical* conditions of existence of norms. This allows me, in Sect. 4, to illustrate the difference between the validity and the existence of legal norms and thus to account coherently for the *mysterious* status of "unlawful law." Lastly, in Sect. 5, I show the function played by validity within this complex ontology and how it is ultimately connected to the objectivity that characterizes our modern legal practices.

2 The Ambiguity About Validity

2.1 The Source of the Ambiguity

"Validity" appears to be one of those concepts for which it is easy to provide examples—"this contract is valid"—but whose definition proves a considerably harder task. While in general parlance the property of being "valid" indicates the state of being in accordance with a set of criteria (Beltrán and Ratti 2010), thus distinguishing between "good" and "bad" tokens of a certain type or between members and nonmembers of a certain set, the use of the concept in legal discourse has proved difficult to account for consistently. Carlos Santiago Nino (1996, p. 117), to mention but one, has identified at least six different "cores of meaning" in which validity is used[1]:

- as existence;
- as binding force;
- as applicability;
- as conformity;
- as membership;
- as efficacy.

Nino (1996, p. 118) notes how these "cores of meaning" are not fully autonomous but rather often presented in various combinations—thus contributing to the ambiguity surrounding the use of the concept. Lamond (2014a, p. 113) too observes that, at least in common law jurisdictions,

> [t]he language of validity is ordinarily used to make three types of claim about a legal rule: (i) that is it legally effective (has legal force); (ii) that it is a member of this legal system (a valid rule *of* English Law); and (iii) that is valid*ated* by another law (valid under the relevant primary legislation, not *ultra vires*). There is an important relationship between the three, inasmuch as the standard explanation for why a rule has legal force is that it is a member of the system in question, and the most common basis for a rule being a member of the system is that it is validated by another rule of the system. Validation gives rise to membership, and membership qualifies a rule for normative force. But it is the normative force of rules – their legal effect – that is fundamentally associated with validity (italics original).

I begin by stressing that, as a preliminary methodological matter, the fact that three (or more) properties have "an important relationship" does not warrant the use of one and the same concept for referring to them.[2] More importantly, the ambiguity surrounding the use of this concept goes to a deeper, metatheoretical, level. For two very different questions about law have been simultaneously addressed by it, a "theoretical" and a "normative" one (Peczenik 1989, p. 175). That is, in some cases, validity is conceived of as the hallmark—the "specific mode of existence" as we shall see—of law: as Raz (1979, p. 146) puts it,

> a rule that is not legally valid is not a legal rule at all. A valid law is a law, and invalid law is not.

Here validity is used in a descriptive manner. In other cases instead, validity means a normative, prescriptive judgment regarding legal norms: to say that a norm is valid is to say that it *ought* to be followed or applied. A first level of confusion arises when these two different types of discourse—descriptive and prescriptive—are not kept properly distinguished. This leads us to Hans Kelsen.

---

[1] According to Sartor (2000, 2008) validity should instead be understood as expressing a "doxastic obligation": that rule R is valid means that we ought to accept rule R in our legal reasoning.

[2] See Ferrajoli (2007, pp. 56–57) on why syntactic clarity is a matter of the utmost importance in any analytical reconstruction of law.

2.2 The Ambiguity in Kelsen

In what might be one of the most quoted excerpts in modern legal theory, Kelsen (1946, p. 30) affirms:

> to say that a norm is valid, is to say that we assume its existence or – what amounts to the same thing – we assume that is has "binding force" for those whose behavior it regulates.

Thus, existence, validity, and binding force of law are synonymous; to wit, they express the same property.[3] Or, as Guastini (2016) puts it, there seems to be "conceptual identity" between the three properties. Before looking at the implications of this identification, it is worth noting how, according to Ferrajoli (2016), Kelsen's semantic ambiguity about validity originates in a higher-level *syntactic* ambiguity due to his use of the term "norm". Even though Kelsen (1960) clearly recognizes the fundamental distinction between normative acts—as acts of will that belong to the *Sein*—and norms, which are of those acts the meaning and belong to the *Sollen*, he denotes both of them with the same term "norm." This in turn means that for him (and his followers on this point) it is conceptually impossible to distinguish between the validity of the act that produces the norm and that of the norm itself: hence the equivalence between existence and validity of norms.

What then of the further equivalence with binding force? The passage above is used, among others, by Nino (1978, p. 358) to argue that Kelsen does not hold a purely descriptive concept of validity, but a normative one. In this sense, to predicate the validity of a norm is to make an evaluative judgment about its obligatoriness and justification, that is, to prescribe that the norm ought to be obeyed.[4] The problem is that such an evaluative stance runs against the postulate of purity of Kelsen's theory (Guastini 2016, p. 403). Things are not better if, following Bulygin (1998), we understand Kelsen's validity as expressing merely a *positive* legal obligation, for in this case we preserve the purity of the theory at the cost of running into the problem

[3]Kelsen is not alone in confusing validity for something else: while natural lawyers "tend[ed] to identify legal validity with justice", so that "a norm is 'properly' valid only if it is coherent with certain objective values," legal realists identify validity with efficacy, so that valid norms are only those "implemented in society" (Pino 1999, p. 535). A notable exception is Finnis (2011, pp. 25–29) who, following Aquinas, recognizes the distinction between the existence of positive law—depending on a valid enactment—and its full validity that depends on its "derivation" from natural law.

[4]It is interesting to note that when validity is predicated of moral and social norms, it seems to be meant exclusively in the normative sense—we claim that a moral or social norm is valid when we are saying that it ought to be obeyed. For if we were instead to use validity to address the ontological dimension, the concept would be simply redundant: there is no ontological status other than that of existence for moral and social norms. Anne Ruth Mackor points to me that German terminology seems to warrant my contention, because even though we cannot say of a social norm that it is *Gültig* (since it is not enacted in accordance with certain criteria), we can say nonetheless that is has *Geltung*, which means that it exists and it has binding force. This might help to explain the widespread flattening of the ontological question onto the normative one in legal discourse, and the resulting equation between validity (in the sense of existence) and bindingness.

of the necessary extralegal or nonnormative character of the *Grundnorm* (Guastini 2016, p. 404). In short, either way, the theoretical coherence of Kelsen's theory is compromised.[5]

2.3 The Results of the Ambiguity

For the purposes of this chapter, nothing hinges on whether Kelsen's notion of validity is, after all, descriptive or normative. What matters instead is that in either case, the ambiguous nature of his notion of validity (and of his notion of "norm" before that) yields far-reaching consequences for our understanding of modern legal systems. In particular, the equivalence between existence, validity, and bindingness entails on the conceptual level that

(I) all existing legal norms are also always valid and binding;
(II) invalid legal norms do not exist and have no binding effect;
(III) all that is necessary for a legal norm to be valid and thus binding is the (formal) validity of its source.

These three theses are hard to reconcile with our current legal practices.

(I) implies that validity and binding force become part of the very *definiens* of "legal norm" so that to talk of a nonbinding legal norm amounts to a contradiction in terms (Peczenik 1989, pp. 175–176). Yet even if we conceive of bindingness in purely legal terms, we know that such contradiction does not hold as a matter of logical necessity (in our modern legal systems at least): just think about the disapplication of domestic norms that are in conflict with European Union legislation. Such norms retain their full validity (provided they had it in the first place) and yet "lose" their bindingness (or force of law).

(II) instead makes it impossible to coherently account for a great number of legal norms (as contained in statutes, secondary legislation, or administrative acts) that might be declared invalid by a court at some point and yet have been *part* of the legal system—and might have produced legal effects—for a while.[6]

(III) has the even more paradoxical effect of preventing Kelsen from fully exploring what is likely one of his greatest contributions to legal theory, namely the identification of the static as well as dynamic character of modern legal systems (Ferrajoli 2016).

Kelsen in fact shows us that one of the distinguishing characteristics of law as a normative order is that it regulates its own creation. It does so through the "chain of

---

[5]See Nino (1996, p. 119). MacCormick (2008, p. 162) states that bindingness is not validity, but "one of the consequences" of it.

[6]See Kelsen's (1992, pp. 72–73) strained attempt to account for "*rechtswidriges Recht*" in terms of the contemporary validity of "alternative provisions" (both the valid and the invalid one). In this sense legal norms would always have an implicit alternative clause: see the rebuttal of this idea in Guastini (2016).

validity," which pertains not just to the forms of the acts that produce norms but also to the content of those norms. Yet if we identify the sufficient condition of validity of legal norms with the validity of the acts that produce them, it does not actually matter whether the content of those norms will conflict hierarchically with that of the superior norms.[7] In other words, the material validity of a norm—its *conformity* with higher norms—becomes irrelevant as it is neither a necessary nor a sufficient condition for the existence of the act that produces it (Ferrajoli 2016, pp. 92–93). This leads us to the striking realization that, if we were to take Kelsen at face value on this point, the concept of validity would be ultimately "completely worthless" (Guastini 2016). Is this really the case?

Before we look at the structure of modern legal systems to see whether validity is really a dispensable concept that plays no real function in our understanding of law, we need to clarify what sense of the "existence" of norms is at stake here.

3 Some Remarks on Normative Ontology

As I have mentioned already, the discussion about validity is muddled not only by terminological differences, but also by some deeper conflicts pertaining to the metaphysical nature of norms that are not always brought to the surface of the discussion. In particular, the idea of the "existence" of norms is in many respects puzzling: it amounts to one, if not to the main driver of the naturalistic explanation of law that we know (in its many variants) as legal realism.[8] For one thing, norms do not *exist* in the same way as material objects do as they lack, for instance, mass. In this sense, norms are "mysterious beasts" (Brennan et al. 2013, p. 2) and are more akin to so-called abstract objects, such as mathematical entities and properties (Berto and Plebani 2015). The puzzling metaphysical nature of norms has become relevant again in legal theory since the introduction of linguistic and conceptual analysis and of the key distinction between norms and norm formulations (Narváez Mora 2015).[9] Once it was clarified that norms cannot *be* the norm formulations through which they are expressed—for norm formulations almost always underdetermine norms as their

[7]For the criticism that a purely source-based criterion can never help identify by itself "individual legal norms" see Priel (2011). As we shall see, legal norms are actually always the product of the interpretation of the act adopted according to the rules on its production.

[8]Most legal realists do not dispute that something we ought to call "law" exists in fact—what they contend is that this institutional practice we call "law" is made (also) of metaphysical entities such as norms. Rather, law is exclusively made of human behavior in their view, and as such it is amenable to empirical observation.

[9]For a comprehensive and insightful discussion of the distinction and its ramifications see Pino (2016).

meanings[10]—the question of what kind of entities norms are does not seem to have a readily available answer any longer.[11]

As Guastini (2013, pp. 146–147) points out, when we talk about the existence of norms in jurisprudential discourse, we might be alternatively referring to two different questions: (i) what does it mean that a norm *exists*, in general, and (ii) when does a norm exist in a given legal system, that is, when does a norm *belong* to it? The first is a metaphysical question that refers to norms in general, while the second is a contingent, positive question whose answer depends on the legal system taken into account—as different legal systems have different criteria as to the membership of their norms. Given space constraints, I will not be able to discuss here all the ontological and metaontological commitments underlying the following remarks,[12] but I will nonetheless flesh out a rough account of what it takes for a (legal) norm to exist.

Let us start from the intuition that norms do not make sense *as such* until they are expressed or formulated: in other words, they *do not exist* before someone expresses them. As Kelsen (1949, pp. 483–484) holds, there are no normative principles in the physical world, only regularities of behavior and physical laws (such as gravity). The point is that these regularities and physical laws *exist*—and causally interact with the world—independently of anyone observing and expressing them: they are strongly mind-independent. The same cannot be said of normative principles. A normative principle is such only if it can be potentially acted *upon*, that is, if it can make a difference, by being taken into account, in the practical reasoning of the agent: and in order to do so, it must be *somehow* expressed and recognized as such.[13] In other

[10]Narváez Mora (2015) claims that legal norms "are not entities of any kind" and that the necessity to look for the ontological "substance" of norms is what inevitably leads us into the rule-following paradox. I address this worry in my forthcoming monograph on the distinction between creation and application of law (Sandro 2019, *forthcoming*).

[11]This is a question that belongs to normative ontology in general, and not just to legal theory. I use the definition of normative ontology to distinguish the approach outlined here from the one that pertains to the social ontology of law, on which see the recent debate in *Rechtstheorie* with contributions by Bernal, Canale, Ekins, and Tuzet. In particular, using Tuzet's (2014) terminology, here I am chiefly concerned with "entity-ontology," while the social ontology approach deals with "process-ontology."

[12]As such a great deal of the analysis that follows is based on the nonreductive ontological account of norms put forward by Brennan et al. (2013). While I do not necessarily subscribe to every element of their proposal (especially when it comes to the analysis of legal norms), it does constitute the most comprehensive account of normative ontology currently available in the literature—and it does have a considerable edge over reductive accounts (like the ones that equate social norms with the underlying practices). For a more general discussion of metaontology I refer the reader to the formidable introduction to the subject by Berto and Plebani (2015). For an application of this line of enquiry to law see Narváez Mora (2015) and Moreso and Chilovi (2016).

[13]I prefer the use of the term "expression" over "formulation" (the one favored by Guastini) given that sometimes norms can remain "implicit," that is not explicitly verbally formulated. Yet even implicit norms must be somehow expressed (through behavior, with reactive attitudes for instance) in order to acquire the capacity to figure in practical reasoning. I owe this remark to Sebastián Figueroa Rubio and Anne Ruth Mackor.

words, a normative principle must have some degree of epistemic accessibility if it purports to guide conduct: as Raz (2011) affirms, it must "be in the world."[14] And as expression is an act of will, one could say then that the normative element in any standard or general requirement is necessarily intentional.[15]

"Expression" seems to be then a necessary, albeit not sufficient, condition for something to be considered normative, for only with its expression does a norm acquire the capacity to interact "causally" with the furniture of the world (Guastini 2013, p. 147).[16] We can call this the *expressive* or *epistemic* condition of existence of norms. In this first sense, to affirm that "norm N exists" means "someone expressed N" (Guastini 2013, p. 147).[17] This might be why many think that norms are a particular kind of abstract object, namely "linguistic entities," and as such bear a special relationship to language (Moreso and Chilovi 2016; Pino 2016).[18] But is this all there is to the existence of norms? Is it enough that someone—*anyone*—expresses or formulates a deontic requirement and this fact alone grounds its existence *qua* norm?[19]

While expression is a necessary condition of the existence of all norms, it is clearly not a sufficient one. I could indeed let you know that "people ought not to listen to music in this city," which is a syntactically and semantically well-formed deontic requirement. But my utterance could only express a genuine norm in light of something else being the case: for instance, if there is a moral principle that prohibits people from listening to music in this city or if the person uttering the deontic sentence is the sovereign of the system and so forth. Thus, in this second sense, to say that norm "N" exists means "something metaphysically grounds normative principle 'N.'" We can call this the *metaphysical* or *grounding* condition of the existence of norms. This grounding relation obtains always between a norm and a "grounding fact," which in turn seems to change depending on the type of norm we are considering (von Wright 1963):

- **Moral norms**: here there is a preliminary distinction to be drawn depending on whether we are talking about an objectively valid moral norm or a norm of positive morality of a given social group.
  - Critical morality: a norm "N" exists if there is an objective normative principle "N" of morality. Here, in other words, we have the conceptual identity

[14]Cf Brennan et al. (2013, p. 31). On how post-modern law is progressively losing its previous mode of "being in the world" see Walker (2009).

[15]For Gaus (2014) norms are "human [normative] artifacts." Cf also Gardner (2012, pp. 59–65, 85–86).

[16]Gardner (2012, p. 86) seems to limit this necessary positive character of norms to legal ones, but I do not see any reason for such limitation. See also the quote by Samuel Pufendorf about the existence of "moral entities" in Westerman's contribution to this volume.

[17]This understanding of ontological parlance in arithmetical terms seems to be similar to the one by Moreso and Chilovi (2016).

[18]Cf Narváez Mora (2015, pp. 43–44).

[19]For an introduction to metaphysical grounding see Tahko and Lowe (2015).

between the truth maker and the proposition that expresses the normative requirement, the problem being instead the existence and epistemic accessibility of such grounding facts (one must be a moral realist, broadly understood).
- Positive morality: if we consider instead a given social group in a given moment in time, a norm "N" exists if the corresponding normative attitudes are displayed by a "significant proportion" of members of the group (and a significant proportion knows about this) (Brennan et al. 2013, p. 29).

What is important to point out is that in both cases, the relevant norm "N" exists but is independent from the underlying N-practice—that is, the social practice that sees "N" as its object, or practice of "N"-*ing*. This is clear in the case of the norms of critical morality, which—postulating the existence of the corresponding objective normative principles—bind irrespectively of the mental states of their addressees, but it is also what, according to Brennan et al. (2013, pp. 58–59), distinguishes the norms of positive morality of a group from its social ones.[20]

- **Social norms**: a social norm "N" exists in a given social group if a significant proportion of members of the group accept "N" and this acceptance is *known* to a significant proportion of members of the group—so that there is an (at least *presumed*) N-practice.[21]
- **Legal norms**: a legal norm "N" exists if it belongs to legal system S, for its existence is tantamount to the membership of the system (Pino 2016; Nino 1996). Now what it takes for a norm to belong to system "S" is a contingent question, the answer to which will be different from system to system. The key point for our purposes—and what distinguishes legal norms (*qua* formal or institutional)[22] from moral or social ones (informal)—is that, in this case, the creation and change and eventual demise of norms is regulated by a second set of rules belonging to

[20]The difference between norms of positive morality and social ones lies in the fact that the former "are constituted by [normative] attitudes that are necessarily *practice-independent*," while the latter are "necessarily *practice-dependent*." In this respect it is worth pointing out that for these authors social norms only entail *presumed* corresponding social practices (p. 76) and not actual ones, thus allowing for the possibility of "universal error" (Gaus 2014) on the existence of such corresponding practices. Now while I agree with Brennan et al. and with many others (see for instance Perry 2015, p. 284 fn.3) that to identify social norms with the corresponding practices amounts to a serious category mistake (to the extent that it is not the case that the existence of a practice is ever sufficient to generate a social norm), I am not convinced that a corresponding social practice needs only be presumed (and not actually obtain) for a social norm to exist. For the purposes of this chapter however nothing fundamentally hinges on this point.

[21]Here (as well as before with norms of positive morality) I leave it open whether this knowledge condition requires *common* or merely *mutual* knowledge amongst members of the group. For an insightful discussion about the acceptance of social rules see e.g. Perry (2015).

[22]Institutionalized normative orders—such as those of a company, or of an association—are to be considered in this respect more similar to law than moral and social orders, as it makes indeed perfect sense to speak of a "valid norm of that association" if by this we refer to the (institutional) fact grounding the creation of such a norm (MacCormick 2008, p. 160).

> the system itself (Hart's secondary rules) that are administered by some type of authority. Law is in this sense reflexive or autonomous. To put it with Kelsen (1946, p. 132), one of its distinguishing features is that it regulates its own creation and application. As such, a legal norm "N" is practice-independent vis-à-vis the corresponding social practice "N" (as much as an equivalent objective moral norm "N^1").[23]

There seems to be then a key difference between moral and legal norms on the one hand and social ones on the other. The latter, but not the former, are necessarily *metaphysically* practice-dependent. In other words, a moral or legal norm does not necessarily need a corresponding social practice (not even a *presumed* one) to exist. This leaves their expression (or formulation) as the only epistemic dimension they might ever "possess," given that the corresponding social practice might never develop.[24] This is clearly shown in the case of legal norms, for example, those that in most countries around the world prohibit the file sharing of copyrighted material. The fact that people do actually share and download illegally copyrighted material on a regular basis—so that the corresponding social practice cannot be said to exist, not even presumably—does not falsify, by itself, the assertion that such legal norms exist (and are valid).

Why is this relevant? According to my analysis, expression is the only ontological (*qua* epistemic) condition that norms of all kinds share. But for moral and legal norms, given their practice-independence, expression might be and remain their only epistemic display—that is, the only way they might "be in the world" to interact with it. Two conclusions stand out then: first, that for these two kinds of norms, it is even more the case that to affirm that they exist is tantamount to saying that someone has expressed or formulated them[25] and that, because of it, the possibility and circumstances of their expression become the real "battleground" in relation to their

[23]While legal norms are practice-independent when considered atomistically vis-à-vis their corresponding N-practices, the legal system as a whole is not so—it is dependent on a different, (general) S-practice of recognizing the authority of the system and on its acceptance by the majority of members of the group. So there seems to be always a social (conventional?) fact that ultimately grounds legal norms and that is not present for objective moral norms, which marks once again the difference between law and (critical) morality. Brennan et al. (2013, p. 49) express this difference (in what seems to me a more convoluted way) by claiming that formal norms (of which legal norms are a subset) need only involve *de re* normative attitudes, and not *de dicto* ones. See furthermore on the concept of "systemic acceptance" Lamond (2014b). This remark seems also to map onto the distinction drawn by Canale (2014, p. 307) between the social practice which originates a legal system and that must be characterized by "collective intentionality" and the subsequent social practice that "warrants the existence of a legal system over time" but need not be characterized by any such "joint action."

[24]We might see epistemic manifestation in the potential judicial decision that applies and enforces the norm, but this is also a manifestation of the underlying S-practice underpinning the authority of the system.

[25]Someone with (normative and not just epistemic) authority, that is. This signals another difference with social and positive morality norms, namely that in this latter case, given their practice-independence, it does not really matter who formulates them (formulation works only as a

existence. In the case of norms of critical morality, the question is whether there are such things as objective moral facts (or goods) and, if there are, whether (and how) we can access them. In the case of legal norms instead, the question is whether whoever formulated the norm had the authority to do so and whether this expressive act was carried out within the formal and material requirements imposed by the higher-ranking norms in the system. This brings us back to the concept of validity.

4 Explaining the Validity Vis-à-vis the Existence of Law

Incidentally, the topic of validity is an example of a certain degree of insulation sometimes displayed by Anglo-American jurisprudential scholarship vis-à-vis its continental and Latin American counterparts. Consider again the paradigmatic statement by Raz (1979, p. 146), for whom a rule that is not legally valid is not a legal rule at all. Like many others in Anglo-American scholarship, Raz identifies the validity of law with its existence. Only valid law belongs to the legal system; invalid law does not. In this regard, laws are like stones: "a non-existent stone is not a stone, though we can talk about such stones and describe some of their properties as we can do about invalid rules" (Raz 1979, p. 148). But is an invalid law necessarily not "law"? Intuitively, one can point to all those instances in our current legal systems in which invalid legal acts—like statutes or administrative measures—may still yield normative consequences, at least until the moment when they are annulled or repealed by a court. These acts, albeit invalid, do *belong* to the legal system—they have some relationship or status within it (Guastini 2013, p. 132).

While the distinction between the existence and the validity of law has come to the fore of Anglo-American scholarship only very recently,[26] it has instead been accepted and discussed for quite some time in continental and South American scholarship, following the seminal work of scholars such as Eugenio Bulygin, Luigi Ferrajoli, and Carlos Nino. These scholars have pointed out that Kelsen's conflation of the existence of a legal norm with its validity conceals what amounts to the key innovation brought about by modern constitutional systems, namely the very possibility of existence of what has been aptly termed by Ferrajoli (2007) "unlawful

"proxy" for the corresponding practice). The same does not clearly apply to law, as we shall see shortly.

[26]This is mainly due to a series of recent contributions by Matthew Grellette. His work, although commendable, cannot "rescue" Anglo-American jurisprudence from the charge of insularity: while Grellette presents the distinction between the existence and the validity of law as "unexplored" (Grellette 2010, p. 38), this distinction has been put forward and discussed in Continental and Latin-American jurisprudence for over 30 years. This does not seem to be due to a lack of resources in English—as Pino's (1999, p. 535) article in *Law and Philosophy* discusses Ferrajoli's idea that the "mere enactment [of a legal norm] does not coincide with validity." Similarly, there is no reference to Munzer's important book *Legal Validity* (1972) where, almost 40 years before Grellette's work, Munzer clearly distinguished not only between formal and material validity (p. 25), but also between the existence and the validity of legal norms (pp. 37–43).

law,"[27] something that would amount to a contradiction in Raz's (and Kelsen's) theory.[28] Yet this constitutes possibly the most striking feature of modern juridical phenomenology: it points to the fact that there are limits to what even the highest legislative authority in a legal system can do—and these limits are *legal* ones, as established in some sort of constitutional settlement (usually codified and entrenched but not necessarily). As such, there are some things that as *a matter of law* the legislator cannot do (Grellette 2010, pp. 26–31): an idea simply unentertainable if we consider the idea of sovereignty as expressed by Bodin (1586) with the idea of *potestas legibus soluta* and that still nowadays proves hard to reconcile with the principle of parliamentary sovereignty in English constitutional scholarship.[29]

4.1 Formal and Material Validity

Only by distinguishing between the existence and the validity of law can we truly understand the meaning of the latter—a property that refers to the conformity of both acts and norms to the hierarchically superior norms governing their production. As already mentioned, in its most general understanding, the property of being "valid" indicates the state of being in accordance or conforming with something. The first step toward understanding how "unlawful law" is even conceivable is to recognize that in institutional-normative systems, validity (as conformity) can assume two different dimensions, the formal and the material one. According to Pino (2014, p. 207), the former pertains to

> the attainment of the formal/procedural conditions regarding the exercise of law-making power, according to which a certain text can be considered as a *legal source*. Formal validity usually coincides with a successful "enactment", and it can be ascertained by means of a factual inquiry about the realization of the relevant law-making procedures (italics mine).

Hence, a bill that is not approved by the Italian Parliament following the prescribed procedure (for instance, a constitutional bill that is approved through the ordinary legislative procedure) is not formally valid, and the Italian Consulta (the Constitutional Court) can quash it (article 136 of the Italian Constitution). Another fitting example is that of a written contract that is lacking one of its essential elements, such as the signature of one of the contracting parties (when this is required by law). Material validity, instead,

---

[27]This is my translation (Sandro 2011) of the original Italian expression "diritto illegittimo." For a discussion of the concept of "unlawful law" see Grellette (2010, p. 36).

[28]Grellette (2010, p. 32) correctly recognizes that early positivists like Austin or Hart took as paradigmatic cases legal systems whose criteria for validity were based purely on conventional practice and hence it would be uncharitable to make too much of their failure to distinguish between existence and validity. The same cannot be said of later positivists, and especially of Kelsen.

[29]Think about the discussion which ensued after recent decisions such as R (*Jackson*) v Attorney General [2005] UKHL 56 and *AXA General Insurance v Lord Advocate* [2011] UKSC 46.

Table 1 Formal and material validity compared

	Formal validity	Material validity
Pertains to	Sources	Norms
Requires	Attainment	Coherence or noncontradiction
Ascertained by	Empirical enquiry (plus minimal interpretive operation)	Interpretative operation

> obtains when a legal norm is coherent (or at least not conflicting) with the relevant higher-rank legal norms. Plainly, material validity is not a matter of fact, but a matter of interpretation: it depends on the content, on the meaning of the relevant norms. More precisely, it requires interpreting both the norm whose validity is to be ascertained, and the (higher) norms that act as the parameter for the validity of that norm (Pino 2014, p. 208).

Going back to the example of a statute, if the normative content of a formally valid statute violates one of the provisions in the Italian Constitution—for instance, by unduly limiting the freedom of the press to publish news about the current government—then the Consulta will be able again to strike the statute down. The same applies, *mutatis mutandis*, in the case of contracts: if a contract, for instance, has an illegal purpose (the infamous contract for murder), no judge will hold that contract valid and enforce it. It is important then to stress how formal validity and material validity work on different levels, pertain to different objects, and are a product of different epistemic endeavors.

As Table 1 illustrates, formal validity pertains to normative sources—acts—and requires the attainment or application of certain formal/procedural conditions to validly exercise a power recognized by the law.[30] As such, it is ascertainable through an empirical enquiry (whether the bill has received royal assent, for instance).[31] Material validity, on the other hand, pertains to norms themselves and requires (at least) the noncontradiction between the content of norms so produced and the relevant, higher, norms. If we look at our current legal practices, this first distinction

[30]By including both formal and procedural conditions in the definition of formal validity I intend to account for a common ambiguity in legal language between "act" as the process of production of it (i.e. the legislative process) and "act" as the product of such process (i.e. the statute): see Ferrajoli (2007, pp. 494–498).

[31]As has been noted, even here there is some degree of interpretive activity, as the formal norms on production will be *used* to verify the correct procedure and form of the law-making act (Ferrajoli 2007, pp. 524, 577). This remark points to the more general idea that norms, as meanings, are always and only the product of interpretation, an idea that is expressed, for instance, by many legal realists of the Genoa School (following Giovanni Tarello) and, more recently by Pino (2016, pp. 24–26). In this sense it would be more correct to claim that norms would not exist before interpretation. This thesis, taken seriously, has far-reaching consequences for the (in)determinacy of law thesis that cannot be discussed here: I only want to note that when it comes to the attainment of formal or procedural norms, this interpretative activity can be considered minimal and predominantly linguistic.

seems rather uncontroversial. What happens, though, when an act is formally valid but the norm so produced is not *materially* so?

4.2 Formally Valid but Not Materially So—The Mysterious Status of "Unlawful Law"

We have seen that for several Anglo-American legal theorists who have been following Kelsen on the point, validity *is* existence and hence validity *is* bindingness. As has been shown instead by those scholars who warn of the unsatisfying theoretical implications of Kelsen's thesis (Munzer 1972; Ferrajoli 2007; Grellette 2010; Guastini 2016), this "flattening" of validity with existence leads to a variety of explanatory shortcomings that leave an important amount of legal practice unsatisfactorily unaccounted for. This discussion has taken place mostly at the constitutional level when some sort of "constitutional entrenchment" is present in a given legal system. Interestingly, the distinction between formal and material validity is operatively present even in common law jurisdictions where such constitutional entrenchment is missing—for bylaws, administrative acts, and contracts can all have either formal/procedural or material requirements. Yet its *general* importance and role as to the ontological status of legal norms in our modern systems has been manifestly undertheorized. Validity in the formal sense only obtains when *all* the formal requirements on the production of a given act (a contract, a statute, a judicial decision, or a will) are attained by the agent(s) in producing it. Guastini (2013, p. 132) aptly reminds us that, "in lawyers' talk," validity means precisely the absence of "vices."[32] But what about the case in which only some of those formal/procedural requirements are attained?

Take the example of a will: a clear formal requirement for a will to be valid is that it is signed (often necessarily in front of some witnesses) by its testator. Now, think about a will whose signature has been forged—it was signed not by its testator but by her nephew, who also (coincidentally) appears to be now the beneficiary of the entire estate. The will *looks like* a formally valid one to the nonexperts—only an experienced calligrapher would be able to ascertain that it was not actually signed by the supposed testator. It is hard to deny that, until the moment in which a judge declares the will invalid because it lacks one of its essential formal requirements, that will *exists*—that is, it *belongs* to the legal system. For one thing, the nephew might have brought some possession claims on the estate on the basis of the forged will. Unless the legitimate heirs to the estate can somehow prove immediately that the will is forged, it is likely that the court will, prima facie, grant the nephew possession of the estate. But even more to the point, the very fact that a court takes the will into

[32]See also Beltrán and Ratti (2010, p. 605) for the claim that "for a rule to be legally valid it must have been produced in a 'legally impeccable way', or is a logical consequence of some impeccably produced rule, and is in any case compatible with superior rules."

consideration and *declares it* invalid implies in the first place that some type of act that is *intelligible* as having a juridical meaning (Ferrajoli 2007, p. 528) must have been produced and hence, for this fact, *exists* for the legal system. This seems also confirmed by the traditional definition of a nullity in law as an act that must be treated *as if it had never existed or taken place*. This logically implies that for a certain amount of time, and precisely from the moment t_0 of creation to the moment t_1 of declaration of nullity by the judge, an act *juridically meaningful* existed for the legal system.[33]

When is it that a will does not even exist for the law then? If we observe our juridical practices, that would be when such a supposed will lacks even some of those foundational requirements that allow for its very *recognizability* as a juridical (type-)act—for instance, a will that lacks the written form. If someone were to tell me in person that she wants to leave her estate to her older child but not to the younger, reckless one, I would never take that to be a speech-act that has any legal relevance whatsoever. Even though my friend is genuinely moved by the desire to make her intentions regarding her estate manifest, no one in her sound mind would take such a speech-act as constituting an enforceable legal act. In other words, the requirement of the written form is so fundamental when it comes to the concept of a will that in its absence there is really nothing we can talk about from the legal point of view.[34,35]

[33]Cf Pino (2016, pp. 24–25). For the purposes of the present chapter, I am leaving aside the discussion regarding the effects of such acts for the system (that is, the difference between nullity and annullability/voidability).

[34]Some civil law expert could rebut: what about nuncupative wills though? It is indeed true that a handful of jurisdictions around the world recognize the existence of oral wills, although they do so only in extreme circumstances where there is no possibility to redact a document following certain formalities. This is the "pure" nuncupative will, that is an oral will whose existence does not depend of any formality whatsoever. It is limited to soldiers at the front and seamen at sea when the death of one of them is imminent. The fact that in these situations no formal requirements whatsoever are requested by the law for the existence and hence validity of the will can be explained by the greater moral bond that arguably develops between human beings before a situation of great peril or danger—like a war or a tempest at sea—and thus by the fact that in these situations one can expect the recipient of the oral will to report it *verbatim* to the authorities. Alas, the possibility of a completely invented will being reported is still looming here, and that is why some commentators argue that in these cases it would still be preferable to leave the distribution of the estate of the deceased according to the rules of inheritance in the given jurisdiction (see Prascina 2009).

[35]It is also true that the oral form was indeed accepted in Roman law. But this did not mean that someone could just report someone's words claiming they were his testamentary dispositions; rather, there were always some procedural requirements—the oral statement, for instance, had to be given in front of a considerable number of witnesses (usually seven) none of whom was going to become a beneficiary (Prascina 2009). What we have experienced is precisely the evolution of the institution of the will from the oral form to the written one. The reasons for this evolution are the same (i.e. epistemic) that underpin the key relevance of understanding validity as a different status from existence in our legal practices. Thus it is safe to say that barring truly exceptional situations, any *existing* will must be written. If the ordinary fellow tells a group of friends about his testamentary intentions and considers that speech-act to be his "will" (and so to have normative effects once he passes away), not only does he not know the law and fails to produce any normative

4.3 The Artificial Ontology of Modern Law

The discussion above points to a key aspect of the difference between juridical existence and nonexistence in modern legal systems. For the vast majority of legal acts (contracts, statutes, administrative and judicial decisions, wills, etc.), most of their necessary requirements to *exist* in the legal system will be knowable and ascertainable by laypeople and not by legal officials only.[36] Anticipating my main claim in the next section, the point is that we can shed light on the complex ontological status of modern law only if we bring to the surface the underlying epistemic issues. Whether a norm belongs prima facie to the legal system or not must be, in normal situations, tendentially knowable and ascertainable by rational and linguistically competent agents in the system. This amounts to a necessary condition—given the practice-independence of legal norms—for law to be *tendentially* objective and thus able to guide the conduct of its addressees.[37]

Whether a feasible inheritance intention has been expressed in written form is something that any person of sound mind can ascertain, and so is whether the document has been signed or not.[38] The same applies, *mutatis mutandis*, to statutes: if the British Prime Minister were to publish a Facebook post with a list of general rules addressed to the public and claiming these were new statutory law, one would take her as either

a) reporting a very recent legislative development no one has ever heard of; or
b) joking; or
c) being delusional.

The point is that *no one* would think that her speech-act could possibly constitute a statute or legislative provision, and if someone did, well that someone would arguably lack the very concept of a statute.[39] Whether a bill has been correctly approved by a given parliamentary commission or whether the signature at the

---

effect regarding the distribution of his assets—more importantly, one could wonder whether his concept of "will" is not defective altogether. True, the friend's speech-act could have several other effects—for example, that of prompting a change in her younger child when he is told about his mother's intentions—but that does change the fact that it cannot by any means purport to have the effects that the legal system acknowledges when a valid token of the (type-)act "will" is performed.

[36]The distinguishing line between requirements that are necessary and sufficient for an act to be existent, and those that are necessary for its formal validity, is a thin one, and seems to resist precise theoretical treatment.

[37]Cf Brennan et al. (2013, p. 10). See also Westerman in this volume: her distinction between type- and token-validity maps onto the one between existence and full validity (albeit from a different viewpoint).

[38]Whereas the question of whether the signature at the bottom of a specific will has been forged or not is something that only an expert might be able to verify (provided that the forgery is apt, of course).

[39]At the very least, a statute is a set of general norms addressed to the public and produced by a *prima facie* legitimate authority according to some given procedure, be it a monarch, a president, a parliamentary assembly, and so forth.

bottom of it by the monarch or the president of the republic is present or not is again an empirical question that can in principle be answered by a great many people in our modern legal systems.

In short, the distinction between (mere) existence and formal validity of an act is premised on the observation that existence requires the application of some of the essential formal norms on the production which make the ensuing (product-)act *juridically intelligible* to every rational and linguistically competent agent in the system.[40] If that act also contains a norm formulation that expresses a deontic sentence, we can say then that a new norm that belongs prima facie to the system has been created. An act that *exists* for the legal system yields a juridical meaning that is recognizable as such by laypeople and officials alike. It might be lacking some formal elements that are necessary to be considered formally valid, or its content might contradict some higher norm and thus be materially invalid, but at this stage it is still the case that upon the mere attainment of some formal/procedural requirements, this act has the potential to produce a change in the normative landscape of its addressees.[41] It is prima facie a source of law.

Table 2 below illustrates the complex ontology of modern law,[42] which is the result of the fundamental distinctions between acts (as containing norm formulations) and norms (as the meaning of those acts) and between their respective existence and validity. According to this model, validity can be predicated of two different entities: of acts (formal validity) and of norms (material validity). The former is (predominantly) a matter of empirical conformity, the latter of interpretive coherence or noncontradiction (Ferrajoli 2016, p. 85). This means that every time someone refers to law as being valid with no further specifications, she usually means the combination of both—a statute is valid only insofar as it is so both formally and materially. This consideration allows us also to make intelligible the status of "unlawful law": that is, all those statutes, regulations, bylaws, judicial decisions, and so forth that albeit extant within the system might be actually *invalid*. As such, the existence of a legal norm (and of the act by which it is expressed) does not imply its validity. Existence is a necessary but not sufficient condition of validity.

[40]Carpentier's contribution in this volume is another very laudable attempt to dispel the ambiguity surrounding the use of the concept of legal validity in legal discourse. While he precisely identifies the distinction between the membership (within a system) of a legal norm as its existence and conformity to "higher-ranking norms" as validity, he still terms both of these properties as (two different types of) "validity," hence somewhat carrying on the ambiguity. I must also confess that I am somewhat not entirely convinced by his claim that conformity with criteria of membership (i.e. existence) is "not a normative, but a conceptual kind of conformity" (original italics). For I do not see any qualitative difference between the test for existence and the test for validity of legal norms in modern constitutional systems (although the former is logically prior to the latter).

[41]Cf Gardner (2012, p. 61).

[42]Cf Pino (2016, p. 42).

Table 2 The artificial ontology of modern law

	Existence	Formal validity	Material validity
Pertains to	Acts (sources) Norms (contents)	Acts (sources)	Norms (contents)
Requires	Attainment of at least some essential elements	Conformity	Coherence or noncontradiction
Ascertainable by	Every rational agent (in normal situations)	Juridical operators (officials, lawyers, etc.)	Courts
Ascertained through	Empirical inquiry (plus minimal interpretive operation)	Empirical enquiry (plus minimal interpretive operation)	Interpretative operation
Normative effect	Force of law	Force of law (enforceability if there are no material norms curtailing the contents)	Force of law and enforceability

Two remarks are in place at the end of this section. Interestingly (and perhaps ironically, given that this chapter is premised on a critical reading of this author), each of the remarks seems to vindicate an important intuition by Kelsen. First, the analysis shows in what sense validity can be conceived of as the *specific* mode of existence of legal norms vis-à-vis social and moral ones. Once validity is "released" from its normativist declination, we are able to appreciate that "valid" is a second and "artificial" ontological status that legal norms—*qua* formal or institutional—can entertain beyond that of "existence." In this sense, validity is a property that originates necessarily from the institutional character of a system of norms[43]—it is a relationship between norms and the acts that create them (Pino 2016, p. 106). This is the way in which law regulates its own creation, which for Kelsen is precisely one of the distinguishing features of law in respect of other normative systems.

The second and generally undertheorized[44] point that our analysis underscores is that, in our modern legal systems, a norm has force of law already with the mere existence of the act that produces it and not just with its (full) validity. Granted, it is necessarily a prima facie force, or, to put it more aptly, there is a presumption of force of any norm produced by an act that *exists* within the system.[45] That presumptions only stands until a norm is scrutinized by a court as the court *will not* enforce invalid norms, only valid ones.[46] But it appears as an undeniable descriptive truth about our legal practices that, until an *invalid* act is brought before a relevant

[43]On the institutionality of law the *locus classicus* is MacCormick (2008); for a very recent take see Ehrenberg (2016).

[44]A notable exception is Ferrajoli (2007, p. 528).

[45]To use Westerman's terminology in this volume, this would be the function of type-validity (as opposed to token-validity).

[46]In reality, it is perfectly possible for a court or tribunal to make an error of law and enforce an invalid norm. If that mistake of law is not rectified by appellate courts, we might well have a change in the law. But the overall objectivity of the system allows us to properly recognize these occurrences for what they are, *mistakes* of law (at least at first).

official for the authoritative declaration of its invalidity, such an invalid act might nonetheless produce normative effects like the equivalent valid one.[47] Hence, *pace* Kelsen, validity and force of law are independent properties that do not entertain any relationship of entailment. An invalid norm, as long as the act producing it exists for the system, can exert force of law, and if it goes unchallenged, the normative consequences thus produced might stand (Grellette 2010, p. 28). This also explains why modern legal systems allow claimants who wish to challenge the validity of a given act to seek "interim injunctions"—measures with which a court might crystallize the (normative) *status quo* while the legal proceedings unfold and until a decision is taken on the validity of the act in question. This central feature of our current legal practices would make no sense if invalid acts were to be considered nonexistent (and thus unable to produce any effect whatsoever).

5 Validity and Objectivity: On the Epistemic Dimension of Law

This chapter started off with the demonstration of how one of the greatest jurisprudential minds has fundamentally misunderstood the relationship between the existence, validity, and bindingness of law. This has subsequently led many more in the literature astray. I have also shown that the consequences of this mistake cannot be possibly underestimated. For validity becomes either a redundant concept that bears no real explanatory capacity vis-à-vis our modern legal practices, leaving a great deal of them unaccounted for, or it must be understood as the expression of an evaluative judgment that implies some form of "ethical legalism" or "ideological positivism" (Guastini 2016). Instead, once properly distinguished from "existence" and conceived of as part of a complex ontological paradigm, the concept of validity is a key element to shed light on the inner structure and workings of modern legal systems (vis-à-vis other normative practices).

In this sense, law is widely held to be, as an institutional-normative practice, a means of social organization and control: not the only one, and not *necessarily* the best one, but a *specific* one (Kelsen 1941). The specificity of law lies in subjecting human conduct to the guidance of norms (Fuller 1969), in this way providing its addressees with reasons for action. Green (1998, p. 121) and Gardner (2012, pp. 205–211) have claimed that law might be a modal and not a functional kind: it would be defined and identified not by *what* it does (for other normative practices such as morality or custom perform the same function) but by *how* it does it. On this point, I stand by Ehrenberg (2009, p. 97) instead when he affirms that

[47] This to the point that, after a certain period of time has passed, such effects might be "stabilized" by the legal system itself in order to endure certainty and protect the *bona fide* expectations of third parties: cf MacCormick (2008, p. 162).

> [w]hat is unique may be neither its form (modality) nor its function but instead the particular way in which the two are joined.[48]

The "particular way," as I noted above, is to use norms to guide people's conduct. This practice might originate from the spontaneous dynamics of a given social group, but once it reaches a certain dimension and level of complexity, the set of (primary) norms as established within those spontaneous practices will no longer be able to effectively and satisfactorily work as a means of group organization and control. Here, of course, I am just picturing in broad strokes Hart's (2012) reconstruction of the evolution from premodern legal systems to modern ones through the union of primary and secondary rules, which I fully endorse.[49] What is important for our purposes is that the evolution from a *set* of (social) primary norms to a *system* of primary and secondary norms entails the ontological independence of those primary norms from the corresponding practices, of which these latter are the most obvious epistemic manifestation in spontaneous social settings. In other words, insofar as social norms are informal and entail the corresponding practices, members of the group have a reliable and conspicuous epistemic source to find out what they ought to do. But when instead the creation of new norms becomes an institutionalized process in the hands of a particular subject (i.e., group leaders or an assembly), a new norm "N" can be created and thus *exist* even if no one (in the most extreme case) in the social group displays the corresponding "N"-normative attitudes.[50] Norms thus created are fully *posited* precisely because there is no necessary relation with the corresponding practices. This requires in turn the centralization of coercive enforcement within the group to "cope" with physiological norm breaching by some members of the group.[51] The positivization of norm creation and the centralization of coercive power appear to be then inextricably related to one another. As Postema (2011, p. 307) puts it:

> [w]ith law comes the institutionalization and centralization of governance or exercise of political power.

The result of these processes is twofold. On the one hand, the positivization of norm creation requires the social group to introduce new norms (and change existing ones) in a way that is epistemically accessible through the institutionalized exercise

[48]Later in the piece Ehrenberg defines law as a "social kind."

[49]"Rule" and "norm" are synonymous for the purpose of this chapter. On the most appropriate way to read Hart's normative "genealogy" see Postema (2011, pp. 306–307). My conclusions are also convergent with Westerman's account of validity as reputation in this volume. In particular see her considerations about the functional advantages entertained by formal institutional orders vis-à-vis informal ones.

[50]As I said, this does not exclude that the social group must somehow *accept* the normative-institutional system in the first place. Without that basic systemic acceptance, there would be no possibility for norms to be detached from their corresponding practices.

[51]In the absence of spontaneous reactive attitudes that come when the practice is there instead. But if the majority fails to comply with the norms coming from the power-holder(s) all the time, one can reasonably doubt whether a legal system is in place at all.

of authority (see Westerman in this volume). In other words, legal norms thus created are ontologically grounded in forms or processes that are empirically observable. This is famously captured by the Hobbesian maxim *auctoritas, non veritas, facit legem.*[52] On the other hand, at this first stage, whatever content can be poured into the *form* of the law; to wit, at this stage, law merely *channels* the exercise of political power, which remains (potentially) unfettered (Ferrajoli 2016). It is only then with a second and *artificial* ontological dimension—validity—that law *itself* regulates its own creation, so that there are *legal* limits to what the authority can and cannot do. And it is precisely with this limitation *of* law *by* law that also comes logically the possibility of "unlawful law," which has proved so hard to reconcile with positivist theories of law (Grellette 2010, pp. 28–37).

Perhaps what many positivists have struggled with is the fact that legal norms are *produced* through an empirical act of creation but also entertain a normative relationship of validation with superior norms (Lamond 2014a; Raz 1979, p. 150). This presupposes Kelsen's binary typology of normative systems that are either "dynamic" (where validity depends on the procedure of creation of that norm) or "static" (where a norm is logically derived from other norms in the system).[53] As should be clear by now, our modern legal systems—no matter whether based on the civil or common law tradition—are static and dynamic at the same time (Ferrajoli 2007; Beltrán and Ratti 2010): there are two logically independent modes of validation of legal norms—one source based (or formal), the other content based—that are at work simultaneously because of two expedients. First, this is because the source-based criterion of validation is already by itself sufficient to give rise to the *force* of law for the norms thus produced, at least prima facie. Second, while the ascertainment of the fundamental elements of legal acts (such as statutes, contracts, wills, etc.) that constitute their recognizability as sources of law can be carried out by every rational and linguistically competent member of a group, the authoritative decision of "invalidation" for the norms thus produced is reserved for a closed group of specialized agents within the system. In other words, unless an act (source) is challenged before the authority entitled to pronounce on its validity, that potentially less-than-valid act might yield the same normative effects as a valid one.[54]

Episodes like these happen regularly in our legal practices. And taken individually, each of these instances of "invalid law" that still produce normative effects constitutes a shortcoming of the system, a *glitch*. But the very possibility of "unlawful law" (and of its occurrences) must be understood as the price we have to pay to have an institutional-normative system that regulates its own change while

[52]The maxim appears for the first time in the 1670 Latin translation of Leviathan (1651): Hobbes (1839).

[53]Kelsen's use of "static" seems very different from Hart's (2012, pp. 92–93).

[54]*Contra* Kirste, in this volume, according to whom only valid law has the "force of law." As I have shown in this chapter, this claim seems hard to reconcile with our current existing legal practices.

being (tendentially) objective and thus allowing for predictability and certainty.[55] The always potential and irreducible tension between the two independent processes of validation of legal norms is resolved by a default rule according to which the source based prevails over the content based, unless there is a supervening authoritative act (by a court) that sanctions the invalidity of the act in question. To put this in Kelsenian terminology, the static character of the system is *partially* sacrificed to its dynamic one (Ferrajoli 2007, 2016; MacCormick 2008, p. 162). Its internal coherence—which would require the logical impossibility of "unlawful" law—is sacrificed toward its certainty and predictability, two features that are necessary to fulfill its guiding function of subjecting human conduct to the guidance of rules (Peczenik 1989, p. 174).

Could this be any different?[56] If "force of law" were only a predicate of the full validity of a norm and not just of the existence of its source, a normative system could fulfill its guiding function only through the following two "routes." Either it would be possible for officials to express an *ex ante* authoritative judgment of validity, both formal and material, for every (token-)act that purports to produce normative effects as recognized by the law, or such authoritative judgments of validity would not have to be reserved to a restricted group of specialized agents (the courts), but would instead have to be *diffused*, in the sense that every agent in the system could authoritatively establish what is valid and thus binding law. The unavoidable problems these two possibilities should be apparent. As to the first possibility, it is not clear how a state of affairs in which officials perform an *ex ante* validity control on each and every act of law creation would be achievable in our large societies, whereas in the second case, law would lose even that (minimal) type of objectivity, that is, intersubjectivity, and become an unavoidably *subjective* practice: one in which everyone in the system is able to say what the law *is*—even the lunatic (Jori 2010). I guess there is no need to stress how such a system—if we can talk indeed of a "system"—would hardly achieve any action-guiding function at all as no one could reliably form any expectation vis-à-vis the behavior of others.

6 Conclusion

Once released from its normative (mis)understanding, the concept of validity assumes a completely different explanatory role vis-à-vis our modern legal practices. As an artificial ontological status that legal norms can possess beyond that of (mere) existence, it allows law to regulate itself (rather than being just the form of exercise of political power), thus creating the logical space for the existence of the only apparently contradictory "unlawful law." This is a crucial point toward shedding

[55]Granted, a system could not fulfill any guiding function if the instances of "unlawful law" were to go beyond a certain, "manageable," threshold.

[56]See for a similar discussion Guastini (2013, pp. 131–135).

light on the relationship between the ontological and the epistemic dimensions of objectivity of modern legal practices. In this sense, due to the ontological practice-independence of legal norms, the institutionalized creation of law must be epistemically accessible for objectivity—which Kramer (2007, p. 46) has termed "transindividual discernibility"—to obtain. In other words, the fact that the existence of a source of law depends on formal, empirical features that are in the majority of situations ascertainable by every rational agent in the system (like the written form of a deed or the fact that it has been signed and so forth) grounds the status of law as a tendentially objective (that is, intersubjective) practice. Importantly, this objectivity is grounded not only on the practice of the officials of the system, as is often held, but on the practice of laypeople as well.[57] This is the epistemic importance of easily identifiable conventional rules that Hart (2012, p. 134) stresses in the Concept as it is this characteristic that allows the law to fulfill its general action-guiding (and thus coordinating) function. A given deed is *easily* recognizable as a source of law (that is, as a token of the juridical type to which the system assigns the production of certain normative consequences) due to the occurrence of some formal characteristics. A statute approved according to the required voting procedures and promulgated in the official gazette is law, whereas a list of norms published on Facebook is not law (at least for the time being).[58] It is this kind of epistemic objectivity that, at a minimum, grounds the rule of law.[59]

Acknowledgements Many thanks to all the participants to the "Public law and public trust" seminar in Groningen from which this contribution originates and in particular to Mathieu Carpentier, Jaap Hage, and Miodrag Jovanović for challenging discussions on the topic of validity. My utmost gratitude goes also to Samuele Chilovi, Sebastián Figueroa Rubio, Riccardo Guastini, Nicolas Kang-Riou, Anne Ruth Mackor, and Anastasia Shesterinina, who provided me with extensive comments on previous drafts. The usual disclaimer applies. Finally, this chapter is dedicated to Pauline Westerman: *per aspera ad astra*.

[57]"Whenever such a rule of recognition is accepted, both private persons and officials are provided with authoritative criteria for identifying primary rules of obligation [...] The existence of this [simple form of] rule of recognition will be manifest in the general practice, on the part of the officials or private persons, of identifying the rules by this criterion" (Hart 2012, pp. 100–101). It has been noted already for quite some time that Hart is ambivalent in the Concept as to whether the rule of recognition is grounded on the practice of officials only, or on that of laypeople as well. I submit here that this ambiguity is due precisely to Hart's lack of distinction between the existence and the validity of law. Once such a distinction is in place, we can understand Hart's claims as describing not a single, but two rules of recognition, one that provides the criteria for the existence of law (this is sometimes called the "rule of identification"), and the other that provides the criteria for its validity.

[58]See again the important contribution by Westerman in this volume. Granted, even the existence and not just the validity of some types of formal acts will be too complex to be ascertained by the nonspecialized members of society; but this technical, more restricted class of acts will still be conceivable only if the general practice of recognizing law's existence holds for the majority of acts in the system.

[59]For an extensive discussion of the relationship between objectivity and the rule of law see Kramer (2007).

References

Beltrán, J.F., and G.B. Ratti. 2010. Validity and Defeasibility in the Legal Domain. *Law and Philosophy* 29: 601.

Berto, F., and M. Plebani. 2015. *Ontology and Metaontology: A Contemporary Guide*. London: Bloomsbury Academic.

Bodin, J. 1586. *De Republica libri sex*. 1st ed. Paris: Apud Iacobum Du-Puys sub signo Samaritanae.

Brennan, G., et al., eds. 2013. *Explaining Norms*. Oxford: Oxford University Press.

Bulygin, E. 1998. An Antinomy in Kelsen's Pure Theory of Law. In *Normativity and Norms: Critical Perspectives on Kelsenian Themes*, ed. S.L. Paulson and B. Litschewski Paulson. Oxford: Clarendon Press.

Canale, D. 2014. Is Law Grounded in Joint Action? *Rechtstheorie* 45: 289.

Ehrenberg, K.M. 2009. Defending the Possibility of a Neutral Functional Theory of Law. *Oxford Journal of Legal Studies* 29: 91.

———. 2016. *The Functions of Law*. Oxford: Oxford University Press.

Ferrajoli, L. 2007. *Principia Iuris: Teoria del Diritto e Della Democrazia*. Vol. 1. Bari: Laterza.

———. 2016. *La logica del diritto: dieci aporie nell'opera di Hans Kelsen*. Bari: GLF Laterza.

Finnis, J. 2011. *Natural Law and Natural Rights*. 2nd ed. Oxford: Oxford University Press.

Fuller, L.L. 1969. *The Morality of Law*. 2nd ed. New Haven: Yale University Press.

Gardner, J. 2012. *Law as a Leap of Faith: Essays on Law in General*. Oxford: Oxford University Press.

Gaus, G. 2014. Review of "Explaining Norms". *Notre Dame Philosophical Reviews* (accessed 28/08/2017).

Green, L. 1998. The Functions of Law. *Cogito* 12: 117.

Grellette, M. 2010. Legal Positivism and the Separation of Existence and Validity. *Ratio Juris* 23: 22.

Guastini, R. 2013. *Distinguendo Ancora*. Madrid: Marcial Pons.

———. 2016. Kelsen on Validity (Once More). *Ratio Juris*.

Hart, H.L.A. 2012. *The Concept of Law*. 3rd ed. Oxford: Clarendon Press.

Hobbes, T. 1839. In *Opera Philosophica Quae Latine Scripsit Omnia*, ed. William Molesworth, vol. 3. London: Joannem Bohn.

Jori, M. 2010. *Del Diritto Inesistente: Saggio di Metagiurisprudenza Descrittiva*. Pisa: ETS.

Kelsen, H. 1941. The Law as a Specific Social Technique. *The University of Chicago Law Review* 9: 75.

———. 1946. *General Theory of Law and State*. Cambridge, MA: Harvard UP.

———. 1949. The Natural-Law Doctrine Before the Tribunal of Science. *The Western Political Quarterly* 2: 481.

———. 1960. What Is the Pure Theory of Law? *Tulane Law Review* 34: 269.

———. 1992 (1934). *Introduction to the Problems of Legal Theory*, Trans. B. Litchewski Paulson and S.L. Paulson. Oxford: Clarendon Press.

Kramer, M. 2007. *Objectivity and the Rule of Law*. Cambridge: CUP.

Lamond, G. 2014a. The Rule of Recognition and the Foundations of a Legal System. In *Reading HLA Hart's 'The Concept of Law'*, ed. L. Duarte d'Almeida, J. Edwards, and A. Dolcetti. Oxford: Hart Publishing.

———. 2014b. Legal Sources, the Rule of Recognition, and Customary Law. *American Journal of Jurisprudence*: 1.

MacCormick, N. 2008. *Institutions of Law: An Essay in Legal Theory*. Oxford: Oxford University Press.

Moreso, J.J., and S. Chilovi. 2016. Il Diritto Come Linguaggio (nella Filosofia Analitica Contemporanea). In *Che cosa e'il diritto. Ontologie e concezioni del giuridico*, ed. G. Bongiovanni, G. Pino, and C. Roversi. Torino: Giappichelli.

Munzer, S. 1972. *Legal Validity*. Leiden: Martinus Nijhoff.

Narváez Mora, M. 2015. Expressing Norms. On Norm-Formulations and Other Entities in Legal Theory. *Revus. Journal for Constitutional Theory and Philosophy of Law* 25: 43.
Nino, C.S. 1978. Some Confusions Around Kelsen's Concept of Validity. *ARSP: Archiv für Rechts- und Sozialphilosophie* 64: 357.
———. 1996. *Introduzione All'analisi Del Diritto*. Torino: Giappichelli.
Peczenik, A. 1989. *On Law and Reason*. Berlin: Springer.
Perry, A. 2015. The Internal Aspect of Social Rules. *Oxford Journal of Legal Studies* 35: 283.
Pino, G. 1999. The Place of Legal Positivism in Contemporary Constitutional States. *Law and Philosophy* 18: 513.
———. 2014. Positivism, Legal Validity, and the Separation of Law and Morals. *Ratio Juris* 27: 190.
———. 2016. *Teoria analitica del diritto I: La norma giuridica*. Pisa: ETS.
Postema, G.J. 2011. *Legal Philosophy in the Twentieth Century: The Common Law World*. Vol. 11. Berlin: Springer.
Prascina, E. 2009. Il Testamento Nuncupativo. *Gazzetta Notarile*: 527.
Priel, D. 2011. The Place of Legitimacy in Legal Theory. *McGill Law Journal/Revue de Droit de McGill* 57: 2.
Raz, J. 1979. *The Authority of Law: Essays on Law and Morality*. Oxford: Clarendon Press.
———. 2011. *From Normativity to Responsibility*. Oxford: Oxford University Press.
Sandro, P. 2011. An Axiomatic Theory of Law. *Res Publica* 17: 343.
———. 2019. *Creation and Application of Law: A Neglected Distinction*. Oxford: Hart/Bloomsbury, forthcoming.
Sartor, G. 2000. Legal Validity as Doxastic Obligation: From Definition to Normativity. *Law and Philosophy* 19: 585.
———. 2008. Legal Validity: An Inferential Analysis. *Ratio Juris* 21: 212.
Tahko, T.E., and E.J. Lowe. 2015. Ontological Dependence. In *The Stanford Encyclopedia of Philosophy*, ed. E.N. Zalta. http://plato.stanford.edu/archives/spr2015/entries/dependence-ontological/ accessed 6 July 2016.
Tuzet, G. 2014. Social Ontology and Legal Practice: A Debate. *Rechtstheorie* 45: 281.
von Wright, G.E. 1963. *Norm and Action: A Logical Enquiry*. London: Routledge.
Walker, N. 2009. Out of Place and Out of Time: Law's Fading Co-ordinates. *Edinburgh Law Review* 14: 13.

Open Access This chapter is licensed under the terms of the Creative Commons Attribution 4.0 International License (http://creativecommons.org/licenses/by/4.0/), which permits use, sharing, adaptation, distribution and reproduction in any medium or format, as long as you give appropriate credit to the original author(s) and the source, provide a link to the Creative Commons license and indicate if changes were made.

The images or other third party material in this chapter are included in the chapter's Creative Commons license, unless indicated otherwise in a credit line to the material. If material is not included in the chapter's Creative Commons license and your intended use is not permitted by statutory regulation or exceeds the permitted use, you will need to obtain permission directly from the copyright holder.

What Is Legal Validity and Is It Important? Some Critical Remarks About the Legal Status of Soft Law

Anne Ruth Mackor

Abstract In this chapter, I shall be concerned with the question what legal validity is and why it is important. The first part of the chapter is devoted to an analysis of the notion of validity, which allows us to answer the question what it means to say that a rule is or is not legally valid. In the second part, I argue that legal validity has practical importance. I illustrate my claim by discussing the legal status of a particular kind of soft law, viz. two Dutch codes of conduct for the judiciary.

1 Introduction

In this chapter, I shall be concerned with the question of what legal validity is and why it is important. The first part of the chapter (Sect. 2) is devoted to an analysis of the notion of validity, which allows us to answer the question what it means to say that a rule is or is not legally valid. In the second part (Sects. 3 and 4), I argue that legal validity has practical importance. I illustrate my claim by discussing the legal status of soft law, more in particular of Dutch codes of conduct for the judiciary. I first show that their legal status (validity) is unclear. Then I argue that to the extent that these codes of conduct have any effect at all, the fact that their legal status is unclear is an important reason to surmise that their actual effect will most likely be contrary to one of the main intended effects, viz. to enhance the trust of citizens in the judiciary.

A. R. Mackor (✉)
Faculty of Law, University of Groningen, Groningen, The Netherlands
e-mail: A.R.Mackor@rug.nl

© Springer International Publishing AG, part of Springer Nature 2018

P. Westerman et al. (eds.), *Legal Validity and Soft Law*, Law and Philosophy Library 122, https://doi.org/10.1007/978-3-319-77522-7_6

2 Existence, Gültigkeit, Geltung, and Efficacy

What does it mean to say that a legal or moral rule is valid or not? I argue that we need to distinguish between two notions of validity. For lack of proper English terms, I follow Hage (1984) in using the German terms Gültigkeit and Geltung to denote them. To say that a rule has Geltung is to say that it generates deontic consequences such as obligations. To say that a rule is Gültig is to say that it has been created in accordance with specific criteria. Both Geltung and Gültigkeit must be distinguished from efficacy. If a rule with Geltung is efficacious, i.e. if it is actually followed and/or enforced, it generates not only deontic consequences but also nondeontic (empirical) consequences, for example that a debtor actually complies or is being forced to comply with his obligation.

Most legal philosophers sharply distinguish between validity and efficacy, but not all of them distinguish between validity and existence. Some even deny the conceptual possibility of the existence of an invalid rule. In this paper, I argue that we should distinguish not only between two notions of validity but also between the validity and existence, as well as between the validity and efficacy, of rules. In this section, I will offer an analysis of the four notions and their interrelations.

2.1 Existence

Let us first discuss the existence of (systems of) rules. (Systems of) rules are peculiar kinds of entities. Elsewhere I have argued that they are abstract objects in that they do not exist in space but exist only in time, even though representations of and evidence for them (e.g., written formulations) can be found in space (Mackor 2012, 2013a, 2016a). Following Searle (1995, 2010) and others, I have claimed that positive law and positive morality exist because and to the extent that people collectively understand them and accept them as systems of rules that guide their behavior, even though this acceptance need not be for moral reasons, let alone be wholehearted. I use the term "recognition" to refer to this collective understanding and acceptance.

However, there are two different ways in which rules can come into existence, and rules can be recognized in two distinct ways, viz. directly or indirectly. A rule can come into existence by being officially enacted. A legal rule can be said to exist as a rule of positive law if its manner of enactment is collectively recognized as a way of coming into existence. If a group recognizes rules that confer power on an authority and prescribe a particular procedure to create rules, then a particular rule that has been enacted in accordance with these rules can be said to exist, even if its existence is not yet collectively known and thus is not yet directly recognized by the group that recognizes the secondary rules that allow for this kind of enactment. In such a case, the rule is recognized indirectly.[1]

It is also possible for rules to exist without being enacted. Rules can come into existence in a less determinate and often more gradual manner. A rule can be said to exist when people refer to a rule or adduce reasons that are based on the rule, when they evaluate each other's behavior. In such a case, we can say that the rule exists because it is directly recognized as a guideline for behavior.

The distinction between the two modes of (coming into) existence—directly via the recognition of the primary rule or indirectly via the recognition of the secondary rules that make it possible to create a primary rule—is not confined to law, but it is most clearly reflected in the distinction between enacted law and customary law and in Hart's (1961, p. 77 ff.) distinction between secondary and primary rules. This distinction takes us to the first notion of validity, viz Gültigkeit.

2.2 *Gültigkeit*

Only rules that are officially enacted can be said to be gültig or ungültig. Customary rules cannot be gültig or ungültig since they are not enacted. Enacted rules are gültig if they are created in accordance with specific criteria; they are ungültig if they are intended to be gültig but erroneously or deceitfully fail one or more criteria.

An enacted rule[2] is gültig

1. if it is created by an authority (person or body) with the competence to do so; if so, then it has formal declarative validity;
2. in accordance with specific criteria; if so, then it has formal procedural validity;
3. if it does not conflict with more authoritative substantive rules; if so, it has substantive or material validity (Munzer 1973, p. 1149; Mackor 2012).[3]

According to this definition, not only legal rules but also rules of sports clubs, professional associations, companies, and churches can be gültig or ungültig. For a rule to be legally gültig, it must be enacted by an authority with the legal competence

[1]If a rule comes into existence through enactment we cannot only say that from then on, this particular rule exists, but also that there is an authoritative and—in most cases—a written rule formulation. Thus, its existence is recognized through its authoritative enactment, its content through its authoritative rule formulation.

[2]Note that not only rules can be gültig. Contracts, tickets, moves in a chess game and goals in a football match can be said to be gültig (or ungültig) too insofar as they are deliberately created in accordance with specific criteria and intended to have deontic consequences (see below Sect. 2.3). Some authors (Hage, this volume) ascribe gültigkeit to the sources of rules and not to the rules themselves.

[3]Some readers might want to subsume criterion 3 (no conflict with more authoritative substantive rules) under criterion 1 (created by an authority with competence to do so). If a rule conflicts with a more authoritative rule, the authority either was not competent to create this rule or he should first change or abolish the more authoritative rules.

to do so and in accordance with a legal procedure and without conflicting with more authoritative legal rules. Accordingly, a rule can only be said to be gültig in relation to or as rule of a particular system, be it the domestic regulations of the rugby club of Haarlem, the guidelines of the Dutch Medical Association, or the Dutch legal system. The mere claim that a rule is gültig is incomplete or even meaningless; a gültige rule of the rugby club of Haarlem is not a gültige rule of the Dutch Medical Association or of Dutch law.

The next question is what the relation is between Gültigkeit and existence.[4] Does it make sense to say that a rule that is ungültig can nevertheless exist[5] and, conversely, that there are gültige rules that nevertheless do not exist? Before answering this question, we should distinguish between rules of hypothetical legal systems and rules of positive legal systems. For a legal system and its rules to be positive, the rules—including the rules that determine how one can make gültige rules—must themselves be recognized within a relevant group. If the rules are not recognized, the rules and the system are merely hypothetical.[6]

Let us first look at the situation in which a rule of a positive system is created in accordance with all three criteria and the rules that contain criteria are recognized in the relevant group. In such a case, the rule is gültig. Its existence can nevertheless be denied if there is no direct collective recognition of the rule whatsoever. This would be the case, for example, if even the judiciary, in cases where the rule is clearly applicable, ignores the rule or openly denies its existence or applicability. However, one might claim that such a rule nevertheless does exist because it has been created as a gültige rule. It could then be said to exist as a dead letter only.

Let us now turn to the question whether ungültige rules can be said to exist. First note that it only makes sense to say that a rule is ungültig if it was deliberately created by a body without the competence to do so, in the wrong manner, and/or in conflict with more authoritative rules. This can happen erroneously, through ignorance or sloppiness for instance, but also purposefully and deceitfully. I believe we should distinguish between two types of situations.

If it is clear to almost anyone that the rule is ungültig and—as a consequence—the rule is not recognized by anyone, let alone collectively recognized, it seems meaningless to say it has come into existence. For example, assume that I declare to have created a legal rule. I am so obviously not competent that it does not make sense to say I created an ungültige legal rule (criterion 1). I did not create a legal rule; in fact, I did not create anything at all, legal or otherwise. The reason my ungültige rule does not exist is that no one will mistakenly recognize me as a legal authority, and

[4]More about the existence of rules in Mackor (2012, pp. 37–39).

[5]Raz's well-known claim (1979, pp. 146, 150) that an invalid rule is not a rule, i.e. does not exist, is not a claim about Gültigkeit, but about Geltung. See Sect. 2.3.

[6]A legal system that is actually recognized by a particular society in a particular period is called a legal order. Thus, whereas it makes sense to talk about a positive legal system, "a positive legal order" is a tautology.

accordingly no one will recognize my rule as a legal rule. In such a case, it seems correct to say that I have not created a rule and that my rule does not exist.[7]

Other situations are more complex. For example, think of an authority that has the competence to create legal rules but that failed on an intricate detail of its own competence (criterion 1) or the procedure (criterion 2) or who created rules that turn out to conflict with more authoritative rules (criterion 3). Perhaps in the first instance the mistake or deceit remains unnoticed and the rule is dealt with as if it is gültig. It might be followed by citizens, and it might even be applied by the judiciary and enforced in concrete cases. In such a case, it would be strange to say that, despite the fact that even legal authorities recognize and apply it, the rule does not exist or that it does not exist as a legal rule. The rule has come into existence despite the fact that it is ungültig. It makes sense to say that it exists because it is collectively recognized as having Geltung, which shows from the role it plays in social and/or legal discourse.

In conclusion, existence and Gültigkeit are not identical. Moreover, Gültigkeit is neither a sufficient nor a necessary condition for existence. The relationship is much more complex. Gültigkeit is not a sufficient condition because even though in most cases a gültige rule also exists, I have offered an example of a gültige rule that does not exist. Gültigkeit is not a necessary condition either. First, even though in most cases ungültige rules do not exist, I have argued that there are ungültige rules that nevertheless do exist. Second, and more importantly, social and customary rules that—by definition—lack the property of Gültigkeit nevertheless exist. This conclusion takes us to the second notion of validity, viz Geltung.

2.3 *Geltung*

What does it mean to say that a rule exists either as a gültige rule—created in accordance with the three criteria mentioned earlier—or as a customary rule that has come into existence in a less determinate way or even as an ungültige rule that is treated as if it were gültig? Can we identify existence with Geltung? Let us first investigate the meaning of Geltung.

Generating Deontic Consequences

To say a rule has Geltung is to say that if the conditions specified by the rule obtain, the rule generates the deontic consequences it claims that follow. For example, if I sign a contract to deliver a good, therewith my obligation to deliver the good comes

[7]Compare this example to the situation in which I create the family rule "shoes are to be placed in the hall." If my family accepts me as an authority to create such a rule and if there is minimally verbal recognition of the rule (but not necessarily a lot of complying behavior), then my rule can be said to exist.

into existence. Note, however, that rules can generate not only obligations but many other kinds of deontic consequences such as rights, powers, liabilities, and immunities. For example, if you and I sign a contract stating that I deliver a good to you, not only my obligation to deliver but also your right to have the good delivered comes into existence.

We can formulate a strong and a weak version of the claim that rules generate deontic consequences. In the strong version, to say that a rule has Geltung is to say that if the conditions specified by the rule obtain, the rule automatically generates the deontic consequences it claims that follow. Thus, if I sign a contract, then I am under an obligation. Obviously, there can be obscurity or disagreement about the question whether the factual conditions obtain and about the interpretation of the rule. However, if there is no obscurity and no disagreement, then we know that the consequences follow.

We can also formulate a weak version.[8] To say that a rule has Geltung is to say that if the deontic conditions as specified by the rule obtain, the rule may not be ignored in practical decision making, and it may be overthrown only in extreme circumstances (also compare Munzer 1973, p. 1149).[9] On the weak version, a rule with Geltung does not "automatically" generate the deontic consequences. The rule is "only" a strong reason in practical decision making that supports the conclusion that the deontic consequences follow. Again, take the rule that if one signs a contract to deliver a good, one then has the obligation to deliver the good. On the weak view, the rule should always be taken into account in the decision making, and in most cases the rule will generate the deontic consequences, i.e. the obligation. However, the consequences are not always generated when the conditions obtain. For example, they might not be generated when this would be unreasonable and unfair in a concrete instance. Geltung is a binary notion, implying that a rule either has Geltung or not, and on the strong view this implies that a rule with Geltung generates the deontic consequences and a rule without Geltung does not. The weak view, however, states that even though Geltung is a binary notion, a rule that has Geltung can have more or less weight in legal decision making, implying that in concrete instances, it can be harder or easier to overthrow it and to deny that deontic consequences follow.[10]

---

[8]The weak view is closely related to Hage's view (see his chapter in this volume) of legal reasoning as reason-based.

[9]Note that to say a rule has legal Geltung only means it cannot be ignored or overthrown from a legal perspective. It does not mean that it cannot be ignored or overthrown from e.g. a moral perspective.

[10]For example, whereas both legal rules and guidelines can be said to have Geltung, most legal rules can less easily be overthrown than e.g. guidelines. Guidelines openly allow for the possibility that their deontic consequences do not follow if special conditions obtain. See Mackor (2016b) about the legal status of medical standards.

The weak view is explicitly expressed, among others, in section 2 subsection 2 of Book 6 of the Dutch Civil Code,[11] which states that a rule that *has Geltung* through an Act, through custom, or through a legal act is nevertheless *not applicable* if that would be unacceptable according to criteria of reasonableness and fairness in the given circumstances. In other words, the section states that if the conditions of a geltende legal rule obtain, the rule nevertheless does not always generate its legal consequences.

Legal Geltung Is About Rules in Words, Not About Rules in Action or Efficacy

To say that a legal rule generates deontic consequences is not to say that a rule generates factual consequences or even that factual consequences will somehow follow. Neither the weak view nor the strong view claims that saying that the rule that signing a contract generates an obligation has Geltung implies that I will actually live up to my obligation and that I will deliver the good voluntarily or that I will be forced to deliver or that I will be held liable for damages. Legal Geltung is not efficacy. Geltung is about "rules in books" or at least about rules in words. It is not about "rules in action," i.e. about what happens in actual practice. For this reason, I reject the use of the term "binding force" as an equivalent of Geltung, precisely because the term "force" seems to suggest a link with efficacy and with nondeontic empirical consequences.

Social Geltung Is Not Efficacy Either

As we can distinguish between the Gültigkeit of legal and non-legal rules, so we can also distinguish between legal Geltung and non-legal Geltung. A rule has legal Geltung if it generates the legal consequences if the conditions formulated in the rule obtain. Similarly, a social or moral rule[12] has Geltung if a rule generates the deontic consequences it claims to generate if the proper conditions obtain. Take the social rule that if one makes a promise, one has the obligation to keep it. Accordingly, if I make a promise, the rule generates my obligation to keep my promise and to deliver on it. As with legal rules, on the strong reading, the deontic consequences automatically follow as soon as the conditions obtain. On the weak reading, the rule plays an important role in practical decision making, and the deontic consequences will follow normally but not always. Sometimes there are overriding

[11]The subsection reads: "Een tussen hen krachtens wet, gewoonte of rechtshandeling geldende regel is niet van toepassing, voor zover dit in de gegeven omstandigheden naar maatstaven van redelijkheid en billijkheid onaanvaardbaar zou zijn."

[12]In this chapter I do not distinguish between social and moral rules since I only discuss positive law and positive morality. I do not talk about validity of rules of natural law and critical morality.

reasons to act differently, and in such a case, the rule, even though it has Geltung, does not generate the obligation.

As with legal rules, to say a social rule has Geltung is not to say that rule is efficacious. It does not mean that factual consequences will follow: it does not mean that I will keep my promise or that I will be forced to keep my promise or that I will be punished for breaking my promise. It only means that if I make a promise, I am under the social obligation to keep it. In other words, not only legal Geltung but also social Geltung is about rules in words and not about rules in action.

Geltung and Existence

Earlier I stated that existence and Gültigkeit should be kept apart. First, some gültige rules only exist as dead letters, and some rules exist despite the fact that they are ungültig. Moreover, not all rules that exist are enacted and thus are gültig. The question now is whether existence and Geltung can be identified or whether Geltung is a necessary and/or a sufficient condition for the existence of a rule.

First, as I have stated above, a gültige rule that is not recognized as geltend can nevertheless be said to exist, albeit as a dead letter. Also, some ungültige rules, the Geltung of which has not yet been settled, can be said to exist. As examples of soft law show,[13] there are rules that have been created, and in that sense clearly exist, and that have been created to have some legal effect (i.e., play a role in legal decision making) even though their legal Geltung is not (yet) settled or is even openly denied. Again, since there are so many different ways for the existence of rules, I believe that we should not identify Geltung and existence. Moreover, Geltung does not seem to be a necessary condition for existence since there are rules that exist as a dead letter. However, unlike Gültigkeit, Geltung does seem to be a sufficient condition for existence: if a rule has Geltung, then it exists.

Because of these different modes of existence, I believe it is better not to identify existence and Geltung but instead to state that "a rule exists as . . .," i.e. as geltende rule, as gültige rule, as efficacious rule, etc. This takes us to the final concept: efficacy.

2.4 *Efficacy*

Internal and External Points of View

I have just argued that both legal and social Geltung should be distinguished from efficacy. A social rule that is not often obeyed or enforced but that people pay (sincere) lip service to—i.e., to the deontic consequences that the rule generates—

[13]More about soft law in Sects. 3 and 4.

can be said to have social Geltung. Thus, even if a lot of promises are broken and the breaking remains unpunished, the social rule that one must keep one's promises has social Geltung as long as people agree, also in concrete instances, that making a promise generates the obligation to keep it. The same holds for legal rules. Legal rules, too, have legal Geltung as long as lip service is paid to them, especially if this is done by officials, in particular by the judiciary. Thus, Gültigkeit and Geltung are characteristics of rules that belong to rules in books or at least to rules in words. They are characteristics we can notice from an internal point of view.

Efficacy, on the other hand, is a characteristic of rules that is primarily observed from an external sociological point of view. I state primarily because the efficacy of a rule can play a role in the internal point of view, too. For example, a judge might take the fact (or rather his belief) that a rule is (or is not) efficacious as evidence for the fact that it does (or does not) exist as a customary rule and thus does (or does not) have legal Geltung.

Accordingly, efficacy—unlike Gültigkeit and Geltung—need not be collectively recognized. On the contrary, a group can be collectively mistaken about the efficacy of a rule; they can believe that a rule they collectively recognize as gültig and/or geltend is efficacious whereas in fact it is not, and they can believe that a gültige and/or geltende rule is inefficacious whereas in fact it is efficacious.

Social and Legal Efficacy

There are at least two ways in which legal rules can lack efficacy. In the first place, a rule can lack social efficacy. It lacks social efficacy when it is hardly ever followed or enforced in a community. Nevertheless, as long as the judiciary applies it and public prosecution, collection agencies, or the parties in the lawsuit themselves actually enforce the verdict, the rule can be said to have not only legal Geltung but also legal efficacy.

A legal rule lacks legal efficacy if the judiciary applies it, but the verdicts are not enforced in a large number of cases. As long as the judiciary applies the rule, it has legal Geltung. However, if it is not enforced, it is neither socially nor legally efficacious.

Existence and Efficacy

I have argued that even though we should not identify Geltung and existence, the primary mode of existence of a rule is its being collectively recognized to generate deontic consequences. One could argue, however, that a rule has a "fuller" existence if it has both Geltung and efficacy than if it only has Geltung.

The question is whether it is possible for a rule to exist as an efficacious rule without having Geltung. At first glance, it seems it cannot. If a rule is not collectively recognized—either directly or indirectly—to generate deontic consequences, then it does not exist, at least it does not exist as a rule. It seems that the borderline of existence of an efficacious rule without Geltung is a rule that is called a rule and in that sense collectively recognized but that is obeyed purely out of fear of sanctions (for example, Mafia protection rules) and that is enforced not because either subjects or enforcers collectively recognize that the rule generates deontic consequences (the obligation to pay and the right to payment) but only because they recognize that enforcers are able to enforce the nondeontic (empirical) consequences (to collect money).

3 Soft Law, Validity, and Trust

3.1 Soft Law

Now that I have distinguished two concepts of validity and argued that Gültigkeit and Geltung should both be distinguished from existence and from social and legal efficacy, we can turn to the question in which sense soft law is or is not legally valid and why its validity matters. In this chapter, I restrict myself to a discussion of domestic soft law, more specifically codes of conduct for the judiciary.[14]

As a rough delineation, I take soft law to be:

1. systems of rules that are explicitly created and encoded, often in accordance with specific criteria,
2. by a body or person without the competence to create legal rules,
3. but that are nevertheless deemed or even intended to have some legal status and influence.

Soft law is like products of legislation in that it is created and encoded and is unlike custom that "grows" and that is unwritten or at least does not have an official rule formulation (criterion 1). What makes these rules soft is that—by definition—the organizations that create them do not have the competence to create legally binding rules (criterion 2). Stated differently, since soft law is explicitly created, often by a specific organ and in accordance with a specific procedure,[15] it can be gültig, but—by definition—it cannot be legally gültig. The reason that these rules are nevertheless qualified as law is that they are deemed or intended to have some legal effect and perhaps even have legal Geltung (criterion 3).

The reason I distinguish between deemed and intended effects is that whereas sometimes societal organizations create regulations at their own initiative (self-regulation), there are also situations in which the legislator legally obliges some body or organization to create guidelines, performance indicators, a code of conduct, or the like to regulate their own activities or those of others (conditional or rather enforced self-regulation). In the former case, soft law sometimes factually has legal

[14]In this chapter I ignore the phenomenon of international soft law.

[15]Compare the criteria of Gültigkeit discussed in Sect. 2.2.

effects and even legal Geltung; in the latter case, soft law is sometimes, but not always, even *intended* to have these legal effects. For example, the former Dutch Act on the Quality of Health Care Institutions (Kwaliteitswet Zorginstellingen, Kwz) obligated care providers to make and use quality systems and performance norms (section 4 Kwz).[16] Even though these performance norms were not legally gültig, they had legal relevance in that they were used to legally assess whether health care institutions have acted in accordance with section 2 Kwz, which obligated them to deliver good care.[17]

The creation of soft law is not restricted to societal organizations. Nowadays, even state organs create their own soft law or have soft law created for them. As with societal organizations, sometimes the legislator legally obliges state organs to create soft law. For example, the Dutch Municipalities Act (Gemeentewet, Gemw) both empowers and obliges municipal councils to make codes of conduct for the mayor and aldermen (section 41c subsection 2 Gemw) and for the municipal councillors (section 15 subsection 3 Gemw). These codes are meant to make the very general legal integrity rules of the General Administrative Law Act (Algemene Wet Bestuursrecht, Awb) and the Municipalities Act more concrete (section 2:4 Awb and sections 14 and 28 Gemw). It is generally agreed, however, that these codes do not legally bind the authorities and councilors. The rules are meant to play a role in guiding their behavior, in facilitating learning and reflection, and perhaps even in internal and informal critiques of their behavior. However, Doornhof and Munneke (2013) and Elzinga (2015), among others, argue that they cannot—as rules of the code—play a role in an official legal procedure against them.

Accordingly, these rules might be gültig (enacted by an authority according to its own procedure and without conflicting with more authoritative rules), but they are not legally gültig. Also, the rules are clearly intended to have social Geltung; more specifically, they are intended to create professional moral obligations, but they are not intended to have legal Geltung, i.e. to create legal obligations. Finally, the aim of these codes is that their rules are socially efficacious, i.e. that they guide behavior and that they are enforced by "soft," i.e. non-legal means. However, to the extent that they have no legal Geltung, it seems that they cannot be legally efficacious in that they are not enforced by legal means, e.g. by the executive power.

3.2 Validity

If soft law lacks both legal Gültigkeit and legal Geltung, what legal status and what legal influence can soft law nevertheless have? On one view, rules of soft law can at most play a role as factual evidence.

[16]From 1 January 2016 this Act has been replaced by the Act Quality, Complaints and Disputes (Wet kwaliteit klachten en geschillen zorg, Wkkgz).

[17]See Mackor (2010) on the legal status of these performance norms.

Again, take codes of conduct as an example. If a legal rule refers to social or professional rules or leaves room for its interpretation in terms of social or professional rules, then the fact that a particular rule is part of a code of conduct could be used as an indication or even as evidence for the truth of the claim that there is an unwritten rule that belongs to the customs of a certain field. On this approach, however, it would not be the rule of the code that is applied. It would instead be the unwritten rule of custom that is applied. Unlike created rules of soft law, rules of (professional) custom often have legal Geltung. Most legal systems recognize and enforce not only rules that belong to the system but also other rules, such as customary rules. The fact that there is an explicitly created rule of soft law with the same content as the unwritten rule of custom can at most be used as evidence for the Geltung of the customary rule with that content. On this view, soft law is at most a source of knowledge of (customary) law but not a source of law.

This claim differs from the claim that the rule of the code itself is applied as a rule simply because it (somehow) is gültig, because it belongs to the code of conduct, and because the code was created by a specific organization according to a specific procedure. This is not to say that this could never happen, on the contrary. Just like customary rules, rules of a code of conduct can become rules with legal Geltung.[18]

Raz (1979, p. 149), for example, argues that rules of private international law ensure that under specific conditions, even legal rules of foreign countries can have legal Geltung, i.e. be recognized in other countries as generating the legal consequences they claim to generate. In a similar way, there are legal rules for the recognition of the legal Geltung of customary rules. Also, it could be possible for legal systems to have legal rules for the recognition of encoded rules of soft law, but to my knowledge these rules do not exist, at least not in the Netherlands.

Of course, soft law can have legal Geltung through a contract that obliges the contracting parties to act in accordance with a particular piece of soft law. For example, Dutch Olympic sports (wo)men signed a contract for the Olympic Games 2016. Article 4 of this contract obliges them to act in accordance with the IOC Code of Ethics. Therewith to the extent that the contract has legal Geltung, the Code of Ethics will in principle have legal Geltung too. It seems, however, that

[18]For example, Dutch Regional Euthanasia Review Committees take into account whether physicians have followed medical guidelines when performing euthanasia. These guidelines do not play a role as rules with legal Geltung. They do not bind the committees and they are not mentioned as a reason in the decisions of the committees. There is one exception: the guideline with respect to the medically correct performance of the euthanasia (dealing among others with the kind and amount of drug to be used) is used as a binding rule and mentioned in the decision, but in a comply-or-explain manner. More on this example and on the legal status of medical guidelines in Mackor (2016b). Another example is the code of conduct of the Netherlands Bar Organization (Gedragsregels van de Orde van Advocaten). The rules of the code are used to interpret article 46 of the Act on Advocates (Advocatenwet). In most cases, however, Councils of Discipline do not refer to these rules. However, compare the decision of the Council of Discipline (Raad van Discipline) 25 January 2016 R. case number 4821/15.131. [Online]. [Accessed 22 February 2017]. Available from: http://tuchtrecht.overheid.nl/zoeken/resultaat/uitspraak/2016/ECLI_NL_TADRSGR_2016_9?DomeinNaam=advocaten&Pagina=2&ItemIndex=12.

contracts for mayor and aldermen, for municipal counselors, and a fortiori for judges that oblige them to act in accordance with soft law cannot have legal Geltung, i.e. not even if they sign a contract, because under the rule of law, members of the legislative, executive, and judicial powers can only be legally bound by hard law.

3.3 Validity and Trust

At this point, the reader and especially a nonphilosophical reader might wonder: what is the relevance of the validity of soft law and of the distinctions I have introduced? Does it matter whether a rule that does not have legal Gültigkeit is invoked as a rule and that it is nevertheless claimed to have legal Geltung, i.e. to generate legal consequences, or whether it is merely invoked as factual evidence for the existence of an unwritten customary rule with legal Geltung?

My answer to the question why we should care about validity in the first place is that it has practical relevance, especially for trust in the state and in state law. There are several reasons why validity seems to be important for trust and why lack of clarity about legal Gültigkeit and legal Geltung can undermine trust.[19]

Rule-Based Decision Making and Trust

First, as Raz (1979) has pointed out, rules function as reasons for behavior; more specifically, they function as exclusionary reasons. If a rule has legal Geltung, then—on the weak reading—normally all first-order reasons that would otherwise have been relevant and that could create deontic consequences or that could prevent deontic consequences from coming into existence should and will be left out.

Why would one prefer the application of rules to the use of primary reasons in decision making? Even though Schauer (1991) convincingly argues that rules have the well-known drawback that they can be over- and underinclusive, rule-based decision making[20] has several possible advantages over first-order reason-based decision making. Among others, it can facilitate stability, efficiency, coordination,

---

[19]There is no room to elaborate on the notion of trust. I follow Hardin (2004, p. 6) in understanding trust in terms of encapsulated interests. On this account A trusts that B will do x if A believes that B has reason to act in the interest of A or at least to take A's interests into account. The question thus is whether clarity about legal Gültigkeit and Geltung can affect the beliefs A has and the reasons B has. More on the relation between validity and trust in Mackor (2017).

[20]Note that I use the term rule-based decision making in the weak reading discussed earlier in Sect. 2.3, viz. that a geltende rule normally, but not without exception, generates its deontic consequences.

and clarity about the allocation of powers.[21] This is not to say that rule-based decision making is an advantage in all situations. For example, it can undermine trust in situations where there is a lot of personal and social understanding, and it can have adverse effects when people have a common interest and strive for the best overall result. However, decision making on the basis of gültige rules, which have been enacted and encoded, which thus clearly have Geltung and that have a more determinate content than rules that have no authoritative formulation, seems an advantage, among others, when people who deal with each other are relative strangers and thus have no shared understanding and when people disagree about almost everything except for the Geltung and the content of the applicable legal rules.

Rule of Law

The advantages of decision making based on gültige and geltende rules with a fairly precise content hold a fortiori for rules that constitute authorities and rules that empower those authorities. Some rules constitute and empower state organs that can create, change, abolish, and apply legal rules. Normally, these rules are accompanied by rules that determine the boundaries of the powers, the obligations that these authorities have, the supervision on the exercise of the powers, etc. It is characteristic of western state law that these rules are laid down in the highest and "hardest" part of state law, viz. the constitution and several other formal laws and international treaties. Therewith, they create not only certainty and efficiency but also clear restrictions on state powers.

If soft law becomes more important, not only in the regulation of nongovernmental organizations but also in the regulation of governmental organizations, this can undermine trust in several ways. It can undermine legal predictability and therewith reliance and efficiency, it can undermine coordination and stability, but most importantly it can undermine trust that the powers and obligations of the most powerful organizations of the state (legislator, executive, and judiciary) are well defined and therewith restricted.[22]

[21]Schauer (1991, pp. 135–166) discusses seven reasons why rule-based decision making can be preferable to (first-order) reason-based decision making, viz. fairness, reliance, efficiency, risk-aversion, stability, coordination and the allocation of powers.

[22]In this chapter I do not explore the ways in which soft law might strengthen trust. For example, a code might contribute indirectly to trust in state organs and officials if it positively affects the behavior of officials directly, thereby indirectly strengthening trust. I only deal with the question whether the unclear legal status of codes can directly contribute to undermining trust in the judiciary. More on this topic in Mackor (2017).

The Judiciary

Lack of clarity about powers and obligations is especially problematic when it comes to the judiciary. On the one hand, the judiciary is often called the least dangerous of the three state powers, among others because it depends on others to begin a case and to execute its decision.[23] On the other hand, the judiciary is powerful in that it is the only state power that does not only decide about the Gültigkeit and the Geltung and about the interpretation of the content of the rules that constitute and regulate the powers and obligations of nongovernmental organizations but also decides about the Gültigkeit, the Geltung, and the content of rules that constitute and regulate the legislative and the executive powers.

Most importantly—in the Netherlands at least—it also decides about the Gültigkeit and the Geltung and the content of rules that constitute and regulate its own powers and obligations. As Bovend'Eert and Kortmann (2013) (also see Mackor 2017) explicate, this shows most clearly from the fact that in the Netherlands, it is the judiciary and the judiciary alone that can decide whether an individual judge has violated a rule and whether disciplinary sanctions are in place. In other words, the judiciary is to a large extent its own supervisor, and it is the only power that can discipline individual judges. These are reasons why we want rules about the conduct of individual judges to be laid down in hard law and not in soft law, in particular not in soft law made by organs that do not have the legal obligation and competence to create these codes in the first place. Especially in the case of judges, it is dubious whether bodies other than the legislator should bind judges on matters closely related to the core of their work and who thus might affect their functional independence, i.e. their independence during the trial and in their decision making in individual cases.

4 The Legal Status of Dutch Codes of Conduct for the Judiciary

In this final section, I discuss a concrete case to illustrate the lack of clarity about the legal Geltung of soft law, more specifically of codes of conduct for the judiciary, and to illustrate how this lack of clarity is more likely to undermine than to enhance the trust of the population in the judiciary.

[23]In the famous words of Alexander Hamilton (2009, p. 368): "the judiciary, from the nature of its functions, will always be the least dangerous to the political rights of the Constitution; because it will be least in a capacity to annoy or injure them. ... it may truly be said to have neither force nor will, but merely judgment."

4.1 Two Codes of Conduct

The Dutch judiciary has two codes of conduct.[24] The judicial council (Rvdr), together with the Meeting of Presidents, created a code in 2010. The professional association of judges and public prosecutors (NVvR) created a code of conduct for judges in 2011.[25]

Bovend'Eert and Kortmann (2013, p. 812) points out that Dutch law has not created a legal obligation, let alone a legal power for either of these organizations or for any other organization to create a code of conduct for the judiciary (also see Mackor 2017). So the question arises, even more pressingly than with regard to the municipal codes mentioned earlier, what the legal status of these codes is. The question is more pressing because whereas in the last instance municipal councils do not and cannot decide about the Gültigkeit, Geltung, and content of their own codes, the judiciary must do so.

Surprisingly, Van Emmerik et al. (2014) state without any hesitation that the Rvdr code has Geltung since the judicial council and the Meeting of the Presidents of Courts have approved it.[26] They do not explicate whether the code has legal Geltung or (only) social Geltung, but they seem to suggest that the codes have "some kind of Geltung" because they are "sort of gültig" because they have been created by an official organization via an official procedure. However, elsewhere the same authors are more hesitant and state that a more deliberate choice must be made whether codes are created as hard or as soft law.[27]

It is often stated that codes of conduct are primarily meant to play a role in learning and reflection, in guiding judges in their behavior, and perhaps even in an internal and informal critique of their behavior and that they are not meant to discipline judges or to function as mandatory prescriptions. For example, on the NVvR website, it is explicitly stated that judicial guidelines are not prescriptions and that all judges and prosecutors must make their own decisions.[28] Unfortunately, the

---

[24]See Di Federico (2012) for an overview of codes of conduct for the judiciary in different countries.

[25]The existence of two codes is remarkable and seems to suggest some disagreement to say the least (see Mackor 2013b, 2014), especially since there are tensions between the Rdvr and a substantial number of judges.

[26]Van Emmerik et al. (2014, p. 23) state: "De Gedragscode Rechtspraak is in 2010 door de Raad voor de Rechtspraak en de Presidentenvergadering vastgesteld en *geldt* sinds 1 mei van dat jaar voor alle rechterlijke ambtenaren."

[27]Van Emmerik et al. (2014, p. 111) state: "Er moet gewaakt worden voor een 'wildgroei' aan leidraden en gedragscodes. De afweging welke normen in *hard law* dan wel *soft law* worden neergelegd, moet meer bewust worden gemaakt" (my emphasis, ARM). Note that they make this claim in a Research Memorandum of the very same judicial council that had created one of the codes.

[28]"De NVvR is de vereniging voor rechters en officieren van justitie in Nederland. In het belang van onze leden stellen wij leidraden op rondom dilemma's waar onze leden mee te maken kunnen krijgen. Deze leidraden kunnen onze leden helpen bij het nemen van hun eigen besluiten. *Deze leidraden zijn daarom géén voorschriften,* onze leden maken zelf hun afwegingen." (my emphasis,

NVvR code itself devotes only one sentence to its status, which states that a code is a guideline to create in judges awareness of the position and possible external influences.[29] In the code itself, however, the term guideline is not explained. Accordingly, to an outsider, but also to judges themselves, it is not clear what the legal status of the code is. This is especially problematic since the NVvR code is not created as an internal document only. On the contrary, it is presented to society at large, and it explicitly states that trust in the judiciary is essential in a democratic state, which is characterized by the rule of law, and that a code is not just for internal use but also a "billboard" for what society can expect of the judiciary as a body and of judges individually.[30]

In conclusion, we find that the NVvR code is a "billboard" that states that society can expect that a judge will conform to the norms of the code, but the code also states that these norms are guidelines, and the website of the NVvR states that guidelines do not bind the judge even though society can expect that judges will abide by these rules. For an outsider, but probably even for judges themselves, it is unclear whether the Rvdr code and the NVvR code are legally and/or socially gültig; whether they have social, let alone legal, Geltung; and whether they can play a role in an official legal procedure against a judge and, if so, in what way. Finally, since there is no evidence that the codes play a role in the professional lives of judges, they not only lack legal Gültigkeit, legal Geltung, and legal efficacy, but they also seem to lack social Geltung and social efficacy.[31]

ARM). [Online]. [Accessed 12 December 2015]. Available from: http://www.nvvr.org/bibliotheek-55.php?action=view&Content_Id=1605.

[29]The NVvR-code p. 1. states: "Dit document beoogt een *leidraad* te zijn om rechters te helpen zich bewust te zijn van hun positie in de samenleving en van de mogelijke interventies en invloeden van buiten." (my emphasis ARM). [Online]. [Accessed 4 August 2016]. Available from: http://www.nvvr.org/view.php?Pagina_Id=50.

[30]On p. 1 of the NVvR-code we find the following claim: "De rechterlijke macht vormt één van de pijlers van onze democratische rechtsstaat. De rechtspraak draagt bij aan de instandhouding van de rechtsstaat en het *vertrouwen* van de burger in het recht. Daarvoor is essentieel dat rechters blijvend *vertrouwen* en gezag genieten in de samenleving." On p. 2 it states: "Een gedragscode is . . . enerzijds van belang als spiegel voor het eigen functioneren van rechters en anderzijds als "uithangbord" van wat de *samenleving* van de rechtspraak en het functioneren van rechters *kan verwachten*." (my emphasis, ARM). [Online]. [Accessed 4 August 2016]. Available from: http://www.nvvr.org/view.php?Pagina_Id=50.

[31]As far as I know, there are no empirical investigations regarding the question whether judges have knowledge of the existence and content of the codes and whether the codes play any role in their professional lives. Based on informal conversations I have had with judges I hypothesize that the codes are not well known and that they do not play a role in their professional decision making.

4.2 A Legal Case

To illustrate how problematic the status of soft law is and to illustrate how likely it is that codes of conduct for the judiciary are more likely to undermine trust than to enhance it, I end with the analysis of a complaint case against an advocate general (AG) of the Dutch Supreme Court.[32]

Briefly, the case is as follows. The person who has filed a complaint about the behavior of an AG of the Supreme Court states, among other claims, that the AG has violated an article of the Rvdr code and an article of the NVvR code. First, the internal complaint procedure is followed, which implies that the complaint goes to the procurator general (PG) of the Supreme Court. The PG then creates a complaint-advice committee. This committee concludes that the complaint is admissible and well founded. Moreover, the committee explicitly states that the Rvdr code binds the AG.[33]

The PG rejects the view of the complaint committee. He states that the AG has not violated the rules of the Rvdr code and the NVvR code.[34] The PG does not discuss, and possibly deliberately leaves undecided, whether these two rules legally bind the AG. A fortiori, he does not answer the question whether the rules bind the AG as rules of these two codes or whether only unwritten customary professional rules (which have roughly the same content as the codified rules) have legal Geltung. In other words, is the code merely evidence for the existence of rules with legal Geltung, or do the rules of the code themselves have legal Geltung?

In the external complaint procedure that follows, the Supreme Court decides that there are rules that bind judges and then states that the articles of the Rvdr code and the NVvR code are illustrative of the content of these rules.[35] In other words, the

[32]In the Netherlands, the PG and the AG's of the Supreme Court are not judges. However, unlike public prosecutors of Courts and Courts of Appeal, they are not part of the Public Prosecution but members of the Judiciary which guarantees more (functional) independence.

[33]ECLI:NL:HR:2014:510, sub 3.: "De Gedragscode wordt door het parket van de Hoge Raad onderschreven en betrokkene is, als lid van dat parket, *gehouden zich daaraan te houden*." (My emphasis, ARM). [Online]. [Accessed 6 July 2017]. Available from: https://uitspraken.rechtspraak.nl/inziendocument?id=ECLI:NL:HR:2014:510&keyword=ECLI%3ANL%3AHR%3A+2014%3A510.

[34]ECLI:NL:HR:2013:2665 sub 5.4: "Voorts was ik van oordeel dat betrokkene *niet heeft gehandeld in strijd met* de in artikel 2.5.4. van de NVvR-rechtscode of de in artikel 7 van de Gedragscode Rechtspraak *neergelegde* gedragsnorm... " (My emphasis, ARM). [Online]. [Accessed 6 July 2017]. Available from: https://uitspraken.rechtspraak.nl/inziendocument?id=ECLI:NL:PHR:2013:2665.

[35]ECLI:NL:HR:2014:510, sub 5.3: "De 'uitoefening van de functie' omvat ook de naleving van de normen die zien op het publieke gedrag van de rechterlijk ambtenaar. Over de niet-naleving van deze normen, voor de inhoud waarvan art. 7 van de Gedragscode Rechtspraak en art. 2.5.4 van de NVvR-rechterscode *illustratief* zijn, kan op voet van art. 13a RO worden geklaagd." (My emphasis, ARM). [Online]. [Accessed 6 July 2017]. Available from: https://uitspraken.rechtspraak.nl/inziendocument?id=ECLI:NL:HR:2014:510&keyword=ECLI%3ANL%3AHR%3A+2014%3A510.

Supreme Court follows the path I sketched earlier, viz. that codes are not legally gültig and do not have legal Geltung and that their existence is merely a fact that can at most point to the existence of unwritten professional rules that do have legal Geltung. The Supreme Court puts even less weight on the existence of the codes than I suggested. The codes are not evidence or an indication; according to the Supreme Court, they are only an illustration of their content.

When we compare the explications of the complaint-advice committee, the PG, and the Supreme Court, the solution that the Supreme Court has chosen is to be preferred because it seems to best fit the demands of the rule of law I discussed in Sect. 3. However, we can doubt whether this sophisticated construction is understandable and convincing to a nonphilosophical "average" citizen who learns that he cannot legally appeal to a rule despite the fact that it has been created as part of the "billboard" for society and that it is supposed to bind judges. As a consequence, I doubt whether the codes are likely to contribute to "the" trust of "the" society in "the" judiciary.[36]

5 Conclusion

I conclude that either the legal power of organs to create codes for the judiciary should be laid down in "hard" law or these organs should be much more explicit about the reason why their codes do not, cannot, and should not have legal Geltung, viz. because that would be an illegal interference with their institutional and functional independence. Therefore, such codes should also not be presented as external "billboards" for society.

My more general conclusion is that we should not think too lightly about creating soft law, that we should be especially critical about creating soft law for state organs, especially for state organs such as the judiciary, which, at least in states that adhere to the rule of law, must be independent and should only be bound by rules that have legal Geltung, either because they are legally gültig or because they are part of legal customary law. To create a third type of rules that are deemed or intended to have some legal effect but that lack legal Gültigkeit and legal Geltung will only create confusion, as the legal case cited shows.

References

Bovend'Eert, P.P.T., and C.A.J.M. Kortmann. 2013. *Rechterlijke organisatie, rechters en rechtspraak*. Deventer: Kluwer.

[36]See Mackor (2017) for a more extensive discussion of the question whether codes of conduct can contribute to trust.

Di Federico, G. 2012. Judicial Accountability and Conduct: An Overview. In *Judicial Independence in Transition*, ed. A. Seibert-Fohr, 87–118. Heidelberg, New York, Dordrecht, London: Springer.

Doornhof, H., and S.A.J. Munneke. 2013. De gedragscode voor raadsleden gewogen . . . en te licht bevonden, *Gemeentestem* 2013/118.

Elzinga, D.J. 2015. Gedragscodes kunnen wet en Grondwet uithollen, *Gemeentestem* 2015/130.

Hage, J.C. 1984. Enkele opmerkingen over geldigheid en gelding. *Algemeen Nederlands Tijdschrift voor Wijsbegeerte* 76 (4): 262–266.

Hamilton, A. 2009. *The Federalist Papers*. New York, 1787. The project Gutenberg EBook, 2009.

Hardin, R. 2004. Distrust: Manifestations and Management. In *Distrust*, ed. R. Hardin, 3–33. New York: Russell Sage Foundation.

Hart, H.L.A. 1961. *The Concept of Law*. Oxford: Clarendon Press.

Mackor, A.R. 2010. Legally Enforced Performance Measurement of Public Services. Crowding-out or Crowding-in of Motivation? *Legisprudence* 4 (3): 227–248.

———. 2012. Legal Doctrine as a Non-normative Discipline. A Refinement of Niiniluoto's and Aarnio's Distinction Between Norm-descriptions, Norm-contentions and Norm-recommendations. *Recht & Methode* 2 (1): 22–45.

———. 2013a. Law as an Abstract Object, Law as an Empirical Object: The Relevance of Ontology and Epistemology for Theories of Legislation. *The Theory and Practice of Legislation* 1 (3): 441–468.

———. 2013b. Gevaarlijke' zinsneden en autonomie. Drie stellingen naar aanleiding van de NVvR Rechterscode. *Trema* 36 (2): 61–65.

———. 2014. Rechterlijke macht: geschraagd of ondermijnd door kernwaarden? *Rechtsgeleerd Magazijn Themis* 175 (1): 6–9.

———. 2016a. Legal Doctrine Is a Non-normative Discipline: An Argument from Abstract Object Theory. In *Facts and Norms in Law: Interdisciplinary Reflections on Legal Method*, ed. S. Taekema, B. Van Klink, and W. De Been, 127–149. Cheltenham: Edward Elgar Publishing.

———. 2016b. Rechtsregels en medische richtlijnen. Een rechtsfilosofisch perspectief op de aard en functie van regels. In *Medische aansprakelijkheid*, ed. S. Heiman, E.C. Huijsmans, and R. Van den Munckhof, 19–40. Oisterwijk: Wolf Legal Publishers.

———. 2017. Rechterlijke gedragscodes. Over hun juridische status en het vertrouwen in de rechtspraak. In *De wisselwerking tussen recht en vertrouwen bij toezicht en handhaving*, ed. H.D. Tolsma and P. De Winter, 87–110. Den Haag: Boom Juridisch.

Munzer, S. 1973. Validity and Legal Conflicts. *The Yale Law Journal* 82 (6): 1140–1174.

Raz, J. 1979. *The Authority of Law*. Oxford: Oxford University Press.

Schauer, F. 1991. *Playing by the Rules*. Oxford: Clarendon Press.

Searle, J. 1995. *The Construction of Social Reality*. London: The Penguin Press.

———. 2010. *Making the Social World*. Oxford: Oxford University Press.

Van Emmerik, M., J.-P. Loof, and Y. Schuurmans. 2014. *Systeemwaarborgen voor de kernwaarden van de rechtspraak*. Een onderzoek in opdracht van de Raad voor de Rechtspraak. Research Memorandum 10(2).

A Fuller Understanding of Legal Validity and Soft Law

Bart van Klink and Oliver W. Lembcke

Abstract Soft law appears to be the "bastard child" of law. Because of its dubious origin, soft law is not officially recognized, in positivist conceptions of law, as legally valid law. At the same time, the legal relevance of soft law is hard to deny. Soft law does generate rights and duties that the parties at hand, and even sometimes state officials, perceive as legally binding. How to make sense of soft law? Is it law or nonlaw, or something in between, law that is emerging or not yet law? Is it really soft and, if so, in what sense? In this chapter, two different approaches to legal validity and soft law will be confronted with each other. Firstly, we will present Kelsen's conception of legal validity, which still is one of the prevailing positivist conceptions and very close to the traditional lawyer's internal perspective on law. Secondly, we will discuss the interactionist theory of legal validity, as developed by Lon L. Fuller. Finally, the two opposing approaches will be compared and evaluated. Building on an interactionist approach, we will explore how we can account for the legal relevance of soft law, without rejecting it all too easily as nonlaw.

1 Of Dubious Origin

One of the haunting questions in the study of law is how to establish that something in the world of fact—e.g., a claim, a decision, or an act—may count as law. How do we know that it is really law? This is the fundamental question of the validity of law. It is not merely a theoretical problem; it has practical relevance too. If we can demonstrate that a certain claim (or a decision or an act) is legally valid, legally

B. van Klink (✉)
Vrije Universiteit Amsterdam, Department of Legal Theory and Legal History, Amsterdam, The Netherlands
e-mail: b.van.klink@vu.nl

O. W. Lembcke
Faculty of Public Affairs and Governance, Erfurt University, Erfurt, Germany
e-mail: oliver.lembcke@uni-jena.de

© Springer International Publishing AG, part of Springer Nature 2018

P. Westerman et al. (eds.), *Legal Validity and Soft Law*, Law and Philosophy Library 122, https://doi.org/10.1007/978-3-319-77522-7_7

binding consequences follow from it. A valid contract, for instance, is binding for the parties involved. If one party does not comply with its terms, the other party is entitled to require the court to enforce it. By contrast, when the contract is not legally valid, the parties have no legal duty to follow it, and therefore they cannot be compelled to do so by the court. According to Raz (1979, p. 153), "[a] rule of law is valid if and only if it has the normative consequences it purports to have." In his view, legal validity presupposes membership and enforceability. A rule is legally valid "if and only if it is valid because it belongs to a legal system in force in a certain country or is enforceable in it" (*ibid.*). A rule that is not a member of a certain legal system is enforceable within that system if the rule is a member of a foreign legal system and is recognized as legally valid within one's own system, for instance when a marriage contracted abroad is recognized as a valid marriage. In that case, however, it has to be demonstrated that the applicable rule or rules belong to the foreign legal system. So membership appears to be crucial for determining legal validity, either as a *sufficient* condition when it comes to rules internal to a legal system or as a *necessary* condition in the case of rules imported from another legal system. A rule is a legally valid rule if it can be shown that it belongs to a legal system, consisting of rules that are already recognized as legally valid.

Ultimately, it is the law itself that determines which facts create law. As Kelsen claims, law takes care of its own reproduction (see Sect. 2). In current, positivist conceptions of legal validity, the source of the rule is decisive. According to Raz (1979, p. 153), "every law has a source."[1] The origin of the rule, where it comes from and by whom it is created, determines whether it may count as law. Problems arise when the source of the rule cannot be determined clearly or is not recognized by the law. In the shadow of the formal law, and sometimes outside it, informal regulations emerge in social interaction the legal status of which is contested or indeterminate. This is the domain of what is often, very loosely, called "soft law." As Westerman (2007b, p. 69) argues, "[a]ll kinds of 'soft law': brochures, informative communications, general guidelines and conclusions suffer from the problem that their legal status is unclear." In her view, the formal law is increasingly supplemented and supplanted by various types of informal regulation such as private lawmaking, different varieties of self-regulation, codes, and certificates. Rules originating from informal regulation do not count as law because "they are not established, applied and enforced in ways that are described and defined by the legal system itself" (Westerman 2013, p. 389). Though not "real" law or really law, soft law seems to be legally relevant since it is closely connected to official law in various ways. For instance, it supports the functioning of an official legal system by clarifying or specifying formal legal rules or by promoting some general policy goal. In this way, soft law figures as an uninvited and uneasy companion to official law.

Soft law appears to be the "bastard child" of law. Because of its dubious origin, soft law is not officially recognized, in positivist conceptions of law, as legally valid law. At the same time, the legal relevance of soft law is hard to deny. Soft law does

[1]This is the so-called "sources thesis."

generate rights and duties that the parties at hand, and even sometimes state officials, perceive as legally binding. How to make sense of soft law? Is it law or nonlaw, or something in between, law that is emerging or not yet law? Is it really soft and, if so, in what sense? In this chapter, two different approaches to legal validity and soft law will be confronted with each other. Firstly, we will present Kelsen's conception of legal validity, which still is one of the prevailing positivist conceptions and very close to the traditional lawyer's internal perspective on law (Sect. 2). Secondly, we will discuss the interactionist theory of legal validity, as developed by Lon L. Fuller (Sect. 3). Albeit Fuller does not provide a litmus test for law (and never pretended to), his approach offers a serious challenge to the mainstream understanding of legal validity. Thirdly, we will apply the two competing conceptions of legal validity to soft law (Sect. 4). On what grounds does Kelsen, as can be expected, dismiss soft law for the most part as nonlaw and not legally relevant? And how could Fuller's interactionist theory make a very different appreciation possible of both hard and soft law? Finally, the two opposing approaches will be compared and evaluated (Sect. 5). Building on an interactionist approach, we will explore how we can account for the legal relevance of soft law, without rejecting it all too easily as nonlaw.

2 A Positivist Conception of Validity

Among positivist conceptions of legal validity, Kelsen's approach occupies an exceptional position. Whereas in most positivist conceptions a *factual* state of affairs or regularity has to account for the validity of law—for instance, certain rules are generally conceived in society as legal rules (legal realism) or the majority of judges within a legal system have accepted its rule of recognition (Hart)[2]—Kelsen tries to construe a *normative* base for legal validity. In his normativist approach, the state constitutes the Archimedean point from which norms can objectively be perceived as legal norms.[3] According to Kelsen (1973, p. 197), the state is "the personification of a legal order." He considers the state to be a "special form of society," "social unity," or a "legal organization" to which all legal norms can be traced back, whether they are produced by state officials, by members of an association, or by individual citizens. Irrespective of how they are created and by whom they are created, legal norms owe their validity to the state and not to society. Taken together, the legal norms of a given legal order build a hierarchical structure (or *Stufenbau*), consisting of different levels of norms and norm applications, starting from the basic norm, moving down to statutes, governmental regulations, court decisions, contracts, and

[2]In *The Concept of Law*, Hart offers two different interpretations of the rule of recognition (see Dyzenhaus 1999, pp. 80 ff.). The first comes very close to the legal realist conception of legal validity, according to which most people in society have to accept the rule of recognition. In the second, more widespread interpretation, only the majority of the judges have to.

[3]This section is to a large extent based on Van Klink and Lembcke (2016, pp. 209–216), with only minor additions and alterations.

so on and ending in the factual execution of a legal command (e.g., the imprisonment of a criminal by a prison officer; see Kelsen 1970, pp. 221 ff.). Because the norms belonging to a given legal order owe their validity ultimately to the basic norm, the basic norm brings unity to the diversity of existing norms. This unity makes it possible to describe the legal order at hand as a coherent set of legal sentences that do not contradict each other (Kelsen 1970, pp. 205–208).

With his pure theory of law, Kelsen intends to offer a critical-scientific conception of law that, purified of metaphysical and empirical references, safeguards the autonomy of law. He seeks to provide a solid scientific foundation for the science of law in order to secure its position among the other sciences, in particular the natural sciences that threaten to become the dominant and only acceptable form of "true" science. For that purpose, the question has to be answered what is typical or unique about the way the science of law understands its object and how it differs from other understandings. Building on the neo-Kantian axiom that in the humanities is and ought are strictly separated,[4] Kelsen (1922, p. 75) argues that the phenomenon of law can be studied from two different perspectives: either how it ought to be (*Sollen*) or how it is (*Sein*). These two perspectives correspond to two different disciplines from which law can be studied: respectively, a *normative* science of law that establishes deductively which rules are valid and an *explanatory* sociology of law that determines inductively a certain regularity for which it tries to find a causal explanation. Thus, in Kelsen's view, the science of law is a normative and deductive science of value, like ethics and logic. However, as a normative science, the science of law does not prescribe what ought to be law but only describes what, according to the conditions set in the law itself, has to count as law. In other words, it is only concerned with the "Is of Ought" (or *Sein des Sollens*). On the other hand, the sociology of law, like other branches of sociology, is a science of reality and conforms more generally to the methodological practices of the natural sciences. It is equally possible and legitimate to study law from both perspectives but not at the same time. According to Kelsen, it is the aim of the science of law to describe the set of valid legal norms in a certain territory at a certain time, irrespective of their ethical value and empirical effects.

Following the dichotomy of facts and norms, Kelsen argues that the validity of law can only be established on normative grounds. In his view, as indicated earlier, a norm is a valid legal norm if it can be demonstrated that a higher legal norm has authorized the creation of this norm on a lower level in the hierarchy of norms that builds the legal system. Ultimately, all legal norms belonging to the same legal system can be traced back to the basic norm. The basic norm holds that all norms that follow from the historically first constitution of a legal order are legal norms. It is a "hypothesis" or "assumption" that makes the scientific description of law in the form of legal sentences possible. Kelsen does not deny that the law may draw its norms from various non-legal sources, such as morality, religion, or custom. However, these norms are not legal norms because religion, morality, or custom dictates them

[4]On the influence of the neo-Kantian epistemology on Kelsen, see Dreier (1990, pp. 56–90).

but because they can be validated by reference to other, and higher, legal norms and, ultimately, to the basic norm. From a legal perspective, as Kelsen (1922, p. 100) claims, it does not matter at all where law derives its content from. Customary law is often said to be based on both *usus* and *opinio necessitatis*. However, mere custom cannot explain why customary law is law, nor can it explain the belief in its legally binding character. From the fact that something used to be done or is expected to be done, it does not follow logically that this should be done. This presupposes the existence of a higher, authorizing legal norm that prescribes or permits the inclusion of law from custom in the interpretation or application of (formal) law.

Kelsen strictly distinguishes the validity of law from its efficacy. In his view, legal norms are valid *as long as* the legal system to which they belong is, by and large, effective but *not because* of its effectiveness. In other words, the efficacy of the legal system is a *conditio per quam* and not a *conditio sine qua non* for the law's validity (see also Dreier 1990, p. 122). If one makes the validity of law dependent on the social acceptance of the norms by the majority of people in society, as in legal realism, one could only establish retroactively that a norm is a legal norm. It is very difficult, if not impossible, to prove scientifically that a norm has been accepted by the majority. In fact, as Kelsen argues, the presumption of social acceptance is a fiction, which, in its turn, is based on the fiction that people know the law, which in most cases is obviously not the case. If the validity of law were to depend on social acceptance, the science of law could no longer fulfill its task of describing the legal system as a unified whole because the various legal norms may be accepted to different degrees by different people. Moreover, actors in legal practice, such as judges, must have an objective criterion to identify the law, not some subjective psychological notion.

In sum, legal validity, in Kelsen's view, is a dichotomous concept: either there is law or there is not. In order to establish whether a norm is a legal norm, a higher norm must be identified that authorizes the creation of this norm on a lower level of the legal system, which, in its turn, is validated by reference to an even higher legal norm and so on—until finally the basic norm is reached, which closes and unifies the legal system.

3 An Interactionist Conception of Validity

3.1 Legislation

In positivist conceptions of legal validity, a strict distinction is made between is and ought. In *The Law in Quest of Itself*, Fuller (1966, p. 34) writes: "Basically the quest of positivism is for some test which will designate plainly the law that is and distinguish it from the law that is merely becoming or merely ought to be." This test could be provided, for instance, by the presupposition of the basic norm (Kelsen) or the acceptance of the rule of recognition by the majority of judges (Hart). Fuller (1966, p. 11) does not believe that such a clear-cut test is possible since he rejects the strict is-ought distinction underlying it: "In the field of purposive human activity, which includes both steam engines and the law, value and being are not two different things, but two aspects of an integral reality." If we acknowledge that law is a purposive activity, as Fuller (1966, p. 14) does, then we have to accept that there are no "neat antinomies." The distinction between law and nonlaw is a gradual affair that involves, in his view, considerations of both efficacy and legitimacy. According to Rundle (2012, p. 79), "the provision of a clear formula for legal validity was not and was never claimed to be a natural starting point for Fuller's jurisprudence, nor its end-game." Fuller never argued, however, that a positivist, source-based standard of legal validity should be rejected completely. It may be seen, therefore, that he only intended to supplement this standard with the basic requirements of legal form, constituting the so-called internal morality of law (see further below). In this reading, Fuller offers a two-step analysis of the notion of legal validity, which Rundle (2012, p. 83) characterizes as "positivism plus form": under normal conditions, a positivist test of validity is applicable, unless some basic requirements of legal form are grossly violated. In Rundle's view, this reading is at odds with Fuller's general conception of law. As Fuller (1969, p. 211) repeatedly stresses, the main task of law is to provide citizens with "a sound and stable framework for their interactions." Law has to show respect for human agency, that is, it should support the aims and aspirations of citizens and treat them as agents in their own right and not as slaves or property. So the requirements of legal form are not merely an additional standard for extreme cases, but they apply to law always, in every instance.[5]

In *The Morality of Law*, Fuller demonstrates, by means of the famous parable of King Rex, various ways in which the legislator may fail to make law. From this negative example, he draws eight requirements that the legislator ought to respect when making law; in short, (1) there must be rules (the requirement of generality); (2) laws must be made known to the public; (3) laws should, in principle, be prospective and not be applied retroactively; (4) laws should be clear and (5) devoid of contradictions; (6) they should not require impossible things from citizens; (7) the legal system has to provide for stability, so laws should not be changed frequently; and (8) there has to be a congruence between official action and declared rule (Fuller 1969, pp. 33–94). These requirements contain principles predominantly of a formal or procedural nature. That is, they do not prescribe what the content of the law should be but only prescribe how the law—whatever its content is—has to be phrased, promulgated, executed, and so on. However, this does not imply, as Fuller (1969, p. 153) argues, that "*any* substantive aim might be adopted without compromise of legality." Moreover, he sees a connection between the formal justice that law offers and substantive justice: "legal morality cannot live when it is severed from a striving toward justice and decency" (cited in Rundle 2012, p. 71). The eight

---

[5]Crowe (2014) also subscribes to this second, "moral" reading and rejects the first, "positivism plus form" reading which he wrongly believes Rundle is supporting. As Rundle (2012, p. 83) argues, "it is clear that, in his [i.e. Fuller's] jurisprudence, law's formal health is a matter that should always be kept in the picture, and not just raised as a concern in the extreme case."

requirements follow both from practical considerations of efficacy and moral considerations. If they are violated, firstly, the law cannot do its job of regulating the interactions of citizens (efficacy). Secondly, it shows no respect for the citizen's capacity of agency (legitimacy). So, contrary to what Hart and others have claimed, the internal morality of law consists in more than just some functional requirements that promote the efficacy of the law. Fuller would deny that law is compatible with "great iniquity."[6] In his view, "law is a precondition of good law" (Fuller 1969, p. 155).

As Rundle (2012, p. 89) argues, "[a] total failure to meet any of these principles does not simply result in a bad system of law, but in something 'that is not properly called a legal system at all.'"[7] In this "moral" reading of Fuller's conception of legal validity (Gur 2014, p. 90), the internal morality of law is a means to assess whether some self-acclaimed instance of legislation really is law. However, it does not offer and does not pretend to offer a clear-cut test that can distinguish in a simple and unequivocal way law from nonlaw. It is no "checklist" but a set of principles that can be observed to a greater or lesser degree. For the most part, they belong to the "morality of aspiration"; the only exception is the second requirement of publication, which constitutes a duty (Fuller 1969, pp. 5 ff.). Westerman (1999, p. 66; original italics) draws an analogy with language: "If we think of law as similar to language and of lawmaking as similar to writing, as a dynamic and tentative enterprise which can sometimes be routinized but more often not, it becomes clear that Fuller's requirements can be better understood as guidelines that *range from simple grammar rules to stylistic requirements*." As a consequence, law becomes a gradual concept. According to Fuller, law may consist of rules that are in the process of becoming law, for instance, when their norm content becomes more and more clear. Moreover, law may consist partly of legal rules and partly of something that is not properly called law because it completely denies the possibility of human agency (as in the case of Nazi law according to Fuller (see also Rundle 2012, p. 81)). It is never a black-and-white matter, but it requires an evaluation based on the eight principles of the internal morality of law, which have a practical as well as a moral quality.

3.2 Other Forms of Social Regulation

The previous considerations pertain in particular to one form of social regulation, namely legislation, or the official law created and enforced by the state. Against Kelsen and other positivists, Fuller argues that law is no closed, unified, and hierarchical system of legal norms. Moreover, it does not have to emanate from

[6]According to Hart, as cited in Rundle (2012, p. 71).

[7]This is the so-called "strong natural law thesis," to be distinguished from the "soft natural law thesis," defended by Murphy, Finnis and others, according to which "a rationally defective norm or system is merely legally defective" (Crowe 2014, p. 115).

the state. In his interactionist understanding, law consists of sets of rules (formal and informal) that emerge from and are developed in social practice, sustaining and supporting this practice and serving its general purpose. Rules created in the field of academic education, for example, may count as law if they—among other things—contribute to the dissemination of knowledge and the creation of critical minds. In the essays collected in *The Principles of Social Order* by Kenneth I. Winston, Fuller explores various forms of social regulation, as part of his unfinished project called "eunomics," or "the science, theory, or study of good order and workable social arrangements" (Fuller 1981, p. 62). Besides legislation or "officially declared law," he mentions various "principles of social ordering," among which adjudication, mediation, contract, and managerial direction.[8] In his introduction, Winston (1981, p. 27) refers to these five principles as "legal processes." However, it can be questioned whether, in Fuller's view, managerial direction can be conceived as a legal process (or principle). In *The Morality of Law*, Fuller (1969, pp. 207–211) makes a fundamental distinction between two forms of social ordering: law on the one hand and managerial direction on the other hand.[9] Managerial direction consists of detailed regulations aimed at achieving objectives set by a superior, which the subordinates are expected to follow. Law posits, instead of a strict hierarchy, a relation of reciprocity between the law giver and the subject. It enables citizens to pursue their own goals within the boundaries of the law. In Fuller's view, "law furnishes a baseline for self-directed action, not a detailed set of instructions for accomplishing specific objectives" (Fuller 1969, p. 221).[10] In *The Principles of Social Order*, a similar distinction is made between two types of association and their corresponding principles: association by reciprocity, dedicated to the "legal principle," and association to achieve common aims, based on the principle of "shared commitment" (Fuller 1981, p. 71). At the same time, Fuller (1981, p. 212) offers a rather broad definition of law:

> I mean the word *law* to be construed very broadly. I intend it to include not only the legal systems of states and nations, but also the smaller systems – at least "law-like" in structure and function – to be found in labor unions, professional associations, clubs, churches, and universities.

The distinction between law and managerial direction becomes less absolute, when indeed these "smaller systems" are included in the definition of law, since they are usually structured hierarchically around a common aim. In churches, for instance, the shared purpose is to live in accordance with God's will, and religious leaders may issue specific directions to members of the religious community for achieving this purpose. In order to solve this tension, we have to assume—following

[8]For the complete list, see Fuller (1981, pp. 170–171).

[9]Oakeshott (1999) makes a similar, if not identical distinction between *nomocracy*, i.e. a civil association based on noninstrumental rules (such as the Rule of Law), and *teleocracy*, i.e. an enterprise association in which the members pursue the same goal (such as a business company or a church).

[10]For a more detailed analysis of this distinction, see Postema (1999, pp. 271–275).

Fuller's general line of thought—a continuum: at one end, there is law consisting of general rules that respect individual freedom and human agency, and, at the other end, there is managerial direction, which, by issuing concrete orders, reduces the subject's capacity to act of her own accord to a minimum.

Another principle of social order, which Fuller (1981, p. 170) discusses at some length, is "the coordination of expectations and actions that arises tacitly out of interaction." The law that arises from social interaction can be called "implicit law." Implicit law is the product of conduct and not, like legislation, of deliberate creation. As Postema (1999, p. 257; original italics) argues, "implicit rules are not mere *regularities* of the behavior in view; they are *rules* for that behavior." A well-known example of implicit law is customary law. Fuller repeatedly insists that he is not very happy with the concept of customary law and the way it is usually treated in legal doctrine. He characterizes customary law as a "language of interaction," "consisting of the reciprocal expectations that arise out of human interaction" (Fuller 1981, p. 176). According to Fuller (1981, p. 219), customary law creates obligations, not through mere custom or repetition but because mutual expectations have settled themselves in social practice: "a sense of obligation will arise when a stabilization of interactional expectancies has occurred so that the parties have come to guide their conduct toward one another by these expectancies."[11] As a language of interaction, customary law has to be interpreted, just like the words of a contract. It is, however, often quite difficult to establish whether an obligation arises from an act or a series of acts. Fuller (1981, p. 226) calls this "the most crucial and most neglected problem of customary law." The notion of *opinio necessitatis* is not very helpful in solving this problem: either it constitutes a tautology, when customary law has established itself or, in the case that customary law is still in the process of emerging, it offers no guidance. Due to the rise of the nation-state, customary law is no longer conceived as a primary source of law. What legal doctrine fails to see, in Fuller's view, is that customary law is still relevant, even in a (post-)Westphalian legal order. Official law is permeated with customary practices that "enable it to function effectively by facilitating a collaboration among its constituent elements" (Fuller 1981, p. 177). So customary law is not just a secondary source of law; it contributes to the functioning of the official legal system. More precisely, the relation between customary and enacted law is one of mutual dependence (Fuller 1981, p. 246):

> When we view the matter in this light it becomes apparent that in complex modern society enacted law and the organizational principles implicit in customary law are not simply to be viewed as alternative ways of ordering men's interactions, but rather as often serving to supplement each other by a kind of natural division of labor.

[11]In this respect, Fuller's understanding of customary law adds a valuable insight to Jellinek's notion of the "normative force of the factual": a mere regularity in social interaction does not in itself have a normative force, but the *expectations* that arise from social interaction do. More specifically, people expect that a certain regularity will occur again and *has to* occur again. In order words, the regularity is turned into a rule governing their interactions. For a discussion of Jellinek's notion, see Van Klink and Lembcke (2016, pp. 207–209).

Within his unfinished project of "eunomics," Fuller had not developed a conception of validity applicable to the law created in or arising from the various forms of social regulation. He does not spell out, as he did with legislation, what requirements or principles the other forms of social regulation have to follow. So no description can be found of the ways in which, for instance, parties may fail to make a contract, a judge reaches a conclusion unlawfully or people unjustly appeal to an expectation established in custom. However, building on his work, we may find some indications of the parameters along which such a conception might be construed. Three of the main parameters will be discussed here briefly. To begin with, there can be no general conception of legal validity that can be applied to all forms of social regulation. A conception of legal validity should be adapted to a specific form of social regulation and customized to the particularities of the regulation at hand. For example, as Fuller (1981, p. 94) argues, adjudication must be based on sound reasoning, more than any other kind of regulation[12]:

> Adjudication is, then, a device which gives formal and institutional expression to the influence of reasoned argument in human affairs. As such it assumes a burden of rationality not borne by any other form of social ordering. A decision which is the product of reasoned argument must be prepared itself to meet the test of reason.

There may be some overlap between the principles governing the various forms of social regulation, though. For instance, the requirement of clarity applies not only to legislation but also to the language used in court decisions and contracts. Subsequently, the requirements that law has to meet within the various kinds of regulation are not only of a practical or technical nature but also have a moral dimension. Obviously, the law that is created in or arises from various kinds of regulation has to contribute to the well-functioning of a specific legal system (either the "big" system of the official law or some smaller system, such as that of a university or a church) in order to sustain what Fuller would call a "good order" and "workable social arrangements" (as quoted above). Moreover, and more importantly, since law is a purposive activity, it has to serve law's basic moral purpose "to furnish a baseline for self-directed action" (*ibid.*). That means, in general terms, that the law has to respect the possibility of human agency and thus has to treat people as agents in their own right. In *Law in Quest of Itself*, Fuller (1966, p. 133) indicates that, except for legislation, is and ought can never be strictly separated when establishing what has to count as law. In adjudication, for instance, the judge will decide what the law is drawing on what she believes the law ought to be.[13] According to Fuller (1966, p. 137), "[t]he judge in deciding cases is not merely laying down a system of

---

[12]For a discussion of this requirement, see Van Klink (2016).

[13]According to the Dutch legal scholar Paul Scholten, a legal decision has to be intuitively right as well as compatible with the legal sources: "We always search for both: intuitively a decision which we deem 'juist' (rightful) because it satisfies our understanding about what actually ought to be done in this case, [and] intellectually a justification of the decision in terms of authoritative sources." Available at: http://www.paulscholten.eu/research/article/english/, p. 161 (last checked on 1 September 2016).

minimum restraints designed to keep the bad man in check, but is in fact helping to create a body of common morality which will define the good man." Finally, although the conditions for legal validity will inevitably vary, it will always be a matter of gradual assessment to what extent the law at hand meets the practical and moral requirements specific for a form of social regulation. That means that a given instance of regulation can be, to a greater or lesser extent, law or "law-like."

4 Soft Law Revisited

4.1 The Positivist Rejection of Soft Law

Whereas Fuller's interactionist approach allows for gradual assessment, in positivist conceptions of law, such as Kelsen's, legal validity is a matter of all or nothing. Either a specific regulation is law or it is not law, and nothing in between. One could argue, in system-theoretical terms, that the positivist conception of law is a product of the functional differentiation of society: society is fragmented into a great variety of systems, among which is the legal system, which produces and reproduces its own code (see, e.g., Luhmann 1995, chapter 2). The binary code of law, operating with a strict opposition between legal and illegal, does not allow for exceptions and indeterminacies. Within this logic, soft law appears to be an anomaly or just a nonentity. In order to establish the existence of law, one has to find, in Kelsen's pure theory, a higher legal norm that authorizes the creation of the norms under discussion. In the case of soft law, a higher authorizing legal norm will usually be absent. As Westerman indicates (see Sect. 1), soft law is not enacted according to the internal procedures prescribed by the legal system. Otherwise, if these internal procedures were followed, the norms or set of norms would not be soft law but simply law. From a (positivist) legal perspective, "soft law" is a superfluous concept; the adjective "soft" does not add anything meaningful to the noun "law."

In their discussion of communicative legislation, Witteveen and Van Klink (1999) raise the question why soft law is really law. As they argue, law consisting of aspirational norms without an effective enforcement mechanism still has to count as law because it may have significant symbolic effects on public debate, language used in society, and the general mentality or attitude. Kelsen would give a very different and much more straightforward answer: if there is a higher legal norm that authorizes its creation, communicative legislation is valid law. For example, the first article of the Dutch constitution, which promotes equality and prohibits discrimination, enables the enactment of the Dutch Equal Treatment Act. The law is soft in the sense that deterrent sanctions are lacking. In individual cases, people who have a complaint about discrimination at work, for instance, may appeal to the Netherlands Institute for Human Rights, which can solely give nonbinding advice to the parties. Moreover, people can make a claim in court, and the judge is authorized to attach legal consequences to a norm violation (although, in practice, this only happens very occasionally). From a political point of view, one may regret the "softness" of the law at hand, but legally speaking, this is not relevant as long as there is some kind of sanction available. For Kelsen, this is a necessary requirement: the violation of a legal norm has to have some consequence, no matter what.[14] Without any sanction, it would not be law but, for instance, merely a moral appeal or a wish.[15]

In all the other examples of soft law mentioned above—brochures, general guidelines, private lawmaking, self-regulation, codes, certificates, and so on—Kelsen would argue that there is no law if a higher legal norm is lacking. In the absence of an authoritative and authorizing legal source, the norms disseminated or created in these cases have no legal validity and, therefore, no legal relevance. Kelsen would not deny that what is, in his view, confusingly called "soft law" could fulfill useful functions for the legal system, for instance, by giving information about the law's content to legal officials who have to apply the norms or to citizens who have to follow them (as in brochures or general guidelines) or by serving as a source of inspiration for the creation of new law (when, for example, a code of conduct is incorporated into official law). As a source of inspiration, soft law has to compete with other sources, such as religion, morality, or political ideology, with which it stands on equal footing. It has no special legal status, or more precisely, it has no legal status at all, just like the other sources. From a legal perspective, legal officials are in no way bound to apply the norms contained in soft law, nor have citizens a legal duty to follow them. For the most part, they constitute, as Kelsen would argue, social norms to which people may submit themselves, either voluntarily or under social pressure. He would certainly debunk the label of "soft law" as a dubious political attempt to smuggle some norms (social or other) into the domain of the official law.

So in positivist conceptions of legal validity, there is no room for soft law. Soft law disappears in the binary opposition between law and nonlaw: either it is included in the current legal system (as "ordinary" law) or it is excluded from it (as nonlaw). If it is law, one may regret its softness, which is its lack of enforceability, on political grounds (as in the case of communicative legislation). If it is not law, it is basically "noise" for the legal system. It may nevertheless in various, informal ways contribute to the functioning of the formal law, e.g., by disseminating its content to the public or by offering suggestions for its development. However, the problem with soft law is that, after being banned from the legal system, it keeps making its appearance in the law, in the applications of law by legal officials, as well as in public perceptions of what is, rightly or wrongly, considered to be law. How to account for this?

[14]Simply put, in Kelsen's view any legal norm has the following logical structure: if fact X happens (e.g., someone shoots the sheriff), a legal official Y (e.g., the judge) is authorized to inflict sanction Z (e.g., to put the shooter in jail).

[15]Like Kelsen (but unlike Raz), Schauer (2015) considers the possibility of enforcement a necessary element of law.

4.2 The Interactionist Reappraisal of Soft Law

Within an interactionist approach, soft law appears to be less of an anomaly because it is not concerned with a strict demarcation between law and nonlaw; it accepts that the boundaries between them are fluid. Fuller is interested not in a strict test to determine what "really" is law but in an empirical and moral assessment of whatever is recognized, by some standard, as law. As Rundle argues (see above), Fuller does not reject positivist tests of legal validity out of hand. He does believe, though, that they provide only one, and not the most interesting, side of the story. Fuller devotes much more attention to the other side of the story, which situates the law in its social context, within the sphere of human interaction. His main question is not what is law, but how does the law function? How does it contribute to a "good order" and to "workable social arrangements"? Does the law show sufficient respect for human agency? For Fuller, the questions of law and good law, is and ought, are inevitably intertwined. In terms of legal validity: one cannot determine what has to count as law without taking empirical and moral considerations into account. This has several important implications for both hard law and soft law.

To begin with, from Fuller's perspective, so-called hard law appears to be less hard. The official law has to meet various requirements of an empirical and a moral nature. According to Fuller, the main task of law is to provide citizens with "a sound and stable framework for their interactions" (as quoted above). In its empirical aspect, the law has to sustain and support the functioning of the social practice that it regulates. It has to facilitate the interactions among citizens in society and ensure that they take place in an orderly and civilized fashion. In its moral aspect, according to Fuller, the most basic principle is that law has to respect the possibility of human agency. That is, it should treat legal subjects as actors in their own right, not as slaves or property. What this entails, more concretely, has to be specified for the different forms of social regulation. Fuller has done so in particular for legislation. The eight rules of lawmaking, which Fuller discerns, consist of formal conditions to the legislative process: the rules should be general, clear, noncontradictory, accessible to the public, and so forth (see further Sect. 3.1). These formal conditions concern the internal morality of law. In addition, the law may be evaluated from a morality external to the legal system on the basis of substantive principles of justice.[16] According to Fuller (as quoted above), "law is a precondition of good law." His eight principles of lawmaking have thus to be conceived as a first step in a full moral assessment of the law, which goes beyond the mere question of legal validity. As indicated earlier, Fuller has not developed a conception of legal validity applicable to the other forms of social regulation, such as adjudication, mediation, or

[16]As Westerman (1999, p. 167) argues, within Fuller's approach no absolute distinction can be made between formal (internal) and substantive (external) requirements: "If we take the requirements in the maximal sense, as a morality of aspiration, they come very close to principles of 'external morality'." However, Fuller focuses mainly on the formal aspects of law and does not address its content.

implicit law. It is obvious, though, that each form of social regulation has its own internal morality, consisting both of empirical and moral requirements and allowing for a gradual assessment of the law's quality. For instance, adjudication must, more than any other kind of regulation, be based on sound reasoning resulting in a clear ruling.

If a form of social regulation fails to meet the empirical and moral requirements specific to its internal morality—e.g., a statute is not made accessible to the public or the rules are not clear or not general enough—it produces something that cannot be properly recognized (or not entirely) as law. It could be argued, for instance, that communicative legislation is not really law in this sense because it contains general clauses and therefore fails to meet the requirement of clarity. Fuller (1969, p. 64) does not, however, reject the use of standards in law (like good faith or due care) as such: "Sometimes the best way to achieve clarity is to take advantage of, and to incorporate into the law, common sense standards of judgment that have grown up in the ordinary life lived outside legislative halls." So communicative legislation constitutes law if it connects to already existing social norms or, we may add, if its meaning is clarified in subsequent applications and public discussions.[17] On the contrary, for the most part, Nazi law cannot be recognized as law in this sense since, among other things, it was not promulgated in advance, did not contain clear and general rules, and, most seriously, deprived large groups in society (Jews, Sinti and Roma, communists, homosexuals, mentally ill people, and so on) of their capacity to act. Consequently, so-called hard law—whatever its source—may not be law at all when it does not respect (or not sufficiently) the principles of the internal morality of law.

Conversely, soft law seems to be less soft when approached from Fuller's interactionist perspective. Fuller would have no problem in recognizing informal regulations—that is, regulations for which, in Kelsen's terms, no higher authorizing legal norm is available—as long as they comply with the internal morality of law specific to a form of social regulation. As a basic requirement law, should, as indicated earlier, provide citizens with a "sound and stable framework for their interactions." Obviously, informal law should, just like formal law, contribute to a "good order" and to "workable social arrangements." For that purpose, as Fuller would argue, informal regulations should reflect the rules that have established themselves or are emerging in social practice and connect to the reciprocal expectations that arise from human interaction. More fundamentally, legal subjects have to be treated as actors in their own right and be given the freedom, within the limits set by the law, to pursue their own goals. Private lawmaking or self-regulation could, for instance, qualify as law in this sense if it meets sufficiently the applicable principles of lawmaking.

Generally speaking, one could say that in the interactionist approach, soft law gets a more favorable treatment. Many instances of soft law that positivism would

[17]According to Witteveen and Van Klink (1999, p. 127), this is the task of the so-called "interpretive community," constituted by communicative legislation.

easily dismiss as nonlaw and not legally relevant are recognized as law in their own right and are considered to be essential to the well-functioning of various legal (or law-like) systems, including the official legal order. However, interactionism does not accept soft law uncritically or unconditionally. From an interactionist perspective, there are several reasons why one should be cautious with qualifying some instance of regulation as soft law. Firstly, soft law is only recognized as law under the empirical and moral conditions that apply to the various forms of social regulation. Fuller's principles of the internal morality of law go beyond the source-based test provided by positivism and set a high level of aspiration, which law may meet to a higher or lesser extent. In her critical discussion of soft law, Westerman points to the many ways in which informal regulations, in particular goal-oriented governance regulations (in, e.g., universities or hospitals), can fail to produce law. To give a few examples:

(i) Governance regulation threatens the generality of law (against Fuller's first principle): "Under a governance regime, the emphasis on flexibility has led to the demand that rules should be tailored to the specific demands and exigencies of the situation in which the norm addressee finds itself" (Westerman 2007b, p. 70).
(ii) If positive prescriptions are generalized, the regulation may violate the requirement of clarity (against Fuller's third principle): "Negative prescriptions can be general and yet informative, whereas the generalization of positive prescriptions immediately turns them into vague and uninformative norms" (Westerman 2007a, p. 124).
(iii) The goals set by governance regulation, such as "good education" or "good health care," can only be furthered but never fully achieved; they are an inexhaustible source of unspecified duties and may, therefore, seem to demand the impossible (against Fuller's sixth principle; Westerman 2007a, p. 119).

Secondly, in close connection with the last point, informal regulations commonly referred to as "soft law" may not be law at all in Fuller's sense. As indicated, Fuller makes a distinction between law and managerial direction. Managerial direction consists of detailed regulations aimed at achieving objectives set by a superior, which the subordinates are expected to follow. Law, on the contrary, is based on a relationship of reciprocity and enables citizens to pursue their own goals within the boundaries of the law. It may be argued that governance regulations are closer to managerial direction than to law since the goals to be achieved are set in aspirational terms from the top down by the regulator. Detailed instructions are lacking, but the subordinates are expected to devise the specific duties themselves, which they later have to account for. This method of "hanging yourself" threatens the possibility of human agency, which Fuller values so highly. Governance regulation does not, in his words, furnish "a baseline for self-directed action" but prescribes the common goal that all participants have to achieve.

Finally, Fuller—like Kelsen but on very different grounds—would not be very happy with the concept of soft law because it presupposes a prioritization of the formal, "hard" law over the informal, "soft" law. It suggests that soft law is not really law or, at best, only a supplement to the "real," official law. As indicated, Fuller would question this dichotomy. Hard law, i.e., law that passes the positivist source-based test, may fail to meet the requirements of the internal morality of law. Vice versa, soft law may be real law if it manages to meet these requirements. Moreover, soft law may function as customary law by codifying rules that arise from social practice (as, for instance, in codes of conduct). As Fuller would argue, even the official legal system cannot do without the rules provided by soft law. For example, the Dutch circular *Instructions for Legislation*, which offers rules for lawmaking, though not legally binding, is considered to be an authoritative guide for legislative practice.[18] In its turn, soft law depends for its coercive force and efficacy largely on the official legal system. According to Westerman (2013), people tend to follow the prescriptions of soft law because they believe it to be hard law, although it does not constitute formally valid law.[19] Instead of adhering to the false opposition between hard law and soft law, Fuller would prefer to speak of different forms of social regulations, which each in their own right generate law and which mutually supplement and reinforce each other.

With both Kelsen and Fuller, each in their own way, questioning the concept of soft law we may ask: what remains, in the end, of soft law?

5 Taking Soft Law Seriously

As discussed earlier, in a positivist approach, there is no need for the concept of soft law. Soft law is either law, if its creation is authorized by a higher legal norm, or nonlaw, if it is not. From a positivist legal perspective, soft law does not exist as a separate entity. That does not exclude the possibility that what is referred to as soft law may appear, from some other (e.g., social or political) perspective, to fulfill useful functions in society: for instance, as a source of inspiration for the creation of new law or as social norms guiding the behavior of people outside the legal system. The positivist conception of legal validity has several apparent advantages; to name a few, (i) it offers a clear and objective criterion for both the legal scholar and the legal practitioner for identifying valid law (in Kelsen's theory, the availability of a higher authorizing legal norm and, ultimately, the presupposition of the basic norm); (ii) this criterion can easily be applied, without having to take into account empirical and moral considerations (efficacy is only a *conditio sine qua non* for legal validity, not a *conditio per quam*; law and morality are strictly separated); (iii) as a consequence, the legal scholar does not have to accept the legal system she is describing (by means of what Raz (1979, p. 153) would call "detached legal statements"); and (iv) the application of this criterion brings unity to the legal system (norms that

[18]In Dutch: *Aanwijzingen voor de regelgeving*, see: https://www.rijksoverheid.nl/documenten/circulaires/1992/11/18/aanwijzingen-voor-de-regelgeving (last checked on 25 August 2016).

[19]As an example Westerman (2013, pp. 392–393) refers to the case of harbor facilities.

contradict a higher legal norm are not legal norms and have to be nullified) and provides for legal certainty (only those norms that fit in the current legal system count as law). This comes, however, with a price. In the positivist conception, the social context in which the law has to operate is mainly neglected. Law is considered to be a fully normative enterprise, and how, on a factual level, it works out in social reality is considered to be of no legal relevance. The only empirical precondition it presupposes is that the legal system is *grosso modo* effective. Moreover, it cannot say—and, as a result of the strict separation between facts and values, refuses to say—anything about the moral value of the norms identified as law. So anything can be law, however dysfunctional and morally corrupt it is, as long as it passes the source-based test of legal validity.[20] Applied to soft law, it amounts to a total rejection of several types of regulation (such as private lawmaking, self-regulation, and customary law) that in legal practice appear to be highly legally relevant, that are essential for the functioning of the official legal system, and that the participants themselves conceive of as law.

In the interactionist conception of legal validity, both the social context in which norms have to operate and their moral value are essential for the identification of law. In order to establish whether some set of norms may count as law, it has to be established, following Fuller, whether the norms at hand contribute to a "good order"—not just any order but an order that promotes the purposes it is meant to serve in a civilized, morally justifiable manner. In other words, law has to contribute to the well-functioning of a given legal system (not only the official legal system but also "smaller" systems such as universities, churches, or labor unions) and has to be in accordance with the applicable internal morality of law. This may be considered a weak test for the identification of law, but Fuller never meant to provide a strict test. He does, however, set the stakes much higher for the recognition of some set of norms as law than a positivist source-based test. What law is in an interactionist approach is always a matter of degree and involves an assessment based on empirical and moral considerations. Some instances of regulation may succeed to a greater or lesser extent in generating law; it may not yet be law but emerging law or not be law at all but managerial direction instead (as in governance regulation).

From a scientific perspective, Fuller's interactionist approach appears in certain respects to be underdeveloped. It gives rise to several questions, for instance, how exactly should we establish the validity of law? How can we assess whether a set of norms contributes to the well-functioning of a legal system? What exactly does the internal morality of law consist of in the various types of social regulation (besides legislation), and when can they be said to be sufficiently met? More importantly, can law be a matter of degree? How is the unity of law to be achieved in the plurality of legal systems where each generates its own law? And what is the role of authority and power in the determination of law?[21] Although an interactionist approach does

[20]For a more extensive criticism of Kelsen's theory, see Van Klink and Lembcke (2016, pp. 219–221).

[21]On the last question, see more extensively Van Klink (2005, pp. 113–122).

not make the identification of law easier, it does, in our view, provide for an important addition and also correction to the mainstream positivist understanding of legal validity and soft law. Firstly, it takes the social context in which law operates into account, not only in the limited instrumentalist sense that law has to be effective but, more broadly, that it has to sustain a good order and serve its purposes. Secondly, it makes a normative assessment of law possible. Law essentially is a normative concept. Otherwise, we could not distinguish between law and mere exercises of power (by, e.g., a robber gang or the Mafia).[22] Obviously, as scholars and citizens, we can and will continue to argue about the right normative standards to apply. Fuller's internal morality of law offers a baseline of formal requirements, to which more substantive moral principles could be added. These normative standards may help legal officials (for instance, a judge) to identify what in a specific case should be recognized as law, more than positivism is able or willing to do. In his theory of legal interpretation, Kelsen (1976, pp. 94–95) acknowledges that in every application of the law, legal officials have to rely on non-legal values since legal norms offer a "scheme of interpretation" that allows for multiple meanings. But he refrains deliberately, within his pure theory of law, from giving any suggestions as to how the legal official should choose among the different possible interpretations.

Finally, an interactionist approach is able to give a better account than legal positivism of the legal relevance of various types of regulation commonly referred to as soft law. It can show how and under what conditions regulations may be recognized as law and how formal law and informal law intertwine and are dependent on each other. One may try to ban informal law from the official legal system for political reasons because one considers the state to be the only legitimate source of law or for scientific reasons in order to safeguard the "purity" of legal theory. In social practice, though, this distinction does not exist: citizens act upon informal law as if it were "real" law. Moreover, as Fuller argues, the official legal system needs to draw on informal law emerging from social interaction for its proper functioning. Informal law provides for the (mostly implicit) normative background against which formal law is created and applied. It contributes to the well-functioning of the official legal system, for instance, by clarifying, specifying, and disseminating the law's content. No matter how one tries to repress informal law, it will make its return in the official legal system as a "necessary supplement"[23] any time when the formal law falls back on norms emerging or established in social practice.

So, again, what remains of the concept of soft law? Fuller would reject this notion because it implies a preference for the official law emanating from the state. In an interactionist approach, law comes in many shapes and sizes. No form of social regulation can claim to be the only or the "real" law. Whatever its source is, law is a matter of achievement that can be accomplished with varying degrees of success.

[22]As Raz (1979, p. 315) argues, law necessarily makes the moral claim that it has legitimate authority.

[23]For a philosophical exploration of the notion of supplement and its various meanings, see Derrida (1997).

Building on Fuller's work, we are able to draw two important conclusions about what is commonly and unhappily referred to as soft law. First and foremost, in many instances it should be recognized as a new kind of (informal) law in itself, which emerges from or is established in social interactions and which increasingly supplements and supplants formal law. As a consequence of the mainstream positivist understanding of legal validity, we fail to see how formal law and informal law presuppose each other and work together (and sometimes against each other) in establishing the legal order. Subsequently and conversely, in some other instances, so-called soft law does *not* fall within the realm of law and comes close to what Fuller would call "managerial direction." Incorporated in the legal order, it leads to an instrumentalization of law and reduces law to a mere means to achieve a certain pregiven end. As such, it endangers the possibility of human agency. This applies in particular to governance regulations that impose top-down general goals on subordinates, for which they have to devise for themselves an infinite set of specific duties. Either way, soft law should be taken more seriously.

References

Crowe, J. 2014. Between Morality and Efficacy: Reclaiming the Natural Law Theory of Lon Fuller. *Jurisprudence* 5 (1): 109–118.

Derrida, J. 1997. *Of Grammatology*. Baltimore: The Johns Hopkins University Press.

Dreier, H. 1990. *Rechtslehre, Staatsoziologie und Demokratietheorie bei Hans Kelsen*. 2nd ed. Baden-Baden: Nomos.

Dyzenhaus, D. 1999. Fuller's Novelty. In *Rediscovering Fuller: Essays on Implicit Law and Institutional Design*, ed. W.J. Witteveen and W. van der Burg, 78–99. Amsterdam: Amsterdam University Press.

Fuller, L.L. 1966. *The Law in Quest of Itself*. Boston: Beacon Press.

———. 1969. *The Morality of Law*. New Haven: Yale University Press.

———. 1981. In *The Principles of Social Order: Selected Essays of Lon L. Fuller*, ed. K.I. Winston. Durham, NC: Duke Press Paperbacks.

Gur, N. 2014. Form and Value in Law. *Jurisprudence* 5 (1): 85–95.

Kelsen, H. 1922. *Der soziologische und der juristische Staatsbegriff: Kritische Untersuchung des Verhältnisses vom Staat und Recht*. Tübingen: Mohr Siebeck.

———. 1970. *The Pure Theory of Law*. Berkeley: University of California Press.

———. 1973. *General Theory of Law and State*. Chicago: Russell & Russell.

———. 1976. *Reine Rechtslehre: Mit einem Anhang: Das Problem der Gerechtigkeit*. 2nd ed. Tübingen: Mohr Siebeck.

Luhmann, N. 1995. *Das Recht der Gesellschaft*. Frankfurt a.M.: Suhrkamp.

Oakeshott, M. 1999. The Rule of Law. In *On History and Other Essays*, ed. M. Oakeshott, 129–178. Indianapolis: Liberty Fund.

Postema, G.J. 1999. Implicit Law. In *Rediscovering Fuller: Essays on Implicit Law and Institutional Design*, ed. W.J. Witteveen and W. van der Burg, 55–275. Amsterdam: Amsterdam University Press.

Raz, J. 1979. *The Authority of Law: Essays on Law and Morality*. Oxford: Clarendon Press.

Rundle, K. 2012. *Forms Liberate: Reclaiming the Jurisprudence of Lon L. Fuller*. Oxford: Hart Publishing.

Schauer, F. 2015. *The Force of Law*. Cambridge, MA: Harvard University Press.

Van Klink, B. 2005. An Effective-Historical View on the Symbolic Working of Law. In *Social and Symbolic Effects of Legislation Under the Rule of Law*, ed. N. Zeegers, W.J. Witteveen, and B. van Klink, 113–145. Lewiston: The Edwin Mellen Press.

———. 2016. Adjudication and Justification: To What Extent Should the Excluded Be Included in the Judge's Decision. In *Argumentation and Reasoned Action: Proceedings of the 1st European Conference on Argumentation, Lisbon, 2015 (Volume II)*, ed. D. Mohammed and M. Lewinski, 643–655. London: College Publications.

Van Klink, B., and O.W. Lembcke. 2016. Exploring the Boundaries of Law: On the Is-Ought Distinction in Jellinek and Kelsen. In *Facts and Norms in Law: Interdisciplinary Reflections on Legal Method*, ed. S. Taekema, B. van Klink, and W. de Been, 201–223. Cheltenham: Edward Elgar.

Westerman, P. 1999. Means and Ends. In *Rediscovering Fuller: Essays on Implicit Law and Institutional Design*, ed. W.J. Witteveen and W. van der Burg, 145–168. Amsterdam: Amsterdam University Press.

———. 2007a. The Emergence of New Types of Norms. In *Legislation in Context: Essays in Legisprudence*, ed. L.J. Wintgens, 117–133. Aldershot: Ashgate.

———. 2007b. Governing by Goals: Governance as a Legal Style. *Legisprudence/International Journal for the Study of Legislation* 1 (1): 51–72.

———. 2013. Law and Regulation. In *Human Rights and the Problem of Legal Injustice: Annals of the Preparatory Meeting for the XXVI World Congress of the International Association of Philosophy of Law and Social Philosophy*, ed. J. Adeodato, 387–400. Sao Paolo: Editura Noeses.

Winston, K.I. 1981. Introduction. In *The Principles of Social Order: Selected Essays of Lon L. Fuller*, ed. L.L. Fuller and K.I. Winston, 11–44. Durham, NC: Duke Press Paperbacks.

Witteveen, W.J., and B. van Klink. 1999. Why Is Soft Law Really Law? *RegelMaat/Journal for Legislative Studies* (3): 124–140.

Validity: The Reputation of Rules

Pauline Westerman

Abstract If we want to know whether a particular legal construct (rule, contract) is valid, we are interested in ascertaining its relevance. We want to know whether a certain rule can be trusted to have the effect it claims to have. This question in itself rests on the background assumption and collective agreement that in general such legal constructs do matter and make a difference. This article investigates the conditions under which such collective agreement can wax or wane. To that end, the validity of rules is compared with the reputation of persons. Personal reputation is not only dependent on one's pedigree and upbringing but is also informed by present conduct and company, as well as by anticipated future performance. The same applies to the legal order, which is equally informed by considerations concerning past, present, and future. It is explained how these considerations move in circles of interaction and can be self-reinforcing, as well as self-defeating.

1 Introduction

Over recent decades, we have witnessed the emergence of so-called soft law. The term is ambiguous and seems to have two distinct meanings, depending on the context in which it is used.

At the international level, "soft" often means "not yet hard": soft law consists in solemn declarations and principles that are not or hardly enforceable. At the domestic level, however, soft law does not necessarily exhibit these features. There, "soft law" serves as an umbrella term for the products of various forms of regulation: self-regulatory codes, regulation drawn up by supervisory boards, standardization norms drawn up by technical experts, guidelines, and "best practices." This kind of soft law is not only enforced but is also often linked to "hard" law if it is generated in response to formal legislation. This is especially the case in forms of legislation such

P. Westerman (✉)
Rijksuniversiteit Groningen, Groningen, The Netherlands
e-mail: p.c.westerman@rthrug.nl

© Springer International Publishing AG, part of Springer Nature 2018
P. Westerman et al. (eds.), *Legal Validity and Soft Law*, Law and Philosophy Library 122, https://doi.org/10.1007/978-3-319-77522-7_8

as "goal-legislation"[1] or "principles-based regulation."[2] In these forms of legislation, the formal legislator confines itself to imposing some desirable policy goals (good labor conditions, sustainability, etc.) and obliges norm addressees to make and to enforce rules in order to achieve these goals. The products of these activities may be called "soft," but they are connected to hard law.

However, even in domestic law, where soft law seems to be "harder" than in international soft law, doubts may arise as to the validity of these rules, standards, and guidelines. Officials, as well as norm addressees, are not sure whether they should regard such rules as binding rules or just "best practices," whether these rules impose obligations or just offer advice. Norm addressees are often in the dark as to what kind of sanctions they can expect. What to make, for instance, of the rules that are accompanied by the demand to "comply or explain"? Are they just suggestions or more than that? In the legal landscape in which a sharp division is made between valid and invalid rules, soft law emerges in a twilight zone and therefore urges us to reconsider our notion of validity. What is validity? What is its function? Is it a necessarily dichotomous concept? Or should we allow for the possibility that validity can come in degrees?

In order to answer these questions, I do not confine myself to the perspective of the practicing lawyer who just wants to know whether a particular contract or will is valid. In order to understand the particular position of soft law, I want to explore under what conditions such validity examinations make sense. In what circumstances is an investigation of validity important? This article is therefore not intended to investigate the conditions for validity but rather seeks to explore under what conditions such investigations of validity usually make sense at all. Only then can we get a glimpse of the twilight zone of soft law.

2 Validity as Reputation

Despite the abundance of literature on legal validity, relatively little attention is paid to the question why we should bother to find out whether a testament, a contract, or a rule is valid.[3] What is the function of validity? Why would it be useful to demarcate the valid from the invalid? The answers to those questions are usually taken for granted because most authors adopt the point of view of the judge, and for her the most important and obvious function of assessing the validity of a contract or rule is to know whether and to what extent such a contract or rule should be seen as a relevant or even overriding reason for decision making.

---

[1] I analyzed this form of legislation more extensively in Westerman (2007a, b). The phenomenon is the subject of my new book *Outsourcing the Law: A Philosophical Perspective on Regulation* which will be published by Elgar Publishers.

[2] Black (2008).

[3] An exception to this neglect are the contributions of Mackor and Paulo in this volume.

But for other actors, a—rather obvious—function of validity is that it helps them to know whether a certain particular contract, rule, or testament *can be trusted to have the effect that it claims to have*. The heir who wants to know whether his father's will is valid is essentially in the same position as the grocer who examines the 1000 euro bill of his customer in order to see whether it is a real bill or a counterfeit one. Can he trust this bill to have the effect that it claims to have: in other words, can he really buy something with this bill?

In informal settings, such questions are determined by reference to the *personal reputation* of those who procured such documents. As is shown by Goyal in this volume, informal markets in India are to a large extent regulated by intermediaries. The validity and value of the parchis (promissory notes) handled by such intermediaries are guaranteed on the basis of the latter's determination of the reputation of the trader who issued them.

In this article, I will argue that validity is the functional equivalent of reputation. Whereas informal systems rely on the reputations of persons as indications of the extent to which these persons can be trusted, in a formal system people rely on the reputation of legal constructs, categories, and rules. We call this kind of impersonal reputation "validity." Just as reputation informs us of whether a person really *is* what he pretends to be, validity informs us of whether the contract, rule, or will is what it claims to be. It is to be noted, however, that by "reputation," I do not refer to "good reputation." In just the same way, a valid rule may be an unfair or immoral rule. But even if it is an unfair rule, we might expect a valid rule to have the effect it claims to have. Just as we can expect people who enjoy the reputation of a villain will act like a villain.

There are three possible routes to approach questions of validity, which are very similar to the ways in which we seek to ascertain whether a person can be trusted. The first is an inquiry into the origins of such persons. If confronted with strangers, it is not unusual to start the conversation with a "where are you from?" Knowing someone's pedigree is in most cultures the method *par excellence* of ascertaining someone's reputation. Next thing to know is in whose company the stranger is seen. Does she converse with the "right" people (and if so, how often), or is she mostly seen in the company of notorious swindlers? And finally (but not exclusively), someone's reputation is informed by what expected goods or ills this person might bring to us, information that is for the most part derived from his or her past performance.

The same three routes are accessible to those who want to determine the validity of a legal product Y such as contracts, wills, or rules. The first is by starting at the input side, questioning how document/construct Y originated, what the source of Y is, and whether Y was established in the procedurally right way. Hage calls this in his contribution "source-validity." To officials whose daily business it is to determine the validity of legal products Y in order to know to what extent they should weigh these items as reasons for their decisions, this is the most accessible road to take.

But it is not the only route available. If origins are unclear, or if the criteria for pedigree are doubtful, as is the case in soft law in which the authority of the rule makers is often doubtful (think of experts or professional associations), judges may also be guided by considerations of whether Y is actually referred to and taken seriously by other participants of a given institutional order. How do other officials weigh these products? How are they dealt with in the relevant academic literature? To what extent are norm addressees actually guided by such rules? This examination considers the "Geltung," the weight that is generally accorded to Y. I will call this throughput-validity; it refers to the company in which Y is seen, i.e. the esteem in which it is held by participants and how Y appears in their decisions and justifications.

Finally, in order to ascertain the validity of Y, one may look at the output side of that legal product. And with output I don't merely refer to the legal consequences to which these products give rise but to the actual factual consequences that arise from according weight to Y. Output-validity is therefore no more than what Kelsen called "efficacy." This route is only partially available to officials such as judges for they—partially—*determine* the extent to which a rule or covenant is efficacious. That is probably why Kelsen thought of output as legally irrelevant.[4] It is not relevant for a legal decision-maker in deciding whether she should consider Y as a weighty reason because such a serious consideration *contributes* to the Y's output. But for those who are *affected* by the decisions of legal experts, efficacy is of the utmost if not overriding importance. For instance, the protocols and procedures of audit committees are often unclear, sometimes even secret, and the way they are developed is mostly unknown to the parties involved. Nevertheless, no institution would declare, for that reason, such protocols and criteria as irrelevant. Failure to comply with these standards may lead to withdrawal of subsidies or official recognition and in any case damage institutional reputation. They are, therefore, taken very seriously as reasons for the internal policy of such institutions, which would rather choose to conform to nonvalid standards than to jeopardize their own reputation by litigation.

Obviously, the terms "input-validity", "throughput-validity", and "output-validity" do not refer to distinct kinds of validity. The terms refer to the distinct *ways* in which a certain item Y can acquire validity. Input-validity refers to the validity, weight, or importance that a certain Y acquires by virtue of the way Y was established. Throughput-validity refers to the weight that is accorded to Y by relevant actors. And output-validity refers to the validity, weight, and relevance that a certain item Y acquires by virtue of its expected consequences. As we shall see, the term "expected" is of utmost importance. We should not forget that validity is reputation. If someone has the reputation of a villain, this does not mean that he actually and unfailingly will act as a villain. I will come back to this in Sect. 3.

The three ways to acquire validity correspond to the routes that are available to us if we want to examine the validity of a certain item. Some of these three routes are taken by officials, others by norm addressees, some by both. It is only by exclusively focusing on the perspective of the judicial decision-maker that validity can be narrowed down to input-validity. But even within such a judge-oriented perspective,

---

[4]Kelsen (1945), p. 119. Hage, too, in his contribution to this book regards efficacy as a concern of (external) sociologists of law. I hesitate to draw strict boundaries between internal and external here; the non-official participants of a legal order are also interested in efficacy.

the exclusive focus on input-validity does not do justice to the complexities of soft law, which often invite consideration of throughput-validity as well, as we have seen. And even output considerations may influence their decision making, as in the case of a court that anticipates further legislation and will incline in a certain direction even if the rules that cover such a decision are not yet valid.

It is important to note that each of these routes of examination allows for *gradual* answers. Although it is possible to give a yes/no answer to the question whether Y should be considered as being enacted by the formal legislature, such dichotomous answers are not always available. Certification procedures may be more or less correctly established, new and alternative rule-making bodies may be considered as more or less respectable sources. The same applies to throughput considerations. There may be more or fewer actors who recognize the type of Y as weighty and important, and also the degree of esteem in which they are held may differ. If Y is embedded in a so-called best practice, it may even enjoy greater respect than a formal rule. Finally, output-validity can also surface in degrees. In a Chinese context, for instance, documents certifying ownership of houses are not completely worthless. But they enjoy less output-validity than in the Netherlands.

3 Type-Validity

So far I have focused on how the validity of a particular legal product Y, such as a code, a contract, a covenant, or a will, can be examined. But such an examination is only relevant against the background of an institutional order in which types of such products and constructs are *generally* seen as relevant. It is against this background that particular contracts, wills, or rules have a *claim* to validity. As Sandro rightly points out in this volume, the mere fact that a court takes a will into consideration and declares it invalid implies that the will originally had juridical meaning in the sense that it had a claim to legal validity. Left unchallenged, the will, although a counterfeit one, would certainly have brought about legal consequences. This claim to validity is vital. Without it, contracts or wills would be treated as a kind of legal monopoly money that no one would bother to examine seriously. The difference between a policeman who acts in a theater play and an imposter who is clothed in police uniform is just this: no one would for a minute contemplate the possibility that the play actor is a real policeman; he simply does not even claim to be one. The whole matter is expressed eloquently by Carpentier in this volume, who agrees with Sandro in this respect and exclaims: *To put it in a nutshell, in order to be invalid, a norm must be a valid norm in the first place!*

Of course, in this statement, the word "valid" has two rather distinct meanings. The claim to validity is different from actual validity. But it is important to point out that a particular will can only have such a claim against the background belief that in general wills are relevant, inform people's decisions, and have legal as well as factual consequences. A particular will is a *token* of a *type*. Because this type (the *class* of wills) is generally felt to be valid in a legal order, we can sensibly ask whether this particular will is valid. We should therefore distinguish between token-validity and type-validity. Validity of types should be presupposed and forms the background of our inquiries into the validity of a particular legal construct as a token of that type.[5]

In order to understand type-validity more precisely, we might recall John Searle's account of the way our social reality is construed.[6] Searle notices that most of the words that do not directly refer to brute facts such as "ice" or "stone" or "wind" are the result of attribution. Terms like "boundary," "wedding," "greeting," or "flag" are all the result of what Pufendorf had already called *impositio*, our attribution of a certain *meaning or status* to brute facts.[7] A banknote may consist of a piece of paper, but it is not the sheet of paper that turns it into a banknote. It is by virtue of our *agreement* that the piece of paper *counts as* a banknote that we can use it to buy bread. Likewise, the wall of stones can only function as a boundary if we collectively agree on the fact that this wall of stones *counts as* a boundary.

The basic element of our social reality is therefore agreement on the statement that X counts as a Y in context C. I do not want to repeat Searle's ingenious account here, but we should point to two properties of such count-as rules that are relevant to our present inquiry. The first is that a Y-term is invoked in order to carry out a particular function. If we say "this wall counts as boundary," it is because "boundary" can do what "wall" in itself cannot do: it can tell people what they should do and what they should refrain from. Searle therefore remarks that the statement "this rock counts as a chair" is *not* a basic element of social reality; it can carry out its function even without our agreement with the rule. Y-terms are completely dependent on our collective attribution of a *status* in order to fulfill the function for which they were instituted.

The boundary example also clarifies a second property of Y-terms: the function that is exercised by the Y-term is that it confers deontic powers[8] (rights, obligations, permissions, privileges). It imposes on some of us the obligation to stay clear from the boundary, or it may give others permission to kill once the boundary is transgressed. According to Searle, it is only on the basis of continued collective acceptance of such status ascriptions that the Y-terms can successfully exercise their assigned function:

> Because the physical features specified by the X-term are insufficient to guarantee success in fulfilling the assigned function, there must be continued collective acceptance or recognition

---

[5]That is why Hart remarks that in the case of a general disregard of the law it is pointless to inquire into the validity of particular rules. See Hart (1997), pp. 103–104.

[6]Searle (1995).

[7]Pufendorf (1934), remarked that so-called "'moral entities' do not arise out of the intrinsic nature of the physical properties of things, but they are superadded, at the will of intelligent entities, to things already existent and physically complete (...), and indeed, come into existence only by the determination of their authors." I,I,4.

[8]Searle (1995), Ch IV, p. 100.

> of the validity of the assigned function; otherwise the function cannot be successfully performed.[9]

This does not imply that all use of Y-terms presupposes such collective agreement. Of course it is possible to use Y-terms that have no deontic status *for us* and is therefore not dependent on our collective agreement. If we say that this pile of stones is "Hadrian's wall," which in antiquity functioned as a boundary, we may make use of our understanding of the status of the type "boundary," but we clearly do not say that for us it has the status of a boundary; we only describe the fact that among the Romans, these stones enjoyed the status of a boundary that created rights and duties for Romans. We are not then agreeing that X counts as Y but simply describing a historical collective agreement that X counts as Y.[10]

For our purpose, it is important to note that Searle adds to this that we commonly attribute such deontic powers to *types* of X-terms, not to a particular token of an X-term. It should be clear that it is certainly possible to attribute meaning to particular items, but usually we do more than that. We may invent Y-terms on the spot, so to speak, when we draw a line in the sand and tell people they should not transgress this particular line. In fact, such attributions of meaning to particular instances can often be witnessed in children's play when they invent a game and say "this doll is from now on the teacher" or "these marbles are money" but a minute later treat the same doll as their child and the marbles as bullets. But in the social life of adults who are not playing games, this variability and changeability is limited. This is, I think, the result of the fact that "X counts as Y" is only applicable in certain conditions.

These conditions are loosely called "context" by Searle. We might say, for instance, that in the context of the classroom, "raising your arm" counts as "putting a question" but that in the context of an auction, "raising your arm" counts as "making a bid." In such examples, drawn from social life, the context consists of conditions that usually remain implicit. However, in a legal order, such conditions are often explicitly mentioned. If a piece of paper is signed by witnesses, before a notary, etc., it counts as a will. It is important to note, however, that explicit conditions not only explicate the context, but they also serve to *construct a general category: all* pieces of paper that exhibit the following features and that meet the following conditions count as wills.

Since we commonly attribute meanings to a *class* of X-terms, we don't stop each time when we want to spend a dollar bill to read the text written on the bill in order to assure ourselves of the fact that this is a genuine bill and not a counterfeit one. We act on the background assumption that bills of this *type* are valid, i.e. have a status that is collectively agreed upon. This is why counterfeit bills are possible. In the absence of type-validity, they could not even claim to be a genuine bill, and therefore this claim

---

[9]Searle (1995), p. 45.

[10]See also Hart (1997), p. 104.

could not be rejected. It could not be decided that they are counterfeit. They would simply be indifferent, meaningless sheets of paper.[11]

So we might say that any examination of the validity of particular tokens presupposes a world in which people agree on the status that is attributed to types and that confers deontic powers. This means that although the examination of a certain item in terms of validity is brought about by our uncertainty as to whether we can trust *a particular item*, such examination only makes sense in a context of *general* trust, the belief that in general the meanings of such items are shared and considered relevant.

This belief that in general people collectively agree on the fact that types X count as types Y is what I called type-validity. It is the belief that there is a collective agreement on the meanings and statuses that are accorded and that others will act on these shared meanings. Therefore, not collective agreement itself is the ultimate building block of social reality, as Searle thinks, *but the belief* that there is such a thing as collective agreement. It might sound strange to characterize type-validity as a belief. Validity is generally presented as a property of a legal construct that can be more or less objectively attributed and not something that is merely "believed" in. But if we say that a will is valid because it is signed before a notary, we can only say so on the basis of the belief that other relevant actors agree on the fact that if such papers are signed before a notary, they count as wills.

4 Collective Agreement and Functionality

In Sect. 3, I described three routes to ascertain the validity of a particular token, such as a contract or a rule. This examination can only be carried out against the background of assumed validity of the type of which this particular item is a token. We should presuppose that in general type X is accorded the meaning and status of type Y. But how do we know whether these assumptions are warranted? How do we know that in general people agree that a certain *type* X counts as *type* Y? How do we know whether our belief in shared meanings is justified? It seems that

[11]I don't think it is necessary to draw distinctions—as Searle does—between actual count-as statements, such as is the case in "this is a cocktail-party" where people are present and actively attribute the meaning of cocktail party in order to let this particular party function as a cocktail party, and count-as statements which are not dependent on such active recognition, as is the case with a dollar bill which—straight from the press—fell between the cracks of a floor which still counts as money despite the fact that no one ever attributed the meaning 'money' to that particular specimen. There are two issues involved here: whether the instant and actual recognition of a party as a cocktail party is necessary for such a cocktail party to fulfill its function (yes) and whether particular cocktail parties can be recognized as such in the absence of a meaning which is attributed to a general type of parties (no). In order to recognize cocktail parties, we are still making use of a general concept 'cocktail parties' which can only sensibly be attached to an X-term (the physical gathering of people) if it meets several conditions. See Searle (1995), pp. 33 and 53.

once again we are confronted with the task of ascertaining the validity of Y, albeit this time we are required to ascertain the validity not of a token Y but of a type Y.

Searle does not deal with this question since he treats the collective agreement by means of which [type] X counts as [type] Y as a starting point for social reality. He does not raise the question how we arrive at such collective agreement or what makes it stronger or weaker. However, we should not have a static view of collective acceptance as something that is there or not there. Collective acceptance can grow or diminish. Consequently, our *belief* in such a collective agreement may also be strengthened or diminished. The question is, therefore, under what conditions does collective agreement grow and under what conditions is such acceptance on the decline?

The analogy of reputation might again prove helpful in answering this question. We saw in Sect. 3 that like the reputation of persons, the validity of a particular item Y is informed by past performance, present company, and expectations of future consequences. A particular item Y can spring from a more or less respectable source, is referred to by more or fewer actors of more or less esteem, and can more or less successfully be enforced. The same applies to the type-validity we should assume to be enjoyed by type Y. [Type] Y's validity is then equally informed by the respectability of its sources, the position it occupies in a network of other [type] Ys, as well as the consequences that might be expected once [type] Y is declared "valid," i.e. presumed to be collectively agreed upon.

All three considerations determine the status of [type] Y, and here I refer to status in the double sense of the term: "status" as used by Searle as the status that is attributed to X, which enables it (as a Y) to confer deontic powers, and "status" as in ordinary usage indicating the amount of prestige that is accorded to a certain person in relation to the position of others. The advantage of the latter colloquial usage is that it treats status as a gradual affair. Not as something that is or is not attributed to a certain X but as something that can be enjoyed to a lesser or greater degree. In some cultures, people generally accord a higher status to accreditation than in others or more weight to judicial interference than others, and those differences can only be taken into account if we allow type-validity to come in degrees.

One of the factors that influence the degree of status is the degree in which it is believed that the status will entail real consequences. A simple example might clarify this point. According to Malinowski in his study of the Trobriand Islands, the owners of coconut trees who could not keep watch over their trees that grew in distant spots used to attach a palm leaf to the trunk of the trees, indicating that these had to be considered as "property," which implied that the owner had the right to harvest the coconuts for his own household and that others had the obligation to keep clear of them.[12] The palm leaf allows the owner of the trees to extend his control far beyond his physical capacities in both space and time.[13] It indicates the status of the tree as being the property of the owner and thereby confers rights and obligations. But if the

[12]Malinowski (1926), p. 60.

[13]Searle (1995), pp. 80–81.

owners never show up to harvest the coconuts and therefore never really exercise the rights they had claimed, the palm leaf (as a type) will gradually lose its meaning and turn into a dead letter. No one will bother to examine particular palm leaves.

This sounds pretty straightforward and self-evident, but we run into a problem here. Searle pointed out that the very fact that we ascribe a meaning to X helps X (in the capacity of Y) to perform its function. Without such agreement, X could not perform that function. So if there is any function performed by Y, it is solely by virtue of the status that we imposed on X, which turned the X into a Y. But if we say that our collective agreement is partly *dependent* on whether Y indeed performs its functions (the output that we expect from Y), we reason the other way round. We do not say—like Searle—that collective agreement constitutes the functionality of Y, but we say that the functionality of Y informs how weighty Y is for us. Functionality is then at the basis of our collective agreement instead of the other way round.

Both statements seem to be true simultaneously. It is undeniably the case that piles of stones only confer rights and obligations if we collectively agree on the statement that these stones count as a boundary. At the same time, however, the reverse is also true: the failure of Y to exercise its function may in turn undermine collective acceptance of the status of Y (and consequently our belief in such a collective acceptance). It seems then that we are talking in circles here. And this was probably the reason that Searle did not look beyond the fact of agreement, which he just assumes to be the basic starting point and ultimate building block of social reality. But circularity may be the closest we can come to solving these riddles. Apparently, there *are* circles here. Successful performance of the assigned functions strengthens collective acceptance, but repeated failure to perform the functions for which the status was ascribed tends to undermine collective acceptance. Functionality and acceptance are mutually interdependent: they wax or wane together.[14]

Although there is a mutual dependence between functionality and acceptance, I should not be misunderstood as asserting that the status of Y-terms is continuously dependent on what Kelsen called "efficacy" or "Wirksamkeit." I am not referring to efficacy as such; I stress the importance of *perceived* efficacy. Statuses owe their functionality to the degree in which Y-types are *believed or perceived* to successfully exercise their deontic powers and to make a difference in the world. The status of the palm leaf would also be diminished if the coconut owners were only *believed* to be lax in claiming their due. This is why I prefer the term "output-validity" to "efficacy." "Output-validity" makes clear that validity is *attributed,* in other words, that weight is *accorded* to some item Y by virtue of the expectation of a future output. Those expectations might be informed by the real output that is delivered, but not necessarily and not continuously so.

The example of the Mafia might clarify my point. The Mafia is commonly thought to be based on violence. However, in his fascinating book on the Sicilian Mafia, Diego Gambetta describes how violence plays a more limited role. It is used to create an atmosphere of insecurity and fear, which made the product the Mafia

[14]On mutual interdependence, see Homans (1950), pp. 6–10.

could deliver, protection, all the more necessary and valuable. However, at a certain point in the historical development of the Mafia, a display of aggression and violence was no longer needed. The mere *name* "Mafia" was enough to fulfill its function. As soon as the reputation of an effective protector has firmly taken root, it is no longer necessary to exhibit aggressive behavior. As Gambetta notes, whereas manufacturers still have to produce cars, even though they enjoy a good reputation, matters are different with the Mafia, who merchandise protection. The very status of a powerful protector is then sufficient to generate the protection in itself.[15]

This example strongly supports Searle's view that acceptance generates functionality. It suggests that the status of Y-terms, although dependent on perceived efficacy, need not continually be supported by output. This is why I do not think that coercion is the key to understanding obedience to the law, as Schauer asserts.[16] The key is the *belief* that coercion will eventually be applied in accordance with the status of the Y-term or, more precisely, the belief that there is a collective agreement to attribute a status to X, which entails the duty to apply sanctions. That belief in itself helps Y to perform its assigned function. On the other hand, repeated failure to perform that assigned function (think of Mafiosi, who are deprived of their guns or simply jailed) would diminish such a status: not immediately but in the long run. And such a diminished status would eventually even further reduce functionality, which would further decrease status and so on.

5 Sources and Status

There is mutual dependence not only between collective agreement and output-validity but also between collective agreement and input-validity. Lawyers will hardly be surprised to learn that origins and procedural correctness determine the status of the Y-term. In fact, this is how they usually and predominantly determine the validity of a certain token Y. And this applies not only to particular rules or contracts but also to types Y: all rules that pass the Council of State are to be accorded the status of formal law. One may even think that not only tokens, not only types, but also the way in which these types are connected to each other and form a *system* is judged by its input-validity. The ways in which a legal order is instituted, the kind of procedures that were followed elevate the status of such an order. All kinds of conditions may apply in order to assess the degree of input-validity. It is not only formal and procedural conditions that may be believed to be relevant but also moral ones. In such cases, a certain legal order is only declared to be valid if it is established by democratic means or when it is issued by the deity. All these conditions may apply and serve to differentiate the legal from the non-legal and the illegal, and the legitimate from the illegitimate. These are all initial conditions to be

[15] Gambetta (1993), p. 44.

[16] Schauer (2015).

met by some type X to count as type Y or to connections between types Y. It is hardly remarkable to observe then that the degree of input-validity (the degree in which these conditions are believed to be met) enhances the collective agreement that type X counts as type Y.

More surprisingly, however, the reverse also obtains. The more status Y enjoys, the more there is the need to show that it meets the initial conditions. Again, the Mafia example, for all its simplicity, serves as a fine example, for as soon as the status of "Mafioso" has met with such support, that is, has become functional in itself, independent of any further display of aggression, it becomes *all the more important* to be able to show that someone counts as a "genuine" Mafioso. To that end, a set of formal conditions is devised by means of which a genuine (valid) Mafioso can be identified. The Mafioso is converted into a type, and any token Mafioso could from now on be compared to the type in order to see whether he is a "valid" Mafioso. Gambetta tells us that various mechanisms were invented in order to "accredit" someone as belonging to the "real brand": initiation rituals, testimonies of witnesses,[17] as well as the organization of different families whose main business is to exclude counterfeit Mafioso from business.[18]

If we apply these insights to the law, they suggest that criteria for input-validity (the initiation rituals, the correct procedures, the pedigree) are deemed more important to the degree in which the status of Y is secure. The more secure the reputation of the Y-term (whether Mafiosi, wills, or contracts), the more important it becomes to tell the genuine Y from the counterfeit one.

It is tempting to hypothesize that the contemporary and typically legal focus on input-validity as the only form of validity suggests that the status that is generally accorded to legal products in our legal culture is rather secure. In countries and cultures where there is a general distrust or indifference toward legal products, questions of pedigree and procedural correctness may play a far more limited role. In fact, this is in line with what I noted at the beginning of this article that there should be a certain amount of type-validity in order to make the examination of the validity of particular legal products relevant. We can now add to this that presumably the *degree* of type-validity determines the *degree* in which input-validity is deemed relevant.

We have seen that the status of a Y-term both determines and is determined by output-validity: the degree in which Y is expected to have effects. We also saw that the status of a Y-term determines and is determined by input-validity, i.e. the degree in which that item is believed to meet the conditions for type X to count as type Y. What about throughput-validity? What role is played by the perception of [type] Y's status as being considered as weighty and relevant by significant others? In fact, throughput-validity is nothing else than the very status that is actually enjoyed by a Y-term by relevant actors. It is the intersubjective and collective agreement itself that

[17]Even fathers wanted to be convinced that their sons had turned into real Mafiosos after emigration to the US and required (independent) testimonies of a neutral third party. Gambetta (1993), Ch. 5.

[18]See Gambetta (1993), Ch. 6.

is taken as a starting point for the determination of the status of Y. The more we believe that there is collective agreement, the more collective agreement there will be, and the more collective agreement there is, the stronger our belief will be that there is such collective agreement. We have come here indeed full circle. But here again, the circularity of the argument need not detain us from following the argument to its logical conclusion. If all my colleagues take the standardized protocols of the audit committee very seriously, I will most likely follow their judgement, if only in order not to jeopardize my reputation with my colleagues. And this will further enhance the status and concomitant deontic powers of such protocols. There is nothing mysterious in this kind of circularity.

It is clear that throughput-validity, the degree of collective agreement, is dependent on both input- and output-validity. But again, collective agreement need not necessarily and continuously be supported by input- and output-validity. The situation may arise that collective acceptance of the Y-term in itself is secure enough to survive even when no sanctions materialize at all. In that situation, throughput-validity, i.e. the intersubjective and collective agreement on the status of a certain type Y-term is self-sustaining. One attributes a certain status to Y because others do so. References by the courts and academics, being practiced by relevant actors or preached by policy makers, may all add up to the status of Y-terms, which will then be relatively autonomous and independent from input and output. And because all others do so and everybody orients themselves to such Y-terms, they grow more closely connected to other Y-terms and in this way form a network of meanings that can also sustain each other. It is no longer necessary that each [type] Y is supported by input or output considerations. Unsupported elements may be supported by other, better equipped elements of the network. A legal order is born.

I think, but of course more empirical evidence should be adduced, that this latter possibility has materialized in our present-day legal order, which is pervaded by various soft law arrangements. Type-validity (the belief in collective acceptance of types) is so strong that the mere semblance of legality is enough to endow soft law arrangements with (token)-validity. If a certain university curriculum counts as an "accredited curriculum," there is apparently no need to either examine the input-validity or the output-validity of that status. That the accreditation is carried out by an organization without legal mandate or which lacks the sanctions to respond to noncompliance does not make any difference: the status itself ("accredited" curriculum) *carries its own reward*. Regulatory practices in which supervisory boards "advise" the norm addressees to invest in labor conditions by following a detailed set of instructions, for instance, may lack a legal basis and may be unaccompanied by sanctions. Yet norm addressees tremble at the prospect of their visits and go to all lengths to comply with their wishes, even if such actions are contrary to their own better judgement.[19] The very fact that these norm addressees take this "advice" so seriously might induce other actors to attach to them a certain weight as reasons for their judgement. The courts generally attach importance to the views and social

[19]Timmer (2011).

practices that exist in a certain field. References in jurisprudential and academic literature will strengthen the reputation of the advice even further, which will presumably also affect the reputation of the rule makers, in this case the supervisory board. From now on, such advice is seen as relevant and weighty reasons for both norm addressees and judges. The best practices of the norm addressees who adopt these rules as their own will be propagated; more institutions will voluntarily adopt these best practices in order to enhance their own reputation, which will give even more support for officials who use them as reasons for their decisions. After some time, the "advice" has evolved into something that approximates binding law.

6 The Fragility of Validity

So far then I have asserted that an examination of the validity of particular legal constructs such as wills, contracts, or rules is dependent on the background belief that in general such contracts matter and make a difference. Type-validity is nothing more than the belief that there is collective agreement by virtue of which [types of] X count as [types of] Y. Collective agreement can wax or wane, dependent on whether these types meet a set of explicit and shared entrance conditions (input-validity), whether and to what extent they are supported by others—the collective acceptance itself or throughput-validity—and, finally, on their outcome, i.e. the real effects that these Y-terms are believed to exercise. On the basis of these three routes, the reputation (i.e., the validity) of legal constructs in general (as well as their interconnections in a legal order) can be established and determined.

I hypothesized that input-validity, throughput-validity, and output-validity are mutually dependent and reinforce each other. In this way, one might say that trust breeds trust.[20] If I am correct in these hypotheses, which need to be substantiated by further empirical evidence, this is good news for countries that struggle with an apparently weak legal order, i.e. an institutional setting that rests on limited type-validity.[21] The circles of interaction between input, throughput, and output do not presuppose a first mover. It is not imperative that legal orders be instituted by a display of violence or coercion. One may as well begin at the other end, by making sure that entrance conditions are made explicit and shared. Or one might try to generate more throughput-validity. We should not look for the golden key toward a more secure or stable legal order. It may arise out of modest beginnings and expand by virtue of its sheer self-reinforcing dynamism.

However, there also seem to be limits to this self-sustaining and self-reinforcing nature of institutional orders. We should not forget that the whole network of mutually reinforcing considerations is ultimately built on reputation. This may be strong and stable, but once doubt creeps in, it may undermine the whole network of

[20] Feld and Frey (2002).

[21] The so-called failed states; see Acemoglu and Robinson (2012).

mutual dependencies in the same self-reinforcing way, and the collective agreement may vanish just as quickly as it emerged. Doubts concerning the status of the Y-term cause it to function less adequately, which would further undermine throughput-validity. Consequently, the loss of throughput-validity would render input-validity less relevant. This inevitably affects the status of other Y-terms that are linked to it. A negative spiral sets in, not unlike a crash of the financial market.

I do not know at what stage such negative spirals can be expected. The emergence of soft law and the status it has acquired testifies to a considerable amount of type-validity. But how long can the perception of efficacy survive if no real sanctions are administered? The question is particularly relevant for international soft law. How long can human rights retain their status if they remain solemn but impotent declarations that cannot deliver a real outcome that effectively improves the lives of the world's inhabitants?

The dilemma is devilish. If we remain true to Searle's picture of the construction of social reality, we might with some reason cherish the expectation that these Y-terms—by the very fact that they are mentioned in declarations and treaties—acquire meaning by themselves and therefore will give rise to enforceable rights and obligations. They will then gradually acquire a moderate degree of type-validity against which at least *claims* to human rights can sensibly be put forward. We have seen that this hope is not totally groundless. But as we have also seen, acceptance is informed by input, throughput, and output. In all three aspects, the position of human rights is unstable. Their origins are doubtful; they are often mentioned in academic circles but more often disregarded by officials. This means that if these declarations remain dead letters, they may breed a kind of—justified—skepticism that might also spread to those parts of international law that enjoy a more formal status. Not only soft but also "hard" law may be perceived as impotent and futile, more symbol than status.

The same applies, to a lesser extent, to domestic soft law. There is a moment at which everybody will suddenly see that the emperor does not wear any clothes. Domestic soft law might be attributed status, as long as it is still linked by some thin thread to formal hard law, but it remains to be seen how long it would survive after it has been severed from that navel cord and whether throughput-validity in itself can keep the baby alive. Of course, and unlike international soft law, domestic soft law may be revived by threat of real enforcement and sanctions. By strengthening output-validity, the circulation between input-, throughput-, and output-validity could once more be set in motion. Or it may profit from a process of formalization in which conditions are made explicit, which refer to a set of procedural constraints that should be met. It seems to be a risky strategy to rely on throughput-validity alone. Soft law and hard law are not separate entities but are intertwined in the network of a legal order. Just as soft law acquires status from its marriage to hard law, hard law may lose its status from its marriage to soft law as well. If people get used to the fact that law may have spurious origins and uncertain outcomes, they may also tend to be less impressed by hard law.

One might object: is the demise of soft (and hard) law really such a disaster? If a certain legal system is iniquitous or cruel, the diminished reputation of that legal system can even be welcomed. This objection is justified. No one in his right mind would deplore a diminished reputation of the Mafia, and the same would probably apply to many legal systems all around the world. Yet I would like to point to one important function of legal orders, which probably deserves to be maintained, even if they figure in wicked or morally despicable political regimes. In order to see that important function, it is worthwhile to recall to mind once more the examples provided by Goyal in his contribution, which pertain to the regulation of informal markets. As we have seen, type-validity of a formal institutional order is the functional equivalent of personal reputation in such informal settings. But although functionally equivalent, there are some advantages attached to a formal institutional order, which cannot be disregarded too easily. In such a formal order, conditions are made explicit and more or less fixed and stable. This means that reputation is enjoyed by types rather than by tokens. And this in turn ensures that these types can acquire a shared meaning and status that stretches far beyond the confined local contexts of informal settings. Formal legal orders, even morally wicked ones, enable the coordination between people who are far apart in both time and place. The reputation of such legal orders is therefore not something that may be jeopardized without risking the reduction of coordination.

7 Conclusion

The very question whether a certain legal construct is valid or invalid presupposes a world in which types of such constructs are generally regarded as relevant reasons for decision making. We only want to know whether a particular document counts as a valid contract in a world in which contracts generally matter and make a difference. But when do they generally matter? Only if we believe that there is collective agreement on the fact that contracts matter, i.e. generate legal and factual consequences, or, more broadly speaking, if there is a belief in a viable legal order. Such a belief, however, is not something that is either there or not there. It can wax or wane.

But under what conditions do such beliefs grow or diminish? The question is important, not only in order to understand the emergence of soft law in the Western world but also in order to understand when and why legal orders lose relevance and credibility, such as is the case in many "failed states." In fact, such "failed" law is exactly the reverse of soft law. Whereas in Western Europe many soft law arrangements are seen as relevant even if they are not valid law, the failed state can issue and codify laws following strict legal procedures, but these extremely "hard" laws are nevertheless seen as irrelevant and do not figure as reasons for decision making.[22]

[22] Or, if they figure at all, they are used as means to increase the private income of officials.

In order to understand these remarkable phenomena, empirical research is called for. To that end, I have formulated a couple of hypotheses, together forming a theoretical framework for further research, that would enable us to understand the conditions under which a belief in a legal order is strengthened or, instead, jeopardized. The basic assumption underlying these hypotheses is an analogy: it is the assumption that the type-validity of legal systems can be understood in just the same way as the reputation of persons. Validity, just like reputation, is informed by input (pedigree, procedures, sources), by throughput (the esteem in which it is held by significant others), and by output (the degree of actual performance). Input, throughput, and output considerations together inform the extent to which a legal order is deemed credible. Interestingly, these three types of considerations are mutually dependent and interact with each other to the degree that we can even speak of self-reinforcing mechanisms. In this manner, disbelief generates disbelief and trust breeds trust. Reputations—both of persons and of legal systems—are just as rapidly gained as they are lost. In cases where the reputation of the legal order is strong, the emergence of soft law can be explained. The network of legal concepts in which a soft law arrangement is embedded is then so strong and stable that unsupported (soft law) elements are supported by better supported elements. Soft law is then parasitic on the validity accorded to hard law. But in situations where the reputation of the legal order is weak, soft law cannot survive at all and hard law also struggles to be regarded as relevant. In such cases, questions of trust will most likely be resolved by reverting to personal reputation, more limited in scope, time, and place.

References

Acemoglu, Daron, and James A. Robinson. 2012. *Why Nations Fail: The Origins of Power, Prosperity and Poverty*. London: Profile Books.

Black, Julia. 2008. *Forms and Paradoxes of Principles Based Regulation*. London: LSE Law, Society and Economy Working Papers 13/2008, London School of Economics and Political Science, Law Department.

Feld, Lars P., and Bruno S. Frey. 2002. Trust Breeds Trust: How Tax-payers Are Treated. *Economics of Governance* 3: 87–99.

Gambetta, Diego. 1993. *The Sicilian Mafia: The Business of Private Protection*. Cambridge, MA: Harvard UP.

Hart, H.L.A. 1997. *The Concept of Law* (Second Edition, with a Postscript edited by Penelope A. Bulloch and Joseph Raz). Oxford: Oxford University Press.

Homans, George C. 1950. *The Human Group*. New York: Harcourt, Brace and World Inc.

Kelsen, Hans. 1945. *General Theory of Law and State*, tr A. Wedberg. Cambridge, MA: Harvard UP.

Malinowski, Bronislaw. 1926. *Crime and Custom in Savage Society*. New York: Harcourt, Brace and Company. To be accessed at https://archive.org/details/crimecustominsav00mali.

Pufendorf, Samuel. 1934 (1688). *De Jure Naturae et Gentium libri octo*, tr C.H. and W.A. Oldfather. In *The Classics of International Law*. Oxford: Clarendon Press.

Schauer, Frederick. 2015. *The Force of Law*. Cambridge, MA: Harvard UP.

Searle, John. 1995. *The Construction of Social Reality*. New York: The Free Press.
Timmer, Wim. 2011. *Het doel wel gesteld: Een praktijkonderzoek naar de toepassing van doelregelgeving*. Centre for Law and Innovation, Boom Juridisch Uitgevers (dissertation Erasmus University Rotterdam).
Westerman, Pauline C. 2007a. Governing by Goals: Governance as a Legal Style. *Legisprudence: International Journal for the Study of Legislation* 51–72. Oxford: Hart Publishing.
———. 2007b. The Emergence of New Types of Norms. In *Legislation in Context: Essays in Legisprudence*, ed. Luc J. Wintgens, 117–133. Aldershot: Ashgate.

A Short Note on the Validity of Rules Guiding Informal Markets

Yugank Goyal and Pauline Westerman

Abstract We argue in this note that the principles of validity need fresh understanding to explain the elements of private ordering exhibited in the vast swathes of informal markets around the world. Informal markets, by definition, lie outside formal legal systems and yet display a tenacious stability in their norms. We show that these norms are valid because they are driven by reputation rather than any higher order of law. In doing so, reputation drives efficacy into validity. By remolding Kelsen's ideas on validity into Hart's internal point of view, we show how reputation drives efficacy into validity. We illustrate this idea through a case study on a centuries-old footwear cluster in Agra (India).

1 Introduction

Legal philosophy is usually concerned with a formal legal order, which owes its origins to the sovereign state. The study of the norms that regulate social groups or foreign nonstate cultures is left to sociology or anthropology. This has had the result that many informal normative arrangements, usually assembled under the broad and uninformative—if not puzzling—heading of "customary law" have largely remained unexplored terrain as far as legal philosophy is concerned.[1] It is at best conceived as the poor relation of "real" law, vestiges of which remain to be seen in rural regions or in the underdeveloped countries of the world.

The emergence of soft law practices in Western Europe and the United States, however, testifies to the fact that nowadays in the developed world, too, the state is less than ever the sole source of law. On the contrary, in order to cope with the

[1] A notable exception is of course Lon Fuller. See Klink & Lembcke in this volume.

Y. Goyal (✉)
OP Jindal Global University, Sonipat, India
e-mail: ygoyal@jgu.edu.in

P. Westerman
Rijksuniversiteit Groningen, Groningen, The Netherlands
e-mail: p.c.westerman@rthrug.nl

© Springer International Publishing AG, part of Springer Nature 2018

P. Westerman et al. (eds.), *Legal Validity and Soft Law*, Law and Philosophy Library 122, https://doi.org/10.1007/978-3-319-77522-7_9

complexities of the regulatory state, modern legislatures of the Western world often invoke the help of social fields and private partners. By relying on extant customary and informal arrangements, they try to find more effective ways of realizing domestic policies. But in doing so, they rely on forms of "law" that cannot be seen as valid in the usual and strict sense of the word, that is, as in conformity with some higher legal norm that regulates the creation and application of legal rules. Does this mean that these informal forms of soft law have to be denied any validity at all and that we should allow for the emergence of "invalid law"? Or should we revise the concept of validity?

In order to shed some new light on this question, it may be instructive to take a look at informal economies. The economies of more than half of the world are unregulated by formal law. They are guided by all kinds of rules. But there is no formal banking system, there is no access to the formal judiciary, and the norms that guide the way these markets function are not in any sense linked to the formal legal system. In India, more than 90% of the total workforce is engaged in the informal economy.[2]

Examining informal markets also helps us understand the concept of validity across time. As von der Pfordten in this volume reminds us, the history of this concept in philosophy is rather recent, the nineteenth century. This is also the time when formal legal structures were emerging in market-based frameworks around the Western world. To understand the concept from the point of view of formal arrangements alone ignores how human societies have dealt with "validity" across time, and informal markets provide a unique window for us to view it through.

In this article, we will describe the case of the informal arrangements by which the shoe trade and manufacture are regulated in Agra, India. The survey for this research was conducted by Goyal during December 2012–January 2013 and April–June 2013. Since the market is concentrated in a small geographical space and traders are present in their shops every day (except Sunday when the market is closed), this was an ideal locale to collect cross-sectional data. Goyal employed unstructured interviews to understand the market, the credit structure, and risk-sharing institutions. The description of the case will prompt us to raise a couple of questions and observations that may be helpful in developing a concept of validity that may apply to informal and nonstate normative systems.

[2]According to recent ILO estimates, the informal economy provides employment to 71% of nonagricultural workers in sub-Saharan Africa, 71% in Asia, 51% in Latin America and 47% in the Middle East and North Africa.

2 The Case

Agra, the poster city of India's tourism (home of the Taj Mahal), is also famous for its centuries-old leather footwear cluster. It produces more than 40% of the domestic and 20% of the export footwear of India. It has both highly formal manufacturers (in the form of huge export-oriented enterprises and smaller factories), as well as unorganized shoemakers in the form of household artisans or small-scale factories. More than two-thirds of the manufacturing units are located in household artisan-dominated communities. The unorganized trade exists "outside" the legal net since most shoemakers are not registered legally, and even traders, many of whom are indeed registered, conduct businesses without disclosing their incomes to save taxes (shadow or black economy).

Like many trading businesses, trade in the Agra footwear cluster takes place on credit. Artisan shoemakers arrive with their shoes in the market every day in the evening to sell the shoes to the traders. Market norms mandate that they sell the shoes on credit (usually for 3 months). For trade credit to work in any informal market, two conditions are necessary: first, there needs to be a credible commitment from the trader's side to pay the debt, and second, the cost of liquidity to suppliers must be low. In other words, promises to repay the outstanding amount must be kept, and the credit supplier must have sufficient capital that he can withstand the restricted cash flow until the debt is paid. Since the market operates outside the law, it is difficult to make credible commitments. If the trader reneges on his promise, the shoemaker cannot really go to court since there is no explicit contract fulfilling legal obligations. Further, the shoemakers are extremely poor, which makes the cost of liquidity very high for them. They need cash every day to buy raw materials from the market and cannot quite sell on credit unlike the rich suppliers.

The market solves the two problems simultaneously through the institution of a credit note, commonly known as parchi. Whenever the shoemaker sells shoes to a trader, the latter issues a credit note (parchi) to him, noting the details of the outstanding amount, the trader's name, and the due date. When the parchi is returned to the trader on the due date, he is obliged to clear the debt.

2.1 Solving the Credible Commitment Problem

Commitments come from the prevalent high degree of information symmetry in the market as regards reputation. Almost everyone knows everyone else: should a trader renege on his payment, this is quickly known to the entire industry through the many informal channels of information dissemination, that is, discussion, gossip, chats, rumors, and informal gatherings. The market is very cohesive and closely knit, which also explains the relational- and trust-based mechanisms invoked in transactions daily. If one looks at the traders' dwelling patterns, they reside in certain expensive areas in Agra and meet often at social gatherings, make conjugal alliances, and are members of the same town clubs.

Most traders are Punjabis by caste, and the shoemakers belong to the lower castes. The caste networks bring them closer. Laborers live in ghettos, and after work they get together for local drinks and food, sharing stories and rumors, constructing and disseminating information. Opportunities for arbitrage are low. Almost everyone knows everyone else, and impersonation is not easy. Hence, if news of a trader reneging on his dues or canceling a contract is revealed to one, almost every shoemaker will hear of it. The market allows everyone to keep a keen eye on the capital and net worth of the traders.

2.2 Solving the Liquidity Problem

Over the decades, the market has evolved an indigenous way of solving the problem of liquidity. The parchis have assumed the role of a promissory note. This means that the shoemaker can sell the parchi to a third person at a discount. Informal intermediaries have emerged in the market, called *aadhatiyas*, who buy the parchis at interest (which is the discount offered by the parchi seller, the shoemaker). Thus, the shoemaker obtains the liquidity owed, minus interest, perhaps on the same day as the shoes are traded. The trader gets credit. Upon maturity, the *aadhatiya* collects the cash noted on the parchi from the trader who issued it and pockets the interest. In this way, the parchi system institutionally creates liquidity in the market. The system resembles the historical emergence of commercial paper. Parchis are the pivot over which a parallel banking system for the enormous footwear industry in Agra rotates.

The question remains: how is the *aadhatiya* able to monitor and manage the risk in securing his money outside the law? Interest rates play a crucial role in this. The interest rates on the parchi depend solely on the reputation and creditworthiness of the trader who issued the parchi. This means that if A is considered trustworthy and the market values his promise, the interest rate on A's parchi will be lower than C's, who has a lower reputation for fulfilling his promises in the market. This will discourage the shoemaker from approaching C to sell his shoes in the first place: the higher interest rates on C are costly for the shoemaker. To attract shoemakers, therefore, traders have to be trustworthy. Hence, C has an incentive to keep his promises and create a good reputation. The parchi institution therefore creates a self-enforcing mechanism.

Inevitably, there are also cases of unavoidable bankruptcies. Again, they are dealt with by an informal dispute settlement, organized by the local associations of traders and the like. These bodies are headed by veterans of the trade who mediate and order how much the creditors need to be paid, assessing the leftover worth of the bankrupt trader. Settlements are not made with documentary evidence and lawyer-driven arguments. People know the story, and lying is impossible. The judgments of the association members are usually adhered to, and the judicial system of the local courts is seldom invoked.

3 The Attribution of Validity

The parchi system is clearly an institution that functions outside the law. Violations of its rules will not be dealt with by formal courts: the rules are enforced by other market players. The story of the parchi system paints a natural landscape for most transactions in the developing world. These transactions are not backed up by any formal law but work on the basis of reputation mechanisms.

It is clear that the reputation of the trader plays an important role in ascertaining the value of a particular parchi. The better is the reputation, the more it is worth. In fact, we might say that whereas in a formal system the validity of any document is decided by reference to some other—higher—*law*, in an informal system that question is decided by referring to the reputation of the *person* by whom the document is created or forwarded. Personal reputation is therefore a type of what Hage in this volume calls source validity. The worth or validity of the document is determined by reference to its source, and in this case the source is the object of gossip, rumors, and all that idiosyncratic knowledge[3] that builds up a personal reputation. On the basis of this form of knowledge, not only is it decided whether a certain piece of paper is a genuine (valid!) parchi or not (in an all-or-nothing fashion), but its value (in a gradual way) is also determined. In the parchi system, validity and value hang closely together.

Yet we must distinguish here between the validity of a particular parchi and the validity of the parchi system as a whole. At first sight, the notion of the validity of an entire system is somewhat strange and elusive. But we should not understand "validity" as an objectively attributable quality of systems. We think that it is more appropriate to understand validity on the basis of what Hart (1994) called the internal point of view. Validity is then *perceived* validity: the degree to which norms are regarded as standards, deviation from which calls for criticism and justification. In informal systems, validity is perceived not only by officials but by all the participants in that normative order. We might therefore say that the rules of the shoe market are valid if people regard them as standards. They are quite different from, for instance, traffic rules as regarded by Indian drivers in India, for whom they are merely legally valid. Despite their legal validity, people do not choose to follow the traffic rules, even when all these rules are bound by a higher valid norm, leading all the way up to the Constitution of India. They are simply not seen as standards for

[3]Idiosyncratic knowledge is similar to Polanyi's tacit knowledge (Polanyi 1966). It denotes specific knowledge that cannot be easily transferred from one individual to another nor can be aggregated for generalization (See also, Williamson 1975, 1979). If idiosyncratic knowledge is in play, the underlying governance structures and contractual arrangements become highly transaction-specific and are unique. The low degree of formalization of these arrangements means that third parties (for example courts) cannot assess them and hence cannot enforce them. As a consequence the trust relation between the parties involved becomes central to running the transaction successfully. Thereby the routines and practices for maintaining the trust relation also become part of the shared idiosyncratic knowledge.

action. On the contrary, traffic *violation* is an all-pervasive norm, existing, interestingly, as one of the few uniting features in a country as diverse as India.

As Hart rightly points out, the internal point of view is not just a feeling. The acceptance of norms as standards should be expressed in action. The horror that Western visitors go through when being driven in a car in Delhi's streets is in stark contrast to the peaceful demeanor of the Indian driver of that same car. The driver knows the norms and does not flinch one bit when he sees a law violation since for him it does not constitute a norm violation. It is important to stress actual practice: only then can people know other people's internal points of view.

4 Trust and Reputation

What conditions should be fulfilled by rules in order to be accepted as standards? Jellinek's (1905) answer would be simply because these rules exist. In a certain minimal sense, we may concede with Jellinek that, indeed, the bare existence of the system is enough to give it a certain validity. Jellinek argues that it is an observable human psychological fact that people attach normative power to that which exists and repeats itself, a phenomenon already to be witnessed in the child who asks every evening for the same story to be read to him and who considers the slightest deviation from regular practice as abnormal, as a violation of the norm. Jellinek called this *die normative Kraft des Faktischen.* We can concede that there is a grain of truth in this observation at the collective level as well, which is observable in the phenomenon of path dependence. Path dependence also plays a role in our example.[4] The very fact that a certain practice has evolved along particular lines makes it more acceptable to people who consider such a practice not only as that which *is* normal but also as that which *should* be normal. Apart from this, path dependence also turns any change in direction into a costly affair. Change entails both psychological and financial effort.

Yet matters should not be exaggerated: people do not comply out of sheer resignation with the status quo and its well-established patterns of behavior. If they did, we would be able to say that they adopt what Hart would call an *external* point of view toward these rules and standards. They would view these rules mainly

[4]Until independence, the business was dominated by Muslims and Jatavs (a lower caste). But most of the affluent Muslims left for Pakistan during the partition-induced migration, and Agra's shoe industry began deteriorating with poor Jatavs in their unorganized cottage units. When the Punjabis arrived in Agra, they noticed the skills of the Jatavs and poor Muslim shoemakers. They also noticed that: (a) there was a lack of market connectivity, and shoemakers had a tough time finding customers since they could not travel far; (b) the shoemakers themselves were shoe sellers, and selling came at the opportunity cost of making; and (c) shoemaking was done in a very informal and unorganized manner. Further, working with leather was not a taboo within the Punjabi community as it was within traditional Hindu upper castes. In addition, the migrant community was badly in need of a sustainable income, and the potential of footwear trading in Agra caught their attention.

as predictions of what will happen and how others will behave. But compliance to the rules of the parchi system is not at all like that. As we noted above, people's attitude towards these rules is more like Hart's internal point of view, according to which they really see these norms as binding standards and express their acceptance of these norms in outward behavior.

That being said, we should immediately add that people's internal point of view should be corroborated, so to speak, by the outward behavior of the other participants that reveal the same internal point of view. It is only on the basis of a shared understanding of one another's internal point of view that the reputation mechanism can work. One knows then how to adapt one's behavior to the gaze of others so that one's reputation will be improved.

In the shoe market, we see this mechanism clearly at work. Again, reputation plays a pivotal role. The reputation of the trader does not only determine the value and validity of a particular parchi. It is also a sanctioning mechanism. Violation of the norms, such as reneging on one's promises, immediately damages one's reputation. Violation of the norms is therefore punished not by a specialized class of people, such as judges or arbitrators, but by all the other members of the system. Norm conformity is directly translated into an improved position in the social network, whereas norm violation is directly translated into a damaged reputation. Sanctions are not inflicted from "without" but consist in an altered composition of the social network.

In the parchi system, indeed there are two economies at work simultaneously and in parallel: an economy of money and of reputation.[5] If the mechanisms of information and reputation work, these two economies reinforce each other, and there is therefore no need for an additional normative system with sanctions of its own. Nonconformity with the norms can even result in social suicide.

So we see that reputation fulfills four functions simultaneously[6]:

1. It indicates someone's past performance (= among other things compliance with the norms).
2. It determines the value and validity of particular documents.
3. It is the key component in decision making (do I trade with trader X or Y?).
4. It sanctions nonconformity.

5 Conditions for Efficacy

In order to carry out all these functions successfully, two conditions should be fulfilled. In the first place, the stability of the system depends on the possibility of *access* to that reputation. How do we *know* someone's reputation? This is the question that haunts many emigrants who leave their rural surroundings and go to

[5]See Homans (1950, p. 295).

[6]See also, Westerman's chapter in this volume for a larger exposition on validity as reputation.

the big cities, where access to someone's reputation is difficult. So in order for the parchi system as a whole to flourish, it should function in a closely knit community in which perfect information symmetry and coordination are possible. Only then can the mechanisms of the market survive and interest rates be thought to reflect the dynamic information about traders' (non)fulfillment of their promises. The crucial factor allowing the system work seamlessly is therefore the information flow. This information flow concerning someone's reputation creates knowledge of how much to trust: a feeling of certainty in the minds of those who participate in the parchi system. In turn, this stability turns it into a viable and efficacious system. It works in practice. Mackor in this volume engages with this intersection of trust and conduct.

The second prerequisite for the system to work is the belief that others share the same internal point of view. This belief is of course crucial because one does not want to run the risk of being deceived by noncompliant others. But more important is that only on the basis of such a shared point of view can we expect reputation to perform its sanctioning task. In a context in which noncompliance is even considered a virtue (as in the traffic example), violation will not damage but may even fortify one's reputation.

Once the system is perceived to be workable and stable, the very functionality, agility, and utility of the system will be (additional) reasons for people to follow its rules. So in a sense, such an informal system is a self-reinforcing system.

Reputation → workable order → perception of effectiveness → willingness to comply → enhanced reputation.

In an informal normative order, unregulated by explicit laws, it is reputation, or—more precisely—information concerning reputation, that is the most important condition for effectiveness. Only then do we know the value of particular items, and only then will norm violation actually and effectively result in a loss of reputation. If violation of the rules has no effect on one's reputation, that order is ineffective and will also damage the internal attitude toward such rules.

For a viable normative order, every actor presupposes (as Hart 1994 would say) the "truth of the external statement of the fact that the system is generally efficacious," and that is how the concerned actor makes an internal statement concerning the validity of the rules. This means that the degree to which the actor perceives rules to be valid is informed by their efficacy, and at the same time, the degree to which a system is perceived to be efficacious is dependent on the degree to which the actor thinks that people generally adopt an internal point of view of its rules.

In societies where legal enforcement or empowerment is not necessarily strong, this knowledge will be the sole distinguishing factor between what is valid and what is invalid. Even though not in binary or discrete terms, validity may be a very real product of efficacy.

Hart is silent on highly efficacious systems that do not conform to the law (or are invalid through a legal lens), and Kelsen (1970) argued that valid systems must be efficacious but not necessarily the other way round. The parchi system reveals a third possibility in which a system that lacks legal validity nevertheless gains efficacy, as well as a binding force from an internal point of view. Most systems in developing countries are of this nature. Indeed, when states are no longer the sole sources of the law, one must not disregard the possibility of locating meanings of validity outside the traditional source of law, something elaborated upon by Carpentier in this volume.

6 Conclusion

What can a legal philosopher learn from this modest excursion into an informal market? In the first place, that it is not necessary to assume, in a Kelsenian (1970) way, a higher—valid—*legal* rule in order to determine whether a specific document or rule is valid. The validity—and value—of parchis is determined by personal reputation and not by law.

But reputation may also decide the validity of systems as a whole. The degree to which this reputation is or can be known and valued determines the degree to which the system is effective; in turn, the degree of efficacy determines—among other considerations—the degree to which these rules are believed to guide other people's actions, whereby such a shared internal view further reinforces effectiveness.

We have seen that the role of reputation is, however, not only limited to being an indication of validity. If there exists a shared internal point of view, reputation is also the major sanctioning mechanism of such a system. Cheating automatically damages one's reputation. The degree to which this sanctioning mechanism is effective might further strengthen the shared internal point of view concerning the validity of the system as a whole. Efficacy and validity are therefore transmitted and mutually reinforced by means of one and the same mechanism: reputation.

It is not easy to ascertain the position of reputation in the dichotomous Kelsenian world in which *is* and *ought* are separated. On the one hand, what the reputation of a certain person *is* depends on considerations of fact: it really matters whether a certain trader is indeed fulfilling his promises. But on the other hand, the ways in which reputations are evaluated is clearly dependent on norms, such as the norm that he should fulfill his promises, so we might say that in the last resort, validity is determined by (non-legal) norms.

Kelsen also seems right in saying that it is not necessary to assume the efficacy of an entire system in order to determine the value and validity of a particular parchi. Although a valid or invalid parchi presupposes a workable parchi system, its value (i.e., the numerical value of the interest rate) is determined not by that efficacy but by the reputation of the trader. In this sense, indeed efficacy is a *conditio sine qua non* and not a *conditio per quam*.

But in order to understand the validity of a legal order as a *whole*, efficacy does play a role. People should feel secure about its workings in order to participate in such a system. This security is not necessarily attached to the perceived moral qualities of the system—many workable informal markets (often dramatically) fall short of noble moral standards—but thrives mainly on the public accessibility of information that sets the wheels of the system in motion. If the system is hampered by information deficits, it cannot sustain itself in the sense we describe above. So in order to determine the validity of the system as a whole, efficacy is of supreme importance and indeed turns into a *conditio per quam.* Not only should we say that valid law should be efficacious. Efficacious laws must be valid too.

Reputation proves to be a powerful mechanism that performs many essential functions in a normative system. There is only one major shortcoming: it is limited in scope. It is dependent on personal information and idiosyncratic knowledge, which is only available in closely knit social networks. The expansion of trade beyond the confines of such localized contexts naturally called for a substitute for reputation. One such substitute is legal rules. However, times are changing. The kind of information that is required to determine one's reputation is now freely available and accessible on the Internet and can be shared with almost anyone, regardless of distance in time and space. This fact might have contributed to the emergence of soft law, which in large part relies on reputation as well. Rather than analyzing soft law arrangements by wondering to what degree they derive their validity from legal rules, it seems more advisable to inquire into the mechanisms of reputation that are at work in such arrangements. The shoe market of Agra shows how such an analysis could be carried out.

References

Hart, H.L.A. 1994. *The Concept of Law*. (Second Edition, with a Postscript edited by Penelope A. Bulloch and Joseph Raz). Oxford: Oxford University Press.

Homans, G.C. 1950. *The Human Group*. New York: Harcourt, Brace and World Inc.

Jellinek, G. 1905. *Algemeine Staatslehre*. 2nd ed. Berlin: Verlag von O. Häring. https://archive.org/stream/allgemeinestaat00jellgoog#page/n366/mode/2up/search/normative+kraft+des+faktische.

Kelsen, H. 1970. *Pure Theory of Law*. Berkeley: University of California Press.

Polanyi, M. 1966. *The Tacit Dimension*. Chicago: University of Chicago Press.

Williamson, O.E. 1975. *Markets and Hierarchies, Analysis and Antitrust Implications: A Study on the Economics of Internal Organization*. New York: Free Press.

———. 1979. Transaction-Cost Economics: The Governance of Contractual Relations. *Journal of Law and Economics* 22 (2): 233.

Critical Remarks on Alf Ross's Probabilistic Concept of Validity

Katarzyna Eliasz and Wojciech Załuski

Abstract The concept of legal validity is regarded within the dominant—legal-positivistic—account of law as a nongradable concept: a legal rule is either valid or nonvalid. However, this account of validity is criticized by some scholars as being too strict and rigid. Apparently, an attractive alternative might be Alf Ross's probabilistic account of validity. Ross assumed that the stronger the predictions of judicial behavior a given rule generates, the greater the probability of their being valid. However, this account of legal validity is by no means uncontroversial. In this paper, four objections to it are formulated: the objection of the apparent gradability, the objection of the problematic ascertainability, the objection of the normative insignificance of probabilistic information, and the objection of neglecting the normativity of legal rules. These objections are treated in the paper as providing strong reasons for rejecting Ross's claim that predictions of judicial behavior formulated on the basis of rules are conceptually linked to their validity (i.e., they define their meaning); it is argued that they are merely a way of testing empirical hypotheses concerning the application (effectiveness) of legal rules.

1 Introduction

The concept of legal validity is regarded within the dominant—legal-positivistic—account of law as a nongradable concept: a legal rule is either valid or nonvalid.[1] However, this account of validity is criticized by some scholars as being too strict and rigid. Apparently, an attractive alternative might be Alf Ross's account of validity as a probabilistic concept. Ross assumed that the stronger the predictions of judicial behavior a given rule generates, the greater the probability of their being valid. This conception is usually called "predictive," but it may just as well be called "probabilistic": according to Ross, assertions about the legal validity of rules are

[1]C.f. the article by von der Pfordten in this volume.

K. Eliasz (✉) · W. Załuski
Jagiellonian University, Krakow, Poland

© Springer International Publishing AG, part of Springer Nature 2018

P. Westerman et al. (eds.), *Legal Validity and Soft Law*, Law and Philosophy Library 122, https://doi.org/10.1007/978-3-319-77522-7_10

probabilistic, and they are probabilistic precisely because legal rules are a basis for (uncertain) predictions of future judicial decisions. However, as we shall see, this account of legal validity is by no means uncontroversial. In the paper, we formulate several objections to it. Our discussion of these objections will be preceded by a detailed presentation of Ross's conception of validity.

2 Ross's Conception of Validity

Ross's theory of legal validity as a probabilistic concept is an answer to what is considered to be the dominant problem of jurisprudence. Following Kelsen, Ross observed that traditional legal philosophy (especially natural law theories) conceives law as an entity or phenomenon that is simultaneously real (empirical) and ideal (nonempirical). Accordingly, he claimed that legal theorists maintained that the concept "valid law" refers not only to some factual phenomena but also to the metaphysical validity stemming from, for instance, the rational nature of man or divine reason. He argued that such dualism leads to a series of antinomies in legal thought, which he traced and preliminarily resolved in *Towards a Realistic Jurisprudence*. In this book, Ross claimed that the two elements, i.e., the reality and validity of law, are not irreconcilable but, on the right interpretation, constitute two aspects of the same phenomenon.[2] He contended that the concept of validity can easily be explained by means of science, without recourse to metaphysics, as it is in fact an element of reality. In his view, propositions concerning valid law must be interpreted as referring to a specific type of social facts, which are decisions of the courts. He claimed that the scientific procedure that is supposed to confer meaning upon doctrinal assertions about valid law is the procedure of verification.[3] Accordingly, if a doctrinal assertion when tested cannot be verified, it is devoid of meaning and thus should be excluded from the scientific, doctrinal study of law. The scientific legal doctrine, as understood by Ross, is built on cognitive propositions, which are not norms but assertions concerning the norms—and these assertions are to the effect that a certain norm has the character of "valid law." Thus, for Ross the doctrinal study of law is normative, but in the sense of being norm descriptive rather than norm expressive.[4] More precisely, he claimed that the doctrinal assertion that "A" is valid law does not express the law but "is a prediction to the effect that if an action in which the conditioning facts (. . .) are considered to exist is brought before the courts of this state, and in the meantime there have been no alterations in the circumstances which form the basis of A, the directive to the judge contained in the section will

[2]Ross (1946), p. 11.

[3]For more on Ross's account of verificationism c.f. Aarnio (2011), pp. 83–84.

[4]In his debate with H.L.A. Hart, Ross made it clear that his focus is on external assertions (descriptions) as to the validity of law. C.f. Ross (1962), p. 1189.

form an integral part of the reasoning underlying the judgment."[5] Ross treated this kind of analysis of assertions about validity as an application of the method of verification; as he wrote, "a proposition about valid law is to be verified by fulfilling the prescribed conditions and observing the decision."[6] Consistently with his claim that assertions about legal validity are predictions, he maintained that statements concerning valid law always refer to hypothetical judicial decisions in the future, arrived at under certain conditions: "Valid law is never a historical fact but a calculation with regard to the future,"[7] and, in a similar vein, "a statement concerning valid law at the present moment does not refer to the past."[8] It is by no means clear, however, whether Ross's assertion that "valid law is a historical fact" entails the claim that predictions should not be based on past judicial decisions. This seems to have been Ross's claim, but it is controversial, even on his own assumptions (we shall return to this problem in section 3). To return to our exposition of Ross's conception, it bears stressing that the abovementioned reference to the future is not targeted at the result of a case. The possibility of anticipating a future result does not indicate the content of valid law. The legal scholar is to predict the rule on which the judge will base his decision and not the decision itself. According to Ross, such predictions of future applications of the rules are possible on the assumption of the existence of a common judicial ideology, which motivates each single judge and animates his actions:

> If [...] prediction is possible, it must be because the mental process by which the judge decides to base his decision on one rule rather than another is not a capricious and arbitrary matter, varying from one judge to another, but a process determined by attitudes and concepts, a common normative ideology, present and active in the minds of judges when they act in their capacity as judges. It is true that we cannot observe directly what takes place in the mind of the judge, but it is possible to construct hypotheses concerning it, and their value can be tested simply by observing whether predictions based on them have come true.[9]

The common normative ideology that forms the basis of doctrinal predictions is shaped by the sources of law in a proper hierarchy.[10] Thus, the normative ideology consists of directives, which do not determine future judicial decisions but are more like guidelines for judges, on the basis of which they can formulate final rules. Ross conceived the sources of law as the aggregate of factors that underlie a judge's formulation of the rule on which he subsequently bases his decision. Some of the sources provide the judge with a ready rule, while others require interpretation. Ross proposed the following classification of the sources of law depending on the degree of their, as he called it, "objectification": the fully objectivized source (legislation), the partly objectivized source (custom, precedent), and the nonobjectivized source

[5]Ross (1958), p. 42., c.f. Ross (1998), p. 161.

[6]Ross (1958), p. 41.

[7]Ross (1958), p. 22.

[8]Ross (1958), p. 41.

[9]Ross (1958), p. 75.

[10]For more on Ross's conception of the sources of law see Millard (2013).

(reason). The abovementioned "objectification" depends on whether the source provides a judge with a ready rule or is merely an inspiration, material that requires interpretation. The result of this variety of sources of law is that predictions concerning valid law can never be considered as absolutely certain. Thus, doctrinal assertions about valid law may be probable to a greater or lesser degree depending on the basis on which they are made, as Ross claimed:

> The probability is high, and the rule possesses a correspondingly high degree of validity, if the prediction is based on the well-established doctrine sustained by a continuous series of undisputed precedents; or it is based on statutory provision whose interpretation has been established in long and consistent practice. On the other hand, the probability is low, and the rule has a correspondingly low degree of validity, if the prediction is based on a single and dubious precedent or even the "principles" or "reason". Between the two extremes lies a sliding scale of intermediate variations (Ross A. op. cit. 45).

Such a graded conception of validity is in stark opposition to the dominant positivistic view thereof, according to which legal validity is considered to be an irreducible quality of a rule functioning in an "all or nothing manner," given that it is derived from the superior norm. Such an account of legal validity can be found, for instance, in Kelsen—for whom the norm is valid in relation to a *Grundnorm*—and Hart—for whom the rule is valid in relation to the rule of recognition. However, law that is valid in the positivistic sense need not be valid at all in Ross's (realistic) sense or may be valid only to a slight degree. This realistic sense can be most succinctly summarized as "the recognition in court practice," as Ross wrote:

> In general it is assumed as a matter of course that a statute having been put into proper form and duly promulgated is in itself valid law, that is, independently of its subsequent application in the courts. Conversely, it is probably rarely thought that what may be derived from "reason" could on these very grounds have the character of valid law – only the recognition in court practice invests the product of "reason" with such character.[11]

Ross's analyses led him to the conclusion that positivism, with its absolute notion of validity, should be rejected as it does not take into account the variety of factors that form the basis of the common normative ideology.[12] The alternative he proposed was the graded—probabilistic—concept of legal validity, which allows the inclusion, as sources of law influencing judges' decisions, of those sources that were excluded by the legal positivists. Prior to passing to a critical analysis of this concept, it is worth noticing that Ross used it with reference to three "objects," namely:

(a) Doctrinal assertions: "if the doctrinal assertion that a certain rule is valid Danish law is, according to its real content, a prediction that the rule will be applied in future judicial decisions, then it follows that assertions of this nature can never claim absolute certainty but can only be maintained with a greater or lesser

---

[11]Ross (1958), p. 101.

[12]According to J. Hage, the difference between the positivistic and Ross's realistic account of legal validity rests on the fact that positivists (especially Kelsen) discuss validity as a binding force, while Ross perceives validity as efficacy, c.f. the article by Jaap Haage in this volume, section 2D.

degree of probability depending on the strength of the points on which the calculations about the future rest."[13]

(b) Rules of law: "a rule can be valid to a greater or lesser degree varying with the degree of probability with which it can be predicted that the rule will be applied. This degree of probability depends on the material of experience on which the prediction is built (sources of law)."[14]

(c) Sources of law: "to regard a statute in itself as law signifies that we can generally and with a degree of probability bordering on certainty predict that it will be accepted by the judge. Conversely, the rules derived from "reason" are not considered directly as law in themselves because here we can do no more than guess the reaction of the courts."[15]

However, this diversity of the usage of the concept of probabilistic validity should not be regarded as an inconsistency by Ross; it is clear that it is a matter of convention whether one speaks about the validity of the rules themselves or about the validity of legal assertions about them; given that the rules are derived from the sources of law, one can just as well speak about the validity of the latter. It seems therefore that he was justified in applying his probabilistic concept of validity, depending on the kind of analysis he was conducting, to doctrinal assertions about law, rules of law, and sources of law. However, the account of legal validity proposed by Ross is by no means uncontroversial. In the next section, we shall put it to critical scrutiny.

3 Critique

Our critique will embrace four objections: the apparent gradability, the problematic ascertainability, the normative insignificance of probabilistic information, and the neglect of the normativity of legal rules. We shall discuss these objections and analyze their mutual relations in succession.

The objection of apparent gradability: according to this objection, Ross's probabilistic (and thereby gradable) account of legal validity in fact presupposes a nongradable account thereof. This is so because in order to formulate predictions about the extent to which a given rule will be invoked in judicial decisions, one must know beforehand what rules should be taken into account as (potentially) grounding these predictions. It is precisely the positivistic concept of a nongradable, formal validity that provides the criterion of a selection of rules to be taken as the basis of predictions. One can therefore say, if this objection is viable, that the probabilistic concept of validity is *partly* "parasitic" on the formal concept thereof. We use the

[13]Ross (1958), p. 45.

[14]Ross (1958), p. 45.

[15]Ross (1958), p. 102.

term "partly" because this objection applies in its entirety only to the fully objectivized sources of law, namely the rules established by a legislature, which are not the only basis for Rossian predictions. The less objectivized sources, e.g., custom, reason, cultural traditions, can also affect the form of the rule on which a judge bases his decision in a case at hand. However, this reservation does not undermine our objection as the main bases of Ross's predictions are properly established, formally valid rules of law.

The objection of the problematic ascertainability: one might ponder whether the account of validity as a probabilistic concept implies that the assertions about legal validity are themselves probabilistic or, rather, that probability is only a measure of the confirmation of in fact nonprobabilistic assertions about legal validity. Ross is explicit on this point: as mentioned in the previous section, *he endorses the view that assertions about legal validity are themselves probabilistic*. This implies that, for him, assertions of the type "rule *R* is valid" are probabilistic, i.e., one can assign to them a certain value of probability. This account encounters, however, three problems connected with ascertaining the probabilistic values of assertions of validity.

The first problem is that Ross does not explain exactly what the process of determining probabilistic values is supposed to look like or, more precisely, how the probabilistic values should be interpreted. This problem, though, is not very serious since one can supplement his theory by distinguishing two alternative ways of making this kind of determination. The first way consists in the empirical testing of assertions about legal validity *initially* treated as *nonprobabilistic* (in the sense that their values of probability are unknown). Accordingly, the process of determining the probabilistic values of these assertions can be schematically presented in the following way:

> *Nonprobabilistic assertion A*: "rule R is valid" → testing its empirical consequences (predictions concerning the judges' decisions) → the determination of the probability of A → *probabilistic assertion A*: "rule R is valid to a probabilistic degree *p*."

The second way consists in revising, in the light of empirical evidence, *subjectively probabilistic* assertions about legal validity (the values initially assigned to them are *prior* probabilities revised in the process of Bayesian reasoning). Accordingly, the process of determining the probabilistic values of these assertions can schematically be presented in the following way:

> *Probabilistic assertion A*: "rule R is valid to a probabilistic degree *p*" → revising the value of *p* in the process of Bayesian reasoning→ *probabilistic assertion A*: "rule R is valid to a probabilistic degree *q*."

On the first account, the probabilistic assertions about legal validity are of a frequentist character, on the second account, of a subjective character. However, irrespective of which of these two accounts was meant by Ross, two additional (and interconnected) problems arise: (1) it is not clear whether the testing of assertions about legal validity should be limited to future judicial decisions (relative to the moment of testing) or whether they should also include past ones; (2) it is not clear how large must be the set of (legally relevant) situations in which assertions about the validity of a given rule should be tested.

As for problem (1), Ross (as already mentioned in the previous section) claimed that doctrinal assertions concerning valid law are predictions and therefore refer to the future, not to the past. But it is unclear whether he derived from this claim about the *meaning* of these assertions (which is by itself counterintuitive given the assumption that they are empirical) the conclusion that the basis for formulating these assertions (and therefore predictions) should not include past judicial decisions. It would be rather peculiar to claim that past decisions should be left out of the process of assessing the probability values of assertions about legal validity: one could ask *on what basis* predictions about future decisions should be made if not, above all, on the basis of past decisions. Accordingly, the discounting of past judicial decisions in the process of determining the probabilistic values of validity assertions is entirely arbitrary. As we already mentioned, it is not clear whether Ross endorsed this implausible view, according to which probabilistic assessments cannot be based on past decisions. On the one hand, his insistence on the claim that legal rules refer to the future might suggest that he did endorse this view. On the other hand, this claim does not entail the conclusion that only future decisions matter in assessing the probability of assertions about validity; for this reason, one can argue that he did not endorse this view. By way of digression, it should be noted in this context that if we are right that past decisions must be assumed to play an important role in determining the value of the rules' validity (if validity is to be understood empirically), then it is not plausible to maintain (as Ross did) that the meaning of validity assertions can be reduced to predictions; they seem to be, on Ross's theory, both predictions and *reports about the past decisions of judges*. It should be stressed that even if one solves problem (1) by assuming that past decisions play an important role in the process of the probability assessment of the validity of legal rules, the ascertainability objection is still not entirely removed. Problem (2) remains unsolved as it is clear that the probability values assigned to a given rule's validity may be strongly dependent on the number of instances of potential applications of a given rule being considered, and Ross does not specify (because such precision would always be arbitrary) what this number ought to be. It seems therefore that Ross does not satisfactorily solve the problem of how to ascertain the probabilistic values of assertions about legal validity.

The objection of the normative insignificance of probabilistic information: in assuming the view that assertions about legal validity are themselves probabilistic, Ross gets entangled in the following difficulty—given that he does not differentiate the binding force of rules on the basis of their different degrees of validity (i.e., he does not claim that rule *R* whose degree of validity is smaller than that of rule *S* is "less binding," thereby establishing a "weaker" duty), the very idea of probabilistic validity appears to have no normative significance. In other words, irrespective of whether given rules have a degree of validity close to 1, or close to (but different from) 0 (i.e., irrespective of whether they are, to use Ross's phrase, "a strong basis for predictions or not"), they are equally binding for citizens, i.e., citizens have an equal (absolute or *prima facie*) duty to obey them. To be quite strict, Ross contended that legal rules are directed to judges, not to citizens,[16] but this limitation of the application of legal rules appears to be entirely arbitrary. However, the acceptance of this limitation does not weaken our objection because judges, too, when applying a legal rule must treat it as a nongradable concept: the very fact that some norms are a less reliable basis for prediction (i.e., their validity is of a smaller degree) will be of no importance to their decisions. Thus, *while characterizing a given rule "from the side" of its validity, we can drop from our description the information about the degree of their probability, since it has no normative significance*. The probability of a given rule being applied may of course have importance for the decision of the Holmesian "Bad Man" as to whether or not to comply with this rule. But let us repeat the main point of our objection: the information about probability does not carry any significant *normative* content. It might have such content only if one could determine some minimal threshold of probability dividing rules into "valid" and "nonvalid," but it is clear that there are no nonarbitrary criteria of rationality for making such a determination.[17]

It may be worthwhile comparing this objection to Hart's famous critique of Ross's conception of validity. Hart argued that if legal rules are what Ross takes them to be, *viz.* predictions of judges' behavior and their motives, they cannot guide judges' decisions; such a conception, in Hart's view, cannot make sense of the "meaning of judgment of legal validity in the mouth of a judge who is not engaged in predicting his own or others' behavior or feelings"; he added: "'This is a valid rule' said by a judge is an act of recognition; in saying it he recognizes the rule in question as one satisfying certain accepted general criteria for admission as a rule of the system and so as a legal standard of behavior."[18] The core of Hart's argument is that legal rules, as understood by Ross, cannot guide judicial behavior. The argument correctly points to the paradoxical consequence of Ross's assumption that the empirical content of assertions about legal validity (i.e., predictions of judges' behavior and their motives) constitute their meaning. But it omits Ross's important distinction between doctrinal and nondoctrinal assertions about valid law: the latter are not regarded by Ross as predictions of judicial decisions; it is precisely the latter that, according to Ross, are supposed to guide judges' decisions.[19] But this distinction does not seem to safeguard Ross's conception from our objection since if his probabilistic concept of validity is to have any clear meaning, it should apply both to doctrinal assertions about legal rules and to the rules themselves.

The objection of neglecting the normativity of legal rules: the empirical conception of normativity neglects its normative aspect. However complex the way in which we characterize these facts, it will not be possible to derive from them any

[16]Cf. the following quotation: "The real content of a norm of conduct is a directive to the judge, while the instruction to the private individual is a derived and figurative norm deduced from it." Ross (1958), p. 33.

[17]Cf, e.g., Grabowski (2014), Ch. 7, section 5.

[18]Hart (1959), p. 235.

[19]Ross (1998), p. 162, Ross (1962), p. 1190.

reason as to why the rules ought to be treated as normatively binding. Ross might reply that normativity in this—strong—sense, as distinct from psychological facts concerning the judges' motives, is a fictitious notion. But this consequence is inconsistent with the arguably widespread intuitions that the normativity of legal rules cannot be reduced to judges' convictions or motives.

Let us summarize our critique. We have argued that the very concept of probabilistic validity may be both *non-free-standing*, as it presupposes the nongradable concept of validity, and *indeterminable*, as it generates the problem of ascertaining probabilistic values. But, as we have demonstrated, even if one assumes that the probabilistic concept of validity is both free-standing and determinable, one can still formulate against it two other strong objections. Firstly, probabilistic information lacks normative significance: the degree d to which a given rule is valid, provided only that this degree is contained in the interval $0 > d \leq 1$, has no consequences for the normative force of this rule. Secondly, Ross's contention that assertions about legal validity are empirical—sociological and psychological—statements amounts to neglecting the normative aspect of the concept of validity: the mere empirical fact that a given rule is applied by judges and treated by them as binding does not explain why this rule ought to be treated as normatively binding, i.e. as possessing a normative aspect. The fact that Ross's theory does not account for the normative aspect of legal rules is a simple consequence of his neo-positivist assumption that the meaning of assertions about legal validity is their empirical consequences, i.e. empirical predictions formulated on the basis of the assertions. However, it seems that, contrary to what Ross maintains, predictions of judicial behavior formulated on the basis of rules are not conceptually linked to their validity (i.e., they do not define the meaning of doctrinal assertions about legal validity); they are merely a way of testing empirical hypotheses concerning the application (effectiveness) of legal rules. Accordingly, (successful) predictions based on a given rule do not show that a given rule is valid (to a high degree) but, simply, that it is usually applied by judges, i.e. that it is effective.[20] All in all, Ross's account of validity, though *prima facie* plausible in its emphasis on the relevance of "the recognition by the courts" of legal rules to their legal validity, encounters, on closer examination, serious, perhaps insuperable, difficulties.

In the end, we would like to emphasize that our critique of a probabilistic concept of validity does not apply to all gradable concepts thereof. It refers solely to *its empirical* variety, which is based on the assumption that assertions about legal validity refer to empirical facts. A different variety of this concept is the typological one, which formulates certain general features of validity that may be fulfilled to a greater or lesser degree and that do not constitute necessary and sufficient conditions of legal validity (an example of this concept is Lon L. Fuller's conception of the "inner morality of law"). However, a discussion of this kind of nonempirical, gradable concept of validity lies beyond the scope of this paper.

[20]For an analysis of the difference between efficacy and validity c.f. the article by Anne Ruth Mackor (section 2.4) in this volume.

References

Aarnio, Aulis. 2011. *Essays on the Doctrinal Study of Law*. Heidelberg, New York, Dordrecht, London: Springer.

Grabowski, Andrzej. 2014. *Juristic Concept of the Validity of Statutory Law: A Critique of Contemporary Legal Nonpositivism*. Heidelberg, New York, Dordrecht, London: Springer.

Hart, H.L.A. 1959. Scandinavian Realism. *Cambridge Law Journal* 17 (2): 233–240.

Millard, Eric. 2013. Alf Ross and the Realist Conceptions of Legislation. In *The Theory and Practice of Legislation*, ed. Pierre Brunet, Eric Millard, and Patricia Mindus, 77–89. Oxford: Hart Publishing.

Ross, Alf. 1946. *Towards a Realistic Jurisprudence, a Criticism of Dualism in Law*. Copenhagen: E. Munksgaard.

———. 1958. *On Law and Justice*. Berkeley: University of California Press.

———. 1962. The Concept of Law by H.L.A. Hart. *Yale Law Journal* 71 (6): 1185–1190.

———. 1998. Validity and the Conflict between Legal Positivism and Natural Law. In *Normativity and Norms. Critical Perspectives on Kelsenian Themes*, ed. Stanley Paulson and Bonnie Litschewski Paulson, 147–163. Oxford: Clarendon Press.

Sovereignty and Validity: On the Relation Between the Concepts and the Role of Acceptance

Antonia Waltermann

Abstract Austin defined law as the commands of a sovereign. This paper investigates the relation between the concept of sovereignty and legal validity, departing from Austin's jurisprudence by distinguishing between constitutive and constituted sovereignty. The aim of this paper is not to prescribe one particular understanding of law, sovereignty, or validity. Rather, it is to investigate what implications one particular understanding of sovereignty has for our understanding of law and validity. Accordingly, this paper posits that a focus on popular sovereignty, which is constitutive, does not cohere well with certain understandings of legal validity, namely validity from pedigree and validity from reason. The understanding of validity that fits best with a focus on popular sovereignty is from acceptance, and a further distinction can be made in this regard with acceptance of an institutional system of law and acceptance of individual rules.

1 Introduction

John Austin famously described law as the commands of a sovereign (Austin 1869). This definition of "law" has been criticized by Hart (2012) as making no distinction between law and the commands of a gunman. Hart's criticism is convincing, but Austin's understanding of law is nevertheless interesting to consider in light of two observations. The first is that Austin's understanding of law necessarily connects the nature of law with the existence of a sovereign; the second is that on a particular understanding of the term "validity," it also connects validity, sovereignty, and law. Carpentier distinguishes between *validity as conformity* and *validity as membership* in his contribution. If laws are the commands of a sovereign, and validity tells us whether a norm belongs to (is a member of) a particular system of norms, the test whether something is a valid legal norm becomes whether this norm is a command of the sovereign. Austin's theory, influential and important though it has been, is

A. Waltermann (✉)
Maastricht University, Maastricht, The Netherlands
e-mail: antonia.waltermann@maastrichtuniversity.nl

© Springer International Publishing AG, part of Springer Nature 2018
P. Westerman et al. (eds.), *Legal Validity and Soft Law*, Law and Philosophy Library 122, https://doi.org/10.1007/978-3-319-77522-7_11

outdated. While we will nevertheless use it as the starting point for an inquiry into the relationship between the notions of validity and sovereignty, we will do so in a way that incorporates Hart's criticism. With this in mind, the theory that provides the starting point for the present paper should more accurately be described as Austin's theory improved by Hart's or as an amalgam of the two. In particular, we will use Hart's understanding of law in conjunction with the notion of popular sovereignty to investigate the link between sovereignty and validity, given that the notion of popular sovereignty has become increasingly significant and cannot be neglected in an inquiry into the relationship between validity and sovereignty or law and sovereignty. Accordingly, the specific question we will consider in the following is what implications a focus on popular sovereignty has for our understanding of validity. In order to answer this question, we will first consider the notion of sovereignty, both as understood by Austin himself and with improvements on the basis of Hart's theory, focusing on popular sovereignty. Thereafter, we will look at the notion of validity and distinguish three tests for validity found in legal theory. We will consequently determine how each of these tests for validity fits with the notion of popular sovereignty as developed in Sect. 2 of this paper.

It bears mentioning that it is not the aim of this paper to prescribe a particular understanding of law, sovereignty, or validity. This means that the present contribution does not make claims incompatible with critical contributions to this volume, such as von der Pfordten's claim that validity is a mere summary concept, or with more substantive views of validity, such as those put forward by Carpentier. Rather than prescribe or argue for one particular understanding, its aim is to investigate what implications and consequences one particular understanding of sovereignty has for our understanding of law and validity. This does not deny that someone might reject this understanding of sovereignty and hence its implications, nor does it deny that other concepts of sovereignty—for example, in international law—exist. The conclusion of this paper will merely be that one cannot consistently advocate one understanding of popular sovereignty specifically while at the same time rejecting its implications.

The value of this contribution lies not in a reconsideration of validity but rather in connecting existing notions of validity to the notion of popular sovereignty to determine which understanding of validity best coheres with an emphasis on popular sovereignty. Such an emphasis on popular sovereignty is made, for example, in Article 3 of the Portuguese Constitution, Article 1(2) of the Greek Constitution, or Article 3 of the Russian Constitution, all providing that sovereignty belongs to the respective people(s) of those states. This contribution helps us determine which understanding of validity any of these states hold or should hold in order to be consistent with their own constitutions.

2 Sovereignty

The term "sovereignty" appears in many different contexts—think, for example, of constitutional law and international law—and is not always used in the same way or to mean the same thing.[1] In the following, we first examine Austin's understanding of sovereignty and afterward improve it by combining Hart's theory of the rule of recognition with the notion of popular sovereignty.

John Austin described law as the commands of a sovereign—but what is the Austinian sovereign like? A first point to notice is that Austin considered sovereignty to be a matter of (political) fact (Swiffen 2011). This makes determining the sovereign in a given (political) community a matter of empirical investigation, just as one can determine what is law and what is not by means of empirical investigation according to the Austinian theory (Bix 2015). The Austinian sovereign is "defined as a person (or determinate body of persons) who receives habitual obedience from the bulk of the population, but who does not habitually obey any other (earthly) person or institution" (Bix 2015). Hart (2012) criticized Austin's command theory as making no distinction between the state and a gunman robbing a bank. To avoid this criticism, we can instead connect sovereignty to the acceptance of rules, particularly rules regarding the creation of other rules (Swiffen 2011, pp. 72 f.). This means defining sovereignty either in the sense of the power to accept or in the sense of power that is accepted—or in other words, it means we must make a distinction between constitutive sovereignty and constituted sovereignty.

As such, it is possible to combine Austin's command theory of law with an institutional system of law, which is in turn constituted by a people by means of popular sovereignty. Popular sovereignty, in this sense, is *pouvoir constituant*, the extralegal power to constitute, maintain, and deconstruct a legal order (Waltermann 2016), which explains how and in what way "all state power emanates from the people." Popular sovereignty constructs the convention that is the basis for the constituted system of law. Within this system of law, it is still the "commands" of a constituted sovereign (for example, parliament acting in accordance with a certain procedure) that determines what law is.[2] As such, both sovereignty and law remain determinable by empirical inquiry. This picture allows for two kinds of sovereignty: on the one hand, there is popular sovereignty as the power to accept, which constitutes the institutional system. On the other hand, there is the body or institution that creates "commands" and thus corresponds to the Austinian sovereign but that is constituted by the people (power that is accepted).

[1]For only a few examples of the many different ways in which "sovereignty" is used, cf. Besson (2011), Dicey (1915), Goldsworthy (1999), Troper (2012), and Steinberg (2004).

[2]"Commands" here refers not only to rules which regulate conduct and have sanctions attached to them (what Hart would call "primary rules"), but also to rules which regulate the operation and creation of primary rules (what Hart would call "secondary rules"). This is, of course, a departure from Austin's theory.

When it comes to popular sovereignty, we can distinguish between three aspects of it: firstly, in moments of a legal vacuum or outside of the framework of an existing legal system, it is the power to constitute a new legal order by recognising or accepting the rule of recognition of the system in question. Recognition or acceptance should be understood to mean that the people take an internal point of view toward the rules created by the Austinian, constituted sovereign. Hampton (1997, pp. 97 f.) summarizes this as "a convention to regard the norms created by the governing institution(s) as preemptive and final" and calls it the governing convention. Each time an individual follows a rule created by the Austinian sovereign *because* it is a rule by the Austinian sovereign, this instantiates this governing convention and counts as recognition or acceptance of the rule of recognition. Secondly, and in much the same vein, popular sovereignty covers the maintenance of an existing legal order by means of recognition. Thirdly, it is the power to deconstruct an existing legal order by no longer recognising the governing convention or rule of recognition of this legal system. Sufficient instantiation of the governing convention or rule of recognition is therefore a necessary condition for the (continued) existence of a legal system. However, it bears mentioning that because generally legal systems provide for enforcement mechanisms and because instances of rule enforcement count as instantiations of the governing convention as well, deconstructing an existing legal order by no longer recognising the governing convention and rule of recognition may mean an act of revolution.

The governing convention or rule of recognition tells us which norms are valid norms of the legal system. Two conditions need to be fulfilled for such a convention/rule to exist: *efficacy* and *acceptance* (Hart 2012). Efficacy is the requirement that the convention is by and large observed, that is, that the system based on it is by and large efficacious, be it due to effective enforcement mechanisms, due to the cooperative attitude of individuals, or for any other reason. Mere efficacy is not sufficient, however, to distinguish a normative system from pure habit or coercion: the convention also needs to be accepted, or recognized.[3] In other words, sufficiently many individuals must take a particular social attitude toward the convention and thereby toward the system it constitutes. Of course, acceptance of the system will, in all likelihood, also have an impact on the efficacy of the system. It bears mentioning that this understanding of efficacy and acceptance and their relationship differs from the understanding put forward by Hage in his contribution to the present volume. While Hage defines efficacy in terms of acceptance—a rule is efficacious if its consequences are accepted—my understanding of efficacy involves only that the consequences come into being for whatever reason, with acceptance as one possible reason.

It is important to note that it is not individuals as such wielding the power of constitutive sovereignty but rather a people as a collective entity. One individual

[3]The term recognized is used here to emphasise that the social attitude required of people is not a particularly demanding one, in that instantiations of the governing convention do not at all times need to be deliberate acts of instantiation. Individuals may do so unthinkingly.

Fig. 1 Popular sovereignty and habitual obedience

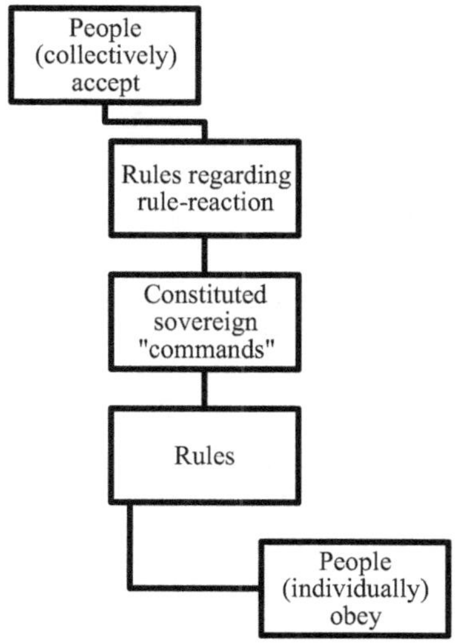

cannot, *individually*, exercise constitutive sovereignty. Collectively, however, this is possible. What is necessary is that there is a governing convention or rule of recognition that is

> [...] constituted by a form of social practice comprising both patterns of conduct regularly followed by most members of the group and a distinctive normative attitude to such patterns of conduct which I have called "acceptance" (Hart 2012, p. 255).

If we combine the elements of popular sovereignty thus defined, an institutional system of law, and a quasi-Austinian constituted sovereign in the form of a body or institution, the commands of which—that is, the rules created by it—receive habitual obedience from the bulk of the population, we get the following Fig. 1:

How does this understanding of sovereignty—or rather of *sovereignties*, as there are two different meanings of it used here—connect to the notion of validity? We will explore this in the next section, distinguishing between three different tests of validity and relating each of them back to an understanding of law and sovereignty, which emphasizes popular sovereignty.

3 Validity

The notion of validity is closely linked to the notion of law. As such, any definition of legal validity that wishes to be conceptually solid immediately requires the answer to a number of questions, and in some ways, simple definitions will appear circular upon close inspection. In particular, the terms "validity" and "law" are closely interlinked. This becomes clear when we ask ourselves whether there can be invalid law. Is an invalid law still law, or is it simply not law at all? To make matters more complicated, the term "validity" has been used in different contexts, meaning different things. Munzer (1972), for example, identifies that "validity" has been understood to mean—inter alia—that a norm is "felt to be socially binding" by Ross, implying an "ought" by Kelsen, or that it "satisfies all the criteria provided by the rule of recognition" (Hart). This lack of a clear definition of validity is by no means an easy obstacle to overcome. In some languages, however, the terminological ambivalence of "validity" is less acute: German, for example, distinguishes between *Geltung* and *Gültigkeit*, both of which translate to validity. Lumer (1999) defines legal validity in the sense of *Geltung* as legal force (*Rechtskraft*) or institutional recognition of laws, and legal validity in the sense of *Gültigkeit* as the legal force (to generate consequences) of, e.g., passports, testaments but also statutes and regulations. In Danish, Ross (1999) identifies a similar distinction between *gyldig* (which corresponds to *gültig* or *Gültigkeit*) and *gældend* (which corresponds to *geltend* or *Geltung*) but distinguishes between not two but three different meanings of the English "validity": firstly, as a term used in legal doctrine to indicate that a legal act has the desired effect; secondly, as a term used in legal theory to indicate the existence of a norm or a system of norms; and, thirdly, as a norm that gives rise to a corresponding (moral) obligation.

We will, in this contribution, focus in particular on validity as *Geltung*. Accordingly, if something is valid, it is law. This leaves us to consider a number of tests of validity that help determine whether something is or is not law and how these tests cohere with a (strong) focus on popular sovereignty. This focus on legal validity necessarily limits this paper in scope in the following way: it excludes discussions resulting from the assumption that validity implies a duty to obey the law, that is, that it implies binding force. Ross considers this to be a conflict regarding the term "validity" and its meaning(s).[4] Without denying this claim, it can also be posited as a conflict about the meaning of "law." The question whether "validity" implies "binding force" can be turned into the question whether "law" implies "binding force," that is, whether all law is binding and what that means. Under the assumption that validity is taken to mean legal validity, and as such separates law from nonlaw, there can be no invalid law, but it may well be possible that there is law that is not felt to have or does not have binding force. Under the assumption that "validity" necessarily implies "binding force," it may well be possible that there is invalid law, namely that which is not binding.[5]

In this paper, as mentioned, validity will be taken as *Geltung*, which means that any of the tests for validity identified in the following will be tests to separate law

[4]Hill, meanwhile, holds that natural law analyses and positivist analyses agree on the fact that legal validity entails binding force; a point which Ross contests (Hill 1970; Ross 1999).

[5]Given that this paper will take validity as membership, the question as to what precisely it means for a norm to have binding force is outside the scope of this paper. The above explanation why the question of binding force is not of immediate concern to the inquiry of this paper shall have to suffice, here. It is worth pointing out, however, that this use of "binding force" as possibly implying a duty to obey the law differs from Hage's technical definition of "binding force" in his contribution to this volume. Hage's technical definition of "binding force" closely corresponds to my use of "legal validity."

from nonlaw. This means also that all laws are *by definition* valid and all nonlaw invalid. This explains why the tests for validity we will consider in the following are so closely linked to theoretical schools concerning the nature of law.

3.1 Validity from Pedigree

The test of validity from pedigree can be linked to the doctrine of hard positivism. This means that the test is a formal one, looking at the origin of a rule rather than its content. Those rules, and only those rules, that were created according to a particular procedure by a person or body with the legal power to do so are valid, meaning only those rules that have this pedigree are legal rules. This corresponds to Austin's understanding of law as something that can be identified by means of empirical investigation—the investigation, in the Austinian case, needs to consider if the rule in question is a command of the sovereign. It equally corresponds to Hart's understanding of law[6] and in fact to the understanding of legal positivists, especially those we can classify as "hard" or "exclusive" positivists. Marmor (2001, p. 49) summarizes this position as follows:

> Legal validity is exhausted by reference to the conventional sources of law: all law is source based, and anything which is not source based is not law.

Importantly, this means that moral or otherwise evaluative standards do not and *cannot* determine what the law is (Marmor 2006). As such, "a norm is never rendered legally valid in virtue of its moral content" (Marmor 2001, p. 50). If legal validity is not and cannot be determined by the moral content of the norm, what determines it? The answer from exclusive positivism is that the source determines legal validity. This means that legal validity is dependent on and determined by the pedigree of a rule: if the rule was created in accordance with the right procedure by an institution or body with the competence to do so, the rule is legally valid.[7] If this is not the case, it is not legally valid (Waluchow 2009; Dworkin 1968). The former is what we will call the pedigree thesis, the latter a claim to exclusivity, that is, the demand that exclusively those rules that satisfy the test from pedigree are legally valid and therefore law. These two elements combined comprehensively describe the test of validity from pedigree.

---

[6]Unless we take the postscript of *The Concept of Law* into account, in which case this point is very much debatable.

[7]Hage, in his contribution, distinguishes between source-validity and validity in the sense of a rule existing and generating legal consequences, the latter is what I call legal validity. The test of validity from pedigree makes source-validity the sole requirement of legal validity. Kirste, in his contribution, equates validity from pedigree as I define it here with legal validity in general, if one assumes that legally established criteria for the enactment of a norm refer exclusively to pedigree. This assumption, however, need not be the case: legally established criteria for the enactment of a norm could, in theory, involve criteria other than or in addition to pedigree.

The test of validity from pedigree is familiar to legal scholars, particularly those with an interest in legal theory. It has existed in this form for several decades now and has during that time sparked a great deal of debate (Shapiro 2007). Of course, its continued existence does not prove its correspondence with (legal) reality or its compatibility with a focus on popular sovereignty.

It is uncontested that there is a great amount of law besides the body of law created by the state legislature in accordance with its legislative procedure and by courts in accordance with their competences. Opinion may differ on whether some of the following items on the list are law, but hardly anyone will hold that from the list of international law, European Union law, the *lex mercatoria*, legal principles, and soft law, none are law and that, at the same time, all law satisfies the test of validity from pedigree.[8] Furthermore, the test of validity from pedigree as described above is subject to all the criticisms that Dworkin famously directed against Hart's theory developed in *The Concept of Law* (Dworkin 1968, pp. 22 f.). The example of hard cases such as *Riggs v. Palmer* shows that the claim to exclusivity, which the test of validity from pedigree makes, fails to account for the fact that legal officials such as judges consider more to be law than is law according to strict pedigree as required by the test of validity from pedigree (Dworkin 1968, pp. 22 f.).

Dworkin's criticism that the test of validity from pedigree does not accurately capture the way in which legal officials distinguish between law and nonlaw is incisive. A further point of contention is that the test of validity from pedigree assumes an institutional system of law and the implications thereof for the importance of popular sovereignty. Law is institutional in the sense that legal rules "derive their existence and status as *legal* rules from being made in accordance with rules that specify how to make legal rules" (Hage 2011, p. 6). This makes the existence and status of legal rules dependent on the operation of other legal rules, describing the institutionalization of law and creating a "legal world." How does this legal world interact with popular sovereignty? As we have seen, popular sovereignty is the power of a people acting collectively, exercised by constituting—or maintaining or deconstructing—such an institutional system of law. However, once such an institutional system is established, the critical reflective attitude of the people regarding rules or principles becomes wholly irrelevant for the classification of those rules or principles as legal or non-legal. Figure 2 below visualizes this.

While this point does not negate the claims of the test of validity from pedigree as such in the same way as Dworkin's criticism does, it shows a certain amount of inconsistency when it comes to the significance of popular sovereignty: popular sovereignty may constitute the legal system, but it cannot be determinative of individual rules of that system as these are determined solely and exclusively by their pedigree. If we acknowledge that the critical reflective attitude of the people is determinative for the existence of the entire system, but within the system, legal validity is determined solely by pedigree, the attitudes of people toward individual

[8] In line with the fact that opinions may differ on whether some of the items on the list are law, opinions may also differ on their relationship.

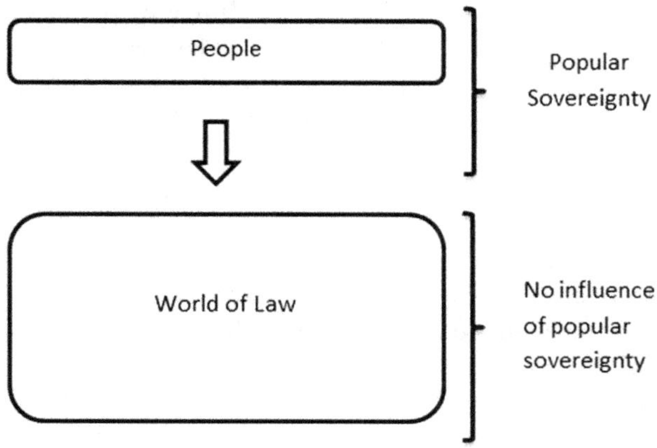

Fig. 2 Spheres of influence of popular sovereignty

rules are irrelevant. The former is consistent with a strong focus on popular sovereignty; the latter seems to deny that popular sovereignty has much significance.

In short, the test from pedigree does not capture legal reality, nor is it compatible with a strong focus on popular sovereignty. In the following section, we will consider an alternative to the test of validity from pedigree.

3.2 *Validity from Reason*

The test of validity from pedigree determines the validity of a rule based on its source. The test of validity from reason is an alternative in which it is not the source of the rule but rather its correspondence to the evaluative standard of rationality and reason that is decisive for legal validity. The test of validity from reason is linked not to the doctrine of legal positivism, much less hard positivism, but rather to the doctrine of natural law. Murphy (2006, p. 8) summarizes the main claim of natural law as follows: "law is backed by decisive reasons for compliance." Decisive reasons to ϕ are present when ϕ-ing is a reasonable act for one to perform and not ϕ-ing is an unreasonable act for one to perform, and "so for law to be backed by decisive reasons is for there to be decisive reasons to perform any act required by that law." This is a claim about the nature of law, in that those "laws" that are not backed by decisive reasons for compliance are not law.[9] For the purpose of this paper, this means that such "laws" as are not backed by decisive reason fail the test of validity from rationality and are therefore *not law*: they lack legal validity. Accordingly, the

[9]Murphy makes the distinction between the strong claim of natural law, whereby a 'law' that is not backed by decisive reason is not a law at all, and the weak claim of natural law, whereby a 'law' that is not backed by decisive reason is either not a law at all, or a defective law. We will here take as representative the strong claim of natural law.

test of validity from rationality is a substantive test to determine the legal validity of a rule and therewith its classification as law or nonlaw.

This separates legal validity from the social fact of acceptance of something as law. After all, those who accept a rule as being a *legal* rule may well be wrong about their judgement. As Murphy (2003, p. 248) holds, the fact that a number of rules have been recognized as law as a matter of social practice "does not make citizens and officials infallible with respect to the philosophical problem of whether these rules insufficiently grounded in reasons are really laws." In short, reason and rationality are the source of substantive standards that determine the validity of a rule; rules that do not comply with these standards are not law.[10] So the test of validity from reason is *substantive* (is this law sufficiently grounded in reason?) instead of *formal* (was this law adopted in accordance with the right procedure?). This means that principles of justice and morality can—and often are—held to be shaping the standard (Hill 1970). This leads to very different conclusions than the test of validity from pedigree:

> [. . .], a law unbacked by reason, while on the strong reading really no law at all, may well have some features of genuine law, most notably the proper pedigree. These features may cause those under it to treat it as a dictate with which they have decisive reason to comply. Indeed, a legal rule may have these features *in order to* cause people to treat it as something with which they genuinely have weighty reasons to comply (Murphy 2006, p. 14).

This conclusion from natural law and the test of validity from reason differs fundamentally from the test of validity from pedigree and the corresponding theory of exclusive legal positivism. For Ross (1999, pp. 254 f.), (one of) the reason(s) why natural lawyers and legal positivists—or adherents of a substantive and a formal test of validity—disagree about the determining factor of legal validity is that they use the term "law" in diverging ways:

> If a natural lawyer wants to reserve the term "law" for a system having some moral value, it is because he wants to emphasize terminologically the moral difference between different systems, and if a positivist prefers to classify as a legal system any factual system, whatever its moral value, that has the same structure as a typical legal system, it is because he wants to emphasize, also terminologically, the factual, structural similarity between diverse systems, whatever their moral qualifications.

Without disputing Ross's argument, there is another difference to the way in which natural lawyers and legal positivists use the term "law," which explains why their tests for legal validity differ so fundamentally: for natural law, and accordingly for the test of validity from reason to be an argument about what law *is* rather than what law *should be*, law cannot be a social construct. If it is,[11] people could construct

[10]Nota bene, however, that these standards will often include legal certainty as a substantive goal. As such, the substantive test whether a law is sufficiently grounded in reason can take into account other criteria besides the content of the law, such as concerns regarding the consequences of disobedience and the relevance of legal certainty. Cf. Finnis (2014).

[11]Alternatively: "if it were." The correct grammatical structure of that sentence fundamentally depends on one's stance on the matter it is meant to describe.

something that does not adhere to the standard to which law must—or, under this formulation, *should*—adhere, and because law *is* whatever is constructed, this would mean they are not and indeed cannot be mistaken about what is law. Popular sovereignty is an explanation of how a people as a collective entity can construct—or constitute—a legal system. As such, popular sovereignty necessarily presupposes that law is a social construct. This means that the test of validity from reason is incompatible with popular sovereignty.

In the following section, we will introduce a test of validity that does not make membership dependent on conformity with some standard, be it formal or substantive, and that coheres better with a strong focus on popular sovereignty.

3.3 Validity from Acceptance

As we have seen, neither the strict test from pedigree nor the test from reason coheres fully with a strong focus on popular sovereignty. The test of validity from reason is in fact incompatible with popular sovereignty, as defined in this paper, because popular sovereignty presupposes an understanding of law as a social construct. While the relationship between popular sovereignty and the test of validity from pedigree does not suffer from that same conflict, we have seen that the test of validity from pedigree's claim to exclusivity is not consistent with a strong focus on popular sovereignty. Let us consider an alternative that avoids these inconsistencies. In the following, we will consider a test of validity from acceptance. There are two possible understandings of the test from acceptance.

Institutional Plus Acceptance

We have already seen how an institutional system of law can have its basis in social acceptance by means of popular sovereignty. This is something the test of validity from pedigree does not deny. However, the test of validity from pedigree claims exclusivity in the sense that *only* those rules that have the right pedigree are legal rules. This means that the entirety of a legal system can be constituted by acceptance, but the attitude of a people toward individual rules of the system is wholly irrelevant for the status of those rules as law or nonlaw, that is, for their validity. The test of validity from acceptance combined with an institutional system disavows this claim to exclusivity but does not disavow the institutional system as such. This means that some rules are legal rules solely by virtue of their pedigree, and for these rules, acceptance is irrelevant. However, some rules or principles are legal not because they have the right pedigree but because they individually are accepted as legal.

Let us first consider whether this is necessary: after all, there are a number of ways in which rules that seemingly do not have the right pedigree—that is, rules that are not created in accordance with the right procedure by a body or institution with the competence to do so—can nevertheless enter the institutional system. One such option is reference: through reference to norms, rules, or principles that do not have the relevant pedigree by rules that do have that pedigree, the existence of these norms, rules, or principles are nevertheless treated as part of the law (Hage 2017). One example of a principle that does not—or did not, at the time—have the relevant pedigree but was nevertheless treated as law is the principle of nondiscrimination on grounds of age in the *Mangold* case before the Court of Justice of the European Union (CJEU). The Court held that "[t]he principle of non-discrimination on grounds of age must thus be regarded as a general principle of Community law" (CJEU (2005) 144/04, para 75). The discriminatory provisions of the German Employment Promotion Act, which were at stake in this case, therefore violated European Union law despite the fact that Directive 2000/78 on employment equality did not yet apply for reasons of its temporal scope (Semmelmann 2013). One could argue that the principle of nondiscrimination on grounds of age is to be regarded and was correctly held by the Court to be part of Community law because Article 6 TEU refers to fundamental rights of the European Convention of Human Rights as "general principles of the Union's law." This is an argument from pedigree that may be acceptable even under the test of validity from pedigree: there is a rule with the right pedigree that refers to this principle; therefore, this principle is law.[12] Another argument is that principles such as the principle of nondiscrimination on grounds of age are treated not as extralegal but *as legal principles* by the officials who apply them, by law students who learn about them as part of the law, and by the laypeople who come in touch with these principles and are for this reason *legal* principles.

The latter is an argument not from pedigree but from attitude. What is decisive for the validity of the principle according to this argument is not the procedure according to which it was laid down but that sufficiently many sufficiently relevant people consider it to be law. With regard to the rules or principles that are broadly accepted, we can distinguish between those accepted for reasons of tradition—*custom*—and those that are accepted because they—or, rather, because their content—are seen as reasonable (Hage 2017). In this way, rationality and the content of a rule enter into the equation again, but they are not the decisive factor for validity; instead, it is the acceptance that is *due* to the rationalist content of the rule that is determinative of validity. An example of such a rule that is broadly accepted and considered a legal rule even though it cannot be identified as one by its pedigree is the rule that the leader of the party that has won a majority in the elections will be appointed as prime minister of the United Kingdom. Equally, the rules surrounding ministerial responsibility in the Netherlands are not legal rules identifiable by pedigree but are nevertheless considered in Dutch constitutional law to be rules that are legal in nature. In other legal systems, these rules are not customary as they are in the Netherlands but laid down in legal documents, such as the Basic Law in Germany

[12]This is very open-ended, however, and exclusive legal positivism would likely reject the principle(s) referenced as law and instead treat the reference as an invitation to the judge to exercise discretion and/or to employ non-legal standards in deciding the case before her.

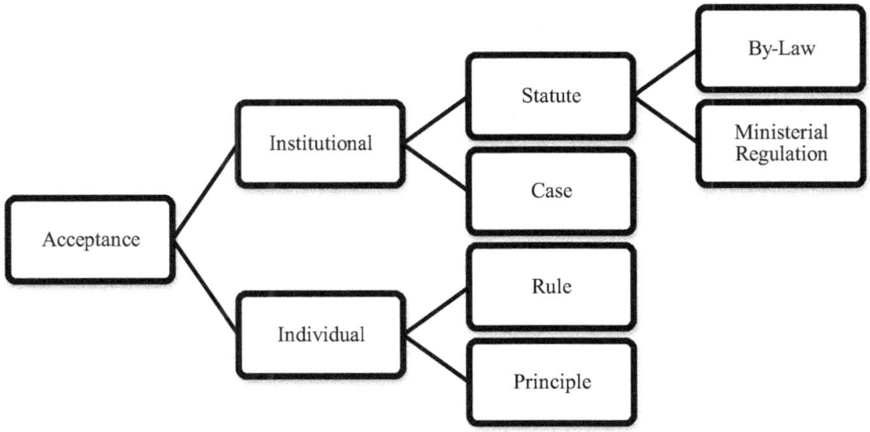

Fig. 3 Institutional and individual acceptance

(see arts. 67 and 68 of the Basic Law). Despite this distinction, the Dutch rules are no less treated as legal rules than the German ones.[13] In short, it is possible to consider that an institutional system of law based on the acceptance of the system as a whole, rather than of its individual rules, can exist side by side with rules not part of the system, which are based on individual acceptance.

Figure 3 shows the institutional system existing side by side with rules and principles whose validity is solely dependent on their individual acceptance as legal. Let us consider the alternative test of validity from acceptance before evaluating both.

Only Acceptance

The alternative test of validity from acceptance makes the validity of all individual rules dependent on their acceptance. Instead of considering that an institutional system and a collection of individual rules the validity of which is based on their acceptance exist side by side, this view disavows the institutional system of rules and the test of validity from pedigree that is determinative within that system.

[13]Prakke and Kortmann (2004, p. 603) and Kortmann (2008, pp. 301 ff.) describe the core of ministerial responsibility in the Netherlands as "an unwritten constitutional norm"; Elzinga and De Lange (2001, p. 188) discuss specifically whether ministerial accountability in the Netherlands is a matter of unwritten *law* or whether it is a constitutional convention in the sense of "constitutional morality" and as such not law, coming to the conclusion that the general consensus is as follows: customary constitutional law (*ongeschreven staatsrecht als gewoonterecht*) exists beside written constitutional law. Customary constitutional law is equal to written law, derives from its own source, may also derogate from written law, and requires custom/precedent as well as the prevalent view that it is law (*algemene rechtsovertuiging*).

Fig. 4 Individual acceptance

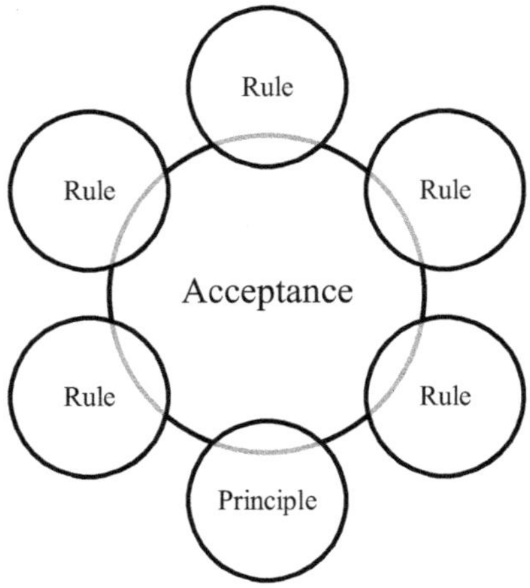

This view makes the validity of each individual rule—and therefore its existence *as a legal rule*—dependent on the collective attitude of people and the efficacy of the individual rule. Figure 4 gives a visual representation of this view.

HLA Hart (2012, p. 103) seems to argue against this view when he states that

> If by "efficacy" is meant that the fact that a rule of law requires certain behaviour is obeyed more often than not, it is plain that there is no necessary connection between the validity of any particular rule and *its* efficacy, unless the rule of recognition of the system includes among its criteria, as some do, the provision (sometimes referred to as a rule of obsolescence) that no rule is to count as a rule of the system if it has long ceased to be efficacious.

While this arguably suggests an institutional system of rules, an alternative interpretation is also possible, namely that efficacy is subservient to acceptance to at least a certain degree. If by efficacy it is meant that the rule actually influences the behavior of people in their day-to-day lives, efficacy may not be a necessary condition for a rule to count as legal. This becomes particularly clear when we consider legal rules that apply only in exceptional circumstances.[14] If, however, a rule does not influence the behavior of people in their day-to-day lives and is rarely relied upon in court, the question might arise whether this rule would be accepted as a legal rule if someone were to rely on it in court after all. If the answer is yes, the test from acceptance holds that this counts as a legal rule. If the answer is no, it does not. The efficacy of the rule is then less relevant to the determination of validity than acceptance, though efficacy can of course play a large role in making people accept something as law.

This has some very concrete implications for our understanding of what counts as law and what does not. Let us consider a few examples. Firstly, what if a traffic

[14]Possible examples of laws applied only exceptionally are those laws which grant far-reaching powers to the executive in states of emergency. However, it admittedly depends on state and circumstances how exceptional their use truly is. In Germany, the Emergency Acts (*Notfallgesetze*) have not been used since their introduction in 1968 (Focus 2008).

regulation stipulates that jaywalking is prohibited but jaywalking is nevertheless a habit widely practiced? This might suggest that the rule individually is not efficacious but that as such does not yet make any statement about its legal validity. What is more relevant is whether the individuals jaywalking have an attitude of awareness that they are breaking a law and whether they would accept a penalty imposed on them by a police officer who catches them jaywalking as unfortunate but legal. Secondly, what about the 1907 rule that makes adultery a class B misdemeanor in the state of New York even today (New York State Penal Law, 255.17)? Assuming an institutional system of law, this section of the state penal law has the necessary pedigree to be considered law whether it is accepted or not. However, section 255.17 is hardly used in legal practice, and even when charges are brought, these are usually dismissed or dropped—to the point that a former federal prosecutor holds that the ban on adultery has no practical significance (Chan 2008). Furthermore, it seems that many individuals in New York do not think that adultery is a crime.[15] In the same vein, validity purely from acceptance without an institutional system beside it that grants validity on the basis of pedigree impacts the classification of soft law instruments such as the Universal Declaration of Human Rights and principles such as the Responsibility to Protect. If the test of validity is from pedigree, these have to be classified as nonlaw. If the test is from acceptance, however, the conclusion may be different depending on the attitude that people (for example, state officials) have with regard to such instruments or principles.

Evaluation

The distinction between the test of validity from acceptance in conjunction with an institutional system or without it may not seem to make much difference in practice for one simple reason: we tend to think of law as an institutional system, and this means that even though we may not know all the legal rules or may not accept (or rather: follow) all of them, we accept that they are legal rules when we are confronted with enforcement by relevant authorities. Furthermore, it is rational for us to accept all these rules for reasons of legal certainty. There is, however, one important reason why making the distinction matters, even if it seems to have, at first glance, little practical relevance: acceptance is a matter of degree rather than an all-or-nothing matter. This means that if we disavow the institutional system, or for those rules that are accepted as legal outside of an institutional system, a test of validity from acceptance means that some rules are less law than others. Under this test, law becomes a matter of degree as well.

A further point of notice is the following: while we have seen that within an institutional system of law popular sovereignty and the command theory can coexist, this is no longer the case if the institutional view of law is rejected and all validity is

[15]Of course, actual empirical studies are necessary to back this claim, which is why it is here phrased in such a qualified manner.

based on acceptance of individual rules rather than acceptance of the system. The institutional system of law is constituted by a people exercising popular sovereignty, and within that institutional system, it is still the "commands" of a constituted sovereign (such as parliament acting in accordance with a certain procedure, for example), which determine what is law. Parliament loses its constituted sovereignty when an institutional system is rejected. This does not mean that parliament acting in accordance with a certain procedure loses its significance, however, because people are likely to accept those rules created by what they accept as an authoritative body acting in accordance with the correct procedure. Nevertheless, while this variant of the test of validity from acceptance coheres with popular sovereignty, it precludes other forms of sovereignty besides itself.

4 Conclusion

The aim of this paper was to consider what implications a strong focus on popular sovereignty has for our understanding of validity. Popular sovereignty as defined in this paper requires two elements, namely efficacy and acceptance. Through their attitude, a people acting collectively can constitute, maintain, and deconstruct legal systems. This understanding was taken as focal point against which three tests of validity were evaluated for their compatibility with popular sovereignty. Validity was taken as determinative of the status of something as legal or non-legal. We have considered three different tests of validity in this paper: the test of validity from pedigree, from content, and from acceptance. With regard to the latter, we have distinguished further between a test of validity purely from acceptance and one from acceptance in conjunction with an institutionalized system in which pedigree is determinative.

The test of validity from pedigree distinguishes between law and nonlaw on the basis of a formal requirement of procedural pedigree: has the rule in question been adopted in accordance with the correct procedure by an entity with the competence to do so? This test has been criticized by Dworkin as too narrow in its approach, but we have seen that for the purpose of this paper, there is another reason to reject or at least question it: it leads to inconsistencies with regard to the role and significance of popular sovereignty. The test of validity from pedigree does not deny that popular sovereignty constitutes the legal system, but it denies that popular sovereignty can play any additional role other than that. Once the system has been constituted, the acceptance, or lack thereof, of individual rules becomes wholly irrelevant.

The test of validity from reason, by contrast, is a substantive test that makes the validity of a rule dependent on it being sufficiently grounded in reason. This test and its proponents hold that peoples or officials are not infallible in determining whether a rule is sufficiently grounded in reason—and hence also not authoritative to distinguish between law and nonlaw. What is relevant is not whether sufficiently many sufficiently important people believe that a rule is legal in nature but whether it is sufficiently grounded in reason. This test of validity must be rejected for the purpose of this paper because it denies that law is a social construct, while popular sovereignty presupposes this. The two are therefore incompatible.

The test of validity from acceptance is, similarly to the test of validity from pedigree, formal in nature. It differs from the test of validity from pedigree, however, in that it disavows either the claim to exclusivity of that test or both the claim to exclusivity and the institutional system that the test of validity from pedigree requires. The test of validity from acceptance can be considered in conjunction with an institutional system of law within which the test of pedigree—minus the claim to exclusivity—is determinative of the status of rules as legal, with some rules being legal rules outside the institutional system, where acceptance is determinative of their status. Alternatively, validity can be dependent solely by acceptance. The test of validity from acceptance in either variant coheres best with a strong focus on popular sovereignty. While it may seem at first as though there is little practical difference between its variants, it is interesting to note that making legal validity dependent on the social fact of acceptance—be it for all rules or only for some—makes law a matter of degree.

Considering the initial aim of this paper to investigate the implications and consequences of a strong focus on popular sovereignty on our understanding of law and validity, we can now conclude as follows: a focus on popular sovereignty as it is defined in this paper precludes an understanding of validity as being determined by reason. A strong focus on popular sovereignty furthermore coheres better with a test of validity from acceptance, whether in conjunction with an institutional system or as the sole determining factor of validity, than it coheres with a strict test of validity from pedigree. Moreover, such a test of validity from pedigree does not accurately capture how people and officials see the law, while a test of validity from acceptance by definition does. As such, the conclusion is that a strong focus on popular sovereignty can and should go hand in hand with an understanding of validity as being determined by acceptance. Given that many jurisdictions explicitly refer to popular sovereignty in their constitutions, this finding has far-reaching implications for many legal systems and our theoretical understandings of them.

References

Austin, J. 1869. *The Province of Jurisprudence Determined*. London: John Murray.

Besson, S. 2011. Sovereignty. In *Max Planck Encyclopedia of Public International Law*, ed. R. Wuolfrum. Oxford Public International Law [Online].

Bix, B. 2015. John Austin. In *The Stanford Encyclopedia of Philosophy*, ed. E.N. Zalta. Spring 2015 Edition. http://plato.stanford.edu/archives/spr2015/entries/austin-john/

Chan, S. 2008. Is Adultery a Crime in New York? *City Room* [Online]. [Accessed 06 November 2015].

Dicey, A.V. 1915. *Introduction to the Study of the Law of the Constitution*. London: Macmillan.

Dworkin, R. 1968. The Model of Rules. *University of Chicago Law Review* 35: 17–24, 29–40.

Elzinga, D.J., and R. De Lange, eds. 2001. *Handboek van het Nederlandse Staatsrecht*. Deventer: Kluwer.

Finnis, J. 2014. Aquinas' Moral, Political, and Legal Philosophy. In *The Stanford Encyclopedia of Philosophy*, ed. E.N. Zalta. Summer 2014 Edition. http://plato.stanford.edu/archives/sum2014/entries/aquinas-moral-political/

Focus. 2008. 40 Jahre Notstandsgesetze.

Goldsworthy, J. 1999. *The Sovereignty of Parliament: History and Philosophy*. Oxford: Oxford University Press.

Hage, J. 2011. A Model of Juridical Acts: Part 1: The World of Law. *Artificial Intelligence and Law* 19: 23–48.

———. 2017. 'Logical Tools for Legal Pluralism. In *Law and the New Logics*, ed. P. Glenn and L.D. Smith. Cambridge: Cambridge University Press.

Hampton, J. 1997. *Political Philosophy*. Boulder: Westview Press.

Hart, H.L.A. 2012. *The Concept of Law*. Oxford: Clarendon Press.

Hill, R.E. 1970. Legal Validity and Legal Obligation. *The Yale Law Journal* 80: 47–75.

Kortmann, C. 2008. *Constitutioneel Rech*. Deventer: Kluwer.

Lumer, C. 1999. Geltung, Gültigkeit. In *Enzyklopädie Philosophie*, ed. H.J. Sandkühler. Hamburg: Meiner.

Marmor, A. 2001. *Positive Law and Objective Values*. Oxford: Oxford University Press.

———. 2006. Legal Positivism: Still Descriptive and Morally Neutral. *Oxford Journal of Legal Studies* 26: 683–704.

Munzer, S. 1972. Introduction: The Subject of Legal Validity. In *Legal Validity*. The Hague: Springer Netherlands.

Murphy, M.C. 2003. Natural Law Jurisprudence. *Legal Theory* 9: 241–267.

———. 2006. *Natural Law in Jurisprudence and Politics*. Cambridge: Cambridge University Press.

Prakke, L., and C. Kortmann, eds. 2004. *Constitutional Law of 15 EU Member States*. Deventer: Kluwer.

Ross, A. 1999. Validity and the Conflict Between Legal Positivism and Natural Law. In *Normativity and Norms: Critical Perspectives on Kelsenian Themes*, ed. S.L. Paulson. Oxford: Oxford University Press.

Semmelmann, C. 2013. General Principles in EU Law Between a Compensatory Role and an Intrinsic Value. *European Law Journal* 19: 457–487.

Shapiro, S.J. 2007. The "Hart-Dworkin" Debate: A Short Guide for the Perplexed. *Public law and Legal Theory Working Paper* [Online].

Steinberg, R.H. 2004. Who Is Sovereign Commemorative Issue - Balance of Power: Redefining Sovereignty in Contemporary International Law. *Standford Journal of International Law* 40: 329–346.

Swiffen, A. 2011. Law Without a Lawgiver: Legal Authority After Sovereignty. *Law, Culture and the Humanities* 7: 66–80.

Troper, M. 2012. Sovereignty. In *The Oxford Handbook of Comparative Constitutional Law*, ed. M. Rosenfeld and A. Sajó. Oxford: Oxford University Press.

Waltermann, A. 2016. *Sovereignties*. Maastricht University (Dissertation).

Waluchow, W. 2009. Four Concepts of Validity: Reflections on Inclusive and Exclusive Positivism. In *The Rule of Recognition and the U.S. Constitution*, ed. M. Adler and K.E. Himma. Oxford: Oxford University Press.

Legal Validity, Soft Law, and International Human Rights Law

Mátyás Bódig

Abstract This chapter looks at international soft law against the background of broader issues about the normativity of law. It explores the ways in which "institutional normativity" operates across legal systems with special focus on the relationship between different constructs of validity. The chapter develops a narrowly defined "core" concept of validity that reflects the minimum conditions for providing effective normative guidance in institutional settings. This concept revolves around the idea that validity establishes a mediated relationship between the legitimacy of law and the internal processes of legal practices. The chapter argues that more specific constructs of validity are political constructs that reflect the concrete political and institutional dynamics of particular legal practices. This point about the coexistence of different constructs of legality and legal validity is demonstrated by an analysis of the relationship between international law and modern state law. The chapter characterise the proliferation of international soft law as one manifestation of the tensions that this coexistence brings about. The growing volume and significance of international soft law has a lot to do with a constraining model of legality in domestic legal systems which have a spillover effect on international law. Soft law often needs to fill normative spaces that have been made hard to access for hard international law. For a more concrete analysis, issues about international soft law in the field of human rights law are picked out. Using the General Comments of the UN Committee on Economic, Social and Cultural Rights as an example, the chapter looks at the legitimacy problems that the proliferation of soft law generates.

1 Introduction

Reflecting on the problems of soft law (especially in respect of international law) can be rewarding for legal theorists. It draws them into a controversy with exciting theoretical implications, as well as practical ramifications. For some, the growing

M. Bódig (✉)
University of Aberdeen, Aberdeen, UK
e-mail: m.bodig@abdn.ac.uk

© Springer International Publishing AG, part of Springer Nature 2018
P. Westerman et al. (eds.), *Legal Validity and Soft Law*, Law and Philosophy Library 122, https://doi.org/10.1007/978-3-319-77522-7_12

volume and significance of soft law instruments poses a dangerous challenge to the very integrity of international law: it has become fertile ground for misconceptions—especially among legal scholars (d'Aspremont 2008). For others, it offers a welcome opportunity to reconsider such fundamental concepts as "legal obligations" and "sources of law" (Goldmann 2010).

In this chapter, I deal with some of the theoretical implications of the proliferation of soft law instruments in international law.[1] To be able to frame the challenge better, I look at soft law against the background of broader issues about the normativity of law. The analysis puts special emphasis on the character of legal validity and its different constructs across different legal orders. Using "validity" as our conceptual focus is an attractive option for making sense of soft law. (This is pretty much the theoretical idea underlying the current volume.) One way of capturing what makes soft law arrangements distinctive is claiming that they deviate from the "formal" validity conditions that apply to hard law. And it is easy to see how this "deviation" may raise concerns. Perhaps soft law instruments extend the scope of legal materials beyond reasonable limits (d'Aspremont 2011, pp. 131–132). Focusing on validity also suggests a way of reining in the proliferation of soft law: perhaps we could resort to some tightening of the conditions under which norms can qualify as "valid law." In this analysis, I am not really concerned with exploring ways of reining in soft law. (Actually, I am more positive about its impact on legal practices than most.) Instead, I use this chapter primarily to test my theoretical intuition that reflecting on soft law may help us understand better the ways in which "institutional normativity" operates. In order to avoid getting stuck with a handful of very abstract points, I relate the analysis to contemporary challenges in international law and scholarship. That is, I rely on particular manifestations of soft law in international human rights law as the object of reflection: the General Comments issued by human rights monitoring bodies at the UN.

The present chapter has two defining ambitions. The first is locating the concept of validity in the account of normativity that I advocate. I hope to provide here a conceptual template to engage with international soft law. Importantly, I do not seek to account for the many ways in which the concept of "validity" features in doctrinal and academic discourses on law. As Dietmar von der Pfordten makes it clear in his chapter,[2] "validity" is a relatively late addition to the vocabulary of lawyering (going back only to the nineteenth century), and the term is used in a dizzying variety of ways. What I work from is a more narrowly defined "core" concept of validity (necessitated by what I like to call "institutional normativity"). In my account, this "core" concept of validity reflects certain minimum conditions of providing effective

[1]For this reason, the current piece is primarily a legal theoretical effort, not really a contribution to international law scholarship.

[2]See in the present volume, von der Pfordten, Validity in Positive Law: A Mere Summary Concept, section 3.

normative guidance. But I think this "thin" concept can be reconciled with the other (more multifaceted) accounts offered in the present volume.[3]

I settle for a thin concept of validity partly because I seek to highlight the ways in which constructs of validity are shaped and embellished depending on the political "profile" of different legal practices (often taking on additional functions and meanings along the way). I am particularly interested in the kind of "formal" validity that became prevalent in modern state law and international law. I contend that the contemporary imagery of formal validity (especially in modern state law) resulted from the convergence of the concept of (formally ascertained) law and political concepts (and ideals) such as "sovereignty," "legitimacy," and the "rule of law." This conceptual development has had a comprehensive impact not just on states but on the institutional parameters of other legal orders as well (and international law in particular).

I hope to use this particular framing to outline a theoretically fruitful account of the proliferation of soft law. The development of international law (as we know it today) was predicated on accepting the central and paradigm-setting role of state law in legal practices. It has led to the coexistence of different constructs of legality and legal validity. However, this coexistence has never been without tensions. Currently, we may go through a period when such tensions become more widespread and more pronounced. Maintaining the paradigm-setting role of state law faces increasing challenges (Bódig 2016, p. 61; Bódig 2015a). I see the proliferation of soft law in international law (as well as certain areas of domestic law) as one manifestation of these tensions. I would like to understand better this dynamic.

My other ambition in this chapter is to look closer into the manifestations of soft law in international human rights law and explore the lessons they hold for our understanding of legal validity. I will not enter the academic debate about the definition of (international) soft law that has been ongoing for a while. Below, I give a clearer, more exact indication of what I mean by soft law. But it may be useful to point out here that the emphasis will be on a rather uncontroversial common feature of the dizzying variety of soft law instruments: they always remain parasitic on hard law.[4] That is, they remain crucially dependent on the constructs of legality in hard international law for their normative significance. This may suggest that the proliferation of soft law reflects a certain narrowness and inadequacy in hard law. Soft law must do some jobs that hard law fails to do. Although this impression is not always warranted, soft law is indeed often the manifestation of the structural tensions that the interactions of international law and domestic legal systems generate. I will argue that the growing volume and significance of international soft law has a lot to do with a constraining model of legality in domestic legal systems which had a

[3]See especially in the present volume Westerman, Validity: The Reputation of Rules; Hage, What Is Legal Validity? Lessons from Soft Law; von der Pfordten, Validity in Positive Law: A Mere Summary Concept. I am probably more distanced from Paolo Sandro's ontological account of validity. See Sandro, Unlocking Legal Validity: Some Remarks on the Artificial Ontology of Law.

[4]Similarly, Pauline Westerman writes that 'soft law acquires status from its marriage to hard law.' See her contribution in this volume, Westerman, Validity: The Reputation of Rules, section 6.

spillover effect on international law. Soft law often had to fill normative spaces that have been made hard to access for hard international law.

I explore this dynamic in a specific context by taking a closer look at the soft law in the General Comments of the UN Committee on Economic, Social and Cultural Rights. I hope to show that, sometimes, soft law provides the only vehicle through which doctrinal development can adjust to the shifting challenges of human rights protection in international law. Admittedly, doctrinal development through soft law raises legitimacy issues about the institutional practices of international bodies. But I do not believe that the problems of soft law can be handled by extending the regulatory ambitions of hard law, and locking international soft law into narrowly defined auxiliary functions. There may be a need to reconsider the constructs of legal validity underlying established doctrines of legal sources. I do not go through with this process of reconsideration here. I do what legal theoretical analysis typically does: I make an attempt at understanding a challenge better.

2 Normativity, Validity, Legitimacy

I need to start with running through a few conceptual points. The terminological parameters for the present analysis are set by my earlier theoretical work on the normativity of law (Bódig 2013a, b). I put forward just a few basic claims: I only seek to make my position intelligible here.[5] Of particular significance is pinning down what I mean by "institutional normativity." That is the concept I will use to capture legal validity and, even more importantly for this analysis, the relationship between legitimacy and validity.

As is rather common among contemporary legal theorists, I organize my account of legal normativity around the idea of "normative guidance." As a starting point for further conceptual analysis, I rely here on just one basic claim: as normative guidance is never physical compulsion (i.e., it works by interfering with the way the addressees' intentions are formed—MacCormick 2008, p. 103—without foreclosing alternative courses of action[6]), it always operates within frameworks of justification that the addressees can relate to. Normative social practices cannot simply be about getting people to act in certain ways: they open up courses of action that are accepted as justified by relevant others in relevant social and institutional contexts. That is, in order for normative claims (such as a statutory provision or a command from a superior) to provide effective normative guidance, they need to fit into a preset framework of justification. I tend to characterize this point about normative guidance in terms of conditions of "success" for normative claims

[5]Most importantly, I set aside how my account presupposes a very specific interpretive methodology. See Bódig (2013a), pp. 120–123.

[6]That is, the act remains 'voluntary.' See Anscombe (1957), pp. 33–34. Normativity (especially in law) operates by using, as opposed to suppressing, agency. See Waldron (2008), p. 26.

(Bódig 2013a).[7] Conditions of success can usefully be broken down into two aspects (mainly because the justificatory capacity of normative claims can be called into question in two basic ways): (1) the "rationale" aspect (as there may be issues about the substantive reasons to conform to normative claims[8]) and (2) the "competence" aspect (as there may doubts whether the given normative claims come from persons competent to set standards for the addressees[9]).

Of course, these basic points are not specific to law. They capture a far broader range of normative phenomena. They would not be enough to capture law anyway as law is not only normative but also "institutional" (Bódig 2013a, p. 119).[10] Legal practices represent complex examples of "institutional normativity" in which patterns of institutionalization interact with the conceptual features of normative guidance.[11]

Perhaps the most conspicuous feature of institutionalized normative practices is the extensive reliance on deliberately and systematically positing and imposing specific "obligations" (as opposed to the incarnations of concrete ethical life that tend to deal in more general constructs of "duties" and "principles" without canonical formulations). Institutional normativity establishes frameworks for consolidating and elaborating "authority relations": developing advanced economies for the distribution of authoritative competences. But foregrounding specific obligations may not actually be the core phenomenon here. It may only be the manifestation of the two basic paradigms of institutionalizing normative guidance. One paradigm is defining set competences for interactions between the participants and the public recognition of designated roles (offices) for key agents. The other is institutionally fixing at least some of the "rules" internal to the social practice (Bódig 2011, pp. 659–660)—most typically by way of public recognition of their canonical formulations. Pinning down specific obligations is an inherent feature of both paradigms.

With a view to the claims I make below, it is worth highlighting two points about this account of institutional normativity. Firstly, the two basic paradigms of institutionalization reflect the two aspects of the success conditions for normative claims

[7]My terminology has its origins in John Searle's *Speech Acts*. See Searle (1969), p. 54 (conditions for 'successful and non-defective performance') and p. 94 ('unsuccessful' acts).

[8]I rely here on Frederick Schauer's profound analysis of how rules are linked with their 'rationale', 'justification' or even 'generating justification.' See Schauer (1991), pp. 5, 26, 53 and 74.

[9]In a similar context, Andrei Marmor speaks about 'identity related' reasons (where the addressee's reason to φ partly depends on the identity of another agent who suggests, requests, or orders the addressee to φ). See Marmor (2011), p. 62.

[10]My views on this point owe a lot to Neil MacCormick. See MacCormick (2008), p. 11.

[11]I use the concept of 'institution' in a relatively narrow sense. I talk of institutionalization in relation to social practices where interaction among the participants is at least partly organized around public and explicit rules and/or fixed role constructions. The term 'institution' itself applies to the set patterns of interaction among the participants—e.g. set procedures (like an election) or normatively constructed and interconnected social relations (like marriage or the relationship between a principal and her agents).

("rationale" and "competence"). Both are eminently open to consolidation and standardization by institutional means. Setting up practice-specific offices institutionalizes normative competences, and when rules are institutionally fixed, they link up substantive normative justification with specific practical judgments.

Secondly, and more importantly, institutionalization has a deep influence on how room is created (and curtailed) for practice-related contestation (on what can and cannot be done with adequate justification). Precisely because of their inherent connection with issues of justification, normative claims in any normative practice invite intense contestation. Institutionalized normative practices achieve higher levels of efficacy mainly because of their ways of dealing with contestation over normative claims. However, even though contestation can bring about uncertainty and confusion, as well as persistent conflict, the point is not that institutionalized normative practices are bound to stifle or block out contestation. The point is that they are designed to rein in and control contestation. This is invariably done by way of channeling practice-relevant contestation through institutional procedures. The specific instances of contestation come to be construed and categorized as distinct forms of "disputes" or (policy) "debates" with a narrow range of possible outcomes.

These points may seem to mark out the place of "validity" claims in the account of institutional normativity quite straightforwardly. Even though lawyers (and legal scholars) talk about "validity" in a variety of senses, perhaps the most characteristic use of the term revolves around the conditions under which legal norms exert influence on the justification of competent legal judgments. (That is, lawyers acknowledge that competent legal judgments cannot be justified without reference to "valid legal norms." The flip side of this point is that if a norm is taken as valid in a given legal practice, there must be situations where competent normative assessment is not possible without making reference to it.)

This close association with legal justification may suggest that legal validity is the specification of the conditions of success for institutionalized normative settings. However, this would be a misleading simplification. We would underestimate the complexity of institutional practices if we simply collapsed issues of background justification for normative claims into criteria of their validity.[12] In fact, directly addressing the success of normative claims is the role of "legitimating processes and discourses" (which link up practice-specific normative processes with values such as "public order" and the "common good", or confer democratic credentials on legal norms). All institutionalized normative practices have legitimating processes in this sense. (Aspects of the legislative process—such as the central role of assemblies and/or sovereign monarchs—obviously fall under this category.)

What about validity, then? I believe that validity (in the sense relevant here) is more helpfully understood as an institutional "substitute": a less than consistently reliable proxy for the success of normative claims (that participants can take as license to rely on given norms in practice-specific normative processes).

[12]That would lead to theoretical trouble e.g. when making sense of civil disobedience.

This important distinction captures one of the key conceptual features of institutional normativity. In institutional normative practices, validity and legitimacy become different (but related) features of publicly recognized normative standards. This can be conceived as a sort of distancing mechanism. Legitimating processes provide substantive and procedural grounds for attributing justificatory force to practice-specific normative claims (norms). Validity claims, on the other hand, mediate between those legitimating processes and the internal operations of the normative practice. This enables participants (and officials in particular) to bracket issues of legitimacy in the day-to-day practice of ascertaining the exact scope and justificatory force of specific normative claims.[13] Hence the point that legal validity traces the manifestations of legitimating processes without guaranteeing that those processes have managed to produce successful normative standards.

This mediated relationship between the success of normative claims and their impact on institutional processes has far-reaching implications. It is because of this mediation that the law is not simply an institutional device that makes it easier for us to do what is justified—all things considered.[14] Due to distancing validity and legitimacy, for legal officials, issues of identifying the relevant rules of law do not collapse into the question of what normative claims could be regarded as justified overall—for the relevant cohort of participants. It also enables officials (and all other participants) to make sense of the distinction between personal and professional judgments on normative requirements. In an important sense, this makes the subjection of agents to the normative requirements of the practice possible—as opposed to subjection to the mere will of the more powerful. Of course, this comes with familiar difficulties and even hazards. Bracketing the substantive justifiability of normative claims leaves open the possibility of enforcing compliance with unsuccessful (sometimes blatantly unjust) normative claims.[15] However, we should not forget that it also makes the law capable of sustaining institutional processes in the face of disagreement and underlying social conflicts. And, of course, it also makes the "rule of law" (as a political ideal) conceptually possible.

---

[13]Elsewhere, I characterize this way of distinguishing between 'external' and 'internal' justification in law. See Bódig (2010), pp. 131–134.

[14]Only a few legal theorists dispute this. Michael Moore is one of them. See Moore (2000), pp. 155–167.

[15]Elsewhere, I call this 'false normativity'. See Bódig (2013b), pp. 216–217. It is one of the typical features of legal practices that people are, on occasion, forced to act in ways that cannot be adequately justified. In this sense, institutional normative practices incur a moral cost that is a matter of legitimate concern for all participants at all times.

3 The Political Context of Formal Validity and the Character of International Law

The previous section outlined a concept of validity that revolves around establishing a mediated relationship between legitimating discourses and the internal processes through which normative guidance operates in institutionalized normative practices. I have argued for a systematic connection between validity and legitimating discourses. In this section, I explore an implication of this systematic connection: constructs of validity cannot be made fully intelligible without regard to the respective legitimating discourses. Importantly for us, this connection makes legal validity in any legal practice laden with political content. For lawyers, validity often looks like a boring technical term, but, actually, it is a remarkably reliable manifestation of the political character of specific constructs of legality.[16]

This should remind us that we need to be more accurate about the scope of the conceptual analysis in the previous section. Even though the points I have made bear some (far from accidental) resemblance to the familiar imagery of formal validity in modern domestic legal systems, it only really captures an underspecified "core" concept of validity. We cannot explore concrete validity constructs without looking at their political underpinnings as well. Without acknowledging this point, we cannot bring down the analysis to the level of concrete legal practices.

In my conceptualization, concrete validity constructs reflect partly the underlying conceptual structures, and partly the concrete political and institutional dynamics of given legal practices. For example, the core concept of validity I offered in the previous section already embodies the vital idea of "formal ascertainment" of rules. As I have argued, institutional normativity distances practical judgments from more direct issues about the success of the underlying institutional rules. As legal theorists have long recognized, this allows participants to develop a perspective on practical judgments that is internal to their specific practices.[17] This internal perspective (on what normative positions knowledgeable participants can plausibly maintain within the parameters of the legal practice) presupposes the possibility of *ex ante* judgments on what rules and competences are internal to the given practice. And only formal criteria of law ascertainment allow for that (Goldmann 2010, p. 678). However, setting concrete criteria for formal validity in a practice remains a matter of specific institutional dynamics or even conscious institutional design—and never simply a matter of conceptual analysis. Of course, this dynamic is comprehensively influenced by the relevant legitimating discourses. So the core concept of validity already implies the idea of the formal ascertainment of norms (i.e., a sense of "formalism"), but as there are different

[16]This connection is actually a conceptual prerequisite: without it, validity could not serve as a proxy for the success of the normative claims.

[17]This indicates that my conceptualization resonates with the (very) useful distinction Jaap Hage draws between 'internal' and 'external' validity claims in his chapter. See Hage, What Is Legal Validity? Lessons from Soft Law. It is clear that the sense of validity I capture here covers only internal validity claims.

models of formal ascertainment, institutional normativity allows for tendencies of both relative "formalization" and "deformalization" in actual legal practices.

For this reason, we cannot bring the analysis closer to our issues about international soft law without engaging with the specific constructs of legality that have created the circumstances for its proliferation in contemporary international law. This is what we have to turn to now.

Perhaps somewhat counterintuitively, we need to start with saying something about the validity construct typical of "modern state law" in particular.[18] As it happens, international law cannot be understood without it. As a (slightly idealized) institutional paradigm, (fully developed) modern state law relies on explicitly formulated and interrelated institutional rules providing the criteria for defining what normative claims carry legal validity. This implies more than just the law regulating its own creation. These rules are exclusive in character: they provide the sole mechanism to ascertain validity, and draw a sharp distinction between norms internal to the given legal system and any other normative claim (as well as between "actual" and "prospective" law). This model of formal validity serves drastically to narrow the scope for contestation on what qualifies as valid law: it makes the truth of all validity claims crucially dependent on the institutional practice of designated (state) officials. By implication, it drastically narrows agency in terms of the ability of shaping and authenticating the law. Nothing is law without authentication by a narrowly defined cohort of legal officials entrusted with the administration of explicit institutional rules.

We should not forget that there can be alternatives to the model of legality underlying this paradigm of formal validity. If officials manage to secure effective consensus on handling the paradigmatic challenges of ascertaining the relevant law (either because they are beholden to shared knowledge and traditions or strongly motivated to act in conformity with one another), institutional normativity can be maintained without defining criteria of validity by way of exclusive rules. Dependence on norms carrying formal validity can also be much less comprehensive. It can be limited to setting procedural parameters, and it can tie legal justification to broader principles—thereby allowing for the importation of normative considerations from a broader range of sources (e.g., religious doctrines) into legal reasoning. Concrete institutional practices can often afford to tolerate much greater peripheral uncertainty than formal validity in modern state law does. Also, some form of ideal law can serve as a reflexive counterpoint to positive law in justifying legal claims—opening up space for second-guessing the normative weight of formally valid law.[19] And also, social life may be characterized by the legal plurality of overlapping legal orders which mutually limit and cross-fertilize each other.[20] Sometimes, legal

[18]For a brief but instructive account of the consolidation of law in the state, see Tamanaha (2017), pp. 107–108.

[19]Berman saw this pattern in how the medieval canonists looked at the relationship between natural law and the prevailing customs of medieval polities. See e.g. Berman (1983), pp. 145–146.

[20]This is how Berman famously characterized the life of the law in medieval Europe. See e.g. Berman (1983), p. 215.

systems operate with some openness to each other (as when rules could be more or less freely imported from Roman law into some European legal systems). Then no group of officials has the final say on what qualifies as relevant law for a polity, and we do not quite see the kind of hardening of the boundaries between legal systems modern state law brings about.

The point is that modern state law offers a particularly constraining model of legality. Its construct of formal validity reflects a political environment in which the clear demarcation of legal systems is of strategic significance. It is a political construct originating from the structural demands of modern statehood (e.g., the more extensive bureaucratic control over populations and the more effective concentration of resources) that sat uneasily with the legal pluralism of premodern political institutions.

Modern state law offers a particular model of ordering the relationship between authority structures within a legal system and between different social practices. It is based on organizing the institutions (carrying intrasystemic normative competence) into a hierarchical authority structure. In unitary states, it also means that authoritative competences are framed as manifestations of a singular claim to state sovereignty. As to the relationship with other normative practices, this model means elevating the normative competences concentrated in the state to the status of sovereign authority—raised over any alternative authority structure (be it subnational, supranational, or religious).[21] State law becomes more than one construct of legality: it is construed as the central case of a legal system.

This suggests a mutually constitutive relationship between the (modern) state and its law. Sovereignty gives an institutional structure the quality of statehood, and the law becomes the sole mechanism through which the exact normative implications of this sovereignty are articulated. Then the primacy of sovereign authority cannot be secured without clearly marking out state law. A fitting model of formal validity for law will provide for this demarcation. Formal processes of law ascertainment patrol the boundaries of state law and guarantee that state officials have the final say on what normative claims carry legal validity. Also, all manifestations of political authority are channeled through the law: there is no exercise of political authority without a legal form of authorization.[22] (That is, sovereign governance internalizes some version of the principles of the rule law.)

---

[21]In a similar context, Neil Walker characterizes the authority claims of (state) law as 'magisterial'. See Walker (2010), pp. 31–32.

[22]It is worth noting that that this model has alternatives. State law can be envisaged as only one of the mechanisms for exercising sovereignty. The sovereign may choose to rely on it (because that is what good governance demands) but may legitimately exercise extra-legal authority (without legal accountability) when necessary. This model is reflected in early modern theories of absolutism. See Bódig (2002), pp. 282–285. The basic idea is also there in Carl Schmitt when he argues that sovereignty must precede the legal order, and can be manifested in decisions that are not subject to legal criteria. See Schmitt (2006). What I claim is that the model I am outlining is dominant and spreading—because this is what underlies constitutional democracy.

Importantly for us, the breadth of the normative scope of state law (and the robustness of its institutional mechanisms) has a comprehensive impact on other, related normative social practices. State law sets out to control and curtail the normative influence of any other authority structure or legal system in all the social settings that fall within the scope of its sovereign authority. (In fact, the normative implications of the claim to sovereign authority are so strong that different incarnations of state law can only coexist by way of territorial demarcation.)

I emphasize that I do not assume that all states (or even all modern states) have state law in this sense. The institutional dynamic I have outlined only really plays out under the conditions of "consolidated statehood"—in a world where many countries are examples of "limited statehood" instead.[23] However, the normative mechanisms through which the relationship of international law and national legal systems are mediated very much presuppose this picture of state law. The construct of modern state law profoundly shapes the way any supranational law can be formed. The interactions of sovereign states will constitute the very normative space international law can inhabit. To be more exact, in modernity, transnational law could not take on the character of "cosmopolitan law"—it could only ever be "international law" (Rawls 2001, p. 36). International institutions cannot have sources of authority independent of the sovereignty of states (loosely construed as all being "nations"). There can be international politics, but no original political authority is generated on the transnational level. The implications of this "living on borrowed authority" are nicely reflected in the clumsy, state-centric procedural mechanisms of creating and amending public international law.

Of course, these points are not meant to cast doubt on the very legal quality of international law. Despite its limited capacity to develop effective and independent enforcement mechanisms, international law establishes a web of obligations that delivers normative guidance: it comprehensively shapes the normative environment in which states operate.

Stepping closer to our more immediate topic, we cannot be surprised that, under the circumstances, the core concept of validity will play out differently in international law. It will still embody formal validity: international law lends itself to formal ascertainment.[24] However, due to the significance of customary international law (which brings intense contestation on actual state practice into the process of finding valid law), the (still considerable) importance of *opinio juris*, and the dearth of officials (specifically assigned to administering international law and not beholden to any national government), the ascertainment of norms is a matter of more controversy and uncertainty than typical in state law.

What we see is that international law represents a different model of institutionalization—that is, a different construct of legality with a different framework for legitimacy (Brunnée and Toope 2010; Franck 1988) and law ascertainment. It inflates (to a quite unusual extent) the role of the consent of duty bearers. Public

[23]For the distinction, see Börzel and Risse (2013).

[24]On this, I agree with Jean d'Aspremont. See d'Aspremont (2011).

international law is not in the position to replicate the ways of law ascertainment familiar from modern state law. International law comes to operate with a different version of formal validity that is shot through with the requirement to resort (again and again) to exploring contested facts about state consent and state practice.

4 Soft Law in International Law

The interesting question is whether its construct of legality (designed to preserve the centrality of state law) allows international law to perform its functions in a world where international cooperation grows ever more intense and multifaceted, and where states have to "lend" large chunks of authority to international bodies. Binding international norms created with the explicit cooperation of state parties (primarily in the form of treaty law) may fall well short of providing adequate normative guidance. This is certainly part of the reason for the growth of a diverse set of institutional authorities on the international level (e.g., the World Trade Organization or the UN Human Rights Committee). And the outcome is a more complex interplay of institutional practices and, as a result, more in the way of subversive developments.

There have been concerns about the institutional setup in which modern international law operates pretty much from the outset, and there are signs of growing structural tensions around it. Some of them are of particular interest for legal theory—such as whether contemporary international law is capable of embodying a viable conception of the rule of law (e.g., Broomhall 2004). And some of them are exacerbated by recent developments—like the emergence of the Responsibility to Protect (R2P) doctrine.[25] One can definitely make the case for the need to reconsider the very construct of legality that international law represents. It is notable that international law scholarship offers ever more ambitious attempts to rethink the foundational concepts of the discipline (such as legal obligations[26]) and that some experiment with alternative, "impact-based" (Kingsbury 2009), or "process-based" (Higgins 1994) models of law ascertainment.

---

[25]See *World Summit Outcome*, GA Res. 60/1., 16 September 2005, ss. 138–140. By entertaining the possibility that the sovereignty of a state can be overridden by the international community (if it is unable or unwilling to discharge its responsibility to protect its population against the most egregious international crimes), the responsibility to protect doctrine offers a template for reworking the very concept of sovereignty. If sovereignty is directly tied to inherent duties toward citizens, it becomes something that can be earned and squandered. And international law, instead of treating state sovereignty as the very ground for its own normativity, may lay claim to setting rules on the conditions under which sovereignty is won or lost. Of course, this conceptual possibility was already implicit in the way human rights obligations were made part of the UN Charter, and also the way in which the *Vienna Convention on the Law of Treaties* limited the treaty-making powers of states (Articles 53 and 64).

[26]As an exciting recent development, one can think of the interactional theory of international legal obligations. See Brunnée and Toope (2010).

As indicated above, I believe that the proliferation of soft law over the past few decades is also a manifestation of the underlying structural tensions in international law. To advance the analysis, I will take a closer look at what drives this proliferation—against the background of the conceptual points I developed in previous sections. I will rely on my earlier work on a paradigmatic example of soft law: the General Comments of the UN human rights treaty monitoring bodies—and the UN Committee on Economic, Social and Cultural Rights (CESCR) in particular (Bódig 2015b, 2016). I emphasize that there is nothing unique about the CESCR General Comments. Similar conclusions could be drawn from similar instruments issued by any other human rights treaty monitoring body at the UN (Human Rights Committee, Committee Against Torture, Committee on the Rights of the Child, etc.).

There is a need to give some indication of the relevant concept of "soft law" here.[27] Once again, I restrict myself to putting forward a few points simply to specify what I mean by the term. Importantly, I offer only one possible conceptualization of (international) soft law that is geared toward accounting for a particular set of analytical challenges.[28] (For other purposes, alternative conceptualizations may work better.)

I have already indicated above that I see soft law as always parasitic on hard law. I need to add three points to this basic claim. Firstly (and most importantly), soft law is *not binding*, or, more exactly, its norms are incapable of creating international obligations in themselves. Even when they speak the language of obligations (as they often do), at best they are articulating obligations established by hard law, or signal normative development toward future hard law.[29]

---

[27] I do not engage with the debates on the very intelligibility of the term among international law scholars, and I grant that the concept may be attributed different meanings. I only aim at providing a particular conceptualization that fits my theoretical agenda here. For the background to my account of international soft law in the literature, see Boyle (2010), p. 128; Shelton (2003), pp. 10–13; Chinkin (2003), pp. 25–31.

[28] I have hinted above that my conceptualization of legal validity can be reconciled with those of Westerman and Hage in this volume. Importantly, that cannot be said about their analysis of soft law. My conceptualization of soft law sharply differs from Westerman's analysis which sees soft law arrangements as carrying token-validity due to a mere 'semblance' of legality. See Westerman, Validity: The Reputation of Rules, section 5. My take on the concept also differs from Hage's account that defines soft law as 'law that can less easily be used in legal arguments than hard law.' See Hage, What Is Legal Validity? Lessons from Soft Law, section 5.

[29] This indicates that I see two basic functions for international soft law. The first is articulating existing obligations. This is what we see in the General Comments I look at more closely in the next section. The second is facilitating the development toward prospective hard law. This is often the case with, e.g., declarations (like the *UN Declaration on the Right to Development*, GA Res. A/RES/41/128., 4 December 1986) or plans of action (like *Transforming Our World: The 2030 Agenda for Sustainable Development*, GA Res. A/REAS/70/1., 25 September 2015) that seek to influence state behavior and the processes of international bodies in ways that make likelier the emergence of certain hard law obligations in the future. Of course, such attempts may fail, and the norms can remain permanently stuck in the status of soft law. (Arguably, this is what happened to the *Declaration on the Right to Development*.)

Secondly, the quality of being soft law derives from *the normative status of the "instruments"* that contain its norms. Normative claims become soft law (as opposed to hard law or mere policy proposals) because they feature in "soft law instruments" (declarations, guidelines, resolutions, etc.). So, for example, norms we can find in the CESCR General Comments (such as "core obligations" in relation to the right to health[30]) are "soft" because they are not binding on state parties, and they have a legal quality because they are issued in official UN documents (instruments) by an international body constituted under international law.

Thirdly, the provisions of soft law are not simply "norms in prospect": they are already *"practiced" in certain ways*. One may justifiably act on them, and some may even need to act on them. I see two basic paradigms here. State representatives (through some international body) may create instruments (e.g., General Assembly Resolutions) that (due to their institutional prestige) exercise normative influence on the practice of international bodies or even the states themselves.[31] Alternatively, expert bodies create instruments that are embedded in their own practice and may even exert normative influence on state behavior ("expert-driven standard-setting"). For example, the CESCR General Comments already set the substantive terms under which the Committee will engage with state parties in its procedures (e.g., when formulating Concluding Observations on State Reports). This reminds us that characterizing, say, the General Comments as nonbinding refers specifically to their normative status in relation to the legal obligations of state parties: it does not mean that they do not guide action.

These features add up to an "institutionally embedded" conception of soft law. Hard law creates the very normative space in which soft law can grow (by establishing, directly or indirectly, the underlying legal competences). The language of obligations in soft law documents depends for its specific legal significance on a background of obligations in hard law. (These are the two main reasons why soft law always remains parasitic on hard law.) By implication, soft law, due to its embeddedness in institutional practices, carries legal validity. If validity is a proxy for the claim to success of normative claims, it must apply to all explicit institutional norms that provide normative guidance. This point is reinforced by the fact that soft law lends itself to pedigree-based identification: it can be subjected to formal law ascertainment.

This does not mean that the construct of validity for soft law will simply fall under the criteria of validity for hard international law. The "triad" of sources of international law (treaty, custom, and general principles) enshrined in the ICJ Statute (which dominates the imagery of international law) do not apply here (*Statute of the International Court of Justice*, Art 38(1)). In my conceptualization, treaty law is never soft law (even when it has nonbinding provisions). Customary law is not soft

---

[30]See CESCR (2000) *General Comment 14* ('The Right to the Highest Attainable Standard of Health') UN Doc. E/C.12/2000/4, ss. 43–45.

[31]This may mean affecting the agenda and language of later documents. For example, the *Declaration on the Right to Development* came to influence the *2030 Agenda for Sustainable Development*.

law either.[32] The construct of soft law presupposes a deliberate and clear distancing from hard law. I would argue that, for soft law, law ascertainment must revolve around "standard instruments."[33] It is not by accident that soft law is deposited in instruments clearly distinguishable from the standard sources of international law. It is on this condition that soft law can speak the language of obligations without subverting the sources doctrine of international law.

5 Soft Law in International Human Rights Law: The CESCR General Comments

I have argued that the constitutive features of soft law differentiate it from hard international law. Nevertheless, we can develop mechanisms of formal ascertainment for them. For this reason, I would be reluctant to accept that soft law represents a trend of deformalization in international law,[34] and I would not contemplate saying farewell to the "sources triad" just because of its proliferation (Riedel 1991, p. 58). The interesting question is whether we can consistently keep soft law limited to the auxiliary role hard law carves out for it. In this section, this is what I will explore in relation to international human rights law and the CESCR General Comments in particular. I seek to demonstrate that the way international law is tailored to the structures of modern state law makes it almost inevitable that hard law proves inadequate, and it keeps fueling the proliferation of soft law. The drawback of the process is that soft law often exacerbates the legitimacy problems of international law.

International human rights law is an especially fertile ground for the growth of soft law. Soft law often serves as the stop-gap mechanism to handle problems generated by inflexible hard law (which is hard to come by and difficult to change). Often, it is only soft law that can maintain the momentum of normative development in the face of shifting political and institutional challenges.

As I have indicated, I look to the CESCR General Comments to explore these points. These are soft law instruments that have been clearly set up for a supplementary role. Their official nature derives from a treaty-based authorization. Most human rights treaties explicitly stipulate that treaty monitoring bodies may issue Recommendations or General Comments based on the examination of State Reports and treaty provisions. In the International Covenant on Economic, Social and

[32]Of course, soft law can be a factor in the development of customary law but it does not change the fact that soft law is *consciously created as* not binding.

[33]I believe Matthias Goldmann has given us an account of standard instruments that we can work with (Goldmann 2010, pp. 691–702)—even though he finds the term of 'soft law' itself too loose and heterogeneous (Goldmann 2010, p. 672).

[34]I disagree with d'Aspremont on this point. See his d'Aspremont (2011), pp. 128–130. Soft law may actually extend the scope of formalism in international law.

Cultural Rights (ICESCR), the relevant treaty provision suggests that General Comments emerge from the communication and cooperation between states parties and the relevant treaty body.[35] When providing an account of the nature of its own General Comments, the CESCR clearly toed this line: it depicted them as by-products of its work on State Reports:

> The Committee endeavours, through its general comments, to make the experience gained so far through the examination of those reports available for the benefit of all State parties in order to assist and promote their further implementation of the Covenant; to draw the attention of the States parties to insufficiencies disclosed by a large number of reports, (. . .) and to stimulate the activities of the State parties, the international organizations and the specialized agencies concerned in achieving progressively and effectively the full realization of the rights recognized in the Covenant.[36]

The suggestion is that the General Comments simply make the CESCR practice more transparent and more directly related to practical issues of implementation. Judged on the terms of their authorization and the Committee's own account of them, the General Comments take on two manifest functions. One is "hortatory": promoting the implementation of economic and social rights among states parties. (This has marginal legal significance, and I set it aside in this analysis.) The other is assisting the implementation of the Covenant rights—e.g., by identifying the practical challenges that states parties need to address. This is best understood as an "obligation-articulating" role: laying out the exact implications of treaty-based obligations for duty bearers. This is obviously the role that drives the normative development of soft law here.

We see here a nicely delimited role for the General Comments and no considerable impact on normative development. However, on a closer look, the CESCR General Comments give a dramatically different impression. They reflect the bold normative ambitions of the Committee—typically providing a partisan account of the implications of treaty rights. They are not descriptive of either current state practice or mandated Committee procedures (Blake 2008): they seek to set the agenda for the professional discourse on economic and social rights. They have become the mechanism through which ideas taken from academic literature can be channeled into CESCR jurisprudence—thereby consolidating an expansive conception of state obligations.

For example, the CESCR General Comments integrate doctrinal constructs like "minimum core obligations"[37] and the distinction between obligations of "respect,"

[35]'The Economic and Social Council may submit from time to time to the General Assembly reports with recommendations of a general nature and a summary of the information received from the States Parties to the present Covenant and the specialized agencies on the measures taken and the progress made in achieving general observance of the rights recognized in the present Covenant.' International Covenant on Economic, Social and Cultural Rights, Article 21. I note that it is the ECOSOC that gets the authorization here. The monitoring powers were delegated to the CESCR by way of Economic and Social Council Resolution 1985/17.

[36]CESCR (1994) *Report on the 8th and 9th Session*, E/1994/23; UN Doc. E/C.12/1993/19. s. 51.

[37]CESCR (1990) *General Comment 3* ('The Nature of States Parties Obligations') UN Doc. E/1991/23(SUPP).

"protect," and "fulfill" into human rights law.[38] These doctrinal innovations are not part of the relevant hard law and cannot even be read off it by way of mere interpretative engagement. Moreover, as the case of "minimum core obligations" shows in particular, such doctrinal devices are sometimes in conflict with the very doctrinal design of the ICESCR.[39] Instead of settling issues about hard law, they tend to exacerbate doctrinal tensions around it.[40]

It is quite clear that the distinctive normative status of the General Comments (as soft law with its own construct of validity) makes this kind of overt deviation from hard law possible at all. In certain ways, CESCR soft law operates like a body of law with its own internal normative dynamics. But the point I want to develop here is not that these ventures beyond the scope of the relevant hard law are necessarily unacceptable. Perhaps the challenge of the meaningful implementation of human rights cannot always be handled within the confines of the hard law we have.

First, it is no accident that CESCR soft law puts special focus on doctrines of state obligations. The practicability of any legal instrument is primarily determined by the clarity and specificity of related obligations. Human rights treaties, however, tend to be particularly vague about the exact obligations they give rise to. They speak a rhetorically elevated language of rights, and the few provisions they contain about state obligations are not specific enough for effective implementation. The CESCR General Comments need to expand on the terms of treaty obligations.

Second, human rights law is underregulated in terms of hard law. As we have seen, international law operates with a rather narrow model for the sources of hard law. This is in stark contrast with the ever-broadening activities of international organizations. Due to the mismatch between the narrowness of hard law and the breadth of institutional practice, international law lacks the web of implementation norms typical of domestic legal systems. This is particularly obvious when we look at economic and social rights. Especially over the past three decades, institutional activity has grown exponentially in the field. In terms of hard law, the burgeoning practice is covered by just a handful treaty provisions. It would be difficult to achieve even remotely adequate coverage of important human rights issues by simply interpreting what is in treaty law. CESCR soft law may have been the most viable option to work out the details of the relevant human rights law. And saying, in different words, what is already in the Covenant would not have been very helpful.

We see here a pattern of the functioning of human rights law that combines slow moving hard law with more flexible and more detailed soft law. In the area of economic and social rights, international law has become increasingly dependent on a body of soft law norms to provide anything approaching a sensible doctrinal framework. Even though soft law does not establish legal obligations in itself, by

[38]CESCR (1999) *General Comment 12* ('The Right to Adequate Food') UN Doc. E/C.12/1999/5.

[39]Talking about 'minimum core obligations' (that are not subject to resource constraints and are immediately applicable) sits very uneasily with the 'progressive realisation standard' in article 2(1) of the ICESCR.

[40]This is clear from the controversy in the literature. See e.g. Young (2008) and Bilchitz (2003).

framing issues of treaty-based obligations, it pervasively influences how institutional practices (even on the national level) go about specifying legal obligations. It has become built into all competent accounts of how to approach the relevant hard law. As I have indicated, the CESCR General Comments behave a lot like a body of law, and it weighs down on the hard law of the ICESCR.

It must also be noted that, when soft law becomes the conduit for innovative doctrinal constructs, it implies some broadening of agency in relation to norm development. The way soft law in human rights law is formed implies the contribution of a broader range of agents. Most characteristically, when General Comments are formulated, treaty bodies must reckon with the challenge of lending credibility to the doctrinal innovations they bring about. They are likelier to stay with the doctrinal constructs that gained acceptance in academic writing[41] and that fit the agenda and ambitions of (mainstream) human rights activism.[42] It is not that scholars and activists cannot make an impact on hard law,[43] but there are far more opportunities to exert influence on soft law. In a limited but important sense, soft law can counteract the agency-narrowing implications of formal validity in international law.

But, of course, it is not enough to list a disparate set of positive features and excuses to justify the doctrinal ambitions manifested in the CESCR General Comments. There are grave legitimacy problems here. Some condemn the gradual reframing and reconstitution of state obligations as an illegitimate use of treaty monitoring authority (Mechlem 2009; Odello and Seatzu 2013, p. 34). There is an unmistakable mismatch with the underlying legitimacy discourse for international law (in which deference to state sovereignty weighs heavily), and that inevitably casts a shadow on the doctrinal work of the Committee. The General Comments stretch the vital conceptual point that soft law is always parasitic on hard law. Here, hard law often seems only the starting point for normative innovations—as opposed to the definitive framework within which normative development needs to take place. It is not a dramatic exaggeration to claim that in, say, CESCR General Comment 14 (on the right to health), we do not really see the clarification of the exact normative content of ICESCR article 12. Instead, we get what a group of experts has to say on a human right in the light of a conception of human rights that is, in certain respects, incompatible with the doctrinal design of the Covenant.

So even though soft law often improves the quality of human rights law, it also exacerbates the tensions around hard law. Soft law can function as a safety valve for hard law when it is in need of some normative development that hard law fails to provide. It circumvents the procedural strictures of renewing or extending treaty law.

---

[41] 'Minimum core obligations' can be traced back to a seminal article by Philip Alston. See Alston (1987). The tripartite classification of state obligations ('respect,' 'protect,' 'fulfill') relies on the work of Henry Shue and Asbjørn Eide. See Shue (1980), pp. 52–60; Eide (2001), p. 24.

[42] Human rights activists, most of whom are minimum core campaigners, and prioritize minimizing goals over lofty ambitions, tend to be sympathetic to 'minimum core obligations.' See Lehmann (2006), p. 180; Bilchitz (2002), p. 500.

[43] The drafting history the *Statute of the International Criminal Court* is an instructive example of the impact of human rights activism on hard international law. See Glasius (2013), pp. 151–154.

But there must be limits to the reasonable use of normative development through soft law. The trouble is that it is difficult to identify where those limits are. This is what makes assessing the norm-creating endeavors of the CESCR so challenging. It forces us to pit respect for state sovereignty against the concern with effective human rights protection, the involvement of a broader cohort of stakeholders, and the importance of improving institutional performance in treaty monitoring.

The main reason for the confusion and uncertainty here is that the legitimacy discourse for soft law is very underdeveloped. The dependence on hard law may suggest that the legitimacy issues are the same as for hard law: soft law borrows its legitimacy from hard law. However, this would be a misleading simplification. If it were true, the problematic normative development we see in CESCR doctrine would be close to impossible: soft law that goes beyond the terms of hard law would fall foul of validity criteria. The mismatches of hard and soft law are made possible by the fact that soft law operates with a different construct of validity (which revolves around standard instruments—not so much state consent).

The implications of this bifurcation of validity criteria and legitimacy in international law are in desperate need of analysis and clarification (which I do not provide here). Without it, we cannot gain an adequate understanding of the scope and limits of "expert-driven standard-setting" that the CESCR General Comments represent. It would be too simplifying (and terribly dogmatic) to say bluntly that the Committee has been acting *ultra vires* (as we would probably do in the context of state law in a similar situation).

Importantly, the legitimacy problems are not simply about soft law here. Few would deny that the root causes of many problems with CESCR soft law are the deficiencies of the ICESCR. And those deficiencies are very difficult to fix. Due to the specific ways in which state law and international law have been reconciled with each other, hard international law simply does not leave adequate space for corrective normative development. (Redrafting a multilateral international treaty is rarely feasible, and even if it does take place, the revised treaty may not attract the critical mass of ratifications.) The tension around poorly drafted treaty law can build over a long period without a resolution in sight. In this context, soft law may seem a rather clever device that opens up international law to some corrective development without sacrificing the centrality of state consent in hard law. With soft law as an option, states (when they experience pressure to agree to new norms) can "wave through" an instrument or two without actually subjecting themselves to new, binding hard law. (We have seen this dynamic with the normative development concerning sustainable development and development assistance.[44]) It is also possible to resort to expert-driven standard-setting (as it happens with the General Comments) that facilitates somewhat improved institutional functioning in many international bodies. However, the result, as we have seen, is the awkward

[44]One can look at the *Millennium Declaration* (GA Res. A/RES/55/2. 18 September 2000), the *Millennium Development Goals* and the *2030 Sustainable Development Agenda*.

coexistence of validity constructs that muddle the underlying legitimacy issues, and leave lingering questions about the very construct of legality in international law.

6 Conclusion

The legal theoretical lesson that this analysis was meant to provide concerns the ways in which theoretical reflection on formal validity in law needs to be deepened and broadened. If we aspire for a more adequate understanding of how legal normativity plays out in a globalized world (characterized by intense interactions between different legal orders), we need to develop multitiered accounts of validity that reckon with the coexistence and interdependence of different constructs of validity. And the theoretical challenge does not really lie in simply clarifying the structural similarities and differences between constructs of validity. We have to see the interplay of validity constructs across legal systems—and sometimes within legal systems.

In this chapter, I tried to straddle an abstract account of legal validity and a more specific analysis of certain developments in international human rights law. I sought to demonstrate that once the core concept of validity develops into specific validity constructs (tailored to particular legal practices), we get tangled relationships between norms and institutional processes. One legal order can influence the way another legal order develops its normative structures, and structural tensions within a legal system can lead to the awkward "cohabitation" of different validity constructs. It is important to make sure that legal theory is capable of reflecting this complexity.

At the beginning of this chapter, I asked whether the proliferation of soft law in international law extends the scope of legal materials beyond reasonable limits and engenders legal uncertainty. This worry was not quite borne out in my analysis. Soft law is not incompatible with formal validity—and not always a significant source of legal uncertainty. However, we have reasons to be concerned when the functioning of international law becomes over-reliant on soft law. The problem is even more pressing when it is due to the dysfunctions of hard law. But the challenge here does not primarily concern validity: it is more about legitimacy. It reminds us that particular constructs of validity always come to reflect the legitimacy discourses that address, directly or indirectly, the criteria of success for normative claims within a particular institutional practice. One of the weaknesses of most legal theoretical analysis about validity is ignoring this connection with issues of legitimacy. We need to unpick the theoretical implications of the relevant legitimacy discourses, and become more conscious of their political underpinnings.

Acknowledgements I am grateful for useful comments from the participants in the Groningen Workshop and subsequent research seminars held in Aberdeen and Debrecen where earlier versions of this chapter were presented. I am particularly thankful to Mátyás Bencze, Irene Couzigou, Tamás Győrfi, Tamás Hoffmann, Andrei Marmor, Paolo Sandro, Robert Taylor, Dietmar von der Pfordten, and Zsolt Ződi. I am also grateful for the anonymous reviewer's comments on my chapter.

References

Alston, P. 1987. Out of the Abyss: The Challenges Confronting the New UN Committee on Economic, Social and Cultural Rights. *Human Rights Quarterly* 9 (3): 332–381.

Anscombe, G.E.M. 1957. *Intention*. London: Basil Blackwell.

Berman, H.J. 1983. *Law and Revolution: The Formation of the Western Legal Tradition*. Cambridge: Harvard University Press.

Bilchitz, D. 2002. Giving Socio-Economic Rights Teeth: The Minimum Core and Its Importance. *South African Law Journal* 119 (3): 484–501.

———. 2003. Towards a Reasonable Approach to the Minimum Core: Laying the Foundations for Future Socio-Economic Rights Jurisprudence. *South African Journal of Human Rights* 19 (1): 1–26.

Blake, C. 2008. *Normative Instruments in International Human Rights Law: Locating the General Comment.* [Online]. New York: Center for Human Rights and Global Justice Working Paper, NYU School of Law. [Accessed 30 August 2017]. Available from: http://chrgj.org/wp-content/uploads/2012/07/blake.pdf

Bódig, M. 2002. Abszolút szuverenitás. In *Államelmélet: A mérsékelt állam eszméje és elemei II*, ed. M. Bódig and T. Győrfi. Miskolc: Bíbor.

———. 2010. Rules, Principles, and the Problem of the Limits of Legal Reasoning. In *On the Nature of Legal Principles*, ed. M. Borowski. Stuttgart: Franz Steiner Verlag.

———. 2011. Legal Positivism and the Limits of the Contemporary Legal Theoretical Discourse. *German Law Journal* 12 (2): 625–662.

———. 2013a. The Issue of Normativity and the Methodological Implications of Interpretivism I: The Idea of Normative Guidance. *Acta Juridica Hungarica* 54 (2): 119–139.

———. 2013b. The Issue of Normativity and the Methodological Implications of Interpretivism II: The Distinctive Normativity of Law. *Acta Juridica Hungarica* 54 (3): 207–218.

———. 2015a. Doctrinal Knowledge, Legal Doctrinal Scholarship and the Problem of Interdisciplinary Engagement. In *Stateless Law? Evolving Boundaries of a Discipline*, ed. H. Dedek and S. Shauna van Praagh. Farnham: Ashgate.

———. 2015b. Doctrinal Innovation and State Obligations: The Patterns of Doctrinal Development in the Jurisprudence of the UN Committee on Economic, Social and Cultural Rights. In *Human Rights Protection in Global Politics: Responsibilities of States and Non-State Actors*, ed. D. Karp and K. Mills. Basingstoke: Palgrave MacMillan.

———. 2016. Soft Law, Doctrinal Development and the General Comments of the UN Committee on Economic, Social and Cultural Rights. In *Tracing the Roles of Soft Law in Human Rights*, ed. S. Lagoutte et al. Oxford: Oxford University Press.

Börzel, T., and T. Risse. 2013. Human Rights in Areas of Limited Statehood. In *The Persistent Power of Human Rights: From Commitment to Compliance*, ed. T. Risse et al. Cambridge: Cambridge University Press.

Boyle, A. 2010. Soft Law in International Law-Making. In *International Law*, ed. M. Evans, 3rd ed. Oxford: Oxford University Press.

Broomhall, B. 2004. *International Justice and the International Criminal Court: Between Sovereignty and the Rule of Law*. Oxford: Oxford University Press.

Brunnée, J., and S. Toope. 2010. *Legitimacy and Legality in International Law*. Cambridge: Cambridge University Press.

Chinkin, C. 2003. Normative Development in the International Legal System. In *Commitment and Compliance: The Role of Non-Binding Norms in the International System*, ed. D. Shelton. Oxford: Oxford University Press.

d'Aspremont, J. 2008. Softness in International Law: A Self-Serving Quest for New Legal Materials. *European Journal of International Law* 19 (5): 1075–1093.

———. 2011. *Formalism and the Sources of International Law: A Theory of the Ascertainment of Legal Rules*. Oxford: Oxford University Press.

Eide, A. 2001. Economic, Social and Cultural Rights as Human Rights. In *Economic, Social and Cultural Rights*, ed. A. Eide et al. Leiden: Martinus Nijhoff.

Franck, T.M. 1988. Legitimacy in the International System. *American Journal of International Law* 82 (4): 705–759.

Glasius, M. 2013. Global Civil Society and Human Rights. In *Human Rights: Politics and Practice*, ed. M. Goodhart, 2nd ed. Oxford: Oxford University Press.

Goldmann, M. 2010. Inside Relative Normativity? From Sources to Standard Instruments for the Exercise of International Public Authority. In *The Exercise of Public Authority by International Institutions: Advancing International Institutional Law*, ed. A. von Bogdandy et al. Heidelberg: Springer.

Higgins, R. 1994. *Problems and Process: International Law and How We Use It*. Oxford: Oxford University Press.

Kingsbury, B. 2009. The Concept of Law in Global Administrative Law. *European Journal of International Law* 20 (1): 23–57.

Lehmann, K. 2006. In Defense of the Constitutional Court: Litigating Socio-Economic Rights and the Myth of the Minimum Core. *American University International Law Review* 22 (1): 163–198.

MacCormick, N. 2008. *Institutions of Law*. Oxford: Oxford University Press.

Marmor, A. 2011. *Philosophy of Law*. Princeton: Princeton University Press.

Mechlem, K. 2009. Treaty Bodies and the Interpretation of Human Rights. *Vanderbilt Journal of Transnational Law* 42 (3): 905–948.

Moore, M. 2000. *Educating Oneself in Public*. Oxford: Oxford University Press.

Odello, M., and F. Seatzu. 2013. *The UN Committee on Economic, Social and Cultural Rights: The Law, Process and Practice*. London: Routledge.

Rawls, J. 2001. *The Law of the Peoples*. Cambridge: Harvard University Press.

Riedel, E. 1991. Standards and Sources: Farewell to the Exclusivity of the Sources Triad in International Law? *European Journal of International Law* 2 (2): 58–84.

Schauer, F. 1991. *Playing by the Rules*. Oxford: Clarendon Press.

Schmitt, C. 2006. *Political Theology*. Chicago: Chicago University Press.

Searle, J. 1969. *Speech Acts*. Cambridge: Cambridge University Press.

Shelton, D. 2003. Law, Non-Law and the Problem of "Soft Law". In *Commitment and Compliance: The Role of Non-Binding Norms in the International System*, ed. D. Shelton. Oxford: Oxford University Press.

Shue, H. 1980. *Basic Rights: Subsistence, Affluence, and U.S. Foreign Policy*. Princeton: Princeton University Press.

Tamanaha, T. 2017. *A Realistic Theory of Law*. Cambridge: Cambridge University Press.

Waldron, J. 2008. The Concept and the Rule of Law. *Georgia Law Review* 43 (1): 1–61.

Walker, N. 2010. Out of Place and Out of Time: Law's Fading Coordinates. *Edinburgh Law Review* 14 (1): 13–46.

Young, K. 2008. The Minimum Core of Economic and Social Rights: A Concept in Search of Content. *Yale Journal of International Law* 33 (1): 113–175.

Soft Law in Public International Law: A Pragmatic or a Principled Choice? Comparing the Sustainable Development Goals and the Paris Agreement

Marcel M. T. A. Brus

Abstract This chapter discusses the role of soft law in international law, in particular in the field of sustainable development law. Soft law is often regarded as nonlaw. However, this qualification increasingly does not match the realities of the development of international law in which many legally relevant statements are made in the form of soft law, while many so-called hard law obligations are rather soft. A comparison between the Sustainable Development Goals (SDGs) and the Paris Agreement on climate change, both adopted in the second half of 2015, is used to illustrate these points. It is argued that the development of international law can be better understood by placing legal statements on a continuum from weak to strong legal pronunciations instead of using the binary approach that distinguishes between hard and soft law and that qualifies soft law as nonlaw.

1 Happy Days in 2015

Governing world affairs is a difficult business. Because of the lack of a central authority with decision-making powers, agreements on how to save our common interests can only be reached through debate and the development of a broad consensus. In 2015, the world saw on two occasions, at least, world leaders united on stage, their hands joined and raised to celebrate the conclusion of two consultation processes. The first one was the conclusion of the discussion on the Sustainable Development Goals (SDGs)[1] as the successor to the Millennium Development Goals in September 2015.[2] The second was the adoption of the Paris Agreement on climate

[1]Transforming Our World: The 2030 Agenda for Sustainable Development, UNGA Resolution A/RES/70/1, 21 October 2015 ('the SDGs').

[2]United Nations Millennium Development Declaration, UNGA Resolution A/RES/55/2, 8 September 2000 ('the MDGs').

M. M. T. A. Brus (✉)
University of Groningen, Groningen, The Netherlands
e-mail: m.m.t.a.brus@rug.nl

© Springer International Publishing AG, part of Springer Nature 2018

P. Westerman et al. (eds.), *Legal Validity and Soft Law*, Law and Philosophy Library 122, https://doi.org/10.1007/978-3-319-77522-7_13

change in December 2015.[3] Both documents reflect the need to find joint answers to collective problems: on the one hand, the problems of poverty, inequality, exclusion of large parts of the world population and the need to develop sustainable societies worldwide and, on the other hand, action to address the causes and effects of human activity on global climate. As many had not expected that any significant outcome would be achievable, the successful conclusion of these negotiations was regarded with great joy. Despite the fact that states have been and will continue to be divided about the precise manner in which the climate problem should be tackled, and who should take the lead, they succeeded in reaching consensus on the way forward. Getting states to endorse a document that sets sustainability targets for realizing significant progress on a broad range of issues seemed even more unrealistic. Yet after an inclusive process that involved states, international organizations, and civil society, a broad consensus was reached—happy days as there was hope that the world is capable of engaging in forms of global governance for the common interest.

Sustainable development has been a key concept since the end of the 1980s. To create sustainable societies at the national and subnational levels, as well as at levels beyond the national, i.e. at the regional and international levels, would require huge efforts. Since the Earth Summit of 1992,[4] it has been recognized that sustainable development involves social, economic and environmental dimensions. Interaction and integration are core notions for achieving sustainability. Climate change cannot be addressed at the national or subnational levels only. By definition, it requires worldwide collaborative efforts. Of course, international consensus about the necessary action has to be translated into effective activities at the national level. The same applies to the topics dealt with in the SDGs, such as poverty reduction, access to education, health care and other basic services, nondiscrimination, and other human rights. To some extent, these topics can be addressed at the national level, but ultimately international cooperation is also necessary: firstly, to provide opportunities for all societies to benefit from economic globalization and, secondly, to develop mechanisms for the international accountability of states and their rulers for not respecting the interests of their population, e.g. in the fields of human rights. In 1992, in the Rio Declaration on Sustainable Development,[5] states formulated core principles of sustainable development, such as the right to development, the principle of common but differentiated responsibilities, the precautionary approach, citizen participation, and scientific cooperation. These broad ambitions have evolved since then in many different ways, including through the use of law. It is this last aspect that forms the core of this contribution. Does law, in particular public international law, play a meaningful role in realizing the ambitions expressed since

[3]UNFCCC, Decision 1/CP.21, 'Adoption of the Paris Agreement' (29 January 2016), UN Doc FCCC/CP/2015/10/Add.1, Annex, 15 December 2015 ('Paris Agreement').

[4]United Nations Conference on Environment and Development (UNCED), Rio de Janeiro, 3–14 June 1992.

[5]The Rio Declaration on Environment and Development, UN Doc. A/CONF.151/26 (Vol. I), 14 June 1992.

1992, culminating in the two 2015 documents? To what extent can these expressions, which are often regarded as so-called soft law, be regarded as valid expressions within the legal system, or should they be regarded as aspirational politics rather than as belonging to the legal domain? This contribution has no ambition to deal with these truly fundamental, comprehensive questions exhaustively. After general remarks characterizing the international legal order and the role of soft law therein, this contribution will focus on a comparison between the two outcome documents, the SDGs (or Agenda 2030 as it is often referred to) and the Paris Agreement. Doing so will illustrate the increasing difficulties that one faces when trying to determine whether we should use the qualification of soft law or hard law to distinguish in a binary manner between nonlaw and law or whether we can place them on a continuum of valid legal expressions raging from weak to strong legal pronouncements. It will be concluded that soft law must be given a constructive role in the international legal system.

2 The International Legal Order at a Crossroads

International law is a complicated phenomenon, although its origins appear simple. The main reason for this is the fact that states, as the creators and primary beneficiaries of international law, accept the need to establish legal rules and procedures at the international level, while at the same time they are scarcely prepared to allow supranational authority into this system to make it work effectively. This is clearly expressed in the traditional doctrines on the sources of international law, as reflected in Article 38 of the Statute of the International Court of Justice.[6] The validity of international law is generally taken as being directly or indirectly based on the consent of states and is linked to the concept of the sovereignty of states. However, Article 38 only mentions a limited number of forms for the expression of international law: treaties, custom, and principles of law recognized by states as primary sources, complemented by subsidiary sources in the form of judicial decisions and the teachings of the most highly qualified publicists. No mention is made of other methods through which legal authority may be given to other outcomes of decision-making procedures, e.g. the decisions by international organizations or their organs. Only in certain cases is it generally recognized that decisions of international organizations have the binding force of law. A major example is the power of the United Nations Security Council to take legally binding decisions. This traditional approach leads to a binary result: either something is law or it is not law.

This approach is rather straightforward, not too complicated, and provides a coherent explanation of many features of international law. However, reality is more complicated than this. First of all, there is the incorporation of new, overarching, legally relevant values and principles that connect participants in the

[6]Statute of the International Court of Justice, 24 October 1945.

international society of humankind. “Elementary considerations of humanity,” as the International Court of Justice once called them, have become an element of the system of law at the international level.[7] In a more recent case, the Court referred to the concept of sustainable development as an apt expression of newly developed norms and standards that have to be taken into consideration in legally assessing the conduct of states. The Court makes reference here to the great number of instruments in which these new norms and standards have been articulated.[8] It does not further specify the nature of these instruments in that particular decision. This ties in with a second point, namely the increasing number of types of normative statements by states made in the context of international organizations, conferences, or treaty bodies that do not fall within the categories mentioned in Article 38 of the ICJ Statute but that nevertheless reflect on what is considered proper behavior in international society. Are such expressions of no legal relevance merely for this reason? A third issue to be mentioned here is that state sovereignty is not a static concept but develops over time. It is increasingly accepted that sovereignty is no longer a shield for states or their rulers that can be used to disregard responsibilities toward their own populations, as well as to world society at large. Being a state, and therefore being sovereign, comes with rights but also increasingly is associated with obligations and responsibilities, for example in connection with the discourse about the responsibility to protect.[9] These and other developments make the traditional Article 38 doctrine less and less convincing.

However, while recognizing these points, there is no clarity about the direction in which international legal society is evolving. There are many inroads into the traditional doctrines, but a convincing alternative has not yet developed. In particular, the criteria and procedures for what may be called legally authoritative international decision making are far from clear. Taking a world government and legislature as the only alternative to the current system is too simplistic. This will not be realized and perhaps should never be our ambition. Nevertheless, responding to societal needs and changes, international law continues to develop, incrementally, and with much confusion and uncertainty. A less rigid approach to what international law is may be a way forward, moving away from the binary approach between law and nonlaw into the direction of positioning legally relevant statements on a continuum from soft to hard law.

[7]International Court of Justice, Corfu Channel case (United Kingdom v. Albania), Merits, Judgment of 9 April 1949, ICJ Reports 1949, p. 22.

[8]International Court of Justice, Gabčíkovo-Nagymaros Project (Hungary/Slovakia), Judgment of 25 September 1997, ICJ Reports 1997, para 140.

[9]International Commission on Intervention in State Sovereignty, 2001. See e.g., Cohen and Deng (2016).

3 Soft Law in International Law

If one approaches law and legal order as basically a mechanism to create predictability and stability in a society, and therewith as more than just a set of rules and procedures, law by definition becomes a dynamic concept. Not only its content but also its form is constantly subject to change as a result of changes in the society in which it is meant to play a role. Societies change as a result of external challenges, e.g. merging of national societies and large-scale migration, as well as through internal changes in dominant values and ambitions. While law and the legal system have a conservative role, namely ensuring that changes take place in an orderly manner through procedures that have been previously agreed upon, law cannot be too rigid as it ultimately must be able to encompass societal developments. The law is a system of rules and procedures for governance, legitimacy, and coherence based on underlying values and principles. It is not the rules and procedures of the legal system as such in which the members of a particular society believe but the fact that these are expressions of their shared concept of what their society stands for or should stand for. Before becoming entangled in a philosophical debate about law, let me explain why this statement is relevant to my perspective on international law and the international legal system.

In the eighteenth and nineteenth centuries, a strong consensus developed that the international legal system is based on shared values and principles that give the state a central role: sovereignty, nonintervention, equality, and the rejection of supranationality. Based on these shared values and principles, at least among the group of states that considered themselves the civilized world, international rules and procedures developed. A coherent legal order emerged, although it remained rather imperfect in comparison to the more fully fledged legal orders that developed within the states at the same time. The international legal order was not capable of channeling conflict effectively with great disasters as a result: wars in the nineteenth century, World Wars I and II, and the great economic depression in the 1920s and 1930s, just to mention a few. The idea of the superiority of the leading states led to the acceptance of colonization, racial inequality, slavery, and economic exploitation. A consensus that change was necessary and new rules needed to be developed that superseded the narrow self-interests of states emerged on some issues, such as the slave trade, limitations to the ever-expanding cruelty of war, and certain economic issues. After the Second World War, it became apparent that the underlying set of values and principles needed to be changed in order to avoid even worse disasters in the future such as the complete annihilation of humankind through (nuclear) war. It became necessary to adopt a less Eurocentric perspective on international affairs and international law as a result of decolonization. The horrors of the Second World War resulted in the incorporation of human rights into international law. The *laissez-faire* approach to international law—what is not prohibited is allowed—became untenable as it increasingly undermined stability in international society. This led to fundamental changes in the international legal system best illustrated by the acceptance of peremptory norms, or *jus cogens*.[10] This is the clearest expression of the fact that the international legal order does not only reflect the interest of (a small group of) states that have only their own interest in mind but that it also contains core values binding international society from which no member of that society can derogate. These norms include protection of fundamental human rights, such as against genocide, crimes against humanity, slavery and the slave trade, discrimination and torture, as well as the right to self-determination of peoples and the prohibition of the use of force in international relations. Crimes against the environment—ecocide—or against sustainability have not yet developed, but it seems a matter of time before we can add these to the list of core values that must be respected.

Accepting *jus cogens* as hierarchically superior norms is an acknowledgement of the fact that international society has become much more complex. This existence of such substantive norms and the ambition to give effect to them in the fabric of international law is at odds with maintaining the traditional approach to the sources of international law. This can be illustrated with an example from the area of human rights protection. The incorporation of international human rights into international law started with the adoption of the Universal Declaration of Human Rights in 1948.[11] This is a declaration accepted by the General Assembly of the United Nations and as such, according to Article 38, not (valid) law. Nevertheless, it is impossible to deny that this document is of utmost importance as a legally authoritative expression of the will of states in the field of human rights. What is its status in the legal system? Is it excluded from what we consider international law? Can it only be regarded as a political expression rather than as legally relevant? According to Brownlie, the "Declaration is a good example of an informal prescription given legal significance by actions of authoritative decision-makers, and thus it has been used as an agreed point of reference."[12] What does legal significance mean? Has it, through the authority of the decision-makers, become law where it was not law before? Did they turn water into wine? Or did it belong to the domain of law from the outset, although needing further elaboration to display its real potential? Puzzling indeed. We will come back to this below.

It is relevant at this point to acknowledge that the level of ambition of international law as an instrument for governing international society has increased greatly. Goals that supersede individual state interests have to be addressed. The best way of doing this, from a legal position, is to agree on legally binding statements that are precise, can be enforced, and are justiciable. However, given the complex nature of international society and the lack of centralized institutions, this ideal type of legal order is still remote. What does this mean for the nature of international legal order?

[10] *Jus cogens* refers to those norms of international law, from which no derogation is allowed. It is prominently formulated in article 53 of the 1969 Vienna Convention on the law of treaties: a treaty will be void "if, at a time of its conclusion, it conflicts with the peremptory norm of general international law." See further e.g. Orakhelashvili (2016).

[11] UNGA Resolution 217 A(III), 10 December 1948.

[12] Crawford (2012), p. 637.

Ultimately, the law is intended to guide behavior in order to realize particular goals. For something to belong to the realm of law, must it completely fulfill all of these characteristics (precision, enforceability, etc.), or can partial fulfillment also be sufficient to be considered as part of it? In other words, is the traditional and predominantly binary approach to validity the best possible option for international law, or can it be placed on a continuum depending on the degree of fulfillment of the relevant criteria? This will be further explored in Sect. 5 and beyond, but it seems undeniable that in the field of international cooperation, various forms of making legally authoritative statements have been developed as an alternative to the impossibility of making legal statements that fulfill the requirements for legal validity of the traditional Article 38 doctrine. In general, these (alternative) legally relevant statements are referred to as soft law.

Soft law in international law is a complex phenomenon as it serves various purposes and takes various forms. It is possible to distinguish at least five different purposes, as has been elaborated upon, among others, by Alan Boyle and Christine Chinkin[13]: (1) as an alternative to treaty law, (2) as an authoritative interpretation of treaties, (3) as guidance to the implementation of a treaty, (4) as a step in the development of international legal principles, (5) as evidence of *opinio juris* in the formation of international customary law.

Treaties may not always be the most ideal instrument for laying down international agreement between states. States may be hesitant to engage in treaty commitments but may agree more easily on a soft law instrument, for example by accepting more specific commitments in soft law than they would in a formal treaty. An obvious reason for this is that soft law instruments are less likely to be enforced in court or other formal procedures. Moreover, soft law instruments do not require domestic ratification. Also, where treaties will only bind the states that ratify them, soft law represents the commitments of a much wider group. There is also much more flexibility in changing or adapting such instruments to new realities. In areas where treaties already exist, soft law may be used to assist in providing authoritative interpretations. Well-known examples of this in the context of the UN Charter are resolutions of the UN General Assembly on the Universal Declaration of Human Rights and the 1970 Declaration on Principles of International Law Concerning Friendly Relations.[14] Other examples are the General Comments given by human rights treaty bodies, such as the Human Rights Committee and the Committee Against Torture, which assist in interpreting the content of the various rights included in the relevant treaty. Soft law may also be used to provide guidance on the implementation of treaties. This is, for example, clearly visible in the field of international environmental law where guidelines or standards developed by technical or scientific bodies established under a treaty are frequently used and recognized for the implementation of the more abstract commitments laid down in the treaty. Besides playing a role in the interpretation and implementation of treaties,

[13]Boyle and Chinkin (2007), Chapter 5.2. See also Boyle (2014) and Abbott and Snidal (2000).

[14]UNGA Res. 217 A(III), 10 December 1948; UNGA Res. 2625 (XXV), 24 October 1970.

soft law may also be of importance in the creation of new international legal norms in the form of legal principles or of international customary law. The principles of sustainable development, as well as of the responsibility to protect, are examples of new principles of international law emerging from soft law declarations.[15] The role of soft law in the development of customary law is widely recognized. Broadly supported UN General Assembly resolutions may have a profound impact on state practice, in other words on (changes in) the actual behavior of states, or may be regarded as expressions of *opinio juris*, the will to adhere to a certain rule.

The fact that in international law legally relevant statements are made in the form of soft law does not mean that they are ineffective. The relevant question is whether states and other actors behave in accordance with such norms and rules. We can observe that soft law does lead to changes in behavior and that it is invoked to assist in interpreting and implementing the principles and rules of international law. But even if states do not comply with soft law norms, this is not necessarily an indication of the lack of a legal character of the relevant statements. Many legally relevant statements in the form of treaties or customary international law are not complied with. Making a binary distinction between political statements and legal statements on the basis of either their formal legal validity according to Article 38 or their compliance is not particularly helpful for appreciating the incremental development of the international legal order. For states, international organizations, judicial and quasi-judicial bodies, and other (international) actors, it is impossible to disregard the fact that they have to operate on the continuum between strictly political and strictly legal statements.

The complexities in this discussion can be well illustrated by taking a closer look at how the concept of sustainable development emerged in international law.

4 The Two-Track Approach to International Law and Sustainable Development

Although the origins of sustainable development as relating to the need to preserve the environment in the process of economic development is not new, in its present form it is based on its articulation in the so-called Brundtland report, the report of the World Commission on Environment and Development (WCED).[16] It was incorporated in the Rio Declaration on Environment and Development in 1992 and has had a profound impact on the further development of international law in the decades thereafter. The concept of sustainable development is mainly aspirational, and its 'definition' as "development that meets the needs of the present without compromising the ability of future generations to meet their own needs"[17] does not provide

[15]The Rio Declaration, note 5, respectively A/RES/60/1 (2005 World Summit Outcome).

[16]Report of the WCED, *Our Common Future*, 1987.

[17]Report of the WCED, Our Common Future, 1987, p. 51.

precise and easily identifiable behavioral guidance. As an integrative principle, aiming at finding a balance between environmental protection and economic and social development, it is by definition a concept that mediates between the various interests and issue areas. Also, more specific notions that help to give content to sustainable development, such as the precautionary principle and the principle of common but differentiated responsibilities as expressed in the Rio Declaration,[18] are by themselves general and principles rather than rules. They need further elaboration in law. States have repeated their commitment to the principle of sustainable development and its connected principles in many documents adopted in an international or regional context.[19]

Many of these documents do not fit within the narrow confines of Article 38 of the Statute of the ICJ. They are typically soft law documents. It is through these expressions that sustainable development and connected principles have become an undeniably legally relevant part of international law, as is recognized, for example, in many decisions by international and domestic courts and tribunals.[20] Moreover, sustainable development is not static but an evolving concept that must be regarded in the context of rapidly expanding scientific knowledge and societal awareness about the urgent need to better integrate the economic, environmental, and social dimensions of development as a basis for stable, secure, and just societies. The continuous references to sustainable development and sustainability in declarations, resolutions, statements, guidelines, and many other types of documents are vital for the building of a legally relevant normative consensus. Trying to encapsulate this in formal treaties or in generally accepted rules of customary international law would be too slow, too static, or leading to abstractly defined commitments, which then require further elaboration, probably through soft law instruments. An important track of the development of the concept of sustainable development has therefore been through soft law.

This does not mean that the more formal sources of international law—treaties and custom—do not play an important role. Reference to sustainable development and its related principles is included in many conventions on a wide range of topics, including environmental protection, natural resource management, human rights conventions, health, and trade.[21] Sustainable development is firmly grounded in treaty law. However, this does not necessarily mean that thereby sustainable development has become a generally enforceable norm of international law. Much depends of course on the way it is incorporated into such treaties and how it is used in their implementation. Some conventions are rather general, and giving them

[18]Se e.g. International Law Association, New Delhi Declaration of Principles of International Law Relating to Sustainable Development, 2002, UN Doc. A/CONF.199/8, 9 August 2002, also available at http://www.ila-hq.org/en/committees/index.cfm/cid/25. In this Declaration the ILA distinguishes seven principles.

[19]See e.g. Barral (2012), French (2010) and Margraw and Hawke (2007).

[20]See e.g. International Law Association, 2012.

[21]Schrijver (2008).

concrete meaning will depend on the treaty implementation bodies, the application and interpretation by the parties, and, where possible, by judicial bodies. Other treaties are much more specific and have a direct impact on particular issues of sustainable development. This is not the place to further expand on this. What is relevant is to recognize that besides the soft law track described above, there clearly is also a treaty law track. This is further supplemented by the development of aspects of sustainable development law and related principles in customary international law. To give one example, the requirement for making a transboundary environmental impact assessment for the activities of one state that might harm the interests of another state has become firmly established in international law as an element of sustainable development. It is included as soft law in the Rio Declaration as principle 17, as treaty law in the 1991 Espoo Convention on Environmental Impact Assessment,[22] and has been recognized as customary international law by the International Court of Justice in the *Pulp Mills* case.[23]

In the dynamic development of international law to address global issues such as sustainable development, a wide range of legal instruments and lawmaking techniques is used. There exists a clear interaction between soft law and the formal expressions of international law in accordance with Article 38 of the Statute of the International Court of Justice.

So far, states have not tried to draft a general treaty on sustainable development. They clearly opted to develop this in an incremental manner and with the intention that it should influence behavior and lead to the development of more specific legal prescriptions. A comprehensive treaty on sustainable development is clearly a step too far. Taking both the soft law and the treaty law track seems to be the most viable option for achieving the commonly shared objectives of sustainable development.

Although from a formal point of view the concept of sustainable development is not a binding rule of international law, neither as treaty law nor customary international law, it has gained its importance by the repeated expression of will by the international state community and the gradual development into a principle of international law that provides legally relevant guidance to assessing what is acceptable or unacceptable behavior of states. However, sustainable development does not prescribe particular behavior and has little enforceability in the courts but as a holistic concept allows and requires choices between alternatives while respecting its core elements of integration, participation, sustainable use and management of natural resources, precaution, equity, and common but differentiated responsibilities.

[22]Convention on Environmental Impact Assessment in a Transboundary Context, Espoo, Finland 1991, 1989 UNTS 309.

[23]Pulp Mills on the River Uruguay (Argentina v. Uruguay), Judgement, ICJ Reports 2010, para. 204.

Table 1 Comparison of the obligations in the SDGs and the Paris Agreement

Content	SDGs	PA
Aims—targets	Specific and general, very ambitious and covering a broad range of topics	General: avoid temperature rise above 2 °C, strengthen adaptive capacity, enhance governance framework
Nature of commitments—form and language	Voluntary, through national planning processes and international cooperation; pledge for action rather than laying down specific individualized obligations for states	Mix of obligations (shall), hortatory provisions (should), and noncommitting statements (recognize)
Timetable	2030 as target for achievement of the goals	Only procedural, in terms of renewing commitments, and periodic reporting and assessment
Implementation mechanism and review procedure	Unspecified at the national and regional level, mainly political at the global level through the High Level Political Forum on Sustainable Development (HLPF)	Reporting obligations, technical expert review, compliance mechanism, and periodical global stock take

5 Comparing the Sustainable Development Goals and the Paris Agreement

Having set out some basic considerations related to the role of soft law in international law, it is now time to try to test these statements by looking at the two concrete examples of the United Nations Sustainable Development Goals (SDGs) and the Paris Agreement on climate change. Both are concerned with creating a global partnership for tackling broad international societal issues related to sustainable development. They have a common pedigree stretching back to the United Nations Conference on Environment and Development in 1992. Whereas the Paris Agreement is a further elaboration of the United Nations Framework Convention on Climate Change, and therefore fits the approach of developing climate action in the form of creating a formal legal framework, the Sustainable Development Goals can be regarded as following the more political track through conference declarations that aspire to create momentum and expectations for concrete action to establish a sustainable international society. Although these seem to represent two diametrically opposed approaches, when one takes a detailed look, both appear to be not that different. In this section, some of these differences and similarities will be highlighted.

To do so, it seems useful to make a distinction between the SDGs and the Paris Agreement based on content and on systemic issues.[24] A summary of this comparison is provided in Tables 1 and 2 below. I will refrain from providing a detailed description of the SDGs and the Paris Agreement.

[24]For a legal characterization of the SDGs and the Paris Agreement see e.g. Kim (2016) and Bodansky (2016).

Table 2 Legal characteristics of the SDGs and the Paris Agreement compared

Systemic	SDGs	PA
Form	Nonbinding declaration	Binding treaty
Authority	Adopted by states in a high-level meeting of heads of states and governments	
Legitimacy	High at adoption, uncertain in the follow-up	Uncertain at the time of adoption, high due to quick ratification by many states
Subjects addressed	States and nonstate actors	States
Specificity	High specificity of targets, not specific on expected behavior	Mixed, a wide range of formulations
Accountability	Weak and mainly political through the HLPF, dependent on further agreement on criteria	Potentially strong, partly expert driven
Justiciability	Low	Low
Enforceability	Absent	Weak

Table 1 compares the SDGs and the Paris Agreement on the basis of content. Such a comparison is, of course, not easy because both documents are very different, although both aspire to create a sustainable international society. The 17 SDGs contain 169 quite precise targets that address a wide range of economic, social, and environmental issues, while the aims and targets of the Paris Agreement only address the specific issue of climate change. Combating climate change has been included in the SDGs as a specific goal. SDG 13 explicitly refers to climate change but acknowledges that the United Nations Framework Convention on Climate Change is the primary forum for this. The aims of the Paris Agreement are quite broad: to keep global temperature rise below 2 °C or if possible below 1.5 °C (mitigation), to assist in dealing with the consequences of climate change (adaptation), and to develop various mechanisms to build a governance structure to jointly address the problem of climate change (strengthening governance institutions). The aims and targets of the SDGs differ insofar as some are specific ("By 2030, achieve universal and equitable access to safe and affordable drinking water for all," SDG 6.1) and others rather unspecific ("Adopt policies, especially fiscal, wage and social protection policies, and progressively achieve greater equality," SDG 10.4).

Although the SDGs are formulated in a rather specific language that sets very clear though ambitious targets, they avoid using language that can be read as laying down legally binding commitments that prescribe the way in which these targets should be achieved. Eradicating extreme poverty everywhere is an abstract target and not formulated as a specific prescription for the behavior of states or other actors (SDG 1). The main intention is that all states, and other relevant actors, prepare the necessary policy plans predominantly at the national level in order to contribute to realizing the specific target. For the realization of many of the SDGs, enhanced international cooperation would be necessary, but the specific form that this should take is left mostly unspecified. In this regard, the Paris Agreement is more concrete. It is addressed to the states parties, either in general (each party) or addressing a specific subset of parties such as the developed country parties or the developing country parties. This makes the Paris Agreement more concrete than the SDGs. However, the nature of the specific commitments and entitlements of the states parties varies significantly. According to the language used, they may be referred to as obligatory (shall), recommendatory (should), and rather general statements that do not commit the parties ("recognize," "share a vision"). But even within these categories, it is possible to distinguish between the natures of the commitments entered into. For example, the core obligation of all parties to "prepare, communicate and maintain successive nationally determined contributions" (NDCs) does not prescribe the level of the contribution that a particular state must make to combat climate change. The main obligation following from this provision is that states must renew their NDCs every 5 years and increase the level of ambition each time. Moreover, parties are under obligation to pursue domestic mitigation measures, with the aim of achieving the objectives of the NDCs. This is a specifically chosen formula that requires parties not to realize their NDCs but to make genuine good-faith efforts to attain them. Although an elaborate analysis can be made about the specific commitments that parties enter into when ratifying the Paris Agreement, for the purpose of this chapter this is not necessary.[25]

The time frame for the implementation of the SDGs is 15 years (2030), although it would be surprising if the drafters of the SDGs really believe this to be achievable. What the SDGs do is set the agenda for the further implementation and concretization of existing ambitions that have been expressed in binding and nonbinding forms by states in the past decades. Where the SDGs refer to human rights goals and environmental ambitions, many of these can be seen as either a further concretization of international agreements in which rights and obligations have been expressed in a less specific manner or as a broadening of such treaty obligations to include non-parties. Many international human rights treaties, in particular on economic, social, and cultural rights, do not contain specific details as to what, for example, the right to housing, health, or education entails. Equally, environmental treaties, for example regarding the management of transboundary water systems, do not contain much detail about the level of ambition for such joint governance. The concrete time frame of the SDGs induces states and other stakeholders to set agendas, formulate concrete ambitions and strategies, and increase the pressure to show substantial improvements by 2030. The Paris Agreement on the other hand does not contain a timetable that determines at what point in time states must have undertaken certain action. In fact, the timetable is determined by scientists with the help of scientific models that provide information relevant for the various pathways that are open to ensure that the global temperature rise does not exceed 2 °C. If more action is taken in the next decade, less will be necessary in the decades to follow, while if nothing is done now,

[25] Rajamani (2016). This article provides a detailed analysis of the entire text of the Paris Agreement.

increased and probably more costly action will be required later. Although the Paris Agreement seems to be taking risks by leaving the decision on concrete measures to the individual parties, this does not necessarily disqualify it from being law, as we will discuss further below. While the Paris Agreement does not provide timetables for mitigation and adaptation, it does contain specific timetables for procedural issues, such as the requirement to periodically submit performance data to the Conference of Parties and the renewal of the NDCs every 5 years. Moreover, from 2023 onward, every 5 years a "global stock take" will take place to assess whether the aggregate implementations of the NDCs is sufficient to meet the target of no more than a 2 °C temperature rise.

The mechanisms for implementation and review in the SDGs are predominantly political and are left to a large extent to the national and subnational levels. As far as the global review of implementation is concerned, this will be left to states in what is called the High Level Political Forum on Sustainable Development (HLPF), functioning under the auspices of the UN Economic and Social Council (ECOSOC). To be able to assess the effective implementation of the SDGs, global, regional, and national indicators will have to be developed. Reaching agreement on these indicators may prove difficult and may frustrate the review process.[26] The Paris Agreement includes provisions on implementation and review at three levels. In general, the Conference of Parties (COP) is responsible for reviewing implementation. The previously mentioned global stock take is an essential mechanism for this. In order to be able to hold states to account for acting on their commitments under the Paris Agreement, states are under the obligation to submit information to the secretariat. This information will be reviewed by technical experts. Moreover, an expert-based mechanism to facilitate implementation and to promote compliance will be established. However, contrary to the noncompliance procedure for the Kyoto Protocol under the Climate Change Convention, this mechanism will not contain enforcement procedures that may penalize noncompliant behavior. It will be a facilitative, non-adversarial, and nonpunitive mechanism.

We can also compare the two instruments at a more systemic level in order to be able to determine their legal character under international law.

The SDGs were adopted in a high-level meeting of the General Assembly of the United Nations in the form of a resolution.[27] As, according to the Charter of the United Nations, the General Assembly in principle adopts recommendations, the resolution is not a decision that creates legal effects in international law *per se*. On the other hand, the Paris Agreement is an agreement linked to the United Nations Framework Convention on Climate Change. It has a status similar to the Kyoto Protocol. It is a legally relevant outcome in accordance with the position expressed in Durban in 2011.[28] The agreement needs the ratification of states before it can enter

[26]See UNGA Doc. A/70/684.

[27]See note 1.

[28]Report of the Conference of the Parties on its seventeenth session, held in Durban from 28 November to 11 December 2011, Decision 1/CP.17 Establishment of an Ad Hoc Working

into force.[29] Some of the confusion around the legal status of the Paris Agreement was caused by the complex position of the United States. The Obama administration needed to stay within the commitments entered into under the United Nations Framework Convention on Climate Change in 1992. If the Paris Agreement had laid down new legal obligations, Obama would have needed the endorsement of the US Congress as required under the US Constitution. Formulating the Paris Agreement as an elaboration of the commitments in the 1992 Convention[30] allowed Obama to deal with the agreement as an executive agreement and to legally bind the United States without the approval of Congress. For the Paris Agreement, this meant that the negotiators had to find compromises that would allow the drafting of a legally meaningful document, without creating new substantial obligations for the United States.[31] This problem underlines what has been said above about the reason to opt for soft law instruments rather than formally binding treaties. In this case, the binding treaty had to be sufficiently soft in its content in order to keep the United States on board.

The term authority in Table 2 is defined as the status of the actor under international law to engage in political and legal decision making, including the power to create legally binding obligations. It is clear that both instruments have been adopted by the best-qualified actors under international law, namely states. The fact that the adoptions took place in high-level meetings of heads of states and governments has no explicit added legal value but underlines the importance attached to the respective documents in terms of the authority and legitimacy of the commitments engaged in.

Legitimacy is a complex phenomenon in (international) law that cannot be dealt with here in any depth. I will only refer to one aspect of the legitimacy debate: its link to the so-called compliance pull.[32] Highly legitimate commitments according to this approach would lead to better implementation and compliance than those with low legitimacy. Whether legitimacy is static or whether the degree of legitimacy can evolve over time is debatable. If we accept that legitimacy can develop over time, two observations may be made. With regard to the SDGs, there is not much doubt that at the time of adoption there was a high level of support and a strong momentum for carrying this agenda forward. However, whether this will remain the case may be dependent on whether the processes through which the implementation will have to take place come to a halt in the quicksand of national and international bureaucracies and endless negotiations about procedural aspects. Many similar documents have been adopted in the past with similar high expectations but have lost momentum after a few years. As to the Paris Agreement, the situation may be the other way

---

Group on the Durban Platform for Enhanced Action, 11 December 2011. The parties agreed to draft no later than in 2015 a "protocol, another legal instrument or an agreed outcome with legal force."

[29]For the status of ratification see http://unfccc.int/paris_agreement/items/9485.php or https://treaties.un.org.

[30]The 1992 Convention was ratified by the USA on 15 October 1992.

[31]See e.g. Werksman (2016) and Bodansky (2015).

[32]Franck (1990).

around. Before the adoption, there was a lot of skepticism about the achievability of a binding agreement, but once it was adopted, states, at an impressively quick pace, endorsed the agreement through ratification.[33] Although this is not a guarantee for the success of the agreement in terms of the adoption of effective measures to combat climate change, it indicates that states consider the outcome as legitimate and are willing to engage in further implementation.

A difference between the two documents is the inclusion of other actors besides states. Having taken the form of a treaty, the Paris Agreement was negotiated by and creates obligations exclusively for states. This occurs despite the fact that nonstate actors, including international governmental organizations, private corporations, and civil society, are not far from the negotiating table and are active in developing their own policies and in creating their own coalitions to prepare for and respond to climate change. However, there is still no explicit role in the Paris Agreement for them. In contrast to this, the SDGs, by not taking the form of a legally binding document, allow for the options of becoming more inclusive and referring to a wider group of stakeholders than states only. The SDGs were drafted after intensive public consultation with stakeholders around the world and with the involvement of the Secretary-General of the United Nations. The constituency for these types of decisions and action programs is broader than simply the state community. A global partnership of state and nonstate actors is being built and referred to at various places in the document, but one has to acknowledge that this is still predominantly a state-centered approach.[34] As international society becomes more complex and multifaceted, a more inclusive approach to international law seems to be unavoidable in the long run. However, it is clear that states are still very reluctant to go that far when creating legal statements in more traditional formats, i.e. in the form of treaties, or regarding monitoring and supervision mechanisms.

Besides the formal aspects of determining the legal impact of a particular instrument, that is the form, the authority, the legitimacy, and the addressees, what might be termed the external aspect, one can also look at a more internal aspect. By internal aspect, I refer to the normative content of the instruments and the type of mechanisms through which effective implementation of the instrument may be ensured. In Table 2, this is referred to as specificity, accountability, justiciability, and enforceability.

To start with the latter, we should acknowledge that justiciability and enforceability are weak aspects of international law in general. The qualification of what are binding obligations under international law does not depend on whether or not a particular obligation can be invoked in court (justiciability) as there are many interstate obligations that cannot be invoked by citizens before national courts.

[33]Within a year, at least 55 Parties to the Convention, accounting in total for at least an estimated 55% of total global greenhouse gas emissions, had ratified the Agreement. Thereby the threshold for entry into force of the Paris Agreement was achieved. It entered into force on 4 November 2016. At the time of writing over 130 of the 197 parties to the Convention have become parties to the Agreement.

[34]See Chasek et al. (2016).

Also, access to international courts is only possible in a limited number of circumstances, and the nature of interstate obligations is often rather unspecified. The same applies to enforceability and actual enforcement. With the exception of the Security Council of the United Nations, and some regional situations, notably the European Union, there is no supranational enforcement capacity in the international community. Enforcement is a decentralized process, which includes various types—military, economic, political, and legal—of sanctions to induce compliance. Its effectiveness depends on a wide range of factors and is very unpredictable. The absence of or the limitations to justiciability and enforceability in international law do not mean that there can be no valid international legal obligations. In this respect, international law is different from domestic law where justiciability and enforceability usually go hand in hand with what is considered binding and valid law. For statements to be characterized as international law, justiciability and enforcement have never been considered determinative.

The justiciability of both the SDGs and the Paris Agreement is rated as low in Table 2 above. Although it seems unlikely that the provisions of these instruments will be directly invoked before courts and tribunals, they may be given legal effect by being used to clarify the obligations of states in other international instruments, e.g. in environmental or human rights conventions. It is highly unlikely that states will seek the enforcement of the SDGs through available interstate sanction mechanisms. There is certainly no supranational authority to do this. With regard to the Paris Agreement, enforcement may be weak but not absent because states or groups of states may use legal or other mechanisms to address the noncompliant behavior of other states. A supranational enforcement capacity, however, is absent from the Paris Agreement.

The Paris Agreement contains a rather elaborate system for ensuring the accountability of the parties. This is the strongest element in the agreement. States seemed to realize that when creating a document in which substantial obligations are formulated in a very open manner and as obligations of conduct rather than results, they need at least relatively strong procedures to monitor and supervise and, if necessary, to assist in correcting the conduct of the parties. A layered approach has been accepted, as already described in relation to Table 1. States have various reporting obligations, there is an expert-based assessment of the reports, there is a supervisory role for the Conference of Parties to the agreement, and there is an expert-based noncompliance system that is intended to address specific noncompliant behavior of states. The noncompliance procedures are somewhat weaker than the noncompliant system accepted under the Kyoto Protocol as that system included the option of correcting states by issuing penalties in cases of serious noncompliance. This was possible as the Kyoto Protocol included very specific, quantifiable targets for states. As the Paris Agreement does not contain such quantifiable targets, such a punitive system would seem to be rather arbitrary. In the SDGs, the predominantly political and aspirational character is reflected in the absence of accountability mechanisms, except for the intention to ensure follow-up and review through the voluntary and state-led HLPF. The HLPF will only meet every 4 years in what is called the Quadrennial Comprehensive Policy Review process.

The last element of the internal aspect of our comparison is the specificity of the normative content of the two instruments. The more specific or precise a provision is, the less room there is for discretion in the application or for self-interpretation by states. At first sight, one would expect that a more precise provision would be legally preferable as there would be less doubt about the expected behavior of actors. However, this will not always be true as a very specifically defined norm will allow an actor to act more freely outside the norm. Prohibiting the dumping of chemical X in a river does not restrain an actor from dumping chemical Y. The norm may not be helpful in realizing the aim of avoiding environmental pollution. The same may be true for combating climate change. A specific percentage of CO_2 emission reduction as an obligation for states might seem a clear solution, but actually it addresses only a small part of the problem. There are many more greenhouse gases; the destruction of sinks (e.g., forests) is not included; prescribing individualized targets to realize collective emission reduction creates a static situation and does not allow for adaptation to new ecological realities. In fact, a wish to increase levels of ambition would require that negotiations on the quantified targets should start all over again in order to find a new balance. More openly formulated targets and rules of conduct rather than results allow for continuous discussion and adaptation to what is perceived as necessary without having to make changes in a formal sense to the agreement. Such a broad normative approach is taken in the Paris Agreement. It creates a normative process that hinges on legally binding due diligence obligations. Whether this is effective, of course, depends on the inclusiveness and legitimacy of the process and the willingness of the parties to engage in a genuine effort to reach the jointly determined goals.[35] Other aspects contribute to making the Paris Agreement even more complex in terms of its legal characterization. It contains a broad range of phrases to express what is considered the expected behavior of states; it varies from clear legal obligations to recommendations and general statements. In terms of hard and soft law, it contains hard law, soft law, and nonlaw, but even within these categories it is possible to differentiate further in terms of hardness or softness.[36] One thing, however, is clear; the agreement does not contain prescriptive rules that are quantifiable at the individual state level. States themselves must individually or cooperatively quantify their actions, which then create legal expectations—the due diligence obligations—as to their fulfillment. This creates a situation that would perhaps not be generally acceptable in any domestic legal system, yet for the international legal system such an approach is an unavoidable reality. Does this "mixed specificity" imply that the Paris Agreement does not qualify as law or qualifies as only partly law? Although not always highly

[35]A possible turning away from the process of an important actor like the United States under the Trump Administration may of course undermine the entire approach. However, such a situation should not be confused with the characterization of the Paris Agreement in legal terms. Anyhow, if strong actors like the USA are determined not to comply with international agreements, there is little that the rest of the world can do to enforce such obligations. This is the political reality within which international law has to operate.

[36]See Rajamani (2016).

specific, it creates legal expectations and constraints state behavior in a process of cooperation. What we can conclude is that there is no particular minimum level of specificity, accountability, justiciability, and enforceability to separate law from nonlaw.

The specificity of the SDGs is of a completely different nature. The goals are formulated as very specific and time bound, e.g. Goal 1.1: "by 2030, eradicate extreme poverty for all people everywhere, currently measured as people living on less than $1.25 a day." However, the specific targets do not translate into individualized and specific normative expectations of states or other actors. Unlike the Paris Agreement, the SDGs do not contain an obligation for states to produce something comparable to the NDCs. They are only encouraged to develop ambitious national responses and to conduct regular reviews of progress.[37]

6 Concluding Observations: The Choice for Soft Law

What can we conclude after this comparison? Firstly, both documents express the shared ambitions of international society as represented by states. These ambitions are based on values such as human dignity, peace and security, and ecological stability and are firmly grounded in the normative context of international law.[38] They contribute to the recognition of international society as a collective entity that exists separately from the states as its main constitutive parts. At the same time, the tension between international law as interstate law and international law as the law of humankind is clearly visible. States are in an impossible position in that they must safeguard their own individual interests in the state-centered legal system while at the same time they increasingly acknowledge that there are overarching interests and ambitions to be realized at a more supranational level. Both the Paris Agreement and the SDGs are designed to serve the commonality rather than individuality in international society. Although this development started in the mid-twentieth century, a firm new balance has not yet been found.

Secondly, when it comes to making choices to serve collective interests, states have to face a number of dilemmas of which the following seem to be most relevant for the present analysis of the legal characterization of their decisions: inclusion versus exclusion, broad versus specific, legal versus political, content versus process, and interstate versus supranational. In regard to collective decisions for the collective interest, it seems rather obvious that the ambition is to be inclusive. Achieving the collective interest with only a small number of the relevant states participating will be difficult, if not impossible. However, trying to keep everybody aboard will in most cases require making compromises. Compromises may be found by reducing the level of ambition but also through more ambiguous language. Be

[37] Note 1, paragraphs 60 and 61.

[38] Note 1, paragraph 10.

that as it may, they will lead to less straightforward legal texts. Similar reasoning applies to formulating behavioral expectations and concrete targets either more broadly or more specifically. Adopting more specific language may lead to fewer participants or may even be impossible or undesirable, given the complexity of the issues at hand. More abstract language, however, creates more space for ambivalence and self-interpretation, given the lack of supranational authority. The choice for a predominantly political rather than a legal form is also linked to these considerations. When a predominantly political form is chosen, such as a resolution of the United Nations General Assembly, it will be easier to reach consensus as states can use as a formal argument the fact that they are not legally bound to such a resolution. It also avoids political difficulties at home as a resolution does not need ratification. However, this does not mean that states voting in favor of such a resolution do not have the intent to lay down legally relevant normative expectations. When the format of a treaty or other formally binding instruments is chosen, this can signify a higher level of ambition and commitment, which can be used both internationally—to put pressure on other states to comply—as well as domestically by requiring or allowing domestic implementation measures. It gives governments the option of using the argument at home that they are legally bound to undertake certain action. A further dilemma is the choice between focusing on the substantive content of commitments or instead engaging in a cooperative process the final results of which will be less certain. The Framework Convention on Climate Change is a good example of the latter: the 1992 Convention does not create many substantive obligations for the parties but has been fundamental to starting the process of developing an international governance model to address climate change. The Paris Agreement is an important output of that process, which in itself creates some substantive expectations, but perhaps even more importantly contributes to a further strengthening of and direction in the governance process. The final dilemma is whether states are willing to engage in a more supranational governance model rather than staying within the strict confines of interstate governance. Are states willing to give up some of their prerogatives by, for example, being subject to the scrutiny of an independent expert committee on compliance or of binding third-party dispute settlement procedures? Depending on the issues at hand, the sense of urgency, the general political climate, and other factors, choices are made and compromises are found regarding these dilemmas in realizing common objects.

Thirdly, the validity of what is an expression of international law should be clearly separated from the form of an international legal statement. Although nobody will disagree that states are the core actors in making international law, there is no clear procedure to determine the validity of an expression as a legal expression and to distinguish such an expression from a political, moral, or other expression. The lack of a predetermined procedure for validity in international society is a fact. A supranational authority in the form of a World Parliament or legislature does not exist. The doctrine of sources assists in identifying expressions that we generally recognize as valid law, but the form does not determine validity: it is content, intent, and authority. This statement links in with the next point and is based on a nonbinary approach to international law.

Fourthly, the binding force of expressions of international law is also not dependent on the form. There is an intricate interplay between the external and internal aspects of legal expressions. Determining legal bindingness requires looking at all these aspects and does not lead to a binary result of being either binding or nonbinding. There are various degrees of bindingness ranging from nonbinding in form and content at one end of the spectrum to fully binding in form and content at the other end. Often expressions can be placed somewhere along the continuum: a formal treaty, with high legitimacy and authority, may be lacking in substantive content and/or meaningful mechanisms to ensure compliance. Such a treaty is usually considered hard law, a valid expression of law, but with soft content. This may be called soft hard law. On the other hand, there may be expressions that lack the fulfillment of external aspects, such as the resolution of an interstate conference, but may have very precise content, a high degree of authority, and legitimacy. This may be called hard soft law. The difference between the two is only a matter of degree. Moreover, both instruments may lack justiciability and enforceability, but this would not influence their categorization as an international legal instrument. It will make implementation dependent on political will.

Fifthly, international law has become complex. It does not only serve the self-interest of states in an interstate community but also increasingly represents the common interest of the entire society of humankind. Interstate law is complemented by global law. This creates tension as there is no historic pedigree for the development of global law. Interstate law has developed over the course of centuries. The development of global law has only recently begun. It is impossible to predict whether it will succeed and what form it will take. That this will not be an easy process is without doubt an understatement.

Sixthly, soft law is a necessary element in both interstate law and global law. In the interstate legal context it may be regarded as a pragmatic choice when a solution creating more elaborate binding commitments is not within reach. Using a carefully drafted and broadly supported declaration of the United Nations General Assembly may be preferred over a treaty without real content but with many ratifications or preferred over a treaty with very precise and binding content yet with only a few states willing to ratify it. Pragmatism will determine in the interstate context what the best option is to achieve results. For climate change, the treaty form has been chosen, while for creating a more sustainable international society the form of a UN resolution seemed to be the more realistic option. It reflects the willingness, or the lack thereof, of states to accept behavior-constraining measures.

On the other hand, in the creation of global law in the common interest, soft law may be considered a principled choice, a deliberate choice for an instrument or procedures that create or assist in clarifying the relevant legal expectations of individual behavior to achieve the common objectives necessary to gradually build an inclusive international normative framework for global governance. It is a deliberate choice for a more policy-oriented approach that moves away from the predominantly state-centered perception of international law. It recognizes that the international legal system serves not only the interest of states but also those of wider human society and requires a more inclusive approach. This will not be achieved through revolutionary steps. It will be a gradual process. Soft law may be regarded as a principled choice to make progress in this perspective. This is not to say that, in this context, soft law is preferred over hard law. Of course, where hard law is attainable, or is the only viable option, it must be chosen. For example, creating an international criminal court cannot be done through soft law.

The SDGs and the Paris Agreement may be regarded as examples of global law rather than interstate law. Although the formats are different, the SDGs in the form of soft law and the Paris Agreement as a treaty, both are rather soft. For the common objective of creating a sustainable international society, it seems that at present the only way forward is through more or less soft instruments.

Finally, for the time being, the difference between the pragmatic and principled approaches is mainly a matter of the theoretical perspectives on the nature of the international legal order. In practice, we will find not much difference. However, engaging in this debate and trying to clarify these points may help those in the position of deciding on the implementation of international law in a situation where the legal rules and obligations are not straightforward in their content and status. A binary approach to international law may seem to make the application easier, but this option does not help decision-makers in their task of contributing to the solution of real existing societal challenges. What legal weight should they give to authoritative expressions about common goals and behavioral expectations that are not formulated in unequivocal legal form and content? What should they choose: the traditional interstate perspective on international law and its interstate objectives as a starting point or the perspective that focuses also on the common interest that international law must increasingly represent? Both are present in the type of instruments discussed in this contribution. The interstate approach is well known and will not lead to much legal controversy. The global-law-oriented approach allows for more flexibility and dynamic development but requires more courage and explanation. It may also meet with rejection. It will certainly not be a simple task. Placing legally relevant expressions on a continuum according to softness or hardness needs further theoretical and practical elaboration. It will require a greater role for umpires with a degree of supranational authority to determine the nature and extent of the legal expectations of, and legal constraints on, actors or, in more traditional terms, their rights and obligations. Much more work needs to be done on the nature of what can be considered valid expressions of international law. Soft law: a pragmatic or a principled choice? This must not be regarded as a binary choice. Soft law is a reality. Without soft law, international law cannot function in the twenty-first century. Incorporating soft law in a constructive manner into international legal theory is our challenge.

References

Books and Articles

Abbott, K., and D. Snidal. 2000. Hard and Soft Law in International Governance. *International Governance* 54: 421–456.

Barral, V. 2012. Sustainable Development in International Law: Nature and Operation of an Evolutive Legal Norm. *The European Journal of International Law* 23: 377–400.

Bodansky, D. 2015. *Legal Options for U.S. Acceptance of a New Climate Change Agreement*. Arlington, VA: Center for Climate and Energy Solutions.

———. 2016. The Legal Character of the Paris Agreement. *Review of European Community and International Environmental Law* 25: 142–150.

Boyle, A. 2014. Soft Law in International Law-Making. In *International Law*, ed. M.D. Evans, 4th ed., 421–456. Oxford: Oxford University Press.

Boyle, A., and C. Chinkin. 2007. *The Making of International Law*. Oxford: Oxford University Press.

Chasek, P.S., et al. 2016. Getting to 2030: Negotiating the Post-2015 Sustainable Development Agenda. *Review of European Community and International Environmental Law* 25: 5–14.

Cohen, R., and F.M. Deng. 2016. Sovereignty as Responsibility. In *The Oxford Handbook of the Responsibility to Protect*, ed. A.J. Bellamy and T. Dunne, 74–93. Oxford: Oxford University Press.

Crawford, J. 2012. *Brownlie's Principles of Public International Law*. 8th ed. Oxford: Oxford University Press.

Franck, T.M. 1990. *The Power of Legitimacy Among Nations*. Oxford: Oxford University Press.

French, D. 2010. Sustainable Development. In *Research Handbook on International Environmental Law*, ed. M. Fitzmaurice, D. Ong, and P. Merkouris, 51–68. Cheltenham: Edward Elgar.

Kim, R.E. 2016. The Nexus Between International Law and the Sustainable Development Goals. *Review of European Community and International Environmental Law* 25: 15–26.

Margraw, D.B., and L.D. Hawke. 2007. Sustainable Development. In *The Oxford Handbook of International Environmental Law*, ed. D. Bodansky, J. Brunnée, and E. Hey, 613–638. Oxford: Oxford University Press.

Orakhelashvili, A. 2016. *Peremptory Norms in International Law*. Oxford: Oxford University Press (Oxford Monographs on International Law).

Rajamani, L. 2016. The 2015 Paris Agreement: Interplay Between Hard, Soft and Non-Obligations. *Journal of Environmental Law* 28: 337–358.

Schrijver, N.J. 2008. *The Evolution of Sustainable Development in International Law: Inception, Meaning and Status*. Leiden: Brill.

Werksman, J. 2016. *The Legal Character of International Environmental Obligations in the Wake of the Paris Climate Change Agreement*. Edinburgh: Edinburgh University and Brodies Environmental Law Lecture Series, 9 February 2016, available at http://www.law.ed.ac.uk/other_areas_of_interest/events/event_documents/BrodiesLectureontheLegalCharacteroftheParisAgreementFinalBICCLEdinburgh.pdf

Documents, Cases, Reports etc.

Convention on Environmental Impact Assessment in a Transboundary Context, Espoo, Finland 1991, 1989 UNTS 309.

International Commission on Intervention in State Sovereignty. 2001. *The Responsibility to Protect: Report of the International Commission on Intervention and State Sovereignty*. Ottawa: International Development Research Centre.

International Court of Justice. 1945. Statute of the International Court of Justice, 24 October 1945.

International Court of Justice. 1949. Corfu Channel case (United Kingdom v. Albania), Merits, Judgment of 9 April 1949, ICJ Reports 1949.

International Court of Justice. 1997. Gabčíkovo-Nagymaros Project (Hungary/Slovakia), Judgment of 25 September 1997, ICJ Reports 1997.

International Court of Justice. 2010. Pulp Mills on the River Uruguay (Argentina v. Uruguay), Judgment, ICJ Reports 2010.

International Law Association. 2002. New Delhi Declaration of Principles of International Law Relating to Sustainable Development. UN Doc. A/CONF.199/8, 9 August 2002, also available at http://www.ila-hq.org/en/committees/index.cfm/cid/25.

International Law Association. 2012. Sofia Guiding Statements on the Judicial Elaboration of the 2002 New Delhi Declaration of Principles of International Law Relating to Sustainable Development, ILA Report of the 75th Conference Held in Sofia August 2012, available at http://www.ila-hq.org/en/committees/index.cfm/cid/1017

Report of the Conference of the Parties. 2011. On its seventeenth session, held in Durban from 28 November to 11 December 2011, Decision 1/CP.17 Establishment of an Ad Hoc Working Group on the Durban Platform for Enhanced Action, 11 December 2011.

Report of the WCED. 1987. *Our Common Future*

Rio Declaration on Environment and Development. 1992. UN Doc. A/CONF.151/26 (Vol. I), 14 June 1992.

Rio Declaration. 2005. A/RES/60/1 (2005 World Summit Outcome).

UNFCCC, Decision 1/CP.21, 'Adoption of the Paris Agreement' (29 January 2016), UN Doc FCCC/CP/2015/10/Add.1, Annex, 15 December 2015 ('Paris Agreement').

UNGA Resolution. 1948. 217 A(III), 10 December 1948

UNGA Resolution. 1970. 2625 (XXV), 24 October 1970.

UNGA Resolution. 2000. A/RES/55/2, 8 September 2000 ('the MDGs'): United Nations Millennium Development Declaration.

UNGA Resolution. 2015. A/RES/70/1, 21 October 2015 ('the SDGs'): Transforming Our World: The 2030 Agenda for Sustainable Development.

CPSIA information can be obtained
at www.ICGtesting.com
Printed in the USA
BVHW040205171218
535775BV00008B/32/P

9 783319 775210